DAILY HEART TO HEART

TALK WITH THE FATHER

By

Mohsen Kazemi

Table of Contents

ACKNOWLEDGEMENT

Every great, precious and practical book has been shaped and influenced by other great and precious works. This book also has been greatly shaped by books by Christian writers such as John Bevere, John MacArthur, Charles Spurgeon, Craig Groeschel, Oswald Chambers and others. However, the most important, essential and interesting book that all the pages of this devotional is based on, is the holy Bible written by Holy Spirit. All the writers that guided my writing were and are amazing servants of my Lord, so I thank my Lord Christ Jesus with all my heart for giving me these words and inspiration to magnify His name and by any means bring many to know Him and deepen their relationships with Him. I would also like to thank my dear friend and mentor, Dr. Tim Berends for encouraging me to create this book in English and Persian. My thanks to Ranji Grace Curtis and Hee Jung Son for their editorial help and encouragement. I thank all the leaders and members of Mohabat Alliance Church, Toronto for their support and prayers. Last but not least, I would like to thank my dear wife, Insook, who introduced me to my lord Jesus and has been my best fan and supporter for more than 30 years.

DEDICATION

To my Lord Jesus Christ and His favorite daughter Insook

INTRODUCTION

On March 15, 2020, I was inaugurated as the senior pastor of Mohabat Alliance Church in Toronto, Canada. A week later Covid 19 restricted attendance of churches to 10 and then 5 people and very soon the doors of the church where we were meeting was closed. My church leaders and I met at my house every Sunday and conducted our praise, worship, and sermons live online. Since most of my congregation were consisted of new believers, to help them grow in their new faith to know Jesus Christ and become familiar with Bible, I decided to post 5–10-minute daily devotionals in Persian on Mohabat Church social media (Telegram Mohabat Alliance Church (Public), Instagram mohabat_church and website www.mohabat.ca) every morning and for a while every evening. Later on, we added English subtitles to these for our English-speaking members. The book you are reading today is the collection of these daily devotionals and you can see the videos on Mohabat Church social media. I continue to post daily devotional in Persian since then and you can share them with your Persian believers or seekers.

This book is designed to be read one day at a time, preferably starting each day with it, pondering and praying through it throughout the day. My intention is to bring you closer to my Lord Jesus and His word so it would transform your life as He did mine.

I hope and pray that Lord Jesus Christ enable you and make you eager to read this devotional and more importantly His Word, the Bible, daily and guide you and bless you by His Holy Spirit. Amen.

JANUARY 1

The thing that we didn't see

2 Corinthians 4:18

While we do not look at the things which are seen, but at the things which are not seen. For the things which are seen are temporary, but the things which are not seen are eternal.

"So, we fix our eyes not on what is seen, but on what is unseen, since what is seen is temporary, but what is unseen is eternal."

HOPE - The Bible speaks of hope as assurance in things not yet seen. In our daily lives, we cling to the hope of promises not yet realized, trusting they will come to pass. This hope becomes our anchor amidst life's storms, propelling us forward.

FAITH - Faith embodies our confidence in the unseen, an unwavering certainty of its manifestation. As the Lord Jesus Christ teaches, live in the present; neither dwell in the past nor be overly anxious about the future. Cherish and act upon the gifts of today.

So, what does hope to represent for us as Christians? Gazing into the future, we anticipate the complete erasure of our sins. We eagerly await Christ's triumphant return. We recognize the transience of death, understanding that through our faith in Jesus Christ, our departure from this world is but a gateway to eternity with Him in heaven. Hope assures us that we will soon reign alongside Christ. Even as we grapple with life's challenges—pain, suffering, and adversities—we remain anchored in this hope. Guided by Jesus Christ, our hope and faith light our path towards the eternal shore.

Charles Spurgeon beautifully encapsulated this sentiment in his writings: "Though this world may present obstacles, causing pain and suffering, we remain confident that our eternal dwelling awaits in the embrace of our Lord Jesus Christ."

May your hope and faith in the Lord flourish with each passing moment.

Amen.

JANUARY 2
Perfect in Christ Jesus

Colossians 1: 28

Him we preach, warning every man and teaching every man in all wisdom, that we may present every man perfect in Christ Jesus.

"So, we tell others about Christ, warning everyone and teaching everyone with all the wisdom God has granted us. We aim to present them to God, perfect in their relationship with Christ.

Often, we scrutinize our reflections, discerning our flaws and errors. "I shouldn't have said that", "I acted rashly there," "That thought wasn't righteous." Indeed, we find ourselves faltering time and again. Yet, God assures us that once we embrace Jesus Christ, we attain perfection through Him. Our imperfections dissolve because Jesus, with His sacrificial blood, purifies us from sin. On the cross, His eternal blood atoned for our transgressions, settling the debt for our misdeeds once and for all. His supreme sacrifice heralded a new dawn.

When God beholds us, He doesn't merely see our earthly identities; He perceives Christ's resurrected spirit within us. He recognizes the indwelling of the Holy Spirit. It's this divine presence that continually refines and sanctifies us. Although we err, each heartfelt plea for forgiveness brings restoration. Whenever we stumble, it's paramount to humbly approach the Lord and plead, "Jesus, purify us. We repent. Wash us anew in Your redeeming blood and elevate us to glorify You."

Our gaze must remain on Jesus Christ, the central figure through whom and for whom all was created. He is the Alpha and the Omega, the nexus of all existence.

Lord, we commit this day to Your divine hands. Illuminate the profound truth that we are complete in You, and that You dwell within us as we reside in the Father, unified in divine harmony. May our focus remain steadfast on You. We offer this prayer in the esteemed name of Jesus Christ, the King of kings. Amen."

JANUARY 3
True repentance

Luke 19:1-11

[1] *And Jesus entered and passed through Jericho.*
[2] *And, there was a man named Zacchæus, which was the chief among the tax collectors, and he was very rich.*
[3] *And he wanted to see who Jesus was; but because he was very short. And because of the crowd, he could not see him.*
[4] *And he ran before, and climbed up a sycamore tree to see him while he was passing that way.*
[5] *And when Jesus came to the place, he looked up, and saw him, and said unto him, Zacchæus, make haste, and come down; for today I must be guest at your house.*
[6] *and came down and received him joyfully.*
[7] *And when people saw that, they all murmured, saying, that he was gone to be guest with a man that is a sinner.*
[8] *And Zacchæus stood, and said unto the Lord Jesus; Behold, Lord, the half of my goods I give to the poor; and if I have taken anything from any man by false accusation, I restore him fourfold.*
[9] *And Jesus said unto him, this day salvation came to this house, so he is also a son of Abraham.*
[10] *For the Son of man is come to seek and to save that which was lost.*

True repentance holds paramount importance in our walk with God. Consider Zacchaeus, a wealthy chief tax collector working for the government. Despite his stature, he was immensely eager to see Jesus. So much so, that he climbed a tree to get a glimpse of Him. It was an action most uncommon for someone of his status and wealth. Yet, his desire to see Jesus surpassed any potential embarrassment.

While Zacchaeus was perched in the tree, Jesus passed by and, knowing him, called out, "Zacchaeus, come down immediately. I must stay at your house today." Zacchaeus eagerly welcomed Him, even knowing the disdain many Jews held for him due to his occupation and perceived dishonesty.

Witness the transformation in Zacchaeus! Overwhelmed with joy and realizing the unconditional acceptance by Jesus, he declared, "Look, Lord! Here and now, I give half of my possessions to the poor, and if I have cheated anybody out of anything, I will pay back four times the amount."

Contrast this with another rich man in Luke 19:63 (Note: I believe you may have misquoted the verse reference; the story of the rich young ruler is found in Luke 18:18-25). This man asked Jesus about inheriting eternal life. When told to keep the commandments, he confidently said he had observed them all. However, when Jesus instructed him to sell all he had and follow Him, the man departed in sorrow, unable to let go of his worldly wealth.

Zacchaeus, on the other hand, eagerly embraced true repentance. He recognized that earthly riches paled in comparison to the transformative power of Jesus Christ's love.

Let's introspect: Is there anything hindering our relationship with God? Is there something that keeps us from truly seeking Him? Are we willing to forsake all to truly know and follow Jesus?

May the love of God the Father, the grace of our Lord Jesus Christ, and the fellowship of the Holy Spirit be with you all. Amen.

JANUARY 4
The amazing giver

Mathew 6:8

Therefore, do not be like them. For your Father knows the things you have need of before you ask Him.

Do not be like them, for your Father knows what you need before you ask him.

Psalm 66:20

Blessed be God, who has not turned away my prayer, Nor His mercy from me!

Blessed be God, who neither rejected nor turned away from me, but instead cared for me, hearing my prayers out of His profound love for me.

This morning, as I awoke, I inquired of God, "Lord, what lesson do You wish to impart today? Which devotional topic should we delve into?" In response, God placed the theme of "Prayer" upon my heart. I hesitated, thinking, "Lord, I just discussed prayer a few days ago, specifically the Lord's Prayer."

Yet, God gently steered my thoughts towards recognizing Him as our "Extraordinary Giver" and the importance of turning to Him in prayer. How intimately does God know you? To what extent does He concern Himself with the intricate details of your life?

God is deeply invested in every nuance of our existence. And while He wishes us to communicate all our concerns to Him, He already knows our needs before they're voiced. This might prompt one to ask: if He is already aware, why then should we pray? Why specify our requests?

At the heart of prayer lies our intimate communion with God. He beckons us, out of love, to approach Him in spirit and in truth. True affection fosters the desire for frequent communication. In this vein, talking and praying to God stand out as the essence of prayer—a testament to the loving relationship we share with the Father and Jesus Christ.

Even as we pour out our hearts—sharing our anxieties and aspirations—God listens. He yearns to hear from us directly.

Though He has generously catered to our every need, the very act of praying, the intimacy of being in God's presence, holds unmatched value.

To be with God is to walk with Him, converse with Him, and bask in His presence.

As you approach Him in prayer today, bring forth all your concerns, but also cherish the moments of communion. The privilege of intimate dialogue with Jesus Christ and our Heavenly Father is truly the greatest gift.

May the love of our Heavenly Father, the grace of our Lord Jesus Christ, and the companionship of the Holy Spirit be with you always. Amen.

JANUARY 5
Tithing and offering (1)

Stewardship and Tithing

Recently, a friend approached me with questions about "Gifts" and "Tithing." He confessed his difficulty in grasping these concepts. It seems for us, the Farsi-speaking community, the idea of gifts and tithing in service to God is not always straightforward. Today, I wish to shed some light on tithing, given its significance in Christianity.

We serve as God's Stewards. Being a Steward implies that we are custodians, the trusted servants of God. But what exactly does stewardship entail? It signifies that all we possess in this world is actually God's property. God has merely entrusted it to us for our sustenance and the advancement of His kingdom. Hence, our primary duty as "Stewards" or "God's custodians" is to optimally utilize what God places in our care, express gratitude, and return a portion to Him.

The practice of tithing predates the Israelites, tracing back to the time of Abraham. After rescuing his nephew Lot and claiming the spoils of victory, Abraham encountered several kings, one of whom was Melchizedek, the king of Salem. Referred to as the "king of peace," Melchizedek remains an enigmatic figure. We know little of his ancestry or lineage. Yet, prophecies about Lord Jesus Christ liken Him to Melchizedek — a priest without precedent. After Melchizedek blessed Abraham, Abraham offered one-tenth of all his spoils, marking the genesis of tithing.

Tithing serves as a reminder: we are custodians of God's trust. God expects us to offer a fraction of our resources as a gesture of gratitude. Although the New Testament doesn't prescribe an exact tithe, scriptural teachings imply that it is the bare minimum. We're encouraged to donate generously, with hearts filled with the love of Jesus. In the "Acts of the Apostles," the early Christians pooled their resources, generously sharing far beyond a mere tenth. Our focus should be on recognizing our role as custodians of God's bounty. By tithing, we express our gratitude and support His divine mission.

I trust this serves as an introduction. Over the next few devotionals, I will delve deeper into the subject of tithing. But for now, let's offer a prayer.

Lord Jesus, we're eternally grateful for Your boundless gifts. As the sovereign over all creation — the heavens, earth, mountains, and plains — You require nothing from us. Yet, You desire that we cultivate generous hearts, reminiscent of Yours, embracing our identity as Your adopted children through Jesus Christ. We beseech You, O Lord, to kindle Your truth in our hearts. Inspire us to prioritize Your kingdom and seek Your approval. May the love of God the Father, the grace of our Lord Jesus Christ, and the fellowship of the Holy Spirit embrace each one of us. Amen.

Gifts and Tithing to God

When we offer our gifts and tithes to God, we're not just giving away a part of ourselves but returning a portion of what God has generously provided. This act is our way of expressing gratitude and thanksgiving.

Let's dive into the Bible to trace the origins of tithing. As I shared previously, the practice has its roots with Abraham. Before being named Abraham, he was known as Abram. This was before God blessed him with a son. Scripture recounts how Abram, after rescuing his nephew Lot and his family from captivity, returned them safely to their homes. Upon his victorious return from the battle against Chedorlaomer and the other kings, Melchizedek met him in the Valley of Shaveh (the King's Valley). Melchizedek, whose name symbolizes "king of righteousness" and "peace," was both the king of Salem and a priest of the Most High God. He brought bread and wine to Abram, blessed him, and proclaimed, "Blessed be Abram by God Most High, Creator of heaven and earth." In gratitude and recognition, Abram gave Melchizedek a tenth of everything, marking the first instance of tithing. Notably, this act preceded any Mosaic laws on tithing.

The enigmatic figure of Melchizedek appears briefly in the Bible. Without documented lineage or background, he's nonetheless recognized as the high priest of the Almighty. Prophetic allusions to Jesus Christ sometimes liken Him to a priest in the order of Melchizedek. The Book of Hebrews speaks of this priestly order, one without start or end, emphasizing the eternal nature of Melchizedek's priesthood. This early incident with Abram underscores that tithing was a recognized practice even before it became a formalized law.

Another mention of tithing is found in Genesis 28:20. Here, Jacob, fleeing his home for his mother's kin, makes a covenant with God. He promises that if God watches over him, providing sustenance and safety, then the Lord would be his God. The stone he set as a pillar would be God's house, and of all that God grants him, he would return a tenth.

From these Biblical anecdotes, we deduce that tithing has been an age-old practice, a way of acknowledging our role as God's "Stewards" and "Custodians." He entrusts us with His resources, expecting us to use them wisely for the benefit of all.

In gratitude, we return a fraction – traditionally 10% – as an offering. As you reflect on this, remember: each time we give, God's blessings are bestowed upon us.

May God's presence envelop you. He never forsakes us; it's often we who drift away, forgetting His constant love and guidance. May the encompassing love of God the Father, through the Holy Spirit, and the grace of our Lord Jesus Christ, be with you always. Amen.

JANUARY 7
Tithing and offering (3)

We will look at when definite tithing principles were laid down. It first started with the Israelites during the time of Moses. God commanded him to write these tithing principles for the Israelites who had been out of Egypt for two years.

Leviticus 27: 30 – 34

> 30 *10% of the earth's crop, whether grain or fruit, belongs to God.*
> 31 *If someone wants to buy their products, they have to add 20% to its price.*
> 32 *10% of all herds and flocks belong to God. When you count them, every tenth one belongs to me.*
> 33 *The owner of the herd or flock should not place the animals in such a way that the bad animal is chosen for me, or replaces the good animal.*
> 34 *If he changes the place of good and bad animals, in that case, both animals will belong to me and he will not have the right to buy it back.*

At Mount Sinai, God delivered a set of commandments to the Israelites through Moses. Among these was the directive to tithe. Unlike a spontaneous act of gratitude, this was a divine mandate.

Where were these tithes directed? They were allocated to the "Tabernacle of the Lord", specifically to the Levites. The Levites, a distinct tribe among the Israelites, held the priesthood. Tasked with maintaining the Tabernacle and later the Temple, they didn't receive land as their inheritance. Instead, their livelihood was drawn from the tithes of the people.

The book of Deuteronomy specifies that the Levites, while receiving a tenth from the populace, should also dedicate a tenth of their collection to God. Additionally, the Torah mentions another essential purpose for these tithes: every third year, a tenth of all produce was to be stored locally and used to support orphans, foreigners, and widows, ensuring they too could eat and offer their gratitude to God.

For contemporary Christians, the principle remains. A tithe is considered a baseline – 10% of our earnings. But God's emphasis is on the disposition of the heart. The Torah recounts that, beyond tithes, the Israelites brought numerous gifts to the Tabernacle, filling it to the brim.

Their generosity was met with divine blessings.

God's blessings aren't merely material. They manifest as health, love, grace, and favor in our undertakings. Some blessings are overt, while others are subtle, like the Israelites' shoes that remained intact during their 40-year journey in the desert.

I urge you all to reflect on this: everything we possess is entrusted to us by God for our benefit. Let's cultivate generous hearts, consistently setting aside at least 10% in gratitude, saying, "Thank you, God." The more grateful we are, the more we're inclined to give. May this message deepen your understanding of tithes and offerings.

May the love of God the Father, through the Holy Spirit, and the grace of our Lord Jesus Christ, envelop each one of you. Amen.

JANUARY 8
Tithing and offering (4)

"Tithing and our Gifts"

Previously, we delved into the concept of tithing and gifts in the Old Testament. Today, let us journey through the New Testament to uncover Jesus Christ's teachings on this matter.

Jesus, in His earthly ministry, often challenged the stringent adherence to the law, especially when it overshadowed its underlying principles. Addressing the Pharisees, Jesus proclaimed, "While you diligently tithe, you've lost sight of the heart of the law: love, generosity, and righteousness."

Let's draw our attention to Matthew 23:23

> *"Woe to you, scribes and pharisees, hypocrites! For you pay tithe of mint, anise, and cumin, and have neglected the weightier matters of the law: justice, mercy, and faith. You should have practiced these, without neglecting the former."*

This scripture paints a vivid picture: it's not enough to simply give tithes. It should be coupled with the embodiment of justice, mercy, and faith. Tithing for mere compliance falls short; it must emanate from a heart full of gratitude, love, and integrity.

Jesus further clarifies His stance on giving in Matthew 6:1-4

> *"Beware of practicing your righteousness before other people in order to be seen by them...When you give to the needy, do not announce it with trumpets...But when you give to the needy, do not let your left hand know what your right hand is doing, so that your giving may be in secret. And your Father who sees in secret will reward you."*

The essence of this teaching? Do not flaunt your generosity for applause. Acts of charity, when paraded, divert the attention from God to ourselves. Our gifts should be discreet, motivated by genuine love and compassion. When we glorify our acts, we settle for human praise, forfeiting the eternal reward from God.

Today, let's meditate on this profound truth. May our hearts align with genuine charity, our acts mirror Christ's love, and our spirits revel in the joy of giving. May the Lord illuminate our paths, enrich our understanding, and draw us closer to His heart. God be with each one of you. Be blessed and be a blessing. Amen.

JANUARY 9
Tithing and offering (5)

"Tithing and our Gifts"

We will return to our study of the New Testament and look at that "Faithful donor".

Our devotional is taken from Mark 12: 41-44

> *41 Jesus Christ was sitting in front of the treasury of the great temple and saw how people cast money into the treasury. Many rich people were pouring a lot of money,*
> *42 but a poor widow came and threw two coins which is worth about two Rials in the box.*
> *43 Jesus called his disciples and said, "Know for a fact that this poor widow paid more than all those who put money in the box,*
> *44 Because they gave of what they have in abundance. But even though this woman is poor, she gave all of her livelihood.*

It's so interesting how Jesus Christ takes the time to observe how people are putting money into the great temple treasury. This shows how God notices the gifts His children offer Him and the sincerity behind their giving. In fact, the focal person in this story is the elderly woman who, with unwavering faith, gave everything she had. What a poignant scene, showcasing her trust in God and her confidence in His provision. Through this, we see how Jesus Christ and God instruct us on how we should perceive giving and the manner in which we should offer. Now, let us delve into the subject of Tithing and Pride.

In Luke 18:9-14

> *9 Jesus also gave this example about those who were confident in their goodness and considered others to be inferior and said,*
> *10 two people went to the temple to pray, one a Pharisee and the other a tax collector.*
> *11 The Pharisee prayed to himself and said, "O God, I thank you that I am not like this greedy, delinquent, and adulterous tax collector.*
> *12 I fast twice a week, I give my tithes,*
> *13 but this tax collector stayed away and didn't even dare to look up in the sky, all he did was to hit his chest and say, "O God, I am a sinner have mercy on me."*

> [14] *Know that this tax collector was forgiven, and went home forgiven but the other one who boasted was humiliated, so whoever humbles himself will be prideful.*

Here, we observe a Pharisee who was proud, complacent, and arrogant. Why? Because he followed God's commandments and fasted out of duty. Meanwhile, the Israelites paid tithes to support the priests, widows, orphans, and strangers in their times of need. In doing so, they were not supposed to feel pride or boast about their deeds to one another. This serves as a reminder to us: when we give gifts, we should do so discreetly, ensuring our actions remain private. Give from the depths of your heart with genuine generosity and do so with humility and love. Let's reflect on this today. Whatever we do, we must do it sincerely, with a heart overflowing with love and humility. May the grace of Lord Jesus Christ and the love of God the Father, through the Holy Spirit, be with you all. Amen.

JANUARY 10
Tithing and offerings (6)

"Tithing and our Gifts – a summary"

We began our discussions with the Israelites when God instructed them to give tithes. The purpose was for them to acknowledge and appreciate the blessings God had bestowed upon them. The concept of tithing wasn't merely an emotional reaction or an obligation; it was an act of gratitude for God's generosity. Furthermore, tithing didn't commence with the Israelites; its roots can be traced back to Abraham. Abraham, Jacob, and other members of God's chosen people offered tithes as heartfelt gratitude, rather than duty. Later, we explored Jesus Christ's perspective on tithing and gifts. Such offerings should always emanate from the heart, reflecting genuine gratitude for God's continuous blessings.

God, the creator of everything, has bestowed all we have upon us. A minimum offering of ten percent as gratitude is a small gesture. Remember, for Christians, this ten percent is a starting point; one can give beyond this. As we embrace this tradition, let's do so with faith and reliance on God, drawing inspiration from the elderly woman who, with unwavering faith, gave all she had, trusting God's providence. I'm not asking you to part with all your assets, but to give wholeheartedly, with faith. When you do, God will shower blessings upon you in diverse ways.

A blessing isn't merely financial prosperity; it can manifest as health, love, familial ties, or even success in your profession. All these are God's gracious gifts to us when we, with full hearts, reciprocate His love. I trust our discussions on tithing and gifts have enriched your understanding of their significance. My wife and I have always prioritized setting aside ten percent of our earnings for God. Before addressing taxes or expenses, we ensure God's portion is dedicated. This principle has always served us well.

Always consider your earnings, minus the ten percent for God. The remaining ninety percent is what we should budget and live on. God promises to amplify the blessings within that ninety percent, much like the Prophet's miracle with the widow's oil. Just as that tiny amount of oil filled multiple jars, similar blessings await us.

Seek God's kingdom foremost, and all else will follow. Pursue God's kingdom with everything you have – your possessions, love, heart, and faith. Amen. May God be with you. Let the love of God the Father, the grace of the Lord Jesus Christ, and the fellowship of the Holy Spirit surround you. Amen.

JANUARY 11
Answer to prayers

Mark 11:23-24

> [23] *For assuredly, I say to you, whoever says to this mountain, 'Be removed and be cast into the sea,' and does not doubt in his heart, but believes that those things he says will be done, he will have whatever he says.*
> [24] *Therefore I say to you, whatever things you ask when you pray, believe that you receive them, and you will have them.*

If you believe in the Lord and harbor no doubt in your heart, you can command even this mountain, "Lift yourself up and cast yourself into the lake," and it will obey.

Whatever you ask in prayer, believe that it has been granted to you, and it will be so.

Today, I stand beside a serene lake, wishing you could share its tranquility with me. I want to discuss the topic of "Answers" to our prayers. What are you fervently praying for today? What is that deep desire of your heart? Do you deem it an impossible feat? In faithful prayer, we affirm God's power to address our challenges. We place our utmost trust in Him, proclaiming, "Lord, we lean on You for this." When He responds, we heed His guidance with humility and hope. If our petition aligns with God's will, He ensures its realization. Conversely, if our plea doesn't reflect His plan for us, He graces us with blessings even greater than our original desires. This is because our Lord Jesus Christ constantly seeks our well-being, out of His profound love for us. He orchestrates events for our ultimate benefit. If we perceive our request to be favorable but it doesn't align with His divine foresight, He refashions our desires with superior outcomes. Now, let's approach God with expectant hearts, trusting His inherent desire to respond to our calls. His answers might not always be swift, but be assured, He will move mountains to heed our petitions. Amen.

May God be with you, for He is ever-present. May you continually sense His enveloping presence. Remember, His arms perpetually remain open, awaiting your embrace. Whatever desires reside within our hearts, whether trivial or paramount, let's lay them at the feet of Jesus Christ. He remains steadfast, always ready to listen and respond.

May the love of God the Father, through the Holy Spirit, and the grace of the Lord Jesus Christ envelop you. Amen.

JANUARY 12
A new thing

Isaiah 43:19

> *Behold, I will do a new thing, now it shall spring forth; Shall you not know it? I will even make a road in the wilderness and rivers in the desert.*

See, I am doing a new thing! Now it springs up; do you not perceive it? I am making a way in the wilderness and streams in the wasteland.

1 Peter 1:3

> *Blessed be the God and Father of our Lord Jesus Christ, who according to His abundant mercy has begotten us again to a living hope through the resurrection of Jesus Christ from the dead.*

Blessed be the God and Father of our Lord Jesus Christ, who by His great grace has given us a new birth and a new hope through the resurrection of Jesus Christ from the dead.

Today, we will discuss the "New" work God has in store for us. "I will do a new thing," the Lord proclaimed to the prophet Isaiah. At times, our hearts yearn for uplifting news, a glimmer of hope for the future. When God conveyed this message to Isaiah, He emphasized that amidst all the prevailing challenges, we should anticipate the forthcoming hope. A new dawn is on the horizon.

Similarly, today, despite the multifaceted obstacles and tumult surrounding us, God reassures us of His omnipotence, wisdom, and boundless love. He is orchestrating fresh endeavors on our behalf. Whether we perceive these changes now or recognize them later, God continues His transformative work, ushering in novel opportunities brimming with endless possibilities. God is forging a distinct path for us, even in seemingly barren terrains. Thus, let us approach this with hearts burgeoning with hope and zest, and walk alongside our Lord Jesus Christ.

Let us anchor ourselves in God's unwavering promise today and embrace it wholeheartedly. I entrust you to God's benevolent care.

May the love of God the Father, channeled through the Holy Spirit, and the grace of our Lord Jesus Christ envelop you. Amen.

JANUARY 13
Real satisfaction

Psalms 42:1-2

> [1]*As the deer seeks cool and flowing waters, and his heart beats for it, my heart beats for you too, O Lord, and longs for you.*
> [2]*My soul thirsts for you, O' God, for the living God. When can I come and see you O' God, and meet with you?*

Once again, we'll discuss a book I've previously mentioned, "Moments of Peace in the Presence of God." How can we truly attain peace?

Consider the deer: it requires water to quench its thirst. Once it drinks, it feels satiated, but with time, thirst returns, driving it back to the water source. We share a similarity with the deer in our innate needs – we require sustenance and hydration for our bodies. However, our needs go beyond the physical. We yearn for love, acceptance, and, most profoundly, a divine connection within ourselves. We might misinterpret this innate yearning, attempting to satiate it with worldly pleasures or material pursuits. Yet, often, these prove inadequate in addressing the profound longing embedded deep within us.

This profound yearning, present in each of us, is fundamentally a longing for God. He is always near, beckoning us closer. Jesus Christ proclaims, "I am the water of life, the bread of life, the way, and the truth. Those who drink from me will never thirst again."

God's eternal presence is our fountain of sustenance. He assures us, "I will never forsake you. I am always by your side." Yet, it's incumbent upon us to seek Him out, to quench our soul's enduring thirst through His grace.

We're eternally grateful, Father, for the privilege to draw near to You. Through Jesus Christ and His redemptive sacrifice, we can freely approach Your throne, seeking the "living water" that promises to satiate our deepest yearnings.

Lord Jesus, we thank You for Your unwavering presence. You are our life's sustenance, our true nourishment. Guide us to continually seek and draw from Your boundless love.

May the love of God the Father, the grace of our Lord Jesus Christ, and the fellowship of the Holy Spirit remain with you always. Amen.

JANUARY 14
The lost son

Luke 15 – This is the story about the "*Lost Son*".

In Luke 15, the Pharisees approached the disciples and asked, "Why do you and your Master eat with sinners?" In response, Jesus told them the parables of the lost coin and the lost sheep. He then continued with the story of the Prodigal son.

There once was a very rich man who had two sons. One day, the younger son approached his father to ask for his share of the inheritance. The father, though saddened by this request, granted it. The boy then left home, taking his money with him to a distant country. There, he lived recklessly and committed many transgressions, eventually squandering all his wealth. When a famine arose, he found himself penniless and starving. In desperation, he sought employment with a landowner, whose job for him was to feed the pigs. His hunger grew so immense that he even began to eat the pigs' food.

The Bible tells us that at this point, he had a moment of clarity. He remembered how, back in his father's house, even the servants had an abundance of food. He resolved, "I'll go to my father and admit that I have sinned. I no longer deserve to be called his son; perhaps he'll let me be one of his servants." With this thought, he began his journey home. From a distance, his father, who had been anxiously waiting for his return, spotted him. Overwhelmed with love and relief, the father ran to his son, embracing and kissing him. The son confessed, "Father, I don't deserve to be called your son for I have sinned against both heaven and you." Yet, the father, in his joy, instructed his servants to dress the boy in the finest clothes, to place a ring on his finger, and sandals on his feet. He declared, "Kill the fattened calf! Let's celebrate, for my son who was lost is now found. He was thought dead, but he is alive."

Meanwhile, the older son, returning from his work, heard the commotion. He inquired of the servants about the cause of the celebration. When told that his brother had returned and a feast was being held in his honor, he became indignant and refused to join the festivities. His father came out to plead with him. The older son retorted, "All these years I've served you, never once disobeying, yet you never gave me even a goat to feast on. Now, this son of yours, who wasted your wealth on prostitutes, returns and you celebrate him?"

The father lovingly responded, "My dear son, everything I have is yours. But today is a day of rejoicing, for your brother was lost and now is found; he was dead and now is alive."

This parable introduces us to three distinct characters: the repentant prodigal son, the resentful older brother, and the ever-loving father. Jesus, through this narrative, illustrates that the Word of God is like a double-edged sword that discerns the heart's intentions. He gave this answer to the Pharisees to highlight the significance of reclaiming lost souls for God.

The Prodigal son represents the sinner, the gracious Father symbolizes our Heavenly Father, and the resentful brother embodies the Pharisee, who shows no compassion for the wayward. Reflect upon these words and may God's presence guide you.

May the love of God the Father, through the Holy Spirit and the grace of our Lord Jesus Christ, be with you all. Amen.

JANUARY 15
Lord's prayer and forgiveness

Based on the "Lord's Prayer".

Several years ago, I searched to find if anyone had set the Lord's Prayer to music in Farsi. To my surprise, I didn't come across any such rendition. So, I took it upon myself to compose a song and now, I'd like to share it with you. Please listen, and afterward, let's raise our voices together in song. Matthew 6:9-14

> 9 *Our Father who art in heaven. Hallowed be thy Name.*
> 10 *Thy will be done, on earth as it is in heaven.*
> 11 *Give us this day our daily bread.*
> 12 *And forgive us our trespasses, as we forgive those who trespass against us.*
> 13 *And lead us not into temptation but deliver us from evil.*
> 14 *For thine is the kingdom, and the power, and the glory, for ever and ever.*
> *Amen.*

When the disciples asked Jesus Christ to teach them to pray, He provided this flawless prayer.

Firstly, He praises God, acknowledging His holiness. Even though we've been brought closer to God through Jesus's sacrifice, and refer to Him as our Father, His sacredness remains undiminished.

He emphasizes the importance of praying for His kingdom on earth and daily sustenance from His hands. God reminds us to live in the present: "Give us this day our daily bread."

Jesus underscores the principle of forgiveness: as we are forgiven, so should we forgive others. God doesn't lead us into temptation but shields us from Satan's snares. He reminds us of the might and glory that belong solely to God.

To elucidate the profound nature of forgiveness, Jesus narrated parables. One recounts a servant who, despite being forgiven a huge debt by a king, refuses to forgive a small debt owed to him. This story serves as a reminder of the boundless forgiveness we receive from Christ and the expectation to extend the same to others.

Forgiveness is a recurring theme in Jesus's teachings. Only through His sacrifice on the cross are we absolved of our countless sins. He beckons us to emulate His example, forgiving others as He has forgiven us.

John Bevere's book, "The Bait of Satan", delves into the pitfalls of holding onto offense. If someone has wronged you, be it justifiably or unjustly, present them before God. Pray, "Lord, I forgive their transgressions because You've pardoned my countless sins. I entrust them to You, praying they find Your path, enter Your kingdom, and receive forgiveness."

We thank God for His unending mercy. May He fortify us with the resolve to forgive, as He does, and to treat everyone with love.

May the love of God the Father, the grace of our Lord Jesus Christ, and the fellowship of the Holy Spirit be with you all. Amen.

JANUARY 16
Indelibly engraved

Isaiah 49:15-16. The title today is "Indelibly engraved."

> *"Can a woman forget her nursing child, and not have compassion on the son of her womb? Surely, they may forget, Yet I will not forget you.*

I will never forget you. Behold, **I have engraved your name on the palm of my hand,** God says this.

In Isaiah 49:23 he says,

> *Kings shall be your foster fathers, and their queens your nursing mothers; They shall bow down to you with their faces to the earth and lick up the dust of your feet. Then you will know that I am the LORD, for they shall not be ashamed who wait for Me."*

You shall know that I am the Lord; whoever puts his trust in me, I will not disappoint him.

This also comes from a book of Devotionals that I use every morning and night. The title of this book is "*Moments of peace in the presence of God*".

In the era of the prophet Isaiah, it was customary among the Israelites to engrave or inscribe the names of their beloved ones on the palms of their hands. This ancient ritual is a testament to a promise from God when He declares, "I will engrave your name on my hand forever." This is not just a symbol, but a profound affirmation of God's unwavering commitment, dependency, and boundless love for each of us. There is absolutely no possibility that God could ever forget any of us; His thoughts are perennially aligned towards our well-being.

If today, or perhaps this very morning, you sense a chasm separating you from Him, take solace in visualizing those divine hands – hands that embody pure love. Remember the sacrifice of Jesus Christ, whose hands were pierced for our transgressions. Our names are etched upon those benevolent hands, and He will always keep us in His memory.

Let's approach God today, asking Him to inscribe His name, love, and peace deep within our hearts. Amen.

May God's presence envelop you today and always. His reassuring presence confirms He's always with us.

Almighty Father, our prayer today is a simple one – with every passing moment, may we feel Your comforting presence ever closer. We remain steadfast in the belief that You will never forsake us, nor ever let us stray from Your path. Guide us, so that our hearts never lose sight of You, enabling us to forever trust and lean on Your strength.

In these challenging times, our reliance is solely upon You, Jesus Christ. You are our unwavering foundation, the very embodiment of God's mighty power within us. During moments of fatigue, desolation, or weakness, You replenish our spirit with renewed vigor.

Our prayers extend to the Christians in Iran, who face persecution. O' Father, in the revered name of Jesus Christ, we trust that Your protective embrace shields them. Lord, use their experiences for the growth of Your kingdom, and similarly, guide us in serving Your divine purpose. We lift these prayers in the cherished name of Jesus Christ, our Lord, Savior, and the King of Kings. Amen.

JANUARY 17
God will save you today

Daniel 6:16

King Cyrus told Daniel, "May your God, whom you serve so faithfully, rescue you".

It also comes from the book we used yesterday, "Moments of Peace in the Presence of God".

Did you know that the prophet Daniel once held the esteemed position of Prime Minister in Persia during King Cyrus's reign? It's a remarkable testament to his character and the favor he found in God's eyes.

The nobles and leaders, envious of Daniel's favor with the king, plotted against him. Recognizing that Daniel was unimpeachable in all matters of state, they targeted his unwavering devotion to God. Aware that Daniel prayed to God thrice daily with his windows open towards Jerusalem, they devised a trap. They persuaded King Cyrus to issue a decree forbidding prayer to any deity but the king himself for thirty days, hoping Daniel would defy it.

True to his faith, Daniel continued his prayer routine undeterred. He was soon reported, arrested, and presented before King Cyrus. Despite the king's affection for Daniel, he was bound by his decree. Reluctantly, with a heavy heart, he said to Daniel, "May the God you serve so faithfully save you."

The scripture in Daniel 6:27 proclaims: "He delivers and rescues; He works signs and wonders in heaven and on earth. He who has saved Daniel from the power of the lions."

Accused and condemned merely for praying to God, Daniel was cast into a den of ferocious lions. King Cyrus, filled with anguish, spent a sleepless night. At dawn, he hurried to the den and cried out, hoping for a miracle. To his overwhelming joy, Daniel replied, detailing how God had sent an angel to seal the lions' mouths since no wrong was found in him.

This miraculous tale reaffirms the nature of our unchanging God. If you ever find yourself maligned or persecuted for your faith in God and the worship of Jesus Christ, remember that the Lord stands by your side. Our God, who shut the jaws of lions to save His servant, is the same God who watches over you today.

Let us, with unwavering faith and devotion, glorify Him and stand firm against any adversity, for He is constant — yesterday, today, and forever. His promises remain eternal.

In gratitude, let us proclaim, "Oh Lord, you continually perform wonders in our lives." We thank You for empowering us to walk in faith and devotion, confident in the knowledge that You are ever-present. In the mighty name of Jesus Christ, we pray. Amen.

JANUARY 18
Always with God

Mathew 28: 20

> *teaching them to observe all things that I have commanded you; and lo, I am with you always, even to the end of the age.*

And lo, I am with you always, even unto the end of the world."
I want to share a special experience from the many years I've been a Christian. Often, our new Christian brethren, when they pray or say goodbye, express hopes like, "I hope God keeps me on the right path" or "I hope God will be with us." However, Jesus Christ assures us of His perpetual presence. He will never abandon us. We are confident in the unwavering truth of the promises made by Lord Jesus Christ and God, our Father. Unlike humans, God never forgets His promises. As the Lord says, "I will always be with you and never leave you alone.

Jesus Christ said in John 14:6,

> *I am the way the truth. No one comes to the Father except through me. I'm the life and resurrection.*

He has also said in Revelation 3:20,

> *I will come and knock on the door of your heart and if you open, I and the Father will come and have dinner with you and we would have relationship with you.*

God is with us every moment. Through Jesus Christ, He established a new covenant with us, assuring us that we are never alone. He is our rock of salvation, a God in whom everything is assured, and who beckons us to trust in Him. Our prayer should reflect this bond: 'Lord, help me to always turn to You. In every situation, let me call upon You. I am confident in Your unwavering presence. Help purify my heart, guide my motivations, and instill in me the kindness and love You embody. Allow me to know You deeper each day.'

As we journey through life, let's hold onto the assurance that Jesus Christ is eternally with us. At times, we might distance ourselves from Him, burdened by our worries, forgetting His call to cast all our anxieties on Him.

In Matthew 6:25-36, He reminds us not to be anxious about life's necessities, pointing to the birds as testament to His provision.

'Look at the birds of the air; they neither sow nor reap nor gather into barns, and yet your heavenly Father feeds them. Are you not of more value than they?' He emphasizes seeking first the Kingdom of God, assuring that all our needs will be met.

Father, we are grateful for today. We thank You, Jesus Christ, for Your sacrifice and triumphant resurrection, making salvation accessible to us. We are anchored in the truth that resides in You. Today, may we draw nearer to You in every facet of our lives, always seeking Your will above ours. Strengthen our bond with You. In the majestic name of Jesus Christ, King of Kings, we pray. Amen.

JANUARY 19
Easter Monday (inner light)

Luke 8:16, 11:33-36

This is where our Lord Jesus Christ talks about our eyes, inner light and the light that enters and leaves us.

> [33] *No one, when he has lit a lamp, puts it in a secret place or under a basket, but on a lampstand, that those who come in may see the light.*
> [34] *The lamp of the body is the eye. Therefore, when your eye is good, your whole body also is full of light. But when your eye is bad, your body is also full of darkness.*
> [35] *Therefore take heed that the light which is in you is not darkness.*
> [36] *If then your whole body is full of light, having no part dark the whole body will be full of light, as when the bright shining of a lamp gives you light.*

Friends, our Lord illustrates the profound truth that the light within us shines outward through our eyes. In the same way, any darkness within is also reflected through them. Scripture tells us that our eyes are the windows to our soul. Through our eyes, we perceive the world and all its inhabitants.

It is essential that we view others through God's perspective — eyes filled with love, kindness, and humility. When we do, our vision becomes clear and luminous. Conversely, when we view the world with jealousy, selfishness, and suspicion, our vision dims, causing sorrow in the heart of God.

May the Holy Spirit purify our eyes and entire being, allowing us to embody God's attributes of kindness, love, humility, and optimism. Let our eyes reflect the Holy Spirit's work, enabling us to see others with kindness, humility, and goodwill. In doing so, may our inner light grow brighter, helping lead others to our Savior, Jesus Christ. May the boundless love of the Father, the grace of our Lord Jesus Christ, and the guiding hand of the Holy Spirit be with you all. May these words uplift and fortify you today. Amen.

JANUARY 20
Our hope

Psalms 130:5

And this is eternal life, that they may know You, the only true God, and Jesus Christ whom You have sent.

I will wait on the Lord, my soul is waiting for him, and in his word my hope is steadfast.

Psalms 43:5

Why are you cast down, O my soul?
And why are you disquieted within me?
Hope in God;
For I shall yet praise Him,
The help of my countenance and my God.

O my soul, why are you despondent? My heart, why are you so heavy? I place my hope in God. Amen? Amen.

Our hope rests in Lord Jesus Christ. Our salvation comes from Lord Jesus Christ. Even when we were unaware of Him, even when we stood as His adversaries, He chose to bear the cross for you and me. He took upon Himself our transgressions and nailed our sins and afflictions to that cross. By embracing Him as the Lord of our hearts and souls, not only are our sins forgiven, but they are also cast aside, remembered no more.

Galatians proclaim that we are reborn – the old self has passed away, and a new self emerges. So, friends, let's march forward today fortified with this promise, this sentiment, this heart. Regardless of the tempests or challenges we face or whatever seeks to trip us up, where does our hope lie? Who is our protector? Who is our redeemer? He holds a name that is exalted above all others, bestowed with power in heaven, on earth, and even below. Our redeemer is a gentle shepherd, ever benevolent and desiring the best for us.

Father, we express our gratitude for Your unending goodness. You are our anchor, our absolute. O God, let every moment of today serve as a reminder of our hope, our guide, our savior. Impress upon our hearts His omnipotence and the fact that nothing is beyond His reach.

Today, we surrender into Your hallowed hands. Father, may we be instruments that magnify Your name. In the name of Jesus Christ, Amen.

JANUARY 21
Night prayer

Psalms 148:4-5

> 4 *Praise Him, you heavens of heavens,*
> *And you waters above the heavens!*
> 5 *Let them praise the name of the* LORD,
> *For He commanded, and they were created.*

Praise Him, all the heavens, and the waters above the skies. Let everything that has breath extol the name of the Lord, for at His command, all things came into being.

Father, today, we approach Your throne with gratitude for the gift of another day. Jesus Christ, we are immensely thankful for Your unwavering presence in every moment and every nuance of our lives. We exalt and magnify Your name. Across the breadth of the earth, the vastness of the heavens, and amidst all creatures, Your name is adored. The harmonious chorus of all creation rises in unified praise to You, O God.

You are our benevolent God, our cherished Father. We are ever grateful for Your boundless love, stretching from the earth to the vastness of heaven. Thank you for the continuous work You orchestrate in our lives, for each instance when You stood by us, and for those moments when unbeknownst to us, You cradled us in Your embrace.

We express our deepest gratitude, Lord Jesus Christ. You are our beacon of hope, and today, we navigated its hours with our trust anchored in You. Tonight, as we lay our burdens at Your feet, we acknowledge that all we do is under Your sovereign will. If we faltered, if we erred, if we trespassed against Your holy commandments, we humbly beseech Your forgiveness. Jesus Christ, sanctify us with Your atoning blood. Holy Spirit, cleanse and elevate our spirits.

Grant us a tranquil night and rejuvenating slumber so that upon dawn's first light, we rise invigorated and renewed. We entrust all into Your sacred care, Jesus Christ. Amen.

JANUARY 22
My helper

Psalms 40

[1] I waited patiently for the Lord. And He inclined to me and heard my cry.
[2] He also brought me up out of a horrible pit Out of the miry clay and set my feet upon a rock and established my steps.
[3] He has put a new song in my mouth. Praise to our God; many will see it and fear and will trust in the Lord.
[4] Blessed is that man who makes the Lord his trust and does not respect the proud or such as turn aside to lies.
[5] Many, O Lord my God, are your wonderful works which you have done; and your thoughts toward us cannot be recounted to you in order; If I would declare and speak of them, they are more than can be numbered.
Amen.

May God's abundant blessings be upon each one of you today.

Today, let us unite our hearts in intercession for all the rulers, presidents, and leaders across the globe. May the Almighty bestow upon them discernment and understanding to safeguard their citizens.

We are deeply grateful for the Government of Canada. Lord, we lift up the Prime Minister before You. In these challenging times, please grace him with unparalleled wisdom to protect and serve every individual under his leadership.

Lord Jesus Christ, You are the steadfast rock upon which we anchor our trust. Firmly planted on this foundation, we raise our hearts in adoration to You. We extol You, O Lord, for the fervor and devotion for Your name burns ardently within us.

May the boundless love of the Father, the redeeming grace of our Lord Jesus Christ, and the guiding assistance of the Holy Spirit be with you all. Amen.

JANUARY 23
God is my shepherd

Psalm 23

> 1 *The Lord is my shepherd The Lord is my shepherd; I shall not want.*
> *He makes me to lie down in green pastures.*
> 2 *He leads me beside the still waters.*
> 3 *He restores my soul He leads me in the paths of righteousness For*
> *His name's sake.*
> 4 *Yea, though I walk through the valley of the shadow of death I will*
> *fear no evil For You are with me Your rod and Your staff, they*
> *comfort me.*
> 5 *You prepare a table before me in the presence of my enemies. You*
> *anoint my head with oil My cup runs over.*
> 6 *Surely goodness and mercy shall follow me. All the days of my*
> *life And I will dwell in the house of the Lord Forever.*
> *Amen.*

I trust, and I hope that you too, believe in these sacred words. Even as we tread through the daunting valley of the shadow of death, we must hold fast to the assurance that God is beside us. The Lord Jesus Christ reassures us, declaring, "I will always be with you." His unwavering presence is our solace. Let us anchor ourselves in His promises, reminding Him, "Lord, you vowed never to abandon us."

We must stand steadfast in our conviction, fully trusting that His Word holds the weight of eternity. Unlike fleeting human promises, often made today and forgotten tomorrow, God's commitments remain eternal. To all who have welcomed Jesus Christ as their Lord and Savior, God's promises extend unceasingly. With resounding faith, we embrace the profound truth that Christ's blood was poured out to cleanse us from every transgression. Empowered by this understanding, we march forward, proclaiming, "God, You are our benevolent Shepherd."

Jesus declares, "I am the good Shepherd. I am the gatekeeper, the guardian who protects His flock from the lurking dangers." Today, and every day, God stands as our vigilant Shepherd.

In reverence and love, we recall our Savior, Jesus Christ. Father, in His precious name, we uplift our friends and loved ones battling ailments, praying for their restoration. Hasten the discovery of a definitive solution to combat the Covid-19 pandemic.

Deliver your children from anguish and distress. With gratitude, we acknowledge Your omnipresent comfort. In the majestic name of Jesus Christ, the King of Kings, we offer this prayer, receiving Your blessings with unwavering faith. Amen.

May the Lord's blessings envelop you all.

JANUARY 24
Why, my soul, are you downcast?

Psalm 42

1 As the deer pants for streams of water, so my soul pants for you, my God.
2 My soul thirsts for God, for the living God. When can I go and meet with God?
3 My tears have been my food day and night, while people say to me all day long, "Where is your God?"
4 These things I remember as I pour out my soul how I used to go to the house of God under the protection of the Mighty One with shouts of joy and praise among the festive throng.
5 Why, my soul, are you downcast? Why so disturbed within me? Put your hope in God for I will yet praise him my Savior and my God
6 My soul is downcast within me; therefore, I will remember you from the land of the Jordan, and from the heights of Sermon, From the Hill Mizar.
7 Deep calls unto deep at the noise of your waterfalls all your waves and billows have gone over me.
8 The Lord will command his loving-kindness in the daytime and in the night His song shall be with me, a prayer to the God of my life.
9 I will say to God my Rock "Why have you forgotten me? Why do I go mourning because of the oppression of the enemy?"
10 As with a breaking of my bones, my enemies reproach me while they say to me all day long "Where is your God?" Why are you cast down, oh my soul?
11 And why are you disquieted within me? Hope in God; for I shall yet praise Him, the help of my countenance and my God.

If today you find yourself submerged in challenges, battling desolation, or entangled in the complexities of life, remember that our God is infinitely mightier than any adversity you face. He is the sovereign ruler of the heavens and the earth. In the book of Genesis, we learn that He cradles entire galaxies within the span of His hand and holds the vast oceans with effortless grace. Our God is omnipotent, transcending all limits.

In the face of trials and tribulations, let us not be overwhelmed by the magnitude of our problems. Instead, let us lift our gaze to the boundless greatness of our Lord Jesus Christ and our Heavenly Father.

We must keep our hearts anchored in the unwavering love and sacrifice of the Lord Jesus Christ who, nearly two millennia ago, endured the cross to secure our salvation. He promises to guide us into the embrace of God's household, making us part of His divine family. As we navigate life's challenges, let us remain steadfast in this truth: our God's might far exceeds any obstacle before us. Amen.

May the grace of God the Father, the love of God the Son, and the guidance of the Holy Spirit be with you always. Let them guide and remind you of today's Word. Ponder upon it, meditate on its truth, and let it illuminate your path. Amen.

JANUARY 25
Bless the Lord, oh my soul

Psalm 103

1 *Bless the Lord, oh my soul and all that is within me.*
2 *Bless his holy name! Bless the Lord, oh my soul and forget not all his benefits.*
3 *Who forgives all your iniquities, who heals all your diseases.*
4 *Who redeems your life from destruction, who crowns you with loving kindness and tender mercies.*
5 *Who satisfies your mouth with good things, so that your youth is renewed like the eagles.*
6 *The Lord executes righteousness and justice for all who are oppressed.*
7 *He made known his ways to Moses his acts to the children of Israel.*
8 *The Lord is merciful and gracious, slow to anger, and abounding in mercy.*
9 *He will not always strive with us, nor will he keep his anger forever.*
10 *He has not dealt with us according to our sins nor punished us according to our iniquities.*
11 *For as the heavens are high above the earth so great is his mercy toward those who fear him.*
12 *As far as the east is from the west, so far, he has removed our transgressions from us.*
13 *As a father pities his children, so the Lord pities those who fear him.*
14 *For he knows our frame He remembers that we are dust.*
Amen.

Dear friends, let's offer our heartfelt gratitude to God for His unwavering promises and the sacred scripture which bears testament to His immense love for us. Through Jesus Christ, He has cleansed our sins, casting them as far from us as the east is from the west. Our God is not only kind and merciful but also our healer, the one who rejuvenates the sick and weary. Know that He never abandons us; His presence is a constant, comforting embrace. I pray that this assurance uplifts your spirit and strengthens your faith. We owe an endless debt of gratitude to the Lord Jesus Christ for the immeasurable sacrifice He made for each one of us on the cross. As we part, I entrust you to the loving embrace of God the Father, Son, and Holy Spirit. Amen.

JANUARY 26

The name of Jesus Christ is above all

Ephesians 1:17-23

This is the prayer of Paul the apostle for the people of Ephesus. I want this prayer to be for us too please pay attention and meditate on it.

> [17] *My prayers that the God of our Lord Jesus Christ, the Father of glory may give to you the spirit of wisdom and revelation in the knowledge of Him.*
> [18] *The eyes of your understanding being enlightened that you may know what the hope of His calling is what are the riches of the glory of His inheritance in the saints.*
> [19] *And what is the exceeding greatness of His power toward us who believe according to the working of His mighty power.*
> [20] *which He worked in Christ when He raised Him from the dead and seated Him at His right hand in the heavenly places,*
> [21] *He raised Him far above all principality and power and might and dominion and every name that is named not only in this age but also in that which is to come.*
> [22] *And He put all things under His feet and gave Him to be head over all things,*
> [23] *The church, which is His body, the fullness of Him who fills all in all.*
>
> *Amen.*

Dear friends, this prayer brims with truth and holds unwavering promises for us believers. The name of Jesus Christ stands exalted above all others. He bore our sins upon the cross, triumphed over death in His resurrection, and now, He sits at the right hand of God, interceding on our behalf. By accepting Him as our Lord, we welcome the risen Jesus into our hearts, and in doing so, we are adopted as heirs and cherished children of God. It's my earnest wish that you recognize the immeasurable power of God manifested in the death and resurrection of Jesus Christ, and may this realization fortify your faith, drawing you ever closer to Him. Let us move forward, empowered by the knowledge that our God is not only great but is always orchestrating the best for us.

May you be enveloped in the love of God the Father, the grace of our Lord Jesus Christ, and find comfort in the companionship of the Holy Spirit. Amen.

JANUARY 27
Solid rock

Luke 6:47-48

> [47] *Whoever comes to me and hears my sayings and does them I will show you whom he is like*
> [48] *He is like a man building a house that dug deep and laid the foundation on the rock. And when the flood arose the stream beat vehemently against that house and could not shake it for it was founded on the rock.*

Our rock in life is Jesus Christ, and we must heed His words and follow His teachings. In storms, floods, and every trial, our reliance should be on Jesus Christ. When we believe in Him and live by His teachings, we have nothing to fear, for our foundation is the steadfast rock of Jesus Christ. Today, let us move forward with this assurance and express our gratitude, saying, "Thank you, Lord, for being our unwavering rock."

In Jesus Christ, we find unwavering trust and companionship. May the love of the Father, the grace of our Lord Jesus Christ, and the guidance of the Holy Spirit be with you always. Amen.

JANUARY 28
He is my refuge and my fortress

Psalms, 91: 1-14

> [1] *He who dwells in the secret place of the Most High shall abide under the shadow of the Almighty.*
> [2] *Will say of the Lord, "He is my refuge and my fortress My God, in Him I will trust."*
> [3] *Surely, He shall deliver you from the snare of the Fowler and from the perilous pestilence.*
> [4] *He shall cover you with His feathers, and under His wings you shall take refuge; his truth shall be your shield and buckler.*
> [5] *You shall not be afraid of the terror by night,*
> [6] *Nor of the arrow that flies by day, nor of the pestilence that walks in darkness, nor of the destruction that lays waste at noonday.*
> [7] *A thousand may fall at your side, and ten thousand at your right hand; but it shall not come near you.*
> [8] *Only with your eyes shall you look and see the reward of the wicked.*
> [9] *Because you have made the Lord, who is my refuge, even the Most High, your dwelling place,*
> [10] *No evil shall befall you, nor shall any plague come near your dwelling.*
> [11] *For He shall give His angels charge over you, to keep you in all your ways.*
> [12] *In their hands they shall bear you up, lest you dash your foot against a stone.*
> [13] *You shall tread upon the lion and the cobra, the young lion, and the serpent you shall trample underfoot.*
> [14] *Because he has set his love upon me, therefore I will deliver him; I will set him on high, because he has known my name.*
>
> *Amen.*

Today, let us meditate on Psalm 91 and lift our hearts in prayer. Always bear in mind that our Lord Jesus Christ will not only stand by us but also bestow upon us the wisdom to protect ourselves. May His divine presence envelop each and every one of you.

May the love of God the Father, the grace of our Lord Jesus Christ, and the guidance of the Holy Spirit be with you. And as His promise declares: He will shelter you safely under His wings. Amen.

JANUARY 29
Remember the dry land

Joshua 3:15-16. "Remember the dry land".

> [15] *And as those who bore the ark came to the Jordan, and the feet of the priests who bore the ark dipped in the edge of the water (for the Jordan overflows all its banks during the whole time of harvest),*
> [16] *that the waters which came down from upstream stood still and rose in a heap very far away at Adam, the city that is beside Zaretan. So, the waters that went down into the Sea of the Arabah, the Salt Sea, failed, and were cut off; and the people crossed over opposite Jericho.*

God, your God, has the power to halt the waters, allowing you to traverse on dry land, reminiscent of the miracle from 40 years prior when He parted the Red Sea. Witness again His great might.

When the second generation of Israelites assembled, on the cusp of crossing the Jordan River, the scriptures recall a divine intervention. As the feet of the priests bearing the Ark of the Covenant touched the water, it surged and heaped on either side. This incredible act is referenced in Joshua 4:23-24: "For the LORD your God dried up the waters of the Jordan before you until you had crossed over, just as the LORD your God did to the Red Sea, which He dried up before us until we had crossed over. This was done so all the peoples of the earth might recognize the hand of the LORD as powerful, instilling perpetual reverence for Him."

During that period, God directed Joshua to have the priests, bearing the Ark, venture into the Jordan River. Despite its raging waters and treacherous currents, an undaunted act of faith was demonstrated. As those carrying the Ark stepped into the water, it receded, standing tall on both sides. Only Joshua and Caleb, from the older generation, remained alive to recall God's intervention at the Red Sea. Their memory of the Red Sea parting under Moses' command fortified their faith, reinforcing the belief that God could repeat such a miracle with the Jordan River. And He did.

If challenges confront you today, remember the Red Sea narrative. God reminds us of His prior acts when we face seemingly insurmountable obstacles.

If you are grappling with a problem today, have faith in Him and acknowledge, "Lord, all is within Your might." Jesus Christ has been bestowed a name that supersedes all, for all is subordinate to Him.

In Jesus Christ's name, every knee shall bow, and every tongue proclaim His lordship. Recollect the instance when He, resting in a boat during a tempest, was awakened by His disciples in panic. He rose, commanding peace, and instantly, all was calm. He possesses dominion over the heavens and the earth; all power resides with Him.

Thus, place your unwavering trust in Him, especially when faced with seemingly impossible odds. Nothing is insurmountable for our Lord Jesus Christ. Let this fortify your spirit and faith, allowing you to deepen your relationship with God, placing undying trust in Him.

In the name of Jesus Christ, Amen.

JANUARY 30
An intermission in your dreams

Genesis 41:52

And the name of the second he called Ephraim: "For God has caused me to be fruitful in the land of my affliction."

God enabled Joseph to be fruitful in the land of his affliction.

In Genesis 39:22-23

[22] The keeper of the prison did not look into anything that was under Joseph's authority, because the LORD was with him; and whatever he did, the LORD made it prosper.
[23] The warden paid no attention to anything under Joseph's care, because the LORD was with Joseph and gave him success in whatever he did.

Here we read how the Lord was with Joseph; and whatever he did, the Lord made it prosper.

In the narrative of Joseph, we see the profound hand of divine intervention. Joseph, as we know, was a dreamer. In one of his dreams, he envisioned himself reigning over not only his brothers but even his parents. Upon sharing this dream, his brothers, fueled by jealousy, sold him to Ishmaelite traders, who subsequently sold him into Egyptian slavery. There, he found himself serving the captain of Pharaoh's guard. But even in these dire circumstances, "The Lord was with Joseph; and whatever he did, the Lord made it prosper."

Despite his honorable conduct, misfortune befell him again when he was falsely accused by the captain's wife. Resisting her advances, he found himself imprisoned due to her false accusations. Yet, even behind bars, Joseph flourished. Why? Because the Lord was with him; and whatever he did, the Lord made it prosper.

A turn of events had Pharaoh's cupbearer and baker imprisoned, both of whom experienced dreams. Joseph, with his God-given ability, interpreted them accurately. Later, when Pharaoh had a perplexing dream, it was Joseph who was summoned to interpret it. His accurate interpretation and wise counsel led to his appointment as the Prime Minister of Egypt, in charge of all food supplies.

Joseph's journey wasn't straightforward. His path, filled with trials and setbacks, might have seemed disconnected from the dreams he had as a young man. However, every challenge was a steppingstone preparing him for the eventual realization of his dream.

If you're holding onto a dream and facing hurdles, remember Joseph's story. Delays, setbacks, and challenges could very well be God's way of preparing you for the bigger picture, the dream He set in your heart. Reflect on this and understand that God remains faithful to His promises; His word never fails.

May the love of the Father, the grace of our Lord Jesus Christ, and the guidance of the Holy Spirit be with you. Amen.

JANUARY 31
No fear in love

1 John 4:18

> *There is no fear in love; but perfect love casts out fear, because fear involves torment. But he who fears has not been made perfect in love.*

There is no fear in love; but perfect love casts out fear.

Hebrews 13:6 we read:

> *So, we may boldly say: "The LORD is my helper; I will not fear. What can man do to me?"*

The Lord is my helper; I will not fear. What can man do to me?

If ever we are afraid of something punishing us or afraid something bad will happen, we must always remember that God is with us. God tells us that he always wants the best for us, things that we cannot even imagine. He tells us that he is our keeper and helper and when he is with us there is no need to be afraid.

When we feel fear, we are saying God we don't trust you but when we are not afraid, we know and show that we trust God to help us. We don't know what will happen in the future, but we know who holds our future because, God with his perfect love, is going to cast out all our fears. When God is with us, we know that not even death will separate us from God's love. We as Christians who believe in Jesus Christ as our Lord and Savior know that when we die, we will be with Jesus Christ in heaven. Death is a step toward our final and heavenly life with the Lord Jesus Christ.

So, friends, let us meditate on this promise of God and principle of faith and know that if there is fear, we should place it at the feet of Jesus Christ because he is good and his perfect love, will cast out all the fears.

May the love of the Father that is perfected and the grace of our Lord Jesus Christ that covers everything be of assistance, help, and guidance by the Holy Spirit be with you. Amen.

FEBRUARY 1
Making a sanctuary for the spirit

Psalms 48:9

> *We have thought, O God, on Your loving kindness, In the midst of Your temple.*

Within your temple, O God, we meditate on your unfailing love.

Psalms 119:147, 148

> 147 *I rise before the dawning of the morning, and cry for help; I hope in Your word.*
> 148 *My eyes are awake through the night watches, That I may meditate on Your word.*
> 47 *for I delight in your commands because I love them.*
> 48 *I reach out for your commands, which I love, that I may meditate on your decrees.*

I rise before dawn, seeking solace and crying out for assistance; my hope anchored firmly in Your word. Throughout the night, my eyes remain open, pondering the messages contained in Your scriptures. We are continually exhorted to be in a state of prayer, to be ever in communion with God.

There's a touching song that resonates with many, expressing the sentiment: "I can approach You anytime, for You are perpetually by my side." Every moment should be an opportunity to spend time with God. While we are free to converse and pray to God at any moment, it's beneficial to allocate specific times and spaces exclusively for this purpose. Doing so allows us to disconnect from worldly distractions and immerse ourselves wholly in divine presence. Such moments rejuvenate our spirits, fostering growth and deeper connection.

Everyone has their unique ritual. Some might find solace in the early morning hours, retreating to the quiet of their basements. Others may prefer the tranquility of their rooms. The manifestation of this personal sanctuary varies.

The Christian movie "War Room" captures this sentiment beautifully. It portrays a woman who transforms her closet into a dedicated prayer space, a sanctified retreat. We find ourselves locked in spiritual combat daily, contending against malevolent forces.

Instead of battling evil head-on, God instructs us to employ prayer as our weapon, summoning divine power to counteract the devil's machinations. Engaging in prayer within your personal sanctuary is deeply fulfilling.

Therefore, I challenge you to identify that special time and place where you can be in solitary communion with our Lord Jesus Christ and the Holy Spirit. Let Him endow you with His power and peace, equipping you to counter the devil's onslaughts. Reflect on these words and find your sanctuary.

May the love of the Father, the grace of our Lord Jesus Christ, and the guidance of the Holy Spirit accompany you always. Amen.

FEBRUARY 2
Peace through faith

Luke 8:48

> *And He said to her, "Daughter be of good cheer; your faith has made you well. Go in peace."*

Then he said to her, "Daughter, your faith has healed you. Go in peace."

Psalms 62:5

> *My soul, wait silently for God alone, for my expectation is from Him.*

Yes, my soul, find rest in God; my hope comes from Him.

The Bible tells the story of a woman who had suffered from a bleeding disorder for over a decade. She had expended all her resources in search of a cure, yet none prevailed. When she heard that Jesus was passing through her town, she was compelled to seek Him out, having heard of His miraculous healings. She thought, "If only I could touch the hem of His garment, I might be made whole."

As Jesus walked through the bustling crowd, people pressed against Him from every side. Suddenly, He paused and inquired, "Who touched Me?" His disciples, perplexed, responded, "Master, the multitudes throng and press You, and You ask, 'Who touched Me?'" But Jesus clarified, "Someone deliberately touched Me, for I felt power go out from Me." Then, the woman, trembling with fear, stepped forward and confessed. Jesus gently lifted her face, smiled, and said, "Daughter, your faith has made you well."

This story prompts us to introspect: Do we possess such unwavering faith? Are we convinced of God's ability to bring peace to our storms and solutions to our longstanding problems? Do we, in our hearts, believe that simply reaching out in faith can bring healing and tranquility? Friends, let us draw nearer to God, not merely to touch the hem of His robe, for through the Holy Spirit, Christ dwells within us. We are in communion with Him at all times. But when we declare, "Lord, I believe You can do this," we acknowledge the peace, healing, and solace that only He can offer.

So, today, let us proceed with renewed faith, expressing our gratitude to the Lord who resides within us. We no longer need to grasp at His robe, for He hears our cries, and through the Holy Spirit, guides our prayers.

Lord, with just one touch from You, all can be made right. We place our trust in You, acknowledging Your sovereignty in every circumstance.

In the powerful name of Jesus Christ, the King of Kings, we pray. Amen.

FEBRUARY 3
Blessed is the believer

Luke 1:45

Blessed is she who believed, for there will be a fulfillment of those things which were told her from the Lord."

Luke 1:46-48

And Mary said: "My soul magnifies the Lord,
47 And my spirit has rejoiced in God my Savior.
48 For He has regarded the lowly state of His maidservant; For behold, henceforth all generations will call me blessed.

Mary is quoted to have said these words after Angel Gabriel met Mary and told her that she is with child. He tells her to name him Emmanuel which means "God is with us", and his name will be Jesus. Mary then says the above words in reverence and obedience to God.

At that time, Mary was probably between 14 to 16 years old, and in that culture, if a woman had a child before getting married, she was condemned and often stoned. Mary was engaged to Joseph, and as we have discussed before, there is the story of how they brought a woman to Jesus, accusing her of committing adultery, and according to the law, she had to be stoned to death. Despite knowing all of this, Mary had strong faith. She was aware of what might happen to her but still praised the Lord because she recognized what a great blessing it was to be the mother of the Messiah.

Mary didn't die for our sins; Jesus did, and Mary was a vessel. Mary had strong faith, and because of this, God used her to bring Jesus into this world. No one can replace Jesus, and we never pray to Mary or to Paul or Peter, because none of them were Christ. Christ died for us on the cross, and it is His blood that cleanses us, for He is the only Son of God who defeated death on the third day.

We should remember that Mary is blessed and thank God for that and for her unwavering faith. Despite everything that could have befallen her, she accepted and said, "God, I know that in the end, all generations will call me blessed."

We too must proceed with faith like this. I too hope that God would work in me to have this kind of faith, so when He says something, I trust that He will do it.

I know God is omnipotent, and He has the power to see it through. So, let us move forward with this power and faith, for our God is able.

Whenever something seems impossible, we must have faith and say, "God, we know you can do it."

In the name of Jesus, may the love of the Father, the grace of Lord Jesus Christ, and the assistance of the Holy Spirit be with you always. Amen.

FEBRUARY 4
God dispels confusion and doubt

Psalms 50:15

> *"...and call on me in the day of trouble; I will deliver you, and you will honor me."*

God says, call upon me when you are in trouble and I will save you and I will show you, my glory.

Psalms 43:3

> *Send me your light and your faithful care, let them lead me; let them bring me to your holy mountain, to the place where you dwell.*

He says, "O God, send your light and your truth, and let them lead me. Let them lead me unto the holy hill and to your sacred tabernacle (tent)."

There are times in life when we face confusion, doubts, and challenges. Perhaps you've relocated to a new place, settled into a new home, and feel disoriented. In such times, God assures us that if we call upon Him, He will guide us through our uncertainties. The God of the Bible invites us, saying, "Come and taste, and see how good I am." Today, let us unite our hearts in prayer. Let us pray together:

Father, in the majestic name of Jesus Christ, the King of kings, we express our gratitude for your boundless love that stretches from heaven to earth. O Father, Creator of heaven and earth, all creation belongs to you. We are profoundly thankful for the sacrifice of your Son, Jesus Christ. We are eternally grateful for His blood shed on the cross, washing away our sins.

We celebrate His resurrection on the third day, through which He was vindicated. We cherish the gift of the Holy Spirit, affirming that we are Your children. Holy Spirit, residing within us, we beseech you to purge any elements not aligned with your divine nature.

O God, dismantle any fortresses of the enemy within us and fill us entirely with the Holy Spirit. We present to You our troubles, doubts, and perplexities, acknowledging that You are the Light of the world, the embodiment of goodness, and the ultimate resolver of all issues.

If you bear a burden, lay it before God's presence now. Present it to Jesus Christ and declare, "O Jesus, I lay these concerns at your feet, trusting you for resolution." O Father, grant solutions to all our problems. Bring healing to the infirm in the mighty name of Jesus Christ. Specifically, bring restoration to those afflicted by the Corona virus. Inspire the discovery of a cure for this virus and guide the creation of an effective vaccine. Bestow wisdom upon our governmental leaders, that they might safeguard our nation and its citizens.

O Lord, equip us with discernment so we always seek You first. We thank You, Father, for heeding our pleas. With faith, we commit this day and all days into Your loving care. In the resplendent name of Jesus Christ, King of kings, we pray. Amen.

May the love of God the Father, the grace of the Lord Jesus Christ, and the fellowship of the Holy Spirit be with you all.

FEBRUARY 5

He should increase and I decrease

John 3:27 to the end of the chapter:

> *John answered and said, A man can receive nothing, except it be given him from heaven.*

John the Baptist was questioned when his disciples informed him, "The one you testified about is baptizing people, and more are flocking to him." John replied, "A man can receive nothing unless it has been given to him from heaven. You yourselves bear me witness, that I said, 'I am not the Christ, but I have been sent before Him. He who has the bride is the bridegroom; but the friend of the bridegroom, who stands by and listens to him, rejoices immensely hearing the bridegroom's voice. Thus, my joy is complete. He must increase, while I must decrease'."

In this chapter, John delves deeper into what John the Baptist proclaimed about Jesus: "He who comes from above is above all; he who is of the earth belongs to the earth and speaks of earthly things. What he has seen and heard; he testifies. He who has accepted his testimony has affirmed that God is truthful. For he whom God has sent utters the words of God, for God gives the Spirit without limit. The Father loves the Son and has placed everything in his hands. He who believes in the Son has eternal life, but he who rejects the Son will not see life, for the wrath of God remains on him."

"He who comes from above is above all; he who is of the earth is earthly." But we must ponder, "Is Jesus Christ growing within us? What does it signify when Jesus Christ thrives in us?" It implies that the nature of Jesus Christ becomes increasingly prominent within us, and our former selves recede. While Jesus is divine and we are of the earth, by embracing Him in our hearts, He and the Holy Spirit dwell within us, initiating a transformation to mold us in His image. Our ultimate aspiration as Christians should be to emulate Jesus Christ, for in doing so, He integrates us into His divine family. Through His sacrifice, He claims us as God's children, allowing us to partake in His divine inheritance. As our elder brother, He labors to refine our spirit to reflect His.

May the Lord Jesus Christ continually transform us, allowing the old self to wane. Let us all be conformed more to the likeness of Christ. May the love of the Father, the grace of our Lord Jesus Christ, and the guidance of the Holy Spirit be with you all.

FEBRUARY 6
The face of forgiveness

In Genesis 33:10

> *And Jacob said, "No, please, if I have now found favor in your sight, then receive my present from my hand, in as much as I have seen your face as though I had seen the face of God, and you were pleased with me.*

2 Corinthians 1:7-8

> 7 *And our hope for you is steadfast, because we know that as you are partakers of the sufferings, so also you will partake of the consolation.*
> 8 *For we do not want you to be ignorant, brethren, of our trouble which came to us in Asia: that we were burdened beyond measure, above strength, so that we despaired even of life.*

"So that, on the contrary, you ought rather to forgive and comfort him, lest perhaps such a one be overwhelmed by excessive sorrow. Therefore, I urge you to reaffirm your love for him."

Why was Jacob fearful of meeting his brother Esau after so many years? Jacob had deeply wronged his brother. He cunningly secured the birthright and, by masquerading as Esau, deceitfully claimed Esau's blessings from their father. Consequently, he fled, fearing Esau's wrath and the possibility of never receiving his brother's forgiveness. Yet, when the moment of their reunion drew near, Esau, upon seeing Jacob, felt an outpouring of love. He raced towards Jacob, embraced him tightly, and kissed him. Esau's forgiveness was a significant relief and blessing for Jacob.

If someone in our lives awaits our forgiveness, let's extend it for the sake of our Lord Jesus Christ. Paul emphasizes in 2 Corinthians the importance of not just forgiving in our hearts but showing the face of forgiveness, much like Esau did. When Esau ran to Jacob, his actions vividly portrayed his forgiving heart. By demonstrating forgiveness, the other person truly comprehends that they are pardoned. This act not only liberates the forgiven but also unburdens the forgiver, enabling spiritual progress and growth. If someone has caused you deep pain, choose to forgive. When sought forgiveness, grant it freely.

Experience the blessings that come with it: the evaporation of anxiety, worry, and sorrow. Let us consistently exhibit the face of forgiveness to all, reflecting the mercy and love of our Savior.

May the Lord Jesus Christ be with you always. May the love of the Father, the grace of our Lord Jesus Christ, and the guidance of the Holy Spirit accompany you on every step of your journey. Amen.

FEBRUARY 7
Pride and humility

Proverbs 16:18-19

Pride goes before destruction, And a haughty spirit before a fall.
[19] *Better to be of a humble spirit with the lowly, than to divide the spoil with the proud.*

The consequence of pride is destruction, and arrogance sets the stage for downfall. It's more honorable to be humble and associate with the oppressed than to share in the spoils of the haughty.

Among all human failings, pride stands as the most grievous. It is the genesis of all sins. It was pride that tempted Adam and Eve in Eden, luring them with the desire to be like God. Similarly, pride led to the fall of Satan, who was once among the most radiant and magnificent of God's angels.

Pride deceives us into thinking, "I am superior to others." Whether it's the pride underlying adultery or betrayal, it remains the root of all sins.

This is why the Lord Jesus Christ consistently preached the virtues of humility. "Those who humble themselves will be exalted, but those who exalt themselves will be humbled." Let us introspect and recognize the seeds of pride within us.

Pride doesn't just lead to destruction; it heralds ruin. Arrogance is a precursor to downfall. It's far nobler to be humble, to sit among the marginalized and those society often overlooks, than to align with the arrogant, regardless of their riches or stature.

God treasures a heart brimming with humility. It's pride that gets wounded when harsh words are thrown our way. It's pride that impedes forgiveness, hinders love, and withholds kindness. Indeed, pride is the root of these transgressions.

Let's unite in prayer:

Heavenly Father, in the majestic name of Jesus Christ, our King, we approach Your throne of grace. We're grateful, Lord, for revealing this profound truth—that pride is the wellspring of all human sins, and it orchestrates our undoing. Lord Jesus, You cleansed our transgressions with Your precious blood, eradicating our inherent pride.

You taught us that through our deeds alone, we cannot attain Your glory, but You bridge that chasm for us.

So, we humble ourselves, recognizing that by our efforts alone, we cannot reach the divine pinnacle. But You, in Your infinite mercy, paid the ultimate price for our redemption. Father, illuminate the areas of pride in our attitudes, behaviors, and actions. Guide us towards humility in every facet of our lives, granting us a gentle heart and spirit. We offer this prayer in the mighty name of Jesus Christ, our King of kings. Amen.

FEBRUARY 8
Trust the Lord with all your heart

Proverbs 3:5-6

> [5] *Trust in the LORD with all your heart and lean not on your own understanding.*
> [6] *In all your ways acknowledge Him, And He shall direct your paths.*

In every aspect of your life, remember the Lord and recognize that all control rests in His hands. Entrust your heart fully to Him, for when you do so, He will guide your every step. "Trust in the LORD with all your heart and lean not on your own understanding; in all your ways submit to him, and he will make your paths straight."

Let's approach the Father with this plea:

Father, in the mighty name of Jesus Christ, our King of kings, we come before You. With unwavering faith, we trust You in every circumstance, with every ounce of our hearts, minds, and very essence.

Jesus, our love for You knows no bounds. You've assured us that when we acknowledge God's hand in everything and recognize all He has accomplished, He will guide and uplift us on our journey.

Today, we place our hopes, dreams, and concerns into Your merciful hands. May Your Holy Spirit guide us, offering the wisdom and strength we need. We wholly rely on You, trusting in Your boundless love and care. Thank You, Father, for being our beacon of hope.

We pray this in the powerful name of Jesus Christ. Amen.

FEBRUARY 9
The excellent guide

Psalms 25:9

> *The humble He guides in justice, And the humble He teaches His way.*

He guides the humble in what is right and teaches them his way or tells them his secrets.

Psalms 25:5

> *Lead me in Your truth and teach me, For You are the God of my salvation; On You I wait all day.*

"Guide me in your truth and teach me, for you are God my Savior, and my hope is in you all day long."

At the core of our spiritual journey, God seeks our humility. It's to the humble in heart and spirit that the Lord unveils His mysteries. The renowned English theologian, Thomas Goodwin, once remarked that the Lord reserves His profound insights for the humble. Yet, to the self-centered and prideful, He remains silent.

When we approach God, it's imperative that we do so with a heart emptied of self-importance, saying, "Lord, You are omniscient while we are but novices. We stand before You, eager to glean from Your wisdom and to be directed by Your hand."

The Lord cherishes such earnestness. He longs for us to earnestly petition Him, admitting our limitations and seeking His divine guidance. It's when we genuinely proclaim, "Lord, my life is Yours to mold as You see fit," that we unlock the treasure trove of His revelations. Are you prepared to take that step?

When we yield to such humility, God's secrets begin to unfurl before us.

We express our gratitude, Lord, for this enlightenment. We recognize that You reserve Your deepest revelations for those with humble spirits. Should arrogance ever cloud our path, we beseech You to guide us back to humility. May we perpetually walk in a manner that pleases You, always radiating humility in Your divine presence. With gratitude, we raise this prayer in the name of Jesus Christ, our King of kings. Amen.

FEBRUARY 10
When things seem unfair remember

Psalms 52:9

For what you have done I will always praise you in the presence of your faithful people.

And I will hope in your name, for your name is good.

O Lord, my heart brims with gratitude for all You've orchestrated in my life. Whenever Your people gather, I lift my voice in worship, praising Your ever-faithful name.

In my trust, I liken myself to a flourishing olive tree rooted in the courts of our God, basking in Your unwavering love for eternity. These sentiments echo in the heart of David when he penned them amidst distress. Before he ascended the throne, David faced severe trials. Israel's king, Saul, driven by envy and fear, sought David's life, knowing that the Lord had anointed David as the future king. This chase led David to seek refuge with the priests of Nob, who, oblivious to the rift between Saul and David, offered him sanctuary. Their innocent act incurred Saul's wrath, resulting in their tragic end.

In Psalm 52, David's anguish is palpable. Torn by confusion and sorrow, he grappled with understanding God's plan amidst the grim circumstances, particularly the fate of the Nob priests. Yet, even when life seemed bleak and devoid of justice, David's faith held steadfast, recognizing that God's sovereignty remains unrivaled and His purposes unfathomable yet always perfect.

In life, when we are ensnared by adversity or face situations that seem harsh and unjust, may we be fortified by the assurance that God's reins are firm. His plans, mysterious as they may seem, are always for our ultimate good.

Romans 8:28 affirms: "And we know that in all things God works for the good of those who love Him, who have been called according to His purpose."

God reassures us that every twist and turn in our journey serves a divine purpose for those who bear His name. With this unwavering trust and profound dependence on Him, let's march ahead, proclaiming:

"O Heavenly Father, no matter the trials and tribulations, we remain ensconced in Your embrace. The horizon might be shrouded in uncertainty, but we rest easy, knowing our future is cradled in the loving hands of our Savior, Jesus Christ, who desires only the best for His flock." Amen.

FEBRUARY 11
Loving behavior

Proverbs 16:27-30

> [27] *An ungodly man digs up evil, and it is on his lips like a burning fire.*
> [28] *A perverse man sows' strife, and a whisperer separates the best of friends.*
> [29] *A violent man entices his neighbor and leads him in a way that is not good.*
> [30] *He winks his eye to devise perverse things; He purses his lips and brings about evil.*

Here, it is mentioned that a godless individual, a vile person, brings forth all the wickedness from beneath the ground, and his words ignite like a raging fire. He speaks of the unclean deeds he unveils from everyone—deeds that are ill-intentioned, events that occurred and are now partially obscured. By revealing these sins, his words turn into a blazing inferno.

An immoral individual or a deviant consistently plants seed of discord, and a person who whispers, speaking gently, estranges close friends. A violent individual misleads his neighbor, guiding him down a perilous path. One who subtly winks, has the power to mislead, diverting individuals down incorrect routes. One who speaks can employ their words for malicious intent. Many speak fondly of love and affection.

In Christianity, love and kindness are not just words but necessitate actions such as compassion, gentleness, and humility. Yet, a mere wink can have sinister motives, negating all prior goodwill expressed. As Christians, we must exercise caution, ensuring we don't reveal those impure thoughts hidden in our minds, and abstain from discussing them with others. In 1 Corinthians 13, it is written: Love shields mistakes; it neither magnifies nor broadcasts them. Love constantly pursues the welfare of others, advocating unity over discord. It refrains from idle talk, does not whisper malevolently into others' ears to inflict harm but instead chooses to shield and protect. Love prioritizes the well-being of one's neighbor and others, never leading them to detrimental situations. Let's direct our prayers to God: Lord, if our actions and words have been inconsistent; if our behavior has caused others to falter and grow apart, we implore your forgiveness.

May you enlighten us swiftly, O God, allowing us to lay our wrongs at your feet. May we echo your love and warmth, emanating a sweet aroma through our deeds, behavior, words, and our very essence.

In our souls linger fortresses of malevolence; O Lord, demolish them. Awaken our spirit, purge us of all that's alien to you, ensuring we grow increasingly in the likeness of your son, Jesus Christ, with each passing day. We offer this prayer in the name of Jesus Christ, the King of kings. Amen.

FEBRUARY 12
Preparation and hope

Our eternal hope lies in Jesus Christ, and it is upon this hope we must act, living lives guided by the Spirit. Let's be primed for action, drawing from the eternal hope embedded in the revelation of Jesus Christ that we've embraced. Let us strive each day to emulate the faith and salvation found in Him, endeavoring always to be more Christlike. How can we grow increasingly in the likeness of Jesus? By immersing ourselves in the Word, delving into the Bible to understand the character of Jesus Christ, and always being receptive to His call.

A methodical reading of the Bible is one way to deepen our relationship with Jesus Christ. If you haven't embarked on this spiritual journey, I urge you to delve into the New Testament. Initiate your reading with the Book of Matthew, committing to a chapter in the morning and one in the evening, and ponder its teachings. Should questions arise, please do not hesitate to reach out to me, Mohsen, so we can explore them together. We've recently embarked on a systematic exploration of the Bible in our church. Currently, our focus is the Book of John. This meticulous approach will bolster our understanding of God's Word, equipping us to lead lives aligned with His desires. May the love of God the Father, the grace of our Lord Jesus Christ, and the fellowship of the Holy Spirit be with you all. Amen.

FEBRUARY 13
A good future

Jeremiah 29:19

For I know the thoughts that I think toward you, says the LORD, thoughts of peace and not of evil, to give you a future and hope.

The Lord says I know the plans that I have for you, plans to prosper, and not harm you. Plans that would give you hope for the future.

Jeremiah 31:16

Thus says the LORD:

"Refrain your voice from weeping, And your eyes from tears; For your work shall be rewarded, says the LORD, And they shall come back from the land of the enemy.

He says, "Don't let your eyes be filled with tears. I will reward you for the things you have done. There's hope for you in the future."

God conveyed this to Jeremiah during the time Judea was enslaved. King Nebuchadnezzar had subjugated them to 70 years of bondage in Babylon. God reassured Jeremiah, saying, "Do not be disheartened by what you witness. Even in the face of such adversities, I remain faithful. I will fulfill my promises." True to His word, after 70 years, God led His people back to their homeland. Even if today feels bleak, even if you find yourself at a seeming impasse, Jesus Christ assures us of His unyielding presence.

The Lord proclaims, "Your future is in my hands." While the intricacies of our future might remain a mystery to us, the one who charts its course wishes only the best for us. His designs are impeccable and for our utmost benefit. Let's anchor ourselves in God's promises, recognizing that whether we face hardship or ailment, God is ever observant, and His designs are invariably for our welfare.

Romans 8:28 articulates: "And we know that all things work together for good to those who love God, to those who are the called according to His purpose."

May this verse fortify you today. During challenging times, always remember: God's presence is unwavering, and He will neither forsake nor abandon you. You are ever enfolded in the Father's love. May the grace of our Lord Jesus Christ and the communion of the Holy Spirit be with each and every one of you. Amen.

FEBRUARY 14
Like an Eagle

Deuteronomy 32:11

As an eagle stirs up its nest, Hovers over its young, spreading out its wings, taking them up, Carrying them on its wings,

It means that like an eagle hover over its young, its spreads its wings, to carry them up and teaches them how to fly.

Psalm 91:4

He shall cover you with His feathers, and under His wings you shall take refuge; His truth shall be your shield and buckler.

It is said that He will cover you with His love, and under His wings, you will find trust and refuge. His truth and His promise act as a shield and a sanctuary.

If you've ever watched a wildlife documentary on eagles teaching their fledgling eaglets to fly, you'll see the profound maternal instinct in action. The mother eagle soars with her young to great heights, then nudges them off the precipice, challenging them to fly. As they falter and fumble, she hovers close by, ever vigilant. Should they plunge downward, she swiftly descends, positioning herself beneath them to catch them on her broad wings. She repeats this until they master the art of flight.

Similarly, in our own lives, God often prompts us to trust Him in situations that seem daunting. When faced with towering challenges, and we feel we're on the precipice of despair, God whispers, "Trust in Me. Just as the eagle safeguards her young, I am with you – above, below, and all around. I will uphold you until you learn to soar with Me." In the face of adversity, God urges us to forge ahead without fear. Though we might feel tentative, teetering on the edge of uncertainty, He reassures us through His Word. He beckons us to trust Him, move forward, and take that leap of faith, confident in the knowledge that He will never let us falter.

Embrace His promises, lean on His Word, and proceed with faith and fidelity. For He counsels us to work diligently and to dispel our fears. With such assurance, we can navigate life, placing unwavering trust and belief in Him.

May the enduring love of the Father, the grace of our Lord Jesus Christ, and the guidance of the Holy Spirit be with you all. Amen.

FEBRUARY 15
No eye has ever seen

1 Corinthians 2:9

> *But as it is written:*
> *"Eye has not seen, nor ear heard, nor have entered into the heart of man The things which God has prepared for those who love Him."*

It is written in God's word that Eye has not seen, nor ear heard nor have entered into the heart of man the things that God has prepared for those who love Him.

Isaiah 64:3

> *When You did awesome things for which we did not look, You came down, The mountains shook at Your presence.*

"When You performed the awe-inspiring deeds, we hadn't anticipated, You descended, and the mountains trembled in Your presence." Elsewhere, it is mentioned that the mountains were shaken.

In our heart's canvas, we paint grand visions—big dreams and spectacular hopes that we believe would usher in joy. Yet, it's essential to recognize that even these grand designs are modest in comparison to the wonders God has in store for those who love Him.

By relinquishing control, by uttering, "Let Your will be done in my life," we pave the way for God's masterful orchestration. The blessings He showers upon us can be so breathtaking that we're left exclaiming, "Wow! I couldn't have possibly fathomed the magnitude of His blessings." Take the Israelites, for instance: cornered at the Red Sea with Pharaoh's elite army in pursuit. Could they have ever envisioned that God would part the vast waters, allowing them safe passage across the dried seabed? It's humbling to realize that our wildest dreams pale in comparison to the majesty of His plans.

So, when we anchor our trust in Him, when we profess our love with genuine fervor, inviting the Father, the Lord Jesus Christ, to work His wonders in our lives, that's when we should take a step back in anticipation. It's then we should proclaim, "Wow! I eagerly await the marvels He's about to unfold." Let us march forth, bolstered by this confidence, constantly reflecting on His boundless love. May the boundless love of God the Father, the abundant grace of our Lord Jesus Christ, and the intimate communion of the Holy Spirit be with you all. Amen.

FEBRUARY 16
Then I will be strong

2 Corinthians 12:10

> *Therefore, I take pleasure in infirmities, in reproaches, in needs, in persecutions, in distresses, for Christ's sake. For when I am weak, then I am strong.*

Paul says therefore I take pleasure in infirmities, in reproaches, in needs, in persecutions, in distresses, for Christ's sake. For when I am weak, then I am strong.

2 Corinthians 11:30-31

> [30] *If I must boast, I will boast in the things which concern my infirmity.*
> [31] *The God and Father of our Lord Jesus Christ, who is blessed forever, knows that I am not lying.*

Paul proclaims, "If I must boast, I will boast of the things that show my weakness." The God and Father of our Lord Jesus Christ, who is eternally blessed, knows I speak the truth. In our moments of vulnerability, it's easier for us to turn to God and admit, "I am weak." Often, when faced with adversity, we might feel that with our skills, talents, and capabilities, we can navigate any situation. We might believe we have it all figured out. However, this isn't always the case. Instead, we should humbly acknowledge, "God, despite the gifts and abilities you've endowed me with, there are areas where I falter. I recognize my frailties and call upon you, for in my weakness, Your strength manifests. In my vulnerabilities, Your might is evident." It's imperative that we lean on Him and not solely on our capacities. We must lay all our concerns at the feet of Jesus, recognizing that with Him, every situation, even those marred by ridicule, belittlement, or pain, becomes an opportunity to witness His strength. Our limitations are the very platforms where God's power is most palpable.

Today, let us approach Jesus Christ and declare: "We are grateful for our weaknesses, for they become the canvas of Your mighty works. In our frailties, Your strength shines brightest. We lay all our inadequacies at Your feet, trusting You to perfect us. We extend our heartfelt gratitude, and in the name of Jesus Christ, we pray. Amen.

FEBRUARY 17
Write it down

Habakkuk 2:2

> *Then the LORD answered me and said:*
> *"Write the vision and make it plain on tablets, That he may run who reads it.*

God says, write down the vision that I show you legibly on a tablet, so that everyone can easily read it.

Revelation 1:19

> *Write the things which you have seen, and the things which are, and the things which will take place after this.*

God instructs John, "Write down what you have seen, the current events, and what will happen thereafter." Why is it crucial to pen down our memories and thoughts?

When we immerse ourselves in God's Word and engage in prayer, it's beneficial to jot down the revelations God grants us during these moments. We ought to document the promises He bestows upon us, the hidden truths He unveils about His scripture, and our petitions to Him.

Recording God's responses to our prayers serves as tangible evidence of our ongoing dialogue and intimate bond with Him. When God imparts a message or assurance, committing it to paper breathes life into His words. This act transforms abstract thoughts into palpable realities. And in moments of doubt or uncertainty, these written records serve as timeless reminders of God's unwavering presence. Moreover, such notes offer future generations — our friends, children, and family — a testament to God's faithfulness and the transformative power of Jesus Christ in our lives.

I encourage each one of you to embark on this practice. Begin today. Chronicle the messages God shares with you and the mysteries He unravels.

May the love of God the Father, the grace of the Lord Jesus Christ, and the communion of the Holy Spirit be with you all. Amen.

FEBRUARY 18
Tears in a bottle

Psalms 56:8

Record my misery; list my tears on your scroll are they not in your record?

It says you number my wanderings; Put my tears into Your bottle Another place it says you know the number of my tears.

Psalm 28:1, 2

[1]To you, LORD, I call; you are my Rock, do not turn a deaf ear to me. For if you remain silent, I will be like those who go down to the pit. [2] Hear my cry for mercy as I call to you for help, as I lift up my hands toward your Most Holy Place.

David penned these words during one of the darkest times in his life, while evading the relentless pursuit of King Saul's soldiers: "To you, O Lord, my Rock, I cry: Do not remain silent towards me. If you are silent, I become like those who descend into the grave. Hear my pleas when I call out to you, when I lift my hands towards your holy dwelling."

Even with God's promise that he would be the king of Israel, David faced tremendous adversity. Saul's intent was clear: David's demise. Yet, amidst all this turmoil, David consistently sought refuge in God. He reminds us that during our moments of despair, God takes note of every tear we shed. The Lord says, "I have collected your tears in a bottle and recorded each one in my book."

When engulfed by life's storms, if we stand firm on God's promises and believe that He will fulfill every word, we can find solace in knowing our tears aren't in vain. God is intimately aware of each one, and He will transform them into moments of joy and contentment. This joy isn't fleeting; it's profound and eternal, emanating from the Holy Spirit dwelling within us.

Our true joy is anchored in God. Our steadfast hope is in Jesus Christ, who sacrificed Himself for our sins. He remains true to His promises and is perpetually faithful. If tears flow from your eyes, take heart in knowing that God witnesses every droplet. He safeguards them, reflecting on His unwavering love, faithfulness, and mercy. Through Jesus Christ's sacrifice on the cross, we are brought near to the Father, not by our deeds but by His grace. Recognized as His children, it is through the Holy Spirit that we are guided towards eternal life. Amen.

FEBRUARY 19
Fully assured

Hebrews 11:1

> [1]*Now faith is the substance of things hoped for, the evidence of things not seen.*
> [2]*For by it the elders obtained a good testimony.*

This verse tells us that faith is the assurance of what we hope for and the belief in what we don't see.

2 Thessalonians 3:5

> *Now may the Lord direct your hearts into the love of God and into the patience of Christ.*

The scripture tells us that God will direct our hearts to His love and into Christ's enduring patience. In contemporary terms, true confidence is rooted in having unwavering trust in what we hope for, even when it remains unseen.

Perhaps you're facing setbacks today, and the dreams you cherish seem distant. Yet, our faith reminds us of God's omnipotence. What seems insurmountable to us is effortless for Him. You might question, "Will He really act on my behalf? Does He truly love me enough to intervene?" The answer resounds: "Absolutely. Wholeheartedly, yes." God's boundless love was manifested in Jesus Christ. But to fully experience this divine love and mercy, we must approach with faith.

Embrace the love and steadfast patience of Jesus Christ, letting Him lead the way. Progress today fortified by this profound conviction. While hope is the anticipation of the unseen, faith is the certitude in its realization. And one undeniable truth remains: both God the Father and Jesus Christ are ever faithful, loving us deeply, ensuring they never let us down.

Dear Heavenly Father, in the mighty name of Jesus Christ, our King of kings, we express our gratitude for the gift of faith and the beacon of hope you've ignited in us. We're confident in your desire for our utmost good. Today, we lay our aspirations before you, seeking your optimal plans for us. Strengthen our faith, O Lord. In Jesus Christ's name, we pray. Amen.

FEBRUARY 20
Justice served

Psalms 58:10-11

[10] The righteous shall rejoice when he sees the vengeance; He shall wash his feet in the blood of the wicked,
[11] So that men will say, "Surely there is a reward for the righteous; Surely He is God who judges in the earth."

This verse says that the virtuous will rejoice when they see the wicked have been punished. And then, in verse 11, it says that in the end, everyone will proclaim that the virtuous are truly rewarded, and there is a God who judges the world.

Have you ever thought that bad people constantly do wrong yet often go unpunished, while when you or I err, we face consequences? However, the reality is that no one can escape the ramifications of their actions. Sins have varied consequences, and God holds accountable all those who commit them.

Though God might not address them immediately, ultimately, He addresses these injustices and wrong deeds. Even in these moments, because God embodies love, He doesn't wish for us to be preoccupied with questions like, "Why wasn't this injustice addressed? Why this incident and not that one?" For, as the Word states, vengeance is God's, and He will exact it in His time. But for you and me, He desires only love and affection. Our role, when faced with injustice, is to pray for the unjust and malicious. Why? So they might encounter God. Because once they truly recognize the Lord Jesus Christ and embrace Him as their Savior and Messiah, they will become aware of their sins.

Subsequently, they will repent and turn to God. Thus, moving forward, let's not dwell excessively on injustices. We should observe, understand, and recognize them, but our reaction should be distinct. Our primary response should be prayer and reflection, aiming for them to discover and follow God. Amen.

Today, if we witness injustice or encounter the wicked, let's swiftly bring them to God, saying, "Lord Jesus Christ, they need You more than anyone else. Enter their lives, cleanse them, so they too might follow You, walk in Your ways, and extol You." Father, in the name of Jesus Christ, we beseech that whenever we witness injustice and wickedness, You empower us to present them to You and pray for them. We pray in the name of Jesus Christ, King of kings. Amen.

FEBRUARY 21
A beautiful message

Isaiah in 52:7

> [7] *How beautiful on the mountains are the feet of those who bring good news, who proclaim peace, who bring good tidings of good things, who proclaim salvation, who say to Zion, "Your God reigns!"*

This verse says, what a great pleasure it is to see the messenger come down from the mountain and bring the good news of peace.

Isaiah in 52:8

> *Your watchmen shall lift up their voices, with their voices they shall sing together; For they shall see eye to eye When the* LORD *brings back Zion.*

In verse 8, it says, "The watchmen lift up their voices with joy, and all the people shout out of joy, and with their own eyes, they witness the return of God to Zion."

In this world, everyone seeks hope, and there are various forms of it. While some hope for material things, we understand that the ultimate hope lies in God. However, perceptions of God differ among people. Some see Him as a deity who merely issues commands, dictating "do this" or "do that." But we, His followers, truly understand His nature. Why? Because we recognize Him as the source of joy, kindness, love, and hope. This is the God we are acquainted with. This is the God whose presence fills us with exuberance and hope.

We understand that God yearns for an intimate relationship with us. He is the loving Father who, even when we were adversaries, didn't hesitate to offer up His son for us. God manifested in flesh as Jesus Christ, recognizing that the sole path to our salvation was to personally descend, bear our sins, and pave the way for us.

He is a God brimming with love, promising us eternal life and an inner joy that remains unshakable. Today, let's reach out to those searching for this profound hope and eternal life. Let's share the good news of God's coming and of Jesus Christ, whose sacrifice and resurrection bestow upon us eternal life and a deep connection with God.

Father, in the name of Jesus Christ, we express our gratitude for today and for Your unwavering love. You've blessed us with the vision to discern that true joy, hope, and truth lie in You and Your son, Jesus Christ.

Today, grant us the bravery and vigor to share this revelation with others, guiding them towards this ultimate hope, inner contentment, and everlasting life. In the name of Jesus Christ, Amen.

FEBRUARY 22
Setting standard

Titus 2:7

In all things showing yourself to be a pattern of good works; in doctrine showing integrity, reverence, incorruptibility,

Paul says, in your life every aspect should be an example of good deeds, be sincere in your teachings and be faithful.

In Titus 3:8

This is a faithful saying, and these things I want you to affirm constantly, that those who have believed in God should be careful to maintain good works. These things are good and profitable to men.

Paul states, "This word is true, and I want you to emphasize it so that those who believe in God remember to dedicate themselves to good deeds. These deeds are beneficial and valuable to people." In Paul's time, the churches on the island of Crete desperately needed leadership. Paul wasn't seeking teachers abundant in knowledge; he stressed the importance of a leader with a noble character, someone intimate with God. While knowledge is vital, it's essential to teach those around us about God through our deeds and daily living, rather than just our words.

Do people see congruence between our professed beliefs and our actions? Do we genuinely love? Are we consistently kind? Do we extend help to the needy? Do we visit prisoners? Or do we merely proclaim the importance of love? Let's strive to live in a way that the essence of Christ in our lives resonates with others. There's an English adage: "Let our actions reflect our faith." By doing so, may others see the reflection of our God in our lives and be drawn to worship Him. Father, in the name of Jesus Christ, empower us today not just to speak but to actualize our words into actions. Our deeds are the fruits borne from the Holy Spirit's work within us. Holy Spirit, perfect your work in us. We express our gratitude, Father.

We pray in the mighty name of Jesus Christ, the King of kings, Amen.

FEBRUARY 23
Bringing the best out

Proverbs 27:17

> *As iron sharpens iron, So a man sharpens the countenance of his friend.*

This verse says that iron polishes and sharpens iron, and in the same way one person sharpens another.

Psalm 119:63

> *I am a companion of all who fear You, and of those who keep Your precepts.*

This verse declares, "O Lord, I am a friend to all who revere you, and to those who uphold your statutes and your righteousness." When one wishes to sharpen a knife, they rub it against another iron or knife, side by side, ensuring both become polished and sharper. However, if the two are rubbed vertically against each other, not only do they fail to sharpen one another, but they may also become dull and damaged.

This same principle is applicable to our relationships with others. Are our friends and close companions living in alignment with God's intentions? Do they cherish God as we do? Or do they possess differing beliefs about God, or perhaps do not acknowledge Jesus Christ at all? If such is the case, are you maintaining these associations? Occasionally, these connections can weaken our bond with God. However, when we surround ourselves with fellow Christians who share our beliefs, our relationship with God is honed and strengthened. The encouragement I offer you elevates you, and the testimonies you share of God's work in your life uplift me. When you seek understanding about God and I provide insight, it bolsters your connection.

Conversely, when I pose questions and you supply the answers, it reinforces both our mutual relationship and our bond with God. Today, let us gravitate towards Christian friends who can enhance our bond with God and with each other, rather than those who might diminish our spiritual sharpness.

Father, in the name of Jesus Christ, we express gratitude for the faithful friends you have placed in our lives. Through them, we refine and enhance one another, deepening our love and understanding of you.

May you grant us opportunities today to foster bonds with those who uplift and edify us in your presence. We pray in the name of Jesus Christ, the King of kings. Amen.

FEBRUARY 24
Keep watch with Me

Matthew 26:38

> *Then He said to them, "My soul is exceedingly sorrowful, even to death. Stay here and watch with Me."*

Jesus Christ tells his disciples, "My soul is exceedingly sorrowful, even unto death. You stay here and stay awake with me".

Mark 14:32

> *They went to a place called Gethsemane, and Jesus said to his disciples, "Sit here while I pray."*

He mentions this when they arrived at a place called Gethsemane. Jesus instructed his disciples, "Stay here while I pray." The Bible recounts that Jesus Christ was profoundly distressed on that final night, to the extent that as He wept, His tears became like drops of blood. Upon reaching Gethsemane, He was so burdened with sorrow that He asked His disciples to remain there. Even though the disciples were unaware of the depth of Christ's sorrow at that moment and didn't understand how to console Him, their mere presence and their prayers offered solace and peace to Jesus. It is heart-wrenching to witness the suffering of our dear ones, especially when we feel helpless in alleviating their pain. However, we can always offer our presence, our unwavering support, and our prayers, ensuring they never feel isolated in their trials. Remember when Jesus went off to pray and the disciples dozed off? Let us not be like those disciples when our friends and family require our spiritual support and comfort. We must remain vigilant for those we care about, accompanying them, standing by their side, and praying with them, assuring them of our solidarity. Amen.

God the Father, in the name of Jesus Christ, we are grateful for setting a perfect example for us. Jesus Christ, despite bearing immense grief, chose to shoulder the sins of the world, to pray, and to fulfill the Father's will. You only asked your disciples to remain, to stay alert, and to pray. Lord, empower us not to succumb to slumber when we should be alert, vigilant, and engaged in prayer. We beseech in the name of Jesus Christ, the King of kings, Amen.

FEBRUARY 25
Bound by love and faithfulness

Proverbs 3:3-4

> *Let not mercy and truth forsake you; Bind them around your neck, Write them on the tablet of your heart, And so find favor and high esteem In the sight of God and man.*

This verse tells us, never lose sight of honesty and truthfulness, bind them around your neck and write them upon your heart.
If you do this, God and people will be pleased with you.

Proverbs 14:22

> *Do they not go astray who devise evil? But mercy and truth belong to those who devise good.*

This verse emphasizes that those who harbor good intentions are blessed with love and trustworthiness. Today, we are called to engrave two virtues on our hearts: love and faithfulness.

When we embrace and embody these two virtues, they shape our character and the path we tread in life. Today, let's radiate our love towards others through compassion, loyalty, and kindness. Let us demonstrate this love with unwavering trust and by continually praising the Lord. Furthermore, let our faithfulness be wholehearted and genuine in every interaction—be it with close ones or mere acquaintances.

Absolute honesty in every circumstance, authentic in all things. Recall our discussions about those who are uncertain, those whose faith wavers, as if one foot is in this realm and the other in the next. Let's march forward with steadfast faith, manifesting our love and loyalty with unwavering belief.

God assures us that if we inscribe love and faithfulness onto our hearts, and navigate our lives with noble intentions, not only will we find favor with our fellow humans, but He Himself will bless and delight in us.

Father, we are deeply grateful today, for you have revealed to us these two pivotal keys to endear both our peers and ourselves: love and faithfulness. Lord, empower us to reflect Your love and loyalty to others. In all our deeds and interactions, may we remain genuine, truthful, and sincere. Let our actions bring a smile to Your radiant face, dear Jesus Christ, Amen.

FEBRUARY 26
Mandatory boundaries

Jeremiah 5:22

> *Do you not fear Me?' says the LORD. 'Will you not tremble at My presence, who have placed the sand as the bound of the sea, By a perpetual decree, that it cannot pass beyond it? And though its waves toss to and fro, yet they cannot prevail; Though they roar, yet they cannot pass over it.*

This verse says, I am the Lord. Why do you not keep my sanctity? Why do you not tremble with fear in my presence? I put the sand at the border of the sea, a border that the seawater never crosses.
Proverbs 16:6

> *In mercy and truth Atonement is provided for iniquity; And by the fear of the LORD one departs from evil.*

David proclaims, "The inheritance you have granted me, and the boundaries you have set for my territory, are splendid." Have you ever pondered the significance of the beach that keeps the vast seas and rivers distinct from the land?

Some of us have witnessed floods and are well aware of the devastation they bring. Yet, God declares, "I have established this border to prevent the waters from trespassing." In a similar vein, God has delineated boundaries for our lives. He has prescribed limits that, if we adhere to, will guarantee our safety, joy, and contentment.

By obeying what God has instructed and refraining from what He has prohibited, we position ourselves within His protective embrace. His commandments, detailed in the Bible, outline these boundaries for our wellbeing, urging us to remain within His protective confines.

Let us turn to God today and exclaim:

"O Lord, you are a marvel of unparalleled magnificence! Your creations are awe-inspiring, and your nature overflows with love and tenderness. We thank You for the protective boundaries You've established for us, for Your unwavering vigilance, and for the countless blessings You bestow upon us. We're eternally grateful for Jesus Christ's sacrificial blood shed on the cross, granting us salvation from the snares of death and darkness, ushering us into Your luminous kingdom. Truly, your deeds are wondrous!

O God, your actions are magnificent. We're profoundly grateful for Your protective embrace and unwavering support. Guide us today, reminding us of the boundaries You've set. Assist us in aligning with Your will and precepts. We are confident in Your promise to stand by us, and we extend our heartfelt gratitude. In the name of Jesus Christ, the King of kings, we pray and embrace Your blessings with unwavering faith, Amen.

FEBRUARY 27
Until our souls are satisfied

Psalms 63:1

> *O God, You are my God; early will I seek You. My soul thirsts for You; my flesh longs for You in a dry and thirsty land where there is no water.*

David says,

> *"O God, you are my God. I'm longing for you like a parched, scorching land; with all my being, I am thirsty for you."*

And later on, he says, "My soul shall be satisfied, and my mouth shall praise you with joyful songs." Sometimes, life and responsibilities drain all of our energy. We then wonder if this is all there is to life. When problems arise and we become mired in them, we question the purpose of life. But during these times, we should turn to God wholeheartedly and say, "O God, we are thirsty for you. We yearn for your presence. Come and quench the dryness in our hearts."

That's when God steps in, banishing our aridness with His refreshing waters, replenishing both body and soul. He replaces our fatigue, despair, anxiety, and confusion with joyous songs, urging us to sing His praises. He is our eternal haven. Jesus Christ is the steadfast rock upon which we can stand.

So, if we find ourselves weary, heartbroken, or feeling lost, let's turn to the King of kings, Jesus Christ, and say, "O Lord, our souls are thirsty for you. Come and satiate our thirst." Father, we thank you for your boundless love and kindness, for always being by our side, and for quenching our parched souls. In the name of Jesus Christ, Amen.

FEBRUARY 28
Hearing our hearts

Romans 8:26

> *Likewise, the Spirit also helps in our weaknesses. For we do not know what we should pray for as we ought, but the Spirit Himself makes intercession for us with groanings which cannot be uttered.*

Paul writes, in this way, that the Spirit of God helps us when we are weak and helpless. Because we don't yet know how to pray, but the God himself intercedes for us with groans that cannot be uttered.

Romans 8:27

> *Now He who searches the hearts knows what the mind of the Spirit is, because He makes intercession for the saints according to the will of God.*

Paul mentions that it is God the Father, who searches the hearts of men, who understands the intentions of the Spirit. The Holy Spirit intercedes for the saints according to the will of God. Sometimes, we reach a point where words fall short, failing to convey our innermost feelings and struggles. We find ourselves at an impasse, doubting whether even the loudest screams can articulate our inner turmoil. In these moments of weariness and uncertainty, the Holy Spirit, who dwells within believers of Jesus Christ, becomes our voice.

When required, the Holy Spirit steps forward, praying to the Father on our behalf. There are instances when the depths of our hearts are too profound to express verbally, but the Holy Spirit, intimately acquainted with every fiber of our being, understands both our conscious and subconscious selves. Being the Spirit of God, the very One who crafted us, He knows our intricacies better than we do. Hence, He can advocate for us with unmatched precision. So, in moments of despair, when words elude us, trust that the Holy Spirit speaks and intercedes for us.

Father, we are deeply grateful for the Holy Spirit residing within us. Through our acceptance of Jesus Christ as our Lord and Savior, He becomes the testament to our unwavering faith and devotion. We invite the Holy Spirit to move freely within us, refining our spirit and casting away elements that aren't of You. Fill us with Your presence, for, without You, we are powerless. We find solace knowing that Your intercession is always aligned with goodness. We offer this prayer in the name of Jesus Christ, the King of kings. Amen.

MARCH 1
Before we knew

Romans 5:8

But God demonstrates His own love toward us, in that while we were still sinners, Christ died for us.

This verse says, when we were sinners, God showed his love and mercy towards us by bringing Jesus Christ to us.

Psalms 13:5

But I have trusted in Your mercy; My heart shall rejoice in Your salvation.

The scripture declares, "I trust in your love, and my heart rejoices because you saved me." We don't have to earn God's love. His love has been our companion from the very beginning before our existence. He loved us even before we came into this world.

God demonstrated this love when, while we were still His enemies, He sent Jesus Christ to us. Jesus Christ, God manifested in human form, came to save us even when we stood against Him. Over 2000 years ago, before we came into being, God showcased His love and mercy towards us. He sent Jesus Christ to Earth to sacrifice for us, knowing that this was the singular path to our salvation, a way to bring us back into His fold. Thus, reestablishing the divine connection that God envisioned for us. It's essential to understand that this bond isn't built on our deeds. We can't earn God's love through acts of charity or kindness. Instead, it's through faith in God and His grace that we've been saved, drawing nearer to Him each day.

Our righteous actions should spring from our faith. These deeds are an expression, a tangible result, of our belief. Faith is paramount, accompanied by the knowledge that God's love is without conditions. We shouldn't harbor the notion that performing certain good acts makes us more deserving of God's love. The sole prerequisite is for you and me to behold the love and mercy in Jesus Christ's eyes and accept Him as our Lord and Savior.

Father, we are deeply grateful for Your love that knows no bounds or conditions, a love so profound that even when we stood opposed to You, You didn't refrain from offering us Your Son. Thank You, Father. Today, we embrace this truth, acknowledging and expressing our gratitude for Your love. A love that demands nothing from us but faith in Lord Jesus Christ. Strengthen our faith, Lord, and fortify our commitment. Amen.

MARCH 2
Above the ark

Exodus 25:22 – God says:

> *And there I will meet with you, and I will speak with you from above the mercy seat, from between the two cherubim which are on the ark of the Testimony, about everything which I will give you in commandment to the children of Israel.*

Psalm 63:2-3 – David says:

> *So I have looked for You in the sanctuary, To see Your power and Your glory. 3 Because Your Loving kindness is better than life, my lips shall praise You.*

In the temple of God in Jerusalem, there was a special place, deeper within, where the Ark of the Covenant was kept – the Holiest of Holies. The word 'Ark' in Hebrew translates to 'coffin', symbolizing the very coffin of God. It's intriguing that God says He will speak from above this coffin, implying a connection with the realm of the dead. The high priest was permitted to enter this sacred place only once a year. By addressing from above the coffin, God demonstrates His supreme power over death, a power that was unequivocally displayed when He raised Jesus from the dead. Jesus Christ is our ultimate salvation.

God's might shines brightest in our moments of despair. When our hopes and dreams feel extinguished, when aspirations seem like a lifeless body in a coffin, that's when God's resounding voice can bring them back to life. As we approach Him with our deepest yearnings, even those that seem impossible or long-gone, we say: "Lord, speak to us above this coffin. Defeat the grasp of death and display Your unmatched love, glory, and magnificence. Breathe life into these dormant dreams and seemingly insurmountable hopes. For Your Son, Jesus Christ, gave His life for our sins on the cross, and through His resurrection, You showcased Your unparalleled power, wisdom, and grace. When we unite with Him, we no longer see death. Instead, we behold the resurrected Jesus Christ within us and reflect His image to the world."

MARCH 3
Why has it happened?

John 9:3

> *Jesus answered, "Neither this man nor his parents sinned, but that the works of God should be revealed in him.*

It says this happened so that the works of God might be revealed in him. When Jesus Christ wanted to heal someone that was born blind, his disciple asked him whose fault it was due to. During those days they believed that if someone was born blind it was because their parents had committed a sin or they were in sin themselves. Jesus Christ corrected them and said this has happened to him so that the power of God can be shown.

Psalms 68:28

> *Your God has commanded your strength; Strengthen, O God, what You have done for us.*

The Scriptures say, "God, show us your strength in the same way you have done for us before." I recall a time when I was fervently praying for someone in need, and I found myself pondering, "Why did this happen?" Despite all the prayers, heartfelt conversations, and physical aid I provided, I struggled to understand the reason behind the ordeal.

Often, when we encounter adversity, we instinctively question, "Did I cause this? Is this my fault?" But as I meditated on this passage from the Psalms, God revealed a profound truth to me: Sometimes, He allows specific challenges to acquaint individuals with the malevolence and depravity of the world. Through these experiences, they gain the insight and compassion required to minister to others and guide them back to God.

So, if you find your prayers seeming unanswered, or you grapple with doubts, wondering if you've erred, remember this: God might be allowing these circumstances to display His mighty power within that individual or group. Much like the blind man in the Scriptures, God desires to manifest His power within us, enlightening our vision and fortifying our faith in Him.

Father, we are profoundly grateful for the revelations You provide through Your Holy Spirit, which helps us discern the purpose behind life's trials. Even when we fail to comprehend, we know we can entrust our uncertainties to You. You are our steadfast rock, the foundation upon which we stand with confidence. May we always place our faith in You, knowing

You will orchestrate the best outcome from every situation. We extol You, Lord, in the cherished name of Jesus Christ, the King of Kings. Amen.

MARCH 4
Answer is coming

Psalm 5:3

> *My voice You shall hear in the morning, O Lord; In the morning I will direct it to You, And I will look up.*

Psalms 85:8

> *I will hear what God the LORD will speak, For He will speak peace To His people and to His saints; But let them not turn back to folly.*

If you rise early in the morning and make conversing with God and reading His Word your initial acts, you will discover the deep joy embedded in such moments.

While we often approach God to communicate our desires, I encourage you to occasionally seek God solely for His presence. Say to Him, "We have conversed numerous times, and now I choose to listen. I yearn to hear Your voice." While we trust that our prayers will be heeded, taking moments of stillness to proclaim, "God, I am here, listening intently. Speak to me," allows for a deeper connection. Our God is a deity of love and connection. He doesn't desire a one-sided relationship. He yearns for a mutual exchange, eager to communicate with us, but He requires attentive ears on our part. So, every so often, when you approach God, instead of listing your requests, simply say, "Lord, while you are familiar with my desires, I seek to hear Your voice today. Guide me in Your ways." And He will respond. When discerning God's voice, always bear in mind that His words will never conflict with the scriptures in the Bible.

Father, in the precious name of Jesus Christ, the King of Kings, we approach Your throne. You are omniscient, knowing all our needs and desires. We are deeply grateful for the mutual bond we share with You. Lord, please converse with each of us, opening our ears so we might discern the sweetness of Your voice. In the name of Jesus Christ, we pray. Amen.

MARCH 5
God is near

Zephaniah 3:17

> *The LORD your God in your midst, The Mighty One, will save; He will rejoice over you with gladness, He will quiet you with His love, He will rejoice over you with singing."*

John 13: 23

> *Now there was leaning on Jesus' bosom one of His disciples, whom Jesus loved.*

When we intentionally distance ourselves from the relentless pace of the world – when we resist the urge to constantly think, "I must do this now or that in two minutes" – and choose to close the door on such frenzy, we find tranquility in God's presence. It's vital to keep in mind that God has assured us, "I will never leave you nor forsake you."

Though we have discussed this before, there are times we might feel estranged from God. However, it's crucial to always recognize His ever-present nature and seek intimacy with Him. Should we not aspire to be like John, whom God cherished deeply? On that final night, John rested his head on Jesus' bosom. It's that very closeness that God desires with each of us. Our God values deep relationships. He longs for us to lean into Him, setting aside all distractions and making Him our foremost priority. We are His, bound by mutual love. And now, let us pray:

Father, in the precious name of Jesus Christ, we express our gratitude for Your unwavering presence and boundless love. No matter our circumstances, You are ever-present. We ask for Your assistance in setting aside the world's distractions, even momentarily, to seek refuge in Your peace. Strengthen us, so that we may advance, living out Your purpose. We thank You, in the name of Jesus Christ, King of Kings, Amen.

MARCH 6
Special salutation

Matthew 6:9,10

In this manner, therefore, pray: Our Father in heaven, hallowed be your name. Your kingdom comes. Your will be done on earth as it is in heaven.

Psalm 67:3

Let the peoples praise You, O God; Let all the peoples praise You.

The disciples of Jesus once observed Him in deep prayer, kneeling in humble communion with the Father. Inspired by what they saw, they approached Jesus and requested, "Teach us to pray, just as John the Baptist taught his disciples."

In response, Jesus imparted a blueprint for prayer that starts by acknowledging and extolling the divine nature of God. He taught them to begin with words of adoration: "Our Father in Heaven, hallowed be Your name. Your will be done on Earth as it is in Heaven."

Prayer, as Jesus revealed, isn't merely about asking for needs or desires. It's about forging a sincere, personal, and intimate connection with God. We're drawn to His boundless love, and in prayer, we express our reciprocal love and submission to His divine will. We acknowledge His sovereignty over everything and profess our understanding of His holy nature.

With hearts filled with gratitude, we approach Him saying, "Thank you, God. You are our cherished Father. We are paramount in Your eyes, just as You are in ours. We exalt You and express our gratitude for the gift of another day, all in the powerful name of Jesus Christ." Amen.

MARCH 7
Choices

Psalms 66:18

If I regard iniquity in my heart, The Lord will not hear.

Psalms 66:8,9

8 Oh, bless our God, you peoples! And make the voice of His praise to be heard,
9 Who keeps our soul among the living and does not allow our feet to be moved.

Every choice we make in life, small or big, shows what our values are. Is our choice based on what God has taught us? In God's view, is it a good choice? Or is our choice based on worldly things? Every choice we make either respects God or disrespects Him.

You may ask about very ordinary things: What should I wear? What food should I eat? Where to go and where not to go? Are these important to God? Yes, they are also essential. God is our Father, and He is a God of details. Every detail demonstrates our respect for Him. In churches, respect is shown in the way we dress. Do the clothes I wear cause my brothers or sisters to sin? Do the clothes I wear arouse lust in them? Especially for men, men are very visual. That's why clothes that expose many parts of the body can be very lustful for men.

So, the way we dress, men too, the way men dress for women, or any of our behaviors, our words, our jokes, do they cause others to sin? Do we respect God in all of them? These small details, these small choices, show our lives to others and indicate whether we are the children of God or not.

So, let us go to God and say, "God, our Father, we are grateful, and we thank you for holding us in your arms. Our lives are in your hands, so please show us the things you love. The things you love are written for us in your book, but open our eyes to see, open our ears to hear. May God give us the strength to obey what He tells us.

In the name of Jesus Christ. Amen.

MARCH 8
Listen to our hearts

Psalms 33:20,21

> [20] *Our soul waits for the LORD; He is our help and our shield.*
> [21] *For our heart shall rejoice in Him, because we have trusted in His holy name.*

Then Psalms 4:7

> *You have put gladness in my heart, more than in the season that their grain and wine increased.*

The special and beloved place for God is our hearts. This is where God lives and speaks to us, for those who have accepted Jesus Christ as Lord and taken Him into their hearts as their Savior. The first condition for this is our belief in Jesus Christ as God, the Savior, the Lord, and King of our lives. When we sincerely hold this belief, God takes residence in our hearts with His Holy Spirit. This communion encompasses all who are believers. It's within our hearts that we grasp the profound depth of God's love for us. It's here that we forge a powerful bond with Him, seeking His guidance with unwavering confidence. From the sanctuary of our hearts, we can candidly and serenely present our needs to God, who perpetually provides for us. Our heart is the sanctified realm where we commune with God. Our heart is imbued with God's presence, enabling us to discern His voice and words, always brimming with love and tenderness towards us. Therefore, lend an ear to your heart today. Remember, the guidance you discern should align with God's word. How can we ascertain that what resonates in our ears and hearts is truly from God? It is by ensuring that it doesn't deviate from the scriptures in the Bible. Father, we're eternally grateful. We thank you, Jesus Christ. We thank you, Holy Spirit, for designating our heart as Your dwelling, allowing us to commune and share fellowship with You at any moment, from anywhere. Inspire us to set aside time for You, to seek You and delve into Your Word.

In the name of Jesus Christ, Amen.

MARCH 9
Speak with a friend

Exodus 3:11

> *But Moses said to God, "Who am I that I should go to Pharaoh, and that I should bring the children of Israel out of Egypt?"*

John 15:15

> *No longer do I call you servants, for a servant does not know what his master is doing; but I have called you friends, for all things that I heard from My Father I have made known to you.*

Prayer is a relationship. As we've previously discussed, a relationship is forged when we communicate with someone familiar. When we approach God in dialogue, in prayer, the Lord Jesus Christ regards us as His friends. With our best friends, there's no apprehension of judgment or humiliation; we can bare our souls to them.

We confide our deepest secrets, our innermost desires. God assures us, "You are my friends, for I've unveiled all my secrets to you. You aren't just my servants or slaves. I've shared everything I know with you." And He documented it all in His Word, the Bible.

Thus, when we approach Him in prayer, we should do so with the sentiment that He is our most cherished friend. Such a friend always desires the best for us, expects no pretenses from us, refrains from judgment, and allows us to be genuine.

Henceforth, as we pray, let's embrace the notion that we're confiding in our dearest, most intimate friend—One who understands us profoundly.

Jesus Christ, we express our gratitude for deeming us worthy of Your friendship, for sharing Your mysteries with us, and for recording those revelations in Your Word. We are thankful that we can approach You like a dear friend, pouring our hearts out without reservations. Lord, we commit this day into Your blessed hands, seeking Your will and guidance in each of our lives. Amen.

MARCH 10
Peace in center of life

Colossians 3:15

> *And let the peace of God rule in your hearts, to which also you were called in one body; and be thankful.*

Philippians 4:7

> *And the peace of God, which surpasses all understanding, will guard your hearts and minds through Christ Jesus.*

When we possess peace in our hearts, this tranquility enables wondrous, beautiful, and incredible events to unfold in our lives and within ourselves. This peace is a gift from God, allowing us to draw near to Him and embrace His love, tenderness, and blessings.

This peace stands tall against the storms, challenges, and disturbances that surround us, quelling their turbulence. Such serenity and steadiness bear testimony to our lives, our understanding, and our faith when we present ourselves before God.

Recognizing God's profound love for us brings forth His peace. This peace bestows upon us the capacity to forgive, and it is this very peace that holds us upright. It reveals God's infinite mercy and the remarkable opportunities He presents in our lives.

God's peace illuminates our path, guiding our decisions. When we sense His peace leading the way, we know we tread on God's path. If that peace is absent in any endeavor or circumstance, it's clear it isn't of God. God embeds this peaceful reassurance and the warmth of His love deep within our hearts. Amen. Dear friends, today let us exclaim, "Oh God, we thank you immeasurably!"

O Father, Jesus Christ, we are grateful for Your peace. Jesus Christ proclaimed, "I grant you My peace, distinct from the peace this world offers." Lord Jesus, we are deeply thankful for the peace You've instilled in our hearts, granting us confidence to navigate life's complexities.

In the name of Jesus Christ, Amen.

MARCH 11
A sponge in ocean

Acts 17:27,28

> [27]*So that they should seek the Lord, in the hope that they might grope for Him and find Him, though He is not far from each one of us;*
> [28]*for in Him we live and move and have our being, as also some of your own poets have said, 'For we are also His offspring.'*

Psalms 33:13,14

> [13]*The LORD looks from heaven; He sees all the sons of men.* [14]*From the place of His dwelling He looks on all the inhabitants of the earth.*

When Paul was in Athens, he felt compelled to speak to its inhabitants, those at the foot of Athens' hill, about the vastness and might of God the Father. Drawing from shared knowledge, he cited an ancient Greek poet who, in his verse, affirmed that we live, move, and have our being in God.

In our childhood, many of us imagined God as a distant figure in the heavens. However, the reality is quite the inverse – the heavens are encompassed by God. God cradles everything within His grasp. He declares that the entire world resides in the hollow of His hand.

Everything exists within Him. Much like sponges submerged in an ocean, we are immersed in the vast ocean of God. We exist within Him. The most comforting realization is our placement in God. It's within this divine embrace that we encounter the authentic love and purpose of God. We live, move, and thrive because of Him.

Let's always remember wherever we stand, God's presence surrounds us. David, in Psalms, poetically inquired, "Where can I go to escape Your presence? Even if I were to delve into the deepest abyss, You would still be with me." Everything is enveloped by God; He is omnipresent, and everything is encompassed within Him.

So, let us approach God and express, O Lord, we are endlessly grateful for our existence within You. We thrive in Your embrace, witnessing Your boundless love through Jesus Christ who sacrificed Himself for our sins. May the love of God the Father, the grace of the Lord Jesus Christ, and the fellowship of the Holy Spirit be with all of us, Amen.

MARCH 12
Some reminders

Exodus 25:9

> *According to all that I show you, that is, the pattern of the tabernacle and the pattern of all its furnishings, just so you shall make it.*

Exodus 29:43

> *And there I will meet with the children of Israel, and the tabernacle shall be sanctified by My glory.*

When God desired to reassure His people of His presence among them, He chose the Tabernacle as His dwelling place, a place where He would meet with His people. This Tabernacle was aptly named the Tent of Meeting, serving as a communal space where the people of Israel could gather with God.

Within this Tabernacle rested a magnificent chest adorned with pure gold, featuring a meticulously crafted lid. This chest was known as the Ark of God or the Ark of the Covenant, and it was revered for its holiness. Safely housed within this chest were the two stone tablets bearing the Ten Commandments, a divine gift from God to His people.

The Ark of the Covenant stood as a testament to God's enduring presence among His people. It wasn't that God resided within the chest, but rather the Ark served as a reminder of His omnipresence. In modern times, various practices and symbols serve a similar purpose. For instance, having a Bible in one's home, or praying daily, can act as gentle reminders of God's presence. Some choose to light a candle during prayer, signifying that their petitions and praises are eternal in God's sight. Others might display a cross, a poignant reminder of the depth of God's love, demonstrated through Christ's sacrifice for humanity. These symbols, while simple, evoke profound spiritual truths, reminding us of God's love, urging us to stay committed in our prayers, and recognizing His ever-present nature.

Father, we are deeply grateful for these tangible symbols that draw our minds and hearts to You. We thank You for Your boundless love and kindness. Thank you for constantly reassuring us that we are never alone.

In the name of Jesus Christ, Amen.

MARCH 13
Give back

2 Chronicles 9:6

However, I did not believe their words until I came and saw with my own eyes; and indeed, the half of the greatness of your wisdom was not told me. You exceed the fame of which I heard.

"Whoever sows sparingly will also reap sparingly, and whoever sows generously will also reap generously."

Malachi 3:10 states, "Bring the whole tithe into the storehouse, that there may be food in my house. Test me in this," says the LORD Almighty, "and see if I will not throw open the floodgates of heaven and pour out so much blessing that there will not be room enough to store it."

The Lord instructs us to bring all our tithes into His storehouse, ensuring there's ample provision within. He challenges us to test Him in this, promising an outpouring of blessings so abundant that we'll lack nothing.

Reflecting on the early church, it's evident that God blessed them in proportion to their giving. The more they shared, the more they received. Recall the story from years past: a luxurious limousine stops beside a destitute man. A well-dressed individual from within asks for a bit of the man's rice. Hesitantly, the poor man obliges, offering three spoonfuls. To his astonishment, he later finds three gold pieces in his bowl. He laments, wishing he had given even more. Our relationship with God mirrors this narrative. The more we give to Him, the more He bestows upon us, multiplying our blessings. These blessings are manifold, encompassing health, relationships, favor, and other intangibles.

We must remember blessings aren't solely financial. God's favor, guidance, and protection are invaluable treasures.

The fundamental principle is this: of all God bestows upon us, we're called to return a tenth willingly and generously. When we consistently tithe from our gross, not our net, we activate God's promise to unleash boundless blessings upon our lives.

May the love of the Father, the grace of the Lord Jesus Christ, and the fellowship of the Holy Spirit increase in your life. Amen.

MARCH 14
You are loved

John 13:34

> *A new commandment I give to you, that you love one another; as I have loved you, that you also love one another.*

Hosea 14:4

> *I will heal their backsliding; I will love them freely For My anger has turned away from him.*

One day, a group of teenagers gathered at a friend's house to play basketball. Suddenly, an argument broke out, escalating quickly. The owner of the ball, frustrated, decided to end the game. As he was asking everyone to leave, he caught sight of his mother watching him. He approached her, remorsefully admitting, "I'm sorry, Mom. What I did was wrong."

His mother replied, "You're right. What you did was not what I expected from you." However, she then drew him into a comforting embrace, adding, "But I still love you."

God's love mirrors this mother's sentiment – it's steadfast and unconditional. Even when we err and allow doubt to creep in, with whispers from the enemy saying, "Look at your mistakes; you're worthless. God will never accept you back," we must remember the truth: God's love never wavers. In moments of weakness, when we return to Him with a contrite heart, He always welcomes us back, assuring, "I will always love you. My love is eternal and without conditions."

Armed with this truth, we should be quick to repent and seek God's embrace whenever we falter. The Holy Spirit, as our guide, will convict us when we go astray. It's then that we must rush back to God, confessing, "Lord Jesus, please forgive me." He will always forgive.

Father, we thank You for Your enduring love and boundless grace. It's a love that saw us when we were still Your enemies and chose us, nonetheless. Father, we love You. Jesus Christ, we adore You. Holy Spirit, work within us today. May we manifest Your love not just in words, but in our every action. Amen.

MARCH 15
Time is everything

Psalm 75:2

When I choose the proper time, I will judge uprightly.

Psalm 75:1

We give thanks to You, O God, we give thanks! For Your wondrous works declare that Your name is near.

Have you ever found yourself in a particular place at a specific moment, and something entirely unexpected unfolds right before you? When seemingly unrelated events align perfectly to culminate in one extraordinary occurrence, it becomes evident: this was no accident. There's a force, a guiding hand at work behind the scenes, orchestrating events in our favor. That force is God.

Such moments train our eyes to discern the hand of God, teaching us to expect wonders from Him. He operates within His divine timetable, bringing disparate pieces together, forging solutions we could never have anticipated. As Romans teaches us, God turns even adversities into blessings for those who love Him and are called according to His purpose. So, when unexpected events transpire, know that they aren't coincidences. God has meticulously pieced them together.

It's essential, then, to place our trust in God, even when things seem awry. Rest assured, He is setting the stage for His grand design, and in His timing, all will be well.

Father, we extend our deepest gratitude. Your word assures us that for those who love You and are chosen by You, all things work together for good. We recognize your boundless love and care, knowing that what You orchestrate for us is always unexpected and wondrous. Today, and every day, we place our trust in You.

In the name of Jesus Christ, Amen.

MARCH 16
Say Amen

2 Corinthians 1:20

> [20] *For all the promises of God in Him are Yes, and in Him Amen, to the glory of God through us.*
> [21] *Now He who establishes us with you in Christ and has anointed us is God,*
> [22] *who also has sealed us and given us the Spirit in our hearts as a guarantee.*

2 Peter 3:18

> *But grow in the grace and knowledge of our Lord and Savior Jesus Christ. To Him be the glory both*
> *now and forever. Amen.*

Have you ever been in church, listening intently to the sermon, and there's that one member who echoes "Amen" to the priest's every word? Sometimes the pastor even encourages the congregation, asking, "Why aren't more of you saying 'Amen'? Everyone, join in!"

The word "Amen" is more than just an affirmation; it's an agreement. When we echo that powerful word, we align ourselves with the message being shared. We are essentially saying, "Yes, I believe!" and "I stand with this truth!".

Let's embrace the promises of God and declare our "Amen" to them. Whether those promises are massive or minute, in Jesus Christ, they are affirmed. By saying "Amen" to God's promises, we show our readiness to participate in His plans. We anticipate His magnificent works in our lives and recognize that He has astounding plans for us — plans beyond our imagination.

The one who began His work within us will bring it to fruition in the most spectacular way. So, let's declare our willingness to be vessels for His glory.

Father, we say "Amen" to Your divine plans. Jesus Christ, we affirm Your work in our lives. Holy Spirit, we are eager and ready for Your guidance.

Together, let us proclaim: Amen.

MARCH 17
A great investment

1 Corinthians 15:58 Paul says:

> *Therefore, my beloved brethren, be steadfast, immovable, always abounding in the work of the Lord, knowing that your labor is not in vain in the Lord.*

2 Chronicles 16:9

> *For the eyes of the LORD run to and fro throughout the whole earth, to show Himself strong on behalf of those whose heart is loyal to Him. In this you have done foolishly; therefore, from now on you shall have wars."*

So, one of the biggest investments we can make is to give ourselves completely to the Lord. There isn't a wiser investment than committing ourselves to God. With this commitment, we gain the power to fulfill God's requests and to receive what He has in store for us.

Paul Tournier, a psychologist, had a profound understanding of the returns on this investment. He believed that nothing defines a man more than his commitments; in other words, commitment is what establishes a person's character. This commitment not only deepens our connection with God, but it also amplifies His will within us.

Commitment aids in completing God's tasks. It allows people to realize the depths of God's love for them. It's this very commitment that elevates us, enabling us to love God with our entire being. Moreover, commitment serves as an investment, unlocking the gifts God has set aside for us.

So, dear friends, let's dedicate ourselves to God, renewing our commitments and saying, "O Lord, we are devoted to You, the one true God whose love spans the heavens and the earth. The God who didn't spare His own son for us. We put our trust in You."

In the name of Jesus Christ, Amen.

MARCH 18
Haven and harbor

Matthew 5:23,24

[23] Therefore if you bring your gift to the altar, and there remember that your brother has something against you,
[24] leave your gift there before the altar, and go your way. First be reconciled to your brother, and then come and offer your gift.

Luke 9:37-38

[37] Now it happened on the next day, when they had come down from the mountain, that a great multitude met Him.
[38] Suddenly a man from the multitude cried out, saying, "Teacher, I implore You, look on my son, for he is my only child.

When we spend time with God alone in prayer, it provides us with the strength and refuge to maintain our faith throughout our daily lives. Our prayers are not only our refuge but also our anchor when we set out into the vast sea of life.

Recall the moment when the Lord Jesus Christ ascended a mountain with three of his disciples. There, he was transfigured, radiating an ethereal light. During this time, he encountered Moses and Elijah, undergoing a profound experience. Strengthened by God, Jesus descended back to the valley, ready to address the multitude seeking his healing and guidance. Similarly, the solitary moments we share with God equip us with the tools needed to venture out and serve the world.

Prayer purifies our spirit, sharpening our senses to recognize those in need. Through prayer, God unlocks the doors of our minds and hearts, directing us towards those who seek our assistance. It stretches our capacity for empathy, allowing our hearts to encompass and nurture those in need.

Father, we are grateful that you always heed our call, remaining forever by our side. Today, we ask you to place someone or something in our hearts. Lead us to someone yearning for kindness, someone in need, or someone seeking encouragement and prayer. Instill them in our hearts, and empower us to extend our hand in aid. We offer this prayer in the revered name of Jesus Christ, the King of kings. Amen.

MARCH 19
Help God to grow you

1 Corinthians 3:6

I planted, Apollos watered, but God gave the increase.

John 5:17

But Jesus answered them, "My Father has been working until now, and I have been working."

God desires our partnership and aims for our growth in our spiritual journeys. Paul and Apollos recognized that while they may plant and water, it is ultimately God who gives the growth. For it is He who brings forth life from the soil.

When discussing spiritual life, the analogy of an oak seed growing into a towering oak tree is often cited. However, our spiritual journey is more intricate than a simple seed. We are endowed with free will, the power to chart our course and set our goals, and the tenacity to achieve them. Our active engagement and commitment to our spiritual objectives can catalyze our growth. Making the decision to press forward is pivotal to spiritual advancement.

Discovering God is akin to unearthing a gold mine. The deeper we delve, the richer our spiritual bounty becomes. Let us approach God with open hearts and eager spirits.

God, we are grateful for Your presence in our lives and for the deepening of our spiritual connection. Lord, guide us as we seek to immerse ourselves in Your Word, for You are the most valuable treasure we can find. You are the gold of our lives. In the name of Jesus Christ, we offer our gratitude and prayers. Amen. Amen.

MARCH 20
New year devotional

Good morning, friends! Happy new Persian year. I extend my warmest Nowruz greetings to each and every one of you. As we step into this new year, my prayer for all of us is to draw nearer to the Lord Jesus Christ. In Him, we find the true embodiment of all the symbols and promises of Nowruz.

This year may our understanding of the Lord Jesus Christ deepen. May our relationship with Him grow stronger. He has called us the light and salt of this world, and so, may we rise to that calling, becoming the beacon of hope and flavor of life to those around us.

I pray that the transformative message of salvation through the Lord Jesus Christ reaches our friends, families, and everyone we encounter. May we be bold and articulate in sharing His love.

When you set up your "haft seen" table and reflect on its symbols, remember that all these symbols point to the character, power, and presence of Jesus Christ.

In gratitude, let's lift our hearts to God:

Thank you, God, for ushering in a new year, symbolizing the revival of all things. We are grateful for the renewal you bring into our lives, making us new creations. Your Holy Spirit dwells within each of us, and for that, we are eternally thankful. You rejuvenate us daily and stand unchanging in your promises. Your consistency is a rock upon which we lean. We are thankful that your desires for us are always for our highest good. May our lives bring joy to your heart, O Lord. We dedicate this year into your loving care. May you reign supreme in our lives. In the mighty name of Jesus Christ, our King of kings, Amen.

MARCH 21
The Lord is able

In the quiet of the morning, we prayed, saying, "O God, though storms may come, we trust in Your protective hand over us." A month prior, as I shared, God revealed this message to me: "Prepare a grand feast in My honor, and on the 2nd of August, perform baptisms. I will not only cleanse them with water but will also anoint them with the Holy Spirit."

He emphasized this thrice, saying, "Host this feast for Me. Witness the spiritual revival I will usher among the Iranians, among the Persian speakers, within Mohabat Church. Beyond the baptism of water, I will bless them with the Holy Spirit."

To those who received baptism, be assured of God's powerful touch upon your lives. Despite the impending storm, God cleared the heavens above us in affirmation of His word that morning: "Act in obedience and witness My wonders."

Just as God halted time for Joshua to vanquish his foes, and for Hezekiah, as a sign of his healing, reversed the shadow, so does He reveal His might and magnificence. Scripture assures us that He who has made promises to you can fulfill them, even when hope seems distant.

Our God is not a distant deity but a living, active Lord. A friend remarked that satellite imagery revealed rain and thunderstorms all around, save for our location. If you were present, I pray you felt the tangible might of God. I certainly did, and it was awe-inspiring. It's miraculous that not a drop of rain fell as we made our way to the lake.

Beloved, our God is not just alive; He is life itself. Jesus Christ lives, and His Spirit dwells within us. Unified with the Father and the Holy Spirit, He beckons us into this divine unity.

May we all be continually enveloped in the power, majesty, love, and grace of Jesus Christ, our King of kings. Amen.

MARCH 22
Lord, my protector

Psalm 91:7

A thousand may fall at your side, and ten thousand at your right hand; But it shall not come near you.

"You will witness firsthand the fate of the wicked. But because you have sought refuge in God and declared the Almighty as your protector, no disaster will strike you, and no harm will approach your dwelling. Why? Because He will order His angels to guard you wherever you journey. They will lift you in their embrace, ensuring you don't stumble upon a stone. Remember when Satan attempted to tempt Jesus, suggesting He leap from a pinnacle because angels would save Him from harm? This promise stands true for us too.

You shall tread upon the lion and the cobra, asserting dominion over them. Recall the roaring lion when Daniel was cast into a den teeming with ferocious lions? Yet God sealed their jaws. Why? Because Daniel saw the Lord as his shelter and the Almighty as his advocate. Daniel faced the lions because of his unwavering devotion.

Consider Paul, who, after surviving a shipwreck near Malta, was bitten by a venomous snake as he gathered firewood. The islanders expected him to succumb, but when he did not, they recognized the divine hand upon him. Why? Because Paul regarded God as his sanctuary and the Almighty as his shield. So, when we claim Jesus as our sanctuary, and God as our bastion, adversity cannot hold us. For God declares that those who cherish Him will find salvation.

God proclaims, 'In my name, they find solace. When they call upon me, I respond. In tribulations, I stand beside them, delivering them to triumph. I will bless them with longevity and ensure their safety.' Amen.

Today, let's embrace these divine assurances, knowing that when we turn to God as our refuge and entrust ourselves to Him wholeheartedly, He never falters in His care. Amen.

May the boundless love of God the Father, the endless grace of our Lord Jesus Christ, and the sweet fellowship of the Holy Spirit be upon you always. Amen.

MARCH 23
Always more

1 Corinthians 13:12

For now, we see in a mirror, dimly, but then face to face. Now I know in part, but then I shall know just as I also am known.

What we see now is like a blurry mirror image, but in time we will see everything in front of us. What we see now is partial and incomplete, but then our knowledge will be complete, that is, as perfect as God's knowledge of us.

1 Timothy 3:16

And without controversy great is the mystery of godliness:
God was manifested in the flesh,
Justified in the Spirit,
Seen by angels,
Preached among the Gentiles,
Believed on in the world,
Received up in glory.

Undoubtedly, the essence of our faith is profound: Christ manifested in flesh, vindicated by the Spirit. Witnessed by angels, He was proclaimed among nations; believed on in the world and ascended in glory.

Consider our eyes, designed to perceive a spectrum of colors from red to purple. Yet, there exist hues—like infrared and ultraviolet—beyond our visual grasp. Similarly, our comprehension of God only scratches the surface of His vastness. Beyond our most profound insights lies the immeasurable expanse of God's nature and majesty.

God's sovereignty, splendor, and love are unparalleled. While His magnificence leaves us lost for words, His boundless love remains immeasurable. Regardless of our depth of knowledge, there remains an infinite expanse of God yet to be explored—and He beckons us toward it.

Let's continually seek Him, recognizing our limited understanding and embracing humility. Despite the scriptures we've read and the revelations we've had, the mystery of His essence, His radiance, and His love will always surpass our grasp.

O Sovereign Lord, we thank You for Your boundless love and immeasurable glory.

We are grateful for the glimpses of Your mysteries You've granted us, and pray for a deepening intimacy with You each day. May we continually be drawn into Your embrace and overwhelming affection.

Father, we dedicate this day to Your divine care.

In the precious name of Jesus Christ, Amen.

MARCH 24
Like God

Genesis 1:27

> *So, God created man in His own image; in the image of God, He created him; male and female He created them.*

God created man in his own image, and in his image, he created male and female.

Psalms 92:13-14

> *Those who are planted in the house of the LORD shall flourish in the courts of our God. [14] They shall still bear fruit in old age; They shall be fresh and flourishing,*

Those who are deeply rooted in the dwelling of our Lord will flourish. They shall be like thriving trees, laden with fruit, enduring gracefully through the seasons.

Imagine a 16-year-old stepping into an elevator. A woman casts repeated glances over him, observing each detail. He shifts uncomfortably, perplexed by her scrutiny. Recognizing a familiar likeness, she finally inquires, "Are you David's son?"

In a similar manner, we bear the divine imprint. Fashioned in God's image, we are the reflection of His very essence. It's as if a mere glimpse of a young boy playing could remind a woman of an old friend, David. The boy's appearance triggers memories of another. So too, we, in our being, resonate with the attributes of God, showcasing His love, compassion, and joy.

The characteristics of God are engraved upon us. These traits not only speak of His profound love but also His unwavering faithfulness. So, who are we? We are the beloved of God, shaped in His image. Emanating from God, we unequivocally belong to Him. This sense of belonging is heightened when we surrender our hearts to Jesus Christ. As He dwells within us, we are continually molded to mirror His divine countenance. Amen.

Heavenly Father, our gratitude knows no bounds, for You have loved us so passionately that we are sculpted in Your image. Holy Spirit, work freely within us, refining us to emulate Jesus Christ more closely each day. This day, we rest in Your benevolent care, Amen.

MARCH 25
God is great

Deuteronomy 10:17

> *For the LORD your God is God of gods and Lord of lords, the great God, mighty and awesome, who shows no partiality nor takes a bribe.*

Your Lord is Highest, above all gods and all powers. He is the almighty, great and powerful and must be obeyed.

Job 37:5

> *God thunders marvelously with His voice; He does great things which we cannot comprehend.*

God raises his voice in a miraculous way like the thunderbolt of a storm; he does great things that we cannot even comprehend. If you and I go to God and let go of all the things that distract us and clear our minds of all the noise and interruptions, we see God in front of us. He is with us, and He is the only one there. At the funeral of Louis XVI, the whole cathedral was lit with many candles. Those candles symbolized the greatness of the king. When the priest went to speak, he shook his head, prompting some of the servants to extinguish all the candles. The whole cathedral was plunged into darkness. The priest spoke in that darkness, emphasizing that only God is great and almighty. No one is as great as God. Only He creates and sustains the whole world. Only God holds you and me in the palm of his hand. Father, we thank you that you are the great and almighty God. We thank you for all that you are doing for us. We thank you for your son, Jesus Christ, who paid the price for our sins on the cross, and on the third day, He rose from the dead and brought us justification. And thank you, Father, that we can come to you and call you Father and be one with you; for your Holy Spirit is in us. As Christ says, "I am one with the Father, I am one with you, we are all one." Father, let us move forward with this power and this awareness and spend time with you alone.

In the name of Jesus Christ, Amen.

MARCH 26
Raised up

Colossians 2:12

> *Buried with Him in baptism, in which you also were raised with Him through faith in the working of God, who raised Him from the dead.* "When you were baptized, you were buried with the Lord Jesus Christ, and then you were raised to life."

Colossians 3:1

> *If then you were raised with Christ, seek those things which are above, where Christ is, sitting at the right hand of God.*

This means that if you were raised with the Lord Jesus Christ or you were resurrected, seek the things which are above, where Jesus Christ is. Here, Paul isn't referring to the future resurrection but rather the present experience of a resurrected life. You and I have died with that suffering, and we have been resurrected with a new life and a new opportunity.

During World War II, a church in London was preparing to celebrate Thanksgiving. Among the items they brought to the church was a bunch of corn. However, before they could conduct the program, bombings began, and the church was destroyed. When spring arrived following the destruction, people noticed green shoots emerging from the ruins. By summer, a significant portion of the ruins was covered in corn.

You and I believe in the resurrected life of the Lord Jesus Christ and the resurrected life within us, propelling us forward. We believe that our life possesses a strength and significance surpassing even death. Just as corn rises from the rubble, in this world riddled with wickedness and evil, you and I are empowered to rise like corn stalks. This growth signifies the impact of our resurrected life in Jesus Christ. Amen.

Thank you, Father, for the power of your resurrection that operates within each of us. Jesus Christ, we are grateful for your blood shed on the cross, allowing us to experience this resurrected life more profoundly.

In the name of Jesus Christ, Amen.

MARCH 27
Come to Me

Matthew 11:28-30

> 28 *Come to Me, all you who labor and are heavy laden, and I will give you rest.*
> 29 *Take My yoke upon you and learn from Me, for I am gentle and lowly in heart, and you will find rest for your souls.*
> 30 *For My yoke is easy and My burden is light."*

Jesus says, "Come to me if your load is heavy, and give me your load, and take mine, for my load is light."

Today, as I reflected on our devotional topic, a thought related to today's subject crossed my mind. God said, "Come to me."

Do we approach God in everything we undertake, whether significant or minor? We must grasp that God is the Creator of the heavens, the earth, and all that they contain. He is the God who understands the mysteries of all things, the God whose wisdom surpasses all fields of knowledge.

For instance, today a query emerged regarding the Chiropractic program in the Chiropractic journal. I pondered; how should I respond? It was then I understood that our God knows everything. After all, He is the Creator of it all. He is omniscient. He is the God who intricately designed every detail, the God familiar with all laws. Everything we study or discover has been orchestrated by Him.

God takes interest in every facet of our lives, be it spiritual, physical, or intellectual. He desires to be included in all. We must turn to God, for both God the Father and Jesus Christ beckon us, saying, "Come to me, bring me all your burdens, and lay them at my feet."

However, our challenge is that, burdened as we are, we often consider God our last resort. If we made Him our first point of contact when faced with dilemmas, we'd find solutions more swiftly than if we exhausted all other avenues before approaching Him.

From this day forth, in the name of Jesus Christ, may we always seek God first when faced with challenges. Jesus assures us, "Ask the Father in my name, and it shall be granted unto you." What will be given? Those things that align with God's will and are beneficial for us.

Sometimes, we might not receive an answer immediately, either because it might not serve God's kingdom or might not be in our best interest. Yet, God always responds.

Father, we are grateful that we can approach You with any concern, big or small. Your strength, kindness, and love are unparalleled, and You cherish our every word.

May we, from this moment forward, consult You first with any challenge or question we encounter.

In the name of Jesus Christ, Amen.

MARCH 28
More about Christ

Ephesians 4:13

> *Till we all come to the unity of the faith and of the knowledge of the Son of God, to a perfect man, to the measure of the stature of the fullness of Christ;* When they become mature, as mature as Christ, they too will be fully formed in his image.

Hebrews 6:1

> *Therefore, leaving the discussion of the elementary principles of Christ, let us go on to perfection, not laying again the foundation of repentance from dead works and of faith toward God,*

When we move beyond our initial understanding of Jesus Christ and seek a deeper connection with God, that's when we truly mature.

There's a hymn that resonates deeply with this sentiment, urging us to delve deeper into the knowledge of Jesus: More about Jesus would I know, More of His grace to others show; More of His saving fullness see, More of His love who died for me.

This song echoes in our hearts, encouraging us to evolve and mature in our relationship with Jesus Christ. The lyrics speak to growth, elevation, and the aspiration to embody more of Jesus Christ in our lives.

By dedicating time to God, we grant Him the space to guide our spiritual journey. Over time, this beckons us to venture further, to explore grander spiritual landscapes, and to deepen our understanding of Him.

The moments we share with God are precious, for they illuminate the essence of His nature. They help us grasp His grandeur and recognize His workings in our lives.

The more time we dedicate to God, the closer our bond becomes. And as we expand our spiritual horizons, we simultaneously enhance our relationship with Him.

O Lord, we are eternally grateful for Your boundless love and kindness, and for the sacrifice You made for us on the cross. May our bond with You continually deepen and may our understanding of You grow day by day.

In the name of Jesus Christ, Amen.

MARCH 29
Under same management

Philippians 1:6

Being confident of this very thing, that He who has begun a good work in you will complete it until the day of Jesus Christ.

God, who has begun his good work in you, will perfect it until the day of Jesus Christ.

Hebrews 13:8

Jesus Christ is the same yesterday, today, and forever.

When we make time to spend with God, we observe greater stability from Him in our lives. As we consistently and routinely commune with God, we discern His strong presence woven intricately into the fabric of our existence.

At such moments, we come to understand that God's presence is constant and unchanging.

God's unwavering nature aids us in making sound decisions. Knowing that He remains consistent, never changing, and always desiring the best for us, gives us the assurance that He is always ready to answer, and His answer is invariably for our benefit.

With the knowledge that God is by our side and for us, our lives brim with confidence. We are assured that He will neither abandon nor forsake us. He is always present, unchanging, and steadfast.

Father, we are grateful for your constancy, knowing you remain unchanging. And Jesus Christ, you are the same yesterday, today, and forever. You are consistent, always desiring our company, always wanting the best for us.

We place today in your blessed care.

In the name of Jesus Christ, Amen.

MARCH 30
What Faith Sees

Matthew 21:21

> *So, Jesus answered and said to them, "Assuredly, I say to you, if you have faith and do not doubt, you will not only do what was done to the fig tree, but also if you say to this mountain, 'Be removed and be cast into the sea,' it will be done.*

Jesus said after he told the fig tree to dry, and it dried the next day. He said that if you have faith and have no doubts, I promise you, you can do the same thing as I did with this tree. In the same way you can tell the mountain to lift up and throw itself into the sea, and it will be done.

Galatians 2:20

> *I have been crucified with Christ; it is no longer I who live, but Christ lives in me; and the life which I now live in the flesh I live by faith in the Son of God, who loved me and gave Himself for me.*

Paul said, "I was crucified with Christ, and I no longer live, but Christ lives in me. The life I now live in the body, I live by faith in the Son of God, who loved me and gave himself for me."

Faith empowers us to achieve beyond our wildest imaginations. It transforms us into visionaries, enabling us to see further. Faith instills principles and guidelines in our hearts and souls, leading us to a life that surpasses our expectations.

Through faith, we perceive possibilities previously unimaginable. By faith, Thomas Edison illuminated the darkness; the Wright brothers conceived human flight. By faith, Martin Luther King Jr. envisioned a route to freedom and equality unseen by many.

Guided by faith, we approach challenges, analyze them, and gather the courage to surmount them. Our aspirations and convictions guide our real-world actions, all through the grace and assistance of Jesus Christ.

Father, Lord, we express our gratitude for granting us the insight and wisdom to understand as you do. Today, fortify our resolve to live by faith. Regardless of our circumstances, come what may, we trust in your omnipotence. We believe that you will never forsake us; you remain ever-present, always desiring the best for us.

In the name of Jesus Christ, Amen.

MARCH 31
Why do we do it?

Luke 10:40

> *But Martha was distracted with much serving, and she approached Him and said, "Lord, do You not care that my sister has left me to serve alone? Therefore, tell her to help me."*

Martha was distracted by all the things she had to do for dinner, and came to Jesus Christ and said: Master, don't you care that my sister is sitting here and not helping me with preparing the food?

In Romans 11:31

> *Even so these also have now been disobedient, that through the mercy shown you they also may obtain mercy.*

Paul says, "Everything comes from Him, everything happens through Him, and everything ends in Him." Always glory, always worship. Yes, yes, yes.

This story tells of Christ's visit to the home of Mary and Martha. Eleazer was invited to dinner, and Martha was responsible for preparing the meal and setting the table. Understandably, she was engrossed in her tasks, deciding which dishes to prepare, serving them, and ensuring the table was impeccably set. Meanwhile, Mary chose to sit at Jesus' feet, absorbing His words.

When Martha expressed her frustration to Jesus about Mary's lack of help, Jesus responded, "Martha, you're worried about many things, but only one thing is necessary." Mary had chosen what was better. Martha might have been taken aback, perhaps thinking, "After all I've done, is this how you see it?"

It serves as a reminder: when we act in God's name, our motives matter. Our actions should be driven by a desire to honor and glorify Him. So, whatever we undertake, let it be for God.

Father, we humbly approach You. May everything we do be in Your name and for Your glory. Help us maintain our focus on You, seeking always to magnify Your name through our actions.

In the name of Jesus Christ, Amen.

APRIL 1
Shouting news

Psalms 32:11

> *Be glad in the LORD and rejoice, you righteous; and shout for joy, all you upright in heart!*

It says be glad in the LORD, and rejoice, all those who are righteous and upright; shout with joy, all those who are righteous in their hearts.

Revelation 19:5

> *Then a voice came from the throne, saying, "Praise our God, all you His servants and those who fear Him, both small and great!"*

A voice emerged from the throne of the LORD, declaring, "Praise God, all His servants, both great and small, and everyone who honors Him."

If you were to pick up a pencil and start cataloging the deeds God has done for you, noting every gift and blessing, you'd soon realize the pages are too few and the pencil too short. Every grace, talent, and ability He has endowed upon you would exhaust the paper's space.

Upon completing this list, take a moment to recount each one, expressing your gratitude to God for His countless blessings and favors. Let your heart overflow with praise, holding nothing back, and tell Him of the wondrous ways He has enriched your life.

Acknowledge the magnitude of your blessings and communicate to God your awareness of His benevolence.

Father, we thank You for the infinite blessings You've bestowed upon us. If we were to jot them all down, all the paper in the world wouldn't suffice. We recognize that every good thing stems from Your benevolent hands and through Your son, Jesus Christ. With heartfelt gratitude and zealous passion, we exclaim joyfully, "Thank You, God." Amen.

APRIL 2
Not the spirit of fear but spirit of power, love ....

2 Timothy 1:6

> *Therefore, I remind you to stir up the gift of God which is in you through the laying on of my hands*

Paul writes to Timothy, saying, "I remind you to fan into flame the gift of God which is in you through the laying on of my hands." For God did not give us a spirit of timidity, but of power, love, and self-discipline. The verse reiterates that God did not endow us with a spirit of fear, but with power, love, and a sound mind. This sound mind suggests discipline and correct thinking. So, have we neglected God's gift, the faith He entrusted to us, or have we cherished it, nurturing its growth?

Recall the exhilaration you felt when you first encountered Jesus Christ, the warmth of His presence kindling a blaze within you. Remember, God has not bestowed upon us a timid spirit, but one filled with power, love, clarity, and right thinking.

Paul urges us not to be ashamed of bearing witness to our Lord. If our faith is aflame, we won't cower in His presence. Paul adds, "Do not be ashamed of me." We should stand by our leaders and companions, leaning into divine strength to endure the trials of the gospel. God has saved us, summoning us to a holy life, not by our deeds, but through His purpose and grace. This grace, granted to us in Christ Jesus before time began, has now been manifested through the coming of our Savior. He has vanquished death and illuminated the path to eternal life.

If fear ever resides within us, know it's not of God's doing, for He imbues us with power, love, and a clear conscience through the grace of Jesus Christ.

Father, we are eternally grateful for gifting us not with fear but with love, discipline, and correct thinking. Guide us today and always.

In the mighty name of Jesus Christ, the King of kings, Amen.

APRIL 3
What can't He do?

Psalms 96:7

> *Give to the LORD, O families of the peoples, Give to the LORD glory and strength.*

It says, call on the Lord, all his family and his people, give unto the Lord glory and strength.

Psalms 96:2, 13

> *Sing to the LORD, bless His name; Proclaim the good news of His salvation from day to day. For He is coming, for He is coming to judge the earth. He shall judge the world with righteousness, And the people with His truth.*

It is written, "Sing to the Lord and worship His name. Proclaim His salvation day after day. He will judge the world with fairness and the nations with truth."

It might surprise you, but there are certain things that even God cannot do. While He possesses all power and everything is within His reach, there are actions that are contrary to His very nature. For instance, because God is holy, He cannot lie or go back on His promises to us.

God does not wield His infinite knowledge for malevolent purposes; He exclusively employs His vast wisdom for good and to assist us. God's love is boundless, and He cannot simply withdraw it or stop loving us. This love is intrinsic to His character. Hence, He cannot stand idly by when we tread the wrong path, a path that may lead us to stumble or suffer. It is for this very reason He granted us salvation through Jesus Christ.

Why? Because His love for us is so profound that He desires us to be with Him for all eternity. Let's embrace God's love today and put our trust in Him. In trusting Him, He will never let us down or put us to shame, for He is a loving and exceptional God.

Father, we thank You for Your holiness and immeasurable love. Your ways overflow with love and compassion. We are grateful that we can always rely on You. You are magnificent, and through Jesus Christ, the King of kings, we approach You. Amen.

APRIL 4
Welcome pursuit

Psalms 9:10

> *And those who know Your name will put their trust in You; For You, LORD, have not forsaken those who seek You.*

It says, O Lord, those who know your name, and trust in you, will never be disappointed. Those who seek you, you'll never be abandoned.

Psalms 9:16

> *The LORD is known by the judgment He executes; The wicked is snared in the work of his own hands. Meditation. Selah*

It is written, "God has revealed Himself to us." When we chase after fame, power, and social status, we quickly find that our foundation becomes increasingly shaky, making us progressively weaker.

If we attempt to quench our innermost desires with wealth, relationships, or constant activity, our sense of fulfillment gradually diminishes. When we resort to alcohol, drugs, or other means to escape our problems, we merely intensify our feelings of isolation. However, by seeking and following God, our joy grows exponentially, and He unveils grand opportunities for us.

He not only provides us with a firm foundation upon which to stand but also nourishes our souls. God enriches our lives with His omnipresent love, goodness, and purpose. Let's unite in our journey towards Him, seeking God in all our actions and with our whole heart. By doing so, we will undoubtedly discover what our souls truly yearn for. Together, let's pray:

Father, we are grateful that You surpass all else that might satisfy us. We thank You, for everything we need is found in You, and You never withhold Your blessings. Today, we place our trust in Your benevolent hands.

In the name of Jesus Christ, Amen.

APRIL 5
If it was not because of the Lord

Psalms 124

> [1] *"If it had not been the LORD who was on our side, "Let Israel now say—*
>
> [2] *"If it had not been the LORD who was on our side, When men rose up against us,*
> [3] *Then they would have swallowed us alive, When their wrath was kindled against us;*
> [4] *Then the waters would have overwhelmed us, the stream would have gone over our soul;*
> [5] *Then the swollen waters Would have gone over our soul."*
> [6] *Blessed be the LORD, Who has not given us as prey to their teeth.*
> [7] *Our soul has escaped as a bird from the snare of the fowlers; The snare is broken, and we have escaped.*[8] *Our help is in the name of the LORD, Who made heaven and earth.*

It is written: "What would have happened if God had not been on our side? If He hadn't been there when our enemies turned on us, they would have swallowed us alive in their burning anger. We would have been swept away by the floodwaters, overwhelmed by the torrential rush and dragged under by the tempest. But blessed be the Lord, who did not allow us to be torn apart by their teeth. Like a bird, we escaped the hunter's trap; the trap was broken, and we were set free. Our only source of help is in the name of the Lord, the Maker of heaven and earth."

Psalms 127 states: Unless the Lord builds the house, its builders labor in vain. Without His protection, city watchmen are on guard in vain. It is fruitless to rise early and go to bed late, toiling for food to eat, for God provides for His beloved even as they sleep. God's greatest blessings are children; they are a reward from Him. Like arrows in a warrior's hands are the children of one's youth. Those with a quiver full of them are truly fortunate, for they will never be shamed when confronting their adversaries.

This reminds us that without God's hand guiding our efforts, our labor is in vain. When we place our faith in the Lord Jesus Christ, the Savior, Shepherd, Friend, and King of Kings, we are given profound promises.

We become children of God, with Him as our loving Father who never withholds His blessings and always looks after us. He is a fervent Father, sometimes disciplining us to guide us back to the right path.

Our Heavenly Father, who is also the Father of Jesus Christ, the King of Kings, desires only the best for us. Without His protective hand and providence, our endeavors would be in vain. Without belief in Jesus Christ, the Son of God, who sacrificed His life for our sins and defeated death with His resurrection, all our undertakings are meaningless.

We are eternally grateful, dear Father, for the ultimate sacrifice made by Jesus. For the unfathomable love You showed by not sparing Your Son for our sake. Let us be continually reminded of Your handiwork behind all things, expressing our gratitude and recognizing Your blessings.

In the precious name of Jesus Christ, Amen.

APRIL 6
Reason for confidence

Psalms 20:4

> *May He grant you according to your heart's desire and fulfill all your purpose.*

May God give you what you desire and make all your plans a success.

Psalms 20:7-8

> [7]*Some trust in chariots, and some in horses; But we will remember the name of the* LORD *our God.*
> [8] *They have bowed down and fallen; But we have risen and stand upright.*

It is written: "Some place their trust in chariots and horses, but we place our trust in the name of the Lord our God. They collapse and fall, but we rise and stand firm."

Throughout the Bible, we find numerous individuals who faced life's adversities with exceptional resilience and emerged victorious. Moses, Joshua, David, and Paul all encountered immense challenges. Yet, they remained unyielding, pressing forward. How could they accomplish this? The answer isn't rooted in their personal strength or capabilities. Instead, their unwavering trust in the omnipotence of God fueled their determination.

Their faith was grounded in the understanding that no matter the gravity of their situation or the seemingly insurmountable odds, with God, all things are possible. After all, the world and all its power are within His domain.

When God calls upon us to act, we must rise, placing our unwavering trust in Him, saying, "Lord, You who have called us to this task, will see it through to completion." As we do so, we witness the manifold blessings He bestows upon our lives. While worldly riches and possessions may abound, our most invaluable treasure remains our Lord Jesus Christ, the King of Kings, and the mightiest of all.

In Him, we find our victory, always and in all places.

Dear Father, we are deeply grateful for being such a trustworthy God. With all our heart, mind, and soul, we trust in You, confident that You always desire the best for us.

In the name of Jesus Christ, Amen.

APRIL 7
Real, abundant life

Psalms 36:9

> *For with You is the fountain of life; In Your light we see light.* Tells us, O Lord, with you is the foundation of life, and in your light, we see the light.

Psalms 36:5-7

> [5]*Your mercy, O LORD, is in the heavens; Your faithfulness reaches to the clouds.*
> [6] *Your righteousness is like the great mountains.*
> *Your judgments are a great deep; O LORD, You preserve man and beast.*
> [7] *How precious is Your lovingkindness, O God! Therefore, the children of men put their trust under the shadow of Your wings.*

O Lord, your love reaches the heavens, and your faithfulness extends to the clouds. No price can be placed on your immortal love. Children of men find refuge in the shadow of your wings. When you think about a full life, what comes to your mind? Some people believe that a perfect life is filled with wealth, luxury, and prosperity. Others feel that an ideal life means being surrounded by loved ones, spending time with friends, acquaintances, family, and relatives. However, when we examine these notions, we realize that something is missing.

John 17:3 states, "And this is eternal life, that they may know You, the only true God, and Jesus Christ whom You have sent."

O Lord, eternal life is found in knowing you. You, my Lord, are the only true God who sent Jesus Christ. This is why we seek God. When we genuinely discover God, we encounter a meaningful and authentic life. A life filled not just with purpose but also abundant love and hope. Dear friends, do you feel that something is missing in your life?

If you harbor this sentiment, it's the Spirit of God knocking on your door, suggesting that the missing piece, the one you need to acquaint yourself with more, is the loving Lord, Jesus Christ, the King of kings, the Savior.

Through His blood, our sins are washed away, and as we get to know Him, all our fears and anxieties vanish, replaced by hope, love, affection, and a purposeful life.

Father, in the name of Jesus Christ, King of kings, we are grateful that we can approach and know you, and your arms remain perpetually open to us. No arms are as welcoming as those of the Lord Jesus Christ on the cross, forever outstretched to embrace us. God, may we seek your embrace in every moment, every situation, every storm, in both good times and bad.

In the name of Jesus Christ, Amen.

APRIL 8

It Is Friday, but Sunday is coming

The renowned message, "It is Friday, but Sunday is coming."

Many might jest, asking, "What do you mean by 'Good Friday"? This is the day Jesus Christ was crucified. Why aren't you mourning? Shouldn't it be called 'Bad Friday'?" But it was on this very day, although Jesus Christ, the King of kings and the Son of God, was crucified, He willingly went to the cross. He did so to liberate us, paying the price for our sins with His blood and reconciling us to the kingdom of God.

Below is the famed text, "It's Friday, but Sunday's coming." This piece was authored by African-American preacher, Rev. S.M. Lockridge, who lived from 1913 to 2000. He served as the Pastor of Calvary Baptist Church in San Diego from 1953 to 1993. This narration encapsulates the essence of Good Friday and the events that unfolded. Yet, it underscores that our ultimate hope is anchored in the resurrection of Sunday. Amen.

Let's read together.

It's Friday. Jesus is praying. Peter's asleep. Judas is betraying. But Sunday's coming.

It's Friday. Pilate's struggling. The council is conspiring. The crowd is vilifying. They don't even know that Sunday's coming.

It's Friday. The disciples are running like sheep without a shepherd. Mary's crying. Peter is denying. But they don't know that Sunday's coming.

It's Friday. The Romans beat my Jesus. They robe Him in scarlet. They crown Him with thorns. But they don't know that Sunday's coming.

It's Friday. See Jesus walking to Calvary. His blood dripping. His body stumbling. His spirit burdened. But, you see, it's only Friday. Sunday's coming.

It's Friday. The world's winning. People are sinning. Evil's grinning.

It's Friday. The soldiers nail my Savior's hands to the cross. They nail my Savior's feet to the cross. And then they raise Him up next to criminals. It's Friday. But let me tell you something: Sunday's coming.

It's Friday. The disciples are questioning what has happened to their King. And the Pharisees are celebrating that their scheming has been achieved. But they don't know it's only Friday. Sunday's coming.

It's Friday. He's hanging on the cross, feeling forsaken by His Father, left alone and dying. Can nobody save Him? Oh, it's Friday. But Sunday's coming.

It's Friday. The earth trembles. The sky grows dark. My King yields His spirit. It's Friday. Hope is lost. Death has won. Sin has conquered. And Satan's just laughing.

It's Friday. Jesus is buried. A soldier stands guard. And a rock is rolled into place. But it's Friday. It is only Friday. Sunday is coming!

May the grace of the Lord Jesus Christ be with you. May this piece resonate within your soul, spirit, and mind. May the Holy Spirit lift you up today, revealing the secret that God has shown us – the secret of saving this world through the death and resurrection of Jesus Christ, events we commemorate this week. Amen.

APRIL 9
Good Thursday and Jesus' prays for us

John 17:20-26

> 20 *I do not pray only for these, I do not pray for my disciples, the disciples of that time; But also, for those who will believe in me through their message and testimony,*
> 21 *so that all of them may be one, just as you, O Father, are in me, and I am in you, and they are one in us. So that the world may believe that you have sent me.*
> 22 *I have given them the glory that you have given me, so that they may be one as we are one,*
> 23 *I am in them and you are in me; That they may be completely one, and that the world may know that you have sent me, and you love them as you love me.*
> 24 *O Father, I desire that those whom you have given me be with me where I am, so that they see the glory which you have bestowed upon me before the world began.*
> 25 *I know you; and they know that you have sent me, and I will make them known unto you, and I will make them known again.*
> 26 *So the love which you have for me may be in them, and I in them.*

Some people refer to the day before Good Friday as "Good Thursday." It is the day when Jesus Christ had the Last Supper with His disciples and shared His final words with them. On this day, He prepared Himself for the sacrifice that lay ahead, knowing He would die on the cross to save us from our sins. His blood, being divine, is infinite and sufficient to atone for the sins of everyone, past, present, and future, reuniting them with the kingdom and family of God.

The Bible recounts how Jesus instructed His disciples to prepare a place for the Last Supper. Notably, only in the Gospel of John is it recorded that Jesus prayed for His disciples and for those who would come to believe in Him through their testimonies. Today, I wish to share with you this prayer that Jesus prayed on our behalf, reminding us of His love and the magnitude of His sacrifice. I'll read from the Mojdeh translation.

Friends, the essence of our Lord's prayer is unity. Jesus desires for us to be united with Him and the Father, such that we all are interconnected. Jesus Christ lives within us; the Father abides in Jesus Christ, Jesus resides in us, and we are intimately unified with God the Father, Jesus Christ, and the Holy Spirit.

Lord Jesus Christ, we give thanks for Your incarnation, for taking on a human form and walking among us. You endured the world's sufferings, faced countless temptations, yet remained sinless. On Good Friday, You willingly went to the cross for our transgressions, knowing it was the sole path to our redemption. We are forever grateful for Your resurrection on the third day, a testament to Your divine power. May we always remain united in You, bonded by love and compassion. I place all present into the hands of the Lord Jesus Christ. Join us tomorrow as we commemorate Good Friday together.

May God bless each one of you in the name of Jesus Christ. Amen.

APRIL 10
Night devotional

Psalms 51:10-12

> [10] *Create in me a clean heart, O God,*
> *And renew a steadfast spirit within me.*
> [11] *Do not cast me away from Your presence,*
> *And do not take Your Holy Spirit from me.*
> [12] *Restore to me the joy of Your salvation,*
> *And uphold me by Your generous Spirit.*

O God, create in me a pure heart and renew a steadfast spirit within me. Do not cast me from your presence, nor take your Holy Spirit from me. Restore to me the joy of your salvation and uphold me with your gracious spirit. Let us draw near to God.

Father, thank you for speaking to each one of us today. We are grateful for all you have done for us this day.

Jesus Christ, we thank you for guarding us and bringing us together to praise your name. We are grateful for today's blessings, and even for the challenges, which shape us and mold us more into your image.

O God, if we have faltered, if we have strayed from your path or failed to glorify you, please forgive us. We repent and ask that you create a clean heart within us and renew our spirits. Do not cast us away from your presence and do not withhold your Holy Spirit from us. Instead, fill us even more with your presence.

We have faith that you will do this, and we express our gratitude for all you have done. May you grant each one of us a peaceful and restful night.

In the name of Jesus Christ, Amen.

APRIL 11
Grow in grace!

2 Peter 3:18

> *But grow in the grace and knowledge of our Lord and Savior Jesus Christ. To Him be the glory both now and forever. Amen.*

As we've discussed before, grace is a gift we don't deserve. It's not just a gift we haven't earned; if justice prevailed, we'd deserve the exact opposite — punishment. But grace is this undeserved gift, given to us by God out of love. Our calling in Christianity is to grow in this grace. Where is the grace of God found? It is in Jesus Christ. So, our goal is to know Him more and more. Why? Because a lover always yearns to be with the beloved and to continually deepen that relationship.

Thus, if there's a reluctance in our hearts to know Jesus more, we must examine our love for Him, questioning if we truly love Him and if we're genuinely aligned with Him. So, let us pray: Father, in the name of Jesus Christ, the King of kings, we come before you. We love our Savior, our teacher, Lord Jesus Christ.

Lord, help us to deepen our knowledge of Him. May we strive every moment to know Him more, to be enveloped in His abundant grace. And we recognize, Lord, your promise: ask in my name, and you shall receive more of the Holy Spirit.

May the Holy Spirit move freely within each one of us, filling us and guiding us today to understand the Lord Jesus Christ better, to embody humility, and to extend His love and compassion to others.

In the name of Jesus Christ, Amen.

APRIL 12
Blessings on you

Matthew 5

The Sermon on the Mount

This is where the Lord Jesus Christ goes to the top of the mountain and speaks to the crowd. It is known as the Sermon on the Mountain.

> [3]*Blessed are those who are aware of their spiritual poverty, for theirs is the kingdom of heaven.*
> [4]*Blessed are the mourners, for they shall be comforted.*
> [5]*Blessed who are humble, for they shall inherit the earth.*
> [6]*Blessed are those who hunger and thirst for the goodness of God, for they will be filled.*
> [7]*Blessed are the merciful, for they shall obtain mercy.*

The English Bible says:

> *Blessed are the merciful because they will see the Lord.*
> [8]*Blessed are the pure in heart, for they will see the Lord.*
> [9]*Blessed are the peacemakers, for they shall be called the children of God.*

As I reflect on this, I realize that for those of us redeemed by the blood of Christ, these blessings are already prepared. We were summoned to recognize our spiritual destitution. Aware of our spiritual poverty, we've approached God and pleaded for salvation, a salvation He grants us daily.

We must never view ourselves as superior to others. We've been called to humility; called to hunger and thirst for righteousness. We've been beckoned to show mercy as we've received mercy, to forgive as we've been forgiven. We are tasked with cleansing our hearts daily through God's word and prayer. If we hold fast to all that the Lord Jesus Christ has bestowed upon us, and if we exhibit the fruits of the Holy Spirit, which encompass all these virtues, then all these blessings will be ours.

Father, we express our profound gratitude for Your word, Your unwavering love, Your promises, and for the bountiful fruits of the Holy Spirit. O Holy Spirit, work within each of us. Manifest Your fruits in our lives. Purify and sanctify us, so that with each passing moment, we become more like Jesus Christ.

We commit this day into Your loving care and submit ourselves for Your transformative work. Let Your work be so evident in us that others, witnessing these fruits, are drawn closer to Your embrace, Lord Jesus Christ. In the name of Jesus Christ, Amen.

APRIL 13
He separated light from darkness

Genesis 1:4

> *And God saw the light that it was good; and God divided the light from the darkness.*

God saw the light, and it was good. He separated the light from the darkness with just His words. Light and darkness are distinct, having no relation to each other. Similarly, the Light of the world, Jesus Christ, has no association with darkness and its deeds.

We too are bearers of this light, having accepted Jesus Christ as our Savior. He, the Light of the world, illuminates our hearts. In His likeness, we too must distance ourselves from darkness.

Thank you, Father, for guiding us to remain within Your light. Jesus, you declared your unity with the Father and expressed the same unity with us. We partake in your divine nature and blessings. Being the Light of this world let Your brilliance shine through us so radiantly that others witness it and glorify the Father.

Today, we express our gratitude for Your work within and for us. If ever we've strayed into darkness, we humbly approach You, seeking forgiveness and guidance to perpetually walk in Your light.

We entrust this night to Your loving care. May Your radiant light continuously shine upon us, granting us a peaceful and serene night.

In the name of Jesus Christ, the King of kings and the Light of the world, Amen.

APRIL 14
Love your enemies

Matthew 5:43-44

> [43] *"You have heard that it was said, 'You shall love your neighbor and hate your enemy.'*
> [44] *But I say to you, love your enemies, bless those who curse you, do good to those who hate you, and pray for those who spitefully use you and persecute you.*

This continues Jesus Christ's teachings from the Sermon on the Mount, where He instructed: "You've heard it said, 'Love your neighbor and hate your enemy.' But I say to you, love your enemies and pray for those who persecute you. This way, you'll be children of your Father in heaven. He causes His sun to rise on the evil and the good and sends rain on the righteous and the unrighteous."

Let us begin our day reflecting on these profound words, urging us to love our adversaries and offer aid when they're in need. If we are reviled, we shouldn't retaliate in kind. Instead, we should counteract malevolence with benevolence. When we're disparaged, rather than retaliating, we should offer a prayer for them.

Father, Jesus, this teaching challenges us deeply. Yet, you provide the blueprint for emulating such divine love. May God's grace empower us today to love our foes, intercede on their behalf, and react to malevolence with kindness. Should we face ridicule or persecution, let our hearts be stirred to pray for those individuals. They perhaps need Your presence in their lives more than most.

Lord Jesus, remind us that you sacrificed everything, stretching out your arms on the cross for humanity, hoping all might come to know and be reconciled with You. In profound gratitude and humility, we offer this prayer in the name of Jesus Christ, our Lord and Savior. Amen.

APRIL 15
Lord's Prayer

Matthew 6:9-13

> [9] *The Lord Jesus Christ said, in this manner, therefore, pray:*
> *Our Father in heaven, Hallowed be Your name.*
> [10] *Your kingdom come. Your will be done on earth as it is in heaven.*
> [11] *Give us this day our daily bread.*
> [12] *And forgive us our mistakes as we forgive our wrongdoers.*
> [13] *And do not lead us into temptation, but deliver us from the evil one. For Yours is the kingdom and the power and the glory forever. Amen.*

God elaborates further on the significance of forgiveness, emphasizing that if we extend forgiveness towards others, our Heavenly Father will forgive us in kind. However, if we withhold forgiveness, our Father will do the same with our transgressions.

He also touches upon the dangers of hypocrisy and the importance of genuine intentions in our actions. If we fast, it shouldn't be a public display of self-pity or an attempt to garner sympathy. When we pray, it's best to seek solitude, away from prying eyes, as genuine communion with God is intimate and personal. We should not seek human approval but should aim for divine approval. For God, who sees everything—even our hidden thoughts and intentions—rewards authenticity.

Today, let us approach God with gratitude for the teachings and guidance He has provided.

Lord, by the power of Your Spirit, instill in us a heart of forgiveness. Help us release any bitterness or grudges against those who have wronged us, entrusting them to You. May we pray earnestly for their well-being and spiritual enlightenment.

Thank You, Father, for Your unending mercy and love. We place this day under Your watchful care and protection.

In the name of Jesus Christ, our Savior, Amen.

APRIL 16
A new creation

Galatians 2:20

> *I have been crucified with Christ; it is no longer I who live, but Christ lives in me; and the life which I now live in the flesh I live by faith in the Son of God, who loved me and gave Himself for me.*

God elaborates further on the significance of forgiveness, emphasizing that if we extend forgiveness towards others, our Heavenly Father will forgive us in kind. However, if we withhold forgiveness, our Father will do the same with our transgressions.

He also touches upon the dangers of hypocrisy and the importance of genuine intentions in our actions. If we fast, it shouldn't be a public display of self-pity or an attempt to garner sympathy. When we pray, it's best to seek solitude, away from prying eyes, as genuine communion with God is intimate and personal. We should not seek human approval but should aim for divine approval. For God, who sees everything—even our hidden thoughts and intentions—rewards authenticity.

Today, let us approach God with gratitude for the teachings and guidance He has provided.

Lord, by the power of Your Spirit, instill in us a heart of forgiveness. Help us release any bitterness or grudges against those who have wronged us, entrusting them to You. May we pray earnestly for their well-being and spiritual enlightenment.

Thank You, Father, for Your unending mercy and love. We place this day under Your watchful care and protection.

In the name of Jesus Christ, our Savior, Amen.

APRIL 17
O God, listen to my words

Psalms 5

1 Give ear to my words, O LORD, Consider my meditation.
2 Give heed to the voice of my cry, My King and my God, For to You
I will pray.
3 My voice You shall hear in the morning, O LORD; In the morning I
will direct it to You, And I will look up.
4 For You are not a God who takes pleasure in wickedness, Nor
shall evil dwell with You.
5 The boastful shall not stand in Your sight; You hate all workers of
iniquity.
6 You shall destroy those who speak falsehood; The LORD abhors
the bloodthirsty and deceitful man.
7 But as for me, I will come into Your house in the multitude of Your
mercy; In fear of You I will worship toward Your holy temple.
8 Lead me, O LORD, in Your righteousness because of my enemies;
Make Your way straight before my face. 9 For there
is no faithfulness in their mouth; Their inward part is destruction;
Their throat is an open tomb; They flatter with their tongue.
10 Pronounce them guilty, O God!
Let them fall by their own counsels; Cast them out in the multitude
of their transgressions, for they have rebelled against You.
11 But let all those rejoice who put their trust in You; Let them ever
shout for joy, because You defend them; Let those also who love
Your name Be joyful in You. 12 For You, O LORD, will bless the
righteous; With favor You will surround him as with a shield.

Hear my prayer, O LORD, and listen to my supplication. O King and my God, hear my voice as I pray to you. O LORD, in the morning you hear my voice; in the morning, I present my prayer to you and eagerly await your response. For you, O God, detest evil. Sinners cannot dwell in your presence, the arrogant cannot stand before you, and you abhor all who do wickedness.

You eliminate those who speak falsehoods and despise the violent and deceitful. Yet, because of your vast love, I may enter your house and worship you in your holy temple with deep reverence. O God, with the many adversaries I face, guide me in the way of truth and righteousness. Amen.

Today, O God, we offer this prayer to ensure we do not count ourselves among the sinners. Let us not be found among the arrogant, the wicked, the deceitful, or the violent. Instead, may your grace through Jesus Christ work continuously within us, shaping us ever more into the likeness of our beloved Savior, Jesus Christ. Today brings its own challenges and tasks, but you are aware of each one. We can entrust all to you without anxiety, knowing you are our benevolent God and provider.

Thank you, Father. We commit this day into your blessed care, praying in the name of Jesus Christ, the King of kings. Amen. Amen.

APRIL 18
Through His wounds we are healed

Isaiah 53

> *The prophet Isaiah says to God, "Who could believe what we have just heard?"*

Who can fathom the power of God in all these things? God's desire for His servant was for him to grow like a tender shoot in arid land. He possessed neither beauty nor majesty to draw our attention, nor the appeal to catch our gaze. We despised and shunned him, a man of profound sorrow. He was so marred that many turned away; we disregarded him as if he were insignificant. Yet it was our afflictions he bore, our pains he carried. We assumed he was struck down by God, afflicted for some wrongdoing.

But he was pierced for our transgressions and crushed for our iniquities. Upon him was the chastisement that brought us peace, and by his stripes, we are healed. Like wandering sheep, we all went astray, each turning to our own way, but the LORD placed upon him the guilt of us all. He was oppressed and afflicted, yet he did not protest. He was silent like a lamb led to slaughter, and as an ewe before her shearers, he did not open his mouth. He was unjustly taken, tried, and condemned to death, with none to plead his cause. He was cut off from the land of the living, struck for the sins of his people. He was given a grave among the wicked, placed with the rich in his death. Yet he committed no wrong, and no deceit was found in his mouth. This is our Lord Jesus Christ; this is our Savior.

Thank you, Father, for sending your Son, Jesus Christ. Jesus, we are grateful for the immense sacrifices you made on our behalf, for it's by your wounds that we are made whole. For those ailing, know that Jesus Christ is the ultimate healer.

May God extend His healing touch tonight, bestowing both physical and spiritual restoration. We commit this night into your gracious care, praying for peace and love to envelop all.

In the name of Jesus Christ, Amen.

APRIL 19
With favor God will shield us

Psalm 5

From an old Persian book I've read, it says, "All who trust in you shall rejoice, they shall sing to you forever; for you are their refuge. Those who love your name shall exult in you. For you, LORD, will bless the righteous. You will encircle him with favor as with a shield."

In the English version, the word "satisfaction" is rendered as "favor". Favor holds a unique significance; it implies bringing joy to someone. Thus, when we pray, "Lord, grant him favor in the eyes of others," we're asking for others to hold a positive and hopeful view of that person. The word "optimistic" captures this essence better.

God extends this special favor, this unique grace, to His children. While it's said that God doesn't show favoritism, He always seems to make exceptions for His children. God doesn't chastise those who aren't His; He reproves those He cherishes, disciplines the ones He loves, to foster their growth in Him.

The text assures us that God becomes our shield with delight, with gratification. Those who adore His name, those who hold it dear in their hearts, are blessed. The name of Jesus Christ is exalted above every other name, in heaven, on earth, and below the earth. Every knee will bow, and every tongue will confess to this name, proclaiming Jesus Christ as Lord.

Jesus Christ proclaimed, "When you know the truth, for I am the way, the truth, and the light, that truth shall liberate you. Rivers of living water will flow from within you." With these promises, with these affirmations, we come before You to exclaim, "O Lord Jesus Christ, how wondrous and magnificent You are."

Lord Jesus Christ, we commit this day into your blessed hands. May God bestow upon us these blessings, to find favor and joy in the eyes of others. Let us fulfill the tasks You've entrusted us with, and put a smile on Your radiant face, Amen.

APRIL 20
And I will be their God

Jeremiah 31:33

> *But this is the covenant that I will make with the house of Israel after those days, says the* LORD*: I will put My law in their minds, and write it on their hearts; and I will be their God, and they shall be My people.*

God declares, "I will be their God." This sentiment is echoed in the book "Morning by Morning" by Charles Spurgeon. Charles Spurgeon, one of the most renowned English preachers of the 19th century, was often dubbed the "Prince of Preachers." In this context, Spurgeon proclaims, "I will be their Lord." He emphasizes the weight of this divine assurance. Spurgeon elaborates, "Christians, this is the promise.

It is the singular promise that suffices for all our requirements. This assurance caters to all our needs. It's truly all we require." God vows to be our God—the deity who fashioned the heavens, the earth, and all that they encompass. "And I will be your God." In moments when worldly possessions fall short, when myriad distractions fail to satiate us, who then can truly fulfill us? Only an entity without bounds. When He enriches, He doesn't just fill; He pours into us abundantly, replenishing us eternally.

Thus, dear friends, God assures us, "I will be your God"—the God competent to bridge every void. We turn to Him, professing, "Jesus Christ, you are my Lord, my Savior, and my everything." Lord, this evening, we place all our concerns and joys in your capable hands. The elation we feel stems from the knowledge that You are our God. This jubilation surges within us like a bubbling spring. We express our profound gratitude, Lord, for this unparalleled joy. We consign this night to Your care.

In the name of Jesus Christ, Amen.

APRIL 21
Trust the Lord with all your heart

Proverbs 3:5-6

> *"Trust in the Lord with all your heart and lean not on your own understanding. In all your ways acknowledge Him, and He will direct your paths."*

So, let us approach the Father and request, "O Father, may this be true for us today." In the esteemed name of Jesus Christ, the King of kings, we come before You, declaring, "God, our trust resides in You. We confide in You regarding every facet of our lives, wholeheartedly and with every ounce of our being." O Jesus Christ, our affection for You encompasses our very essence. You've assured us that when we credit God for all things, He will then take the reins. It's at this juncture, O God, that You guide, uplift, and shepherd us on our journey. O Father, we consign this day into Your benevolent care. Through the Holy Spirit, may You provide guidance and assistance today. Lord, with unwavering faith, we commit all unto Your gracious and tender hands. We express our gratitude, Father.

In Jesus Christ's name, Amen.

APRIL 22
Why are you fearful?

Matthew 8:24-25

> 24 *And suddenly a great tempest arose on the sea, so that the boat was covered with the waves. But He was asleep.*
> 25 *Then His disciples came to Him and awoke Him, saying, "Lord, save us! We are perishing!"*

When the Lord Jesus Christ was on a boat with His disciples, they journeyed across the Lake of Galilee. As Jesus Christ slumbered in the boat, a ferocious storm emerged, causing the boat to be swamped by high tides and waves. In their panic, the disciples approached the sleeping Jesus and exclaimed, "Lord, please awaken, for we are perishing."

Upon awakening, Jesus questioned them, "Why are you so afraid? O ye of little faith." He then stood up, rebuked the wind and the sea, and all was still. There was no wind, no tumultuous waves.

Astonished, the disciples wondered aloud, "Who is this man, that even the wind and sea obey Him?" Truly, He is the King of Kings and the Lord of Lords. Prophet Isaiah, in his writings, echoes a similar sentiment. He speaks of a God who possesses the power to shift the seas and quell its roaring waves. The Book of Genesis also alludes to such wonders.

Indeed, we serve an extraordinary Lord. Both perfect man and divine, Jesus is the Christ. When we find ourselves in life's tempestuous seas, engulfed by towering waves of challenges and fears, we must turn to Jesus. He will reassure us, asking, "Why are you afraid? Where is your faith?" and then He will bring tranquility to our storms.

Thank you, Father, for gifting us with Your son, Jesus Christ. Lord Jesus Christ, You reign supreme as the Lord of all lords and the King of all kings. May Your will be manifested in each of us. Tonight, we take solace in the knowledge that when we entrust everything into Your benevolent hands, if our lives are steered by You, then who could stand against us? Amen.

APRIL 23
Do not be wise in your own eyes

Proverbs 3:7-8

> [7] *Do not be wise in your own eyes.*
> *Fear the LORD and depart from evil.*
> [8] *It will be health to our flesh,*
> *And strength to your bones.*

"Do not consider yourself wise in your own eyes." This passage advises us against overvaluing our own knowledge. Pride, often considered the root of all sins, convinces us that we are superior to others. It allows us to disregard the rights of others, justifying our wrongdoings and leading us astray. Here, Solomon cautions us against arrogance and self-importance. Instead, he encourages obedience to God. Through this obedience, we embrace humility. In doing so, God brings healing and wholeness to our lives.

Our Father, and O Holy Spirit, we beseech you: when pride arises within us, extinguish it, and grant us the grace of humility.

In our obedience to God, we elevate the name of Jesus Christ above all else. Jesus, you epitomize humility. You left the splendor of heaven, took on human form, and entered this world. Instead of a palace, you were born in a humble stable. Raised in a modest household, you became intimately acquainted with our struggles and challenges. Despite facing immense pain and suffering, you endured, becoming a beacon of hope and the ultimate role model for us all.

O Lord Jesus Christ, may we continuously strive to emulate your character. Heal our wounds, alleviate our pains, and cure our ailments. As Prophet Isaiah proclaimed, "He will bear all our pains, wounds, and diseases." We pray in the majestic name of Jesus Christ, the King of kings and Lord of Lords. Amen.

APRIL 24

Do you believe?

Matthew 9:20-22

> 20 *And suddenly, a woman who had a flow of blood for twelve years came from behind and touched the hem of His garment.*
> 21 *For she said to herself, "If only I may touch His garment, I shall be made well."*
> 22 *But Jesus turned around, and when He saw her, He said, "Be of good cheer, daughter; your faith has made you well." And the woman was made well from that hour.*

There was a woman who had been suffering from a bleeding condition for 12 years. Despite spending all her savings on doctors, no one could cure her. With steadfast faith, she believed that just by touching Jesus's garment, she would be healed. She acted on this belief, aware of the Judaic teaching that a bleeding woman who touches someone renders them impure.

Upon her touch, Jesus immediately sensed it and questioned, "Who touched me?" Surrounded by a multitude, His disciples were puzzled and responded, "In this crowd pressing against you, how can you ask, 'Who touched you?'" Jesus, however, clarified that this touch was different; he felt power flow out from him. Turning to the woman, He acknowledged her faith, declaring that it had healed her. From that moment, she was completely healed.

Are our faith and conviction as profound as that of this woman? If we were to reach out to Jesus, would we too experience healing?

Around the same time, two blind men approached Jesus, crying out, "Son of David, have mercy on us." When questioned about their desires, they simply requested their sight. Jesus asked them about their faith, and upon their affirmation, He healed them, saying, "Let it be done according to your faith." Both men regained their sight.

Do we believe that Jesus, the Almighty God, the King of kings and Lord of lords, to whom all power in heaven, on earth, and below is given, is capable of miracles? Should we even question His capabilities? Or should we have unwavering faith that He can heal our ailments and resolve our challenges?

Father, in the name of Jesus Christ, we approach You acknowledging Your might. We pray for strength in moments of doubt and ask that our faith be fortified today. In the name of Jesus Christ, Amen.

APRIL 25
Does your faith in God increase?

Lord Jesus Christ, with unwavering faith, we approach You, acknowledging that You are the King of kings and the Lord of Lords. To You has been given all authority in heaven, on earth, and beneath the earth.

Do we ever take a moment to examine our faith? It's essential, at times, to introspect and assess the strength and foundation of our beliefs. My hope is that today's collective prayer to Lord Jesus Christ not only tests our faith but also reinforces and deepens our conviction.

Let us now express our heartfelt gratitude, saying, "Thank You, Father. Thank You, Lord Jesus Christ, for Your boundless goodness. Your radiant love envelopes us always. Today, we felt an augmentation in our faith in Your might, Your unwavering love, and Your very essence. O God, we thank You for today's countless blessings, for the gift of life, and for the privilege to worship You.

Lord Jesus Christ, only You are truly deserving of our adoration and praise. We are endlessly grateful for Your love that pulled us from darkness into Your magnificent light. We cherish the honor of being known as Your children, being considered sons and daughters of God. We thank You.

Father, we entrust this night into Your divine hands, praying for a deeper infusion of Your peace, love, purity, and the joy You promise us. Bestow upon us the gift of restful sleep so that we awaken tomorrow renewed and transformed.

In Your Holy name, we pray. In the name of Jesus Christ, Amen.

APRIL 26
You are the witnesses of Christ

Matthew 10:16-20

> 16 *"I am sending you out like sheep among wolves. Therefore, be as shrewd as snakes and as innocent as doves.*
> 17 *Be on your guard; you will be handed over to the local councils and be flogged in the synagogues.*
> 18 *On my account you will be brought before governors and kings as witnesses to them and to the Gentiles.*
> 19 *But when they arrest you, do not worry about what to say or how to say it. At that time, you will be given what to say,*
> 20 *for it will not be you speaking, but the Spirit of your Father speaking through you.*

When the Lord Jesus Christ selected His disciples, as recorded in the book of Matthew, He granted them the power to heal all kinds of illnesses and to cast out demons from the afflicted. He then sent them forth to preach and proclaim the good news of the impending kingdom of God.

Jesus cautioned them, saying, "Behold, I send you out as sheep in the midst of wolves; so be shrewd as serpents and innocent as doves. But beware of men, for they will hand you over to the courts and scourge you in their synagogues; and you will even be brought before governors and kings for My sake, as a testimony to them and to the Gentiles." However, this persecution and questioning served a divine purpose—to bear witness for Christ and bring others to the truth for their salvation.

So, if today you find yourself facing adversity, being questioned, or enduring persecution for your faith in the Lord Jesus Christ, remember that the power of the Holy Spirit is with you. Do not be disheartened or fearful, for in those moments, the Holy Spirit will provide you with the words to speak. Whenever you go out and face such challenges, keep in mind that you are a witness for Jesus Christ.

You need not fear anything, for your purpose is to testify, so that others may see the truth and find salvation in God's hope. Amen.

Father, today we come before You with gratitude, knowing that we need not fear any circumstance, because if God is with us, who can stand against us? With the Lord Jesus Christ by our side, whose name is exalted above all others and who possesses all power on earth and in heaven, we are empowered.

As stated in Romans 8:28, "And we know that in all things God works for the good of those who love him, who have been called according to his purpose," we trust that everything will ultimately work for good for those who love and are called by the Lord. Therefore, we place all things into the loving hands of the Lord, allowing Him to use us for the advancement of His kingdom.

May people come to know the truth about Jesus Christ, the King of kings, the Son of God, who came from God, sacrificed His life for us, bore our sins on the cross, rose from the dead on the third day, and today is our living Savior. Amen.

APRIL 27
He is mighty to save

Isaiah 63:7

> *I will tell of the kindnesses of the Lord, the deeds for which he is to be praised, according to all the LORD has done for us—yes, the many good things he has done for Israel, according to his compassion and many kindnesses.*

It is proclaimed that God is magnificent in salvation and that He saves with power. Jesus Christ indeed possesses the power to save, as He willingly sacrificed Himself on the cross for you and me. Furthermore, He is more than capable of bringing to fruition what He has initiated, even beyond our wildest imaginations.

Not only can Jesus reveal Himself to people, but He also has the authority to humble those who oppose Him and lead them to accept Him as their Lord and Savior. For all power in heaven, on earth, and beneath the earth has been entrusted to Jesus Christ, the King of kings.

Therefore, He has the capacity to bring to completion the work He has initiated in each one of us. I believe that today He will bring to fruition the work He began in each of us this morning. So, Father, we approach You today with gratitude for Your Son, Jesus Christ.

O Jesus Christ, we thank You for Your boundless love, Your selfless sacrifice, Your grace, and the power bestowed upon You, which will ultimately lead every knee to bow before You and every tongue to confess that You are the Lord and Savior of the world. We thank You for calling us out of darkness into the light and rescuing us from the depths of darkness.

We are grateful that You are always with us and never forsake us, and we thank You for all the blessings of today, O God. Shower us with blessings, peace, joy, love, and a restful night's sleep, so that when we awaken tomorrow, we will be filled with renewed energy and ready to praise and exalt You. In the name of Jesus Christ, we pray. Amen. Good night, dear friends.

APRIL 28
The excellent name of the lord

Psalms 8

1 *O LORD, our Lord, how excellent is thy name in all the earth! who*
hast set thy glory above the heavens.
2 *Out of the mouth of babes and sucklings hast thou ordained*
strength because of thine enemies, that thou mightest still the enemy
and the avenger.
3 *When I consider thy heavens, the work of thy fingers, the moon,*
and the stars, which thou hast ordained.
4 *What is man, that thou art mindful of him? and the son of man, that*
thou visitest him?
5 *For thou hast made him a little lower than the angels, and hast*
crowned him with glory and honor.
6 *Thou madest him to have dominion over the works of thy hands;*
thou hast put all things under his feet:
7 *All sheep and oxen, yea, and the beasts of the field;*
8 *The fowl of the air, and the fish of the sea, and whatsoever passeth*
through the paths of the seas.
9 *O LORD our Lord, how excellent is thy name in all the earth!*

This Psalm beautifully captures the magnificence and majesty of God. O Lord, our Lord, Your name's excellence is renowned throughout the entire earth, and Your glory transcends even the heavens.

It's awe-inspiring to think that even children and infants praise You, silencing Your enemies. When we gaze upon Your creation, the sky, moon, and stars that You have crafted, we can't help but marvel at how insignificant we are in comparison. Yet, You have exalted us, positioning us just slightly lower than the angels and crowning us with honor and dignity.

You've entrusted us with authority over all Your creation, from the animals on land to the birds in the sky and the creatures of the sea. O Lord, our Lord, Your glorious name encompasses the entire earth.

Together, let us glorify the name of our Lord, the Creator of heaven and earth. Glory be to God the Father, the Son, and the Holy Spirit, who worked in unity during the creation, three distinct personalities within one Godhead.

Just as we are made up of spirit, flesh, and body, and losing any of these components would change who we are, God exists as three personalities in one divine essence.

Let us remember that in the beginning was the Word, and the Word was with God, and the Word was God, which is the Word of Jesus Christ, the Father, the Son, and the Holy Spirit.

O Lord, we thank You for Your love, greatness, goodness, and for considering us, even in our insignificance, as Your sons and daughters through faith in Jesus Christ. You declare us to be Your princes and priests in heaven.

As we entrust this day to Your blessed hands, O Father, continue to work in us, removing all that is not of You and filling us increasingly with Your Holy Spirit. In the name of Jesus Christ, we pray. Amen.

APRIL 29
Heavy burden

Matthew 11:27

> *All things are delivered unto me of my Father: and no man knoweth the Son, but the Father; neither knoweth any man the Father, save the Son, and he to whomsoever the Son will reveal him.*

Jesus' words remind us of the profound relationship between Him and the heavenly Father. He tells us that the Father has entrusted everything to Him, and that only the Father truly knows the Son, and vice versa. It is through Jesus that the Father's nature and character are revealed to those whom Jesus chooses to reveal them.

Furthermore, Jesus extends a loving invitation to all who labor under heavy burdens, offering them rest. He calls us to take His yoke upon ourselves and learn from Him, assuring us that His yoke is kind and humble and His burden is light. This signifies that trying to attain salvation or righteousness through our own efforts and deeds will always be burdensome and fruitless. Instead, Jesus invites us to bring our heavy burdens, our troubles, our sins, and lay them at His feet, accepting Him as our Lord, Savior, and the only way to God the Father.

As Christians, our daily practice should be to place our burdens before Christ and acknowledge that He alone is capable of carrying them. By doing so, we surrender to Him, worship Him, and allow His grace and love to lighten our loads.

Let us pray: Heavenly Father, we thank You for the profound truths shared by Your Son, Jesus Christ. Thank You for inviting us to cast our burdens upon Him and find rest. Lord Jesus, we acknowledge You as our Lord and Savior and lay all our concerns at Your feet. Help us to live each day in the light of Your grace, trusting in Your kindness and humility.

In the name of Jesus Christ, we pray. Amen.

APRIL 30
Did you take your heavy burden?

Your reflection on the importance of placing our cares and worries at the feet of Jesus and finding His peace is a powerful reminder of the comfort and solace we can find in our faith. It's a testament to the transformative power of surrendering our burdens to our Lord and experiencing the peace that surpasses all understanding.

The passage from Proverbs underscores the sovereignty of God over the hearts and actions of both leaders and individuals. It serves as a reassurance that even in the midst of life's uncertainties, God is in control and can guide us like a river, bringing us to where He wills.

Your prayer beautifully expresses gratitude for God's love, kindness, and the peace that He imparts to those who trust in Him. May we all continue to find solace and strength in surrendering our concerns to the Lord and embracing His peace, knowing that He is with us always.

Let us pray: Heavenly Father, we come before You with hearts filled with gratitude for the peace and comfort You offer us. Thank You for carrying our burdens and guiding us in Your love. Lord Jesus, help us continually find solace in Your presence and trust in Your sovereign plan.

In the precious name of our Lord and Savior, Jesus Christ, we pray. Amen.

MAY 1
Heaven is where Christ is

Your reflection on the profound connection between heaven and the presence of the Lord Jesus Christ is a beautiful testament to the central place that Christ holds in the hearts of believers. Indeed, for Christians, the ultimate aspiration is to be with the Lord, where He is, and to experience the fullness of His presence.

The quotes you shared, particularly the one about heaven being with Christ and the idea that heaven without Him is hell while hell with Him is heaven, encapsulate the essence of Christian faith and longing. It emphasizes that our true joy and fulfillment come from our relationship with Christ, regardless of our circumstances.

Your prayer expresses gratitude for the assurance of Christ's constant presence and seeks His perspective in viewing the world around us. It's a reminder that with Christ by our side, even in challenging situations, we can find hope, peace, and a sense of heaven.

Let us pray: Heavenly Father, we thank You for the hope and joy that come from being in the presence of Your Son, our Lord Jesus Christ. May we continually seek to be where He is, finding heaven in His presence. Help us view the world through the lens of faith and hope, knowing that with Christ, every place can be transformed into a glimpse of heaven. We entrust this day and our lives into Your blessed hands.

In the name of Jesus Christ, we pray. Amen.

MAY 2
Where did you lose Christ?

Song of Solomon 3:1

> *By night on my bed I sought the one I love; I sought him, but I did not find him.*

Your reflection on seeking Christ and the analogy of losing Him in the same place where we can find Him is a powerful reminder of the importance of maintaining a close and continuous relationship with the Lord. Charles Spurgeon's question, "Where did you lose your fellowship with Christ?" prompts us to self-reflect and pinpoint the moments or actions that may have caused a separation.

You rightly point out that prayer is a place where we can find Christ again. It serves as a means of reconnecting with Him and reestablishing that vital fellowship. When we confess our sins and turn back to Christ in prayer, His open arms are always ready to receive us, for He never leaves us nor forsakes us.

Your analogy of sitting in the passenger seat and letting Jesus take the steering wheel of our lives is a beautiful illustration of surrendering control to Him. It echoes the importance of trust and reliance on Christ's guidance in all aspects of our lives.

Let us pray: Gracious Lord, we come before You, seeking Your presence and fellowship. Help us to identify the moments or actions that have caused a separation between us and You. May we never lose sight of You due to pride, sin, or neglect. Instead, may we continually seek You in prayer, surrendering control to Your loving hands. Guide us, Lord, and lead us in the way that is best for us.

In the name of Jesus Christ, we pray. Amen.

MAY 3
Five bread and two fish

Matthew 14:14-21

> [14] *And when Jesus went out, He saw a great multitude; and He was moved with compassion for them and healed their sick.*
> [15] *When it was evening, His disciples came to Him, saying, "This is a deserted place, and the hour is already late. Send the multitudes away, that they may go into the villages and buy themselves food."*
> [16] *But Jesus said to them, "They do not need to go away. You give them something to eat."*
> [17] *And they said to Him, "We have here only five loaves and two fish."*
> [18] *He said, "Bring them here to Me."*
> [19] *Then He commanded the multitudes to sit down on the grass. And He took the five loaves and the two fish, and looking up to heaven, He blessed and broke and gave the loaves to the disciples; and the disciples gave to the multitudes.*
> [20] *So they all ate and were filled, and they took up twelve baskets full of the fragments that remained.*
> [21] *Now those who had eaten were about five thousand men, besides women and children.*

This is the story of the Lord Jesus Christ feeding the people. Jesus had just heard that Herod's soldiers had taken the head of John the Baptist. When Jesus Christ learned of this, he was upset and went on a boat to a remote place to be alone with himself. When he got there, he saw that many people had come to greet him and had gathered around him. When Jesus saw them, he sympathized and had compassion for them. He healed their diseases and cast out demons.

When evening came, the people were hungry, and there was no food. The disciples asked him to send people away, but Jesus said, "No, we must feed them." There were 5,000, including men, women, and children. He asked if anyone had brought any food. There was a little boy who had five loaves and two fish given to him by his mother for lunch. Jesus took the food, looked up to heaven, gave thanks to God, and asked the people to sit down.

He broke the loaves and fish and gave it to them, and as he gave, there was more and more bread and fish. All the people ate to the fill, and when they had finished, there was still more food that filled up 12 baskets. We see that Jesus Christ always pays attention to the basic and physical needs of the people and always does the amazing to save them from sin on earth.

Here too, he meets their needs with heavenly food. If we are in that situation with many problems, let us take our problems, like those 5 loaves and two fish, to Jesus Christ and say, "Lord, bless this food, please take our problems and help us solve them." Amen.

Thank you, Father, for helping us with our problems and cares. We know you'll use whatever means to miraculously and incredibly solve all the problems. In the name of Jesus Christ, we entrust ourselves into your hands. Amen.

MAY 4

Why did you doubt?

Matthew 14
he says that after God sent the people to their homes, he sent his disciples to the boat on the lake and went up the mountain alone to pray.

> 23 *Now when evening came, He was alone there.*
> 24 *But the boat was now in the middle of the sea, tossed by the waves, for the wind was contrary.*
> 25 *Now in the fourth watch of the night Jesus went to the disciples walking on the sea.*
> 26 *And when the disciples saw Him walking on the sea, they were troubled, saying, "It is a ghost!" And they cried out for fear.*
> 27 *But immediately Jesus spoke to them, saying, "Be of good cheer! It is I; do not be afraid."*
> 28 *And Peter answered Him and said, "Lord, if it is You, command me to come to You on the water."*
> 29 *So He said, "Come." And when Peter had come down out of the boat, he walked on the water to go to Jesus.*
> 30 *But when he saw that the wind was boisterous, he was afraid; and beginning to sink he cried out, saying, "Lord, save me!"*
> 31 *And immediately Jesus stretched out His hand and caught him, and said to him, "O you of little faith, why did you doubt?"*
> 32 *And when they got into the boat, the wind ceased.*
> 33 *Then those who were in the boat came and worshiped Him, saying, "Truly You are the Son of God."*

It was about 4 o'clock in the morning when his disciples saw a man walking on the water. It was Jesus Christ who was walking on the water toward the boat in the midst of turbulent and strong winds on the sea. They saw this and were very afraid, crying out in fear because they thought it was a ghost. However, Jesus Christ reassured them, saying, "Do not be afraid; it is me."

Then Peter, who was always the first to speak, said, "Lord, if it is truly you, command me to come to you on the water." Jesus then commanded him to come. As Peter took a few steps toward Jesus Christ on the water, he became frightened when he saw the wind and waves and began to sink.

He cried out, "Jesus, please save me!" Jesus Christ reached out, took his hand, and lifted him back onto the boat, asking, "Why did you doubt?" When this happened, the wind ceased, and all the disciples fell to their knees, praising him, saying, "You truly are the Son of God."

So, today, God may call you and me to do something that seems difficult, like going against the wind, against the storm, against all odds.

How should we respond? When we step forward in faith, if we lose our faith, we may feel like we are drowning, and we'll have to cry out, "God, save us!" But when we believe and move forward in faith, God will say to us, "Blessed are you and your faith."

Therefore, Father, grant us faith today. If you call us to do something that appears impossible, help us not to lose faith when we consider all the challenges and storms. Let us fulfill our calling and lift you up.

Father, we thank you and place this day in your blessed hands.

In the name of Jesus Christ, Amen.

MAY 5
The word of the Lord is pure

Psalm 12:6-7

> [6] *The words of the LORD are pure words, like silver tried in a furnace of earth, Purified seven times.*
> [7] *You shall keep them, O LORD, You shall preserve them from this generation forever.*

It says, the word of the Lord is pure, it's pure. Like silver that has been refined in the furnace of the earth seven times.

You, O God, will keep them and protect them from this generation to the last.

Matthew 15:1-7

> [1]*Then the scribes and Pharisees who were from Jerusalem came to Jesus, saying,*
> [2] *"Why do Your disciples transgress the tradition of the elders? For they do not wash their hands when they eat bread."*
> [3] *He answered and said to them, "Why do you also transgress the commandment of God because of your tradition?*
> [4] *For God commanded, saying, 'Honor your father and your mother'; and 'He who curses father or mother, let him be put to death.'*
> [5] *But you say, 'Whoever says to his father or mother, "Whatever profit you might have received from me is a gift to God"—*
> [6] *then he need not honor his father or mother.' Thus, you have made the commandment of God of no effect by your tradition.*
> [7] *Hypocrites! Well, did Isaiah prophesy about you, saying:*

When the Pharisees confronted Jesus Christ, saying, "Why don't your disciples wash their hands before they eat?" Jesus replied, "Why do you break God's commandment with your tradition?"

God commands children to honor their parents, but you say that if they declare their possessions "Corban" (dedicated to God), they are exempt from taking care of their parents. In everything, you have substituted human traditions for God's commandments. God teaches that what enters a person's mouth does not defile them, but what comes out of their mouth reveals the impurity of their heart.

All sins and impurities, such as wicked thoughts, murder, and adultery, originate in the human heart and are expressed through speech.

The Word of God and the Gospel are pure and unaltered. The Bible is inspired by the Holy Spirit and remains uncorrupted, as God will protect it from distortion. When the enemy claims that the Word of God has been altered, it is a complete falsehood. It can even be scientifically demonstrated that the content of the Bible has not changed. One way to confirm the integrity of an ancient book is to find numerous copies from different time periods, compare them, and observe that the content has remained consistent.

Did you know that the Bible is one of the most well-preserved books in the world? Over 1,500 manuscripts dating back nearly 2,000 years have been discovered, and they all agree. This reinforces our faith in the Word of God, which is pure and serves as the manual for our lives. Amen.

Thank you, Father, for your holy Word, which is more precious than gold and silver. Help us read and memorize it daily.

In the name of Jesus Christ, Amen.

May 6
Do you not remember?

Matthew 16:1-4

> [1] *Then the Pharisees and Sadducees came and testing Him asked that He would show them a sign from heaven.*
> [2] *He answered and said to them, "When it is evening you say, 'It will be fair weather, for the sky is red'.*
> [3] *and in the morning, 'It will be foul weather today, for the sky is red and threatening.' Hypocrites! You know how to discern the face of the sky, but you cannot discern the signs of the times.*
> [4] *A wicked and adulterous generation seeks after a sign, and no sign shall be given to it except the sign of the prophet Jonah."*

The passage reveals that the Pharisees sought a sign from Jesus Christ. To which He responded, "I will give no sign except the sign of Jonah the prophet."

Subsequently, as Jesus embarked on a boat with His disciples, He cautioned them, saying, "Beware of the leaven of the Pharisees and Sadducees." The disciples, however, misunderstood, thinking He was referring to the actual bread they had forgotten to bring. Jesus, recognizing their confusion, asked, "Why do you have so little faith? Do you not yet understand? Can't you remember? Have you forgotten the miracle with the 5,000 men fed with just five loaves and two fish? Or the 4,000 men nourished with seven loaves and a few fish, and how many basketfuls of leftovers you gathered?"

The lesson for us is clear. When the Lord communicates with us, He means precisely what He says. Jesus wasn't cautioning them about physical bread but was warning them about the doctrinal impurity and hypocrisy of the Pharisees and Sadducees. These two groups were fastidious about the law's externals, speaking of God with their lips, but their hearts were far from Him.

Sometimes, we interpret God's word or His signs based on our own preconceptions. However, we must approach His teachings holistically and remember His deeds. If He performed miracles before, isn't He capable of doing them again? Our role isn't to superimpose our own understanding but to seek God's true message.

If our perception contradicts His past acts, we must remember: God, who worked wonders in the past, can surely do so again.

Heavenly Father, if You have a word for us today, grant us the discernment to truly grasp it. You spoke plainly: "Beware of the leaven of the Pharisees and Sadducees." It wasn't the leaven but the corrupt teachings and hypocrisy of these groups that were the concern. Lord, when You speak to us today, illuminate our hearts and minds. May we recall the wondrous deeds You've done in our lives. We pray this in the name of Jesus Christ, Amen.

MAY 7
Our Father

Today, we begin our devotional by reflecting upon the prayer that our Lord Jesus Christ taught us.

> *"Our Father in heaven, Hallowed be Your name. Your kingdom come, Your will be done on earth as it is in heaven. Give us today our daily bread, and forgive us our sins as we forgive those who sin against us. Lead us not into temptation but deliver us from the evil one. For Yours is the kingdom, the power, and the glory forever. Amen."*

What are we proclaiming in this prayer? Firstly, we acknowledge and embrace God as our Father. When we address Him as 'Our Father', we are recognizing His boundless love for us. He is a benevolent Father, one who desires only the best for His children.

Christ Himself assured us: if we, being earthly parents, know how to give good gifts to our children, how much more will our Heavenly Father provide for our needs? Indeed, He goes beyond our petitions, blessing us in ways we might not even imagine.

Upon accepting Jesus Christ as our Lord and Savior, and surrendering our hearts to Him, we become God's adopted children. We earn the privilege to call Him, 'Our Father'.

By praying, "Your kingdom come, Your will be done", we are expressing a desire for God's divine will to be manifested here on earth, as perfectly as it is in heaven. We invite God to work in our lives, in our hearts, and throughout our world.

We also ask for His guidance during trials, knowing His promise: He will never allow a temptation to befall us without providing a way out. Thus, we pray that He illuminates that escape route, shielding us from the clutches of the adversary.

"Give us today our daily bread" - with these words, we are expressing our dependence on God for all our needs. We recognize Him as our ultimate Provider, believing that every good thing originates from His benevolence.

We close by acknowledging His eternal sovereignty, "For Yours is the kingdom, the power, and the glory forever." We are forever grateful for His unending love and provisions.

In the name of Jesus Christ, our Savior and Redeemer, Amen.

MAY 8
Greatest in the kingdom of God

Matthew 18:2-6

> 2 *Then Jesus called a little child to Him, set him in the midst of them,*
> 3 *and said, "Assuredly, I say to you, unless you are converted and become as little children, you will by no means enter the kingdom of heaven.*
> 4 *Therefore whoever humbles himself as this little child is the greatest in the kingdom of heaven.*
> 5 *Whoever receives one little child like this in My name receives Me. Jesus Warns of Offenses,*
> 6 *"But whoever causes one of these little ones who believe in Me to sin, it would be better for him if a millstone were hung around his neck, and he were drowned in the depth of the sea.*

Once, the disciples of the Lord Jesus Christ asked Him, "Who will be the greatest in the kingdom of God?" In response, Jesus brought a child to stand among them and declared, "Truly, I tell you, unless you become like this child, you will never enter the kingdom of heaven. Therefore, whoever takes the humble position of this child is the greatest in the kingdom of heaven."

What did Jesus mean by urging us to be like children? Has a young child accomplished notable feats? Can they boast of any grand achievements? Children exemplify pure reliance. They wholly trust their parents, often viewing their fathers as the mightiest figures. Held by their parents' hands, they feel invincible. They see their every need met by those who care for them.

The Lord's message is clear: to achieve greatness in God's kingdom, one must lean wholly on the Heavenly Father and the Son. We should believe that nothing is beyond reach when our lives are guided by God and Jesus Christ. It's about embodying the unwavering faith a child places in their parents. Children often regard their fathers as heroes, believing they can achieve anything. If we anchor our faith in our Heavenly Father, recognizing His unmatched power and boundless love for us, we embrace that childlike trust.

Our pathway to greatness in God's kingdom involves loving Him wholeheartedly, trusting in His plans, and seeing Him as the omnipotent force guiding our every step. We should confide in Him as a child would with their parents, sharing our deepest fears, joys, and desires.

Knowing this, we understand that God always desires the best for us. As Jesus Christ said, "Come to me, all you who are weary and burdened, and I will give you rest. Take my yoke upon you and learn from me, for I am gentle and humble in heart, and you will find rest for your souls."

Father, grant us the grace to approach you with the innocence and trust of a child. Let us recognize Your greatness, might, and unwavering love. May we come to You with all our burdens and find solace in Your embrace. Starting today, help us to continually turn to You with childlike faith.

We pray this in the name of Jesus Christ, Amen.

MAY 9
Perfect in Christ Jesus

Colossians 1:28

> *Him we preach, warning every man and teaching every man in all wisdom, that we may present every man perfect in Christ Jesus.*

Scripture encourages us to be perfect in Christ Jesus. Often, we introspect and spot our own flaws. We regret our ill-advised words or rue our missteps, thinking, "I shouldn't have said that or done this." We're constantly aware of our lapses. However, God's word assures that upon accepting Jesus Christ, we attain perfection in Him. It's Jesus, through His redemptive blood, that washes away our blemishes.

He bore our iniquities and paid the ultimate price for our transgressions on the cross with His eternal sacrifice. Through this unparalleled act, Jesus transformed our destinies.

When the Heavenly Father gazes upon us, He doesn't merely see "Mohsen" or any of us individually. Instead, He beholds the risen Christ within us, the indwelling of the Holy Spirit. It's this Holy Spirit that ceaselessly sanctifies, purifying us with each passing moment.

Indeed, we falter and sin. Yet, the moment we turn in repentance, acknowledging our wrongs and seeking God's mercy, we're cleansed. Our transformation is ongoing, demanding our hearts remain humble. At every misstep, we must hasten to the Lord, seeking His cleansing touch, entreating, "Lord Jesus, purify us with Your precious blood and elevate us to sing Your praises."

Our focus must remain steadfast on Jesus Christ. Scripture affirms that all things were created through Him and for Him. He is the Alpha and the Omega, the entirety of our existence and purpose.

Lord, we commit this day into Your divine hands. Lord Jesus, illuminate our minds to grasp this profound truth: that we're perfected in You, enveloped in Your embrace, and intricately united with the Father. May our hearts and minds fixate on You this day and always.

We pray in the name of Jesus Christ, our King of kings, Amen.

MAY 10
Hope and faith!

2 Corinthians 4:18

> *While we do not look at the things which are seen, but at the things which are not seen. For the things which are seen are temporary, but the things which are not seen are eternal.*

Scripture reveals that hope pertains to things we have not seen, yet we understand that both Hope and Faith are very real. Faith is the assurance of things we do not see but are firmly convinced will come to pass. In guiding our Christian journey, the Lord Jesus Christ instructs us to live in the present. We shouldn't be overly consumed with the regrets of yesterday or anxiously anticipate tomorrow; rather, we should fully embrace today.

Today, we must stand firm in the hope of things unseen, trusting in their eventual manifestation. This hope acts as our beacon, guiding us through the tumultuous storms and challenges of today. So, what is this hope? When we, as Christians, cast our eyes toward the future, what do we envision?

We anticipate a future devoid of sin, a glorious time when Jesus Christ returns. We perceive death not as an end but a brief transition, for if we believe in Jesus Christ, immediately after death we will be united with Him in heaven. Our hope also assures us that we'll eventually sit on heavenly thrones alongside Jesus Christ. Despite the inevitable struggles, pains, and storms of our current lives, it's this hope that allows us to glimpse the distant shore and know we'll reach it. For Jesus Christ is with us every step of the way, guiding and propelling us forward.

In contemplating hope and faith, Charles Spurgeon beautifully penned:

"When the world, my heart is rending with its heaviest storm of care, my glad thoughts to heaven ascending find a refuge from despair. Faith's bright vision shall sustain me till life's pilgrimage is past, fears may vex and troubles pain me, I shall reach my home at last."

Despite the myriad challenges that the world presents, causing pain and distress, it's through our unwavering Hope and Faith that we'll ultimately find our eternal home in the embrace of the Lord Jesus Christ.

May the Lord continually bolster your hope and faith each and every moment. Amen.

MAY 11
The apple of Lord's eye

Psalm 17:8

> *Keep me as the apple of Your eye; Hide me under the shadow of Your wings,*

Scripture conveys, "Guard me as the apple of your eye and hide me in the shadow of your wings, away from the wicked who do me harm, my deadly enemies who surround me." The psalmist laments about these adversaries, highlighting their godlessness and self-centered pride. Yet, by verse 15, the tone shifts, and he declares, "As for me, I shall behold your face in righteousness; when I awake, I shall be satisfied with your likeness. For you have forgiven my sin." Amen.

Today, we approach God with gratitude, recognizing that He sees us as the apple of His eye. We entrust ourselves to His care, seeking His protection and guidance. Lord, listen to the sincere cry of our hearts, and shield us beneath your wings, just as you always have.

It's essential to remember the sacrifices made for us by the Lord Jesus Christ and to recall the numerous blessings He has bestowed upon us throughout our lives. As the song from Bethel goes, "God, you have always been faithful to me. You've been my constant through every season."

Let us keep in our hearts the numerous times the Lord Jesus Christ has uplifted us, being our ever-present help. Jesus, who remains the same yesterday, today, and forever, always desires the best for us. No matter the worldly successes and riches amassed by the wicked, we should heed David's words, focusing instead on the joy of beholding God. Every morning, we are blessed with the knowledge that our sins are forgiven through Jesus Christ.

When we accept Jesus Christ as our Lord, our sins are washed away. Should we falter, His mercy remains unchanging. Christian life isn't about living sin-free but about daily renewal through the blood of Jesus Christ. Every time we err, we run to Him, confessing with open hearts, "Lord, I have sinned. Forgive me, I repent, cleanse me."

So, today, we come before you with hearts full of gratitude. Thank you, God, for treasuring us like the apple of your eye. Thank you, Jesus Christ, for sheltering us beneath your wings. And for the assurance that each morning we are forgiven and embraced by your presence. We commit the rest of this day into your loving and capable hands. In the mighty name of Jesus Christ, Amen.

MAY 12
Opportunity to repent

Today's devotional draws inspiration from the book of Exodus, chapters 3 and 4.

Moses returns to Egypt, and God commissions both Moses and Aaron to approach Pharaoh. Their request? That Pharaoh releases the Israelites so they can worship and celebrate the Lord. However, Pharaoh remains obstinate.

Interestingly, each time God contemplates inflicting a punishment, He first instructs Moses and Aaron to entreat Pharaoh, emphasizing, "Let my people go, that they may serve me." Only after presenting this choice does He warn Pharaoh of impending consequences should he refuse. Why didn't God act immediately? Certainly, He possesses the power to do so. Yet, God consistently offers Pharaoh an opportunity to comply. If Pharaoh remains unyielding, the consequence is deferred to the next day.

Why this delay? It underscores God's compassionate, kind, and merciful nature. The Bible tells us God desires not the demise of anyone but wishes for everyone to find salvation and worship Him. By granting Pharaoh a window until the subsequent day, God possibly hopes for a change of heart and repentance from Pharaoh, averting the disaster.

Despite these chances, Pharaoh consistently resists. This narrative serves as a poignant reminder for all of us. God's message is clear. If we falter or err today, He imparts to us the grace of time, even if it's just until tomorrow.

Remember, today is our day of salvation. Thus, if our actions today were not aligned with His will, may the Holy Spirit bring them to our attention. May we be reminded to humble ourselves, seek forgiveness, and ensure we don't stray again.

Father, if today we strayed from your path, we implore your forgiveness. Illuminate our missteps, so with your guidance, we might not repeat them. We surrender this day into your benevolent hands, for you are incomparably good.

In the name of Jesus Christ, the King of kings, Amen.

MAY 13

The house of prayer

Matthew 21:1-5

> [1] *Now when they drew near Jerusalem, and came to Bethphage, at the Mount of Olives, then Jesus sent two disciples,*
> [2] *saying to them, "Go into the village opposite you, and immediately you will find a donkey tied, and a colt with her. Lose them and bring them to Me.*
> [3] *And if anyone says anything to you, you shall say, 'The Lord has need of them,' and immediately he will send them."*
> [4] *All this was done that it might be fulfilled which was spoken by the prophet, saying:*
> [5] *"Tell the daughter of Zion, 'Behold, your King is coming to you, Lowly, and sitting on a donkey, A colt, the foal of a donkey.'"*

When Jesus Christ enters Jerusalem on a donkey, prophesying Psalm 118, and all the people say, Hosanna, Hosanna to David's son. Hosanna means save right now.

Upon arriving at the temple, Jesus entered and began to cleanse it, driving out those selling sacrifices and exchanging money. Here, we witness the righteous anger of Jesus Christ. When questioned about His actions, He responded, "Have you not read that My house shall be called a house of prayer?"

God's house resides within each of us, manifested in our hearts and souls. Through the Holy Spirit, He dwells in us. Yet, how often do we treat our inner temple as a marketplace? Do we allow transactions of worldly desires and distractions to replace our devotion and prayer? Instead of immersing ourselves in the pursuit of material gains, we should be seeking a deep and meaningful relationship with God.

May we make a commitment today and always to center our thoughts and actions on Him.

Father, in the name of Jesus Christ, the King of kings, cleanse the temple within us, which should be dedicated to prayer and communion with You. Lord, purify our hearts. Remove all that is not of You, all that distracts us, and leads us away from communing with You. Eradicate these distractions, ensuring our inner temple remains a sanctified space for prayer and deep connection with You.

In the name of Jesus Christ, the King of Kings, Amen.

MAY 14
Has God answered our mourning?

In yesterday's devotion, we reflected on the house of God within our hearts. We prayed earnestly for the removal of anything within that space that isn't aligned with His will, anything where the adversary might have established a stronghold. If you genuinely prayed this, I'm confident that God revealed not just one, but perhaps several areas of concern.

Have you taken those revelations to God, laying them at His feet in surrender? Have you dedicated time to be in His presence? Recall our Sunday discussion, where we spoke of Jesus as the true vine and our need to abide in Him through reading His Word, praying, and nurturing our relationship with Him.

If you've already taken these steps, acknowledged your shortcomings, and asked the Lord to fill those voids with His presence, then I believe He is already working in you. But if you haven't yet, know that it's never too late. Approach Him with a contrite heart.

For those who've sought Jesus and repented, let's lift our voices in gratitude:

"Lord, we express our deepest gratitude to You, dear Christ, for illuminating our blind spots and frailties. We are grateful for your guidance when we've strayed. We deeply appreciate Your corrective love, and if there remains any aspect of our lives that grieves Your Holy Spirit, reveal it to us. Grant us the courage to repent and surrender it to You.

Dear Jesus, You bear our burdens and make our yokes easy. We are thankful for another day under Your grace and for the beauty You bring into our lives. We commit the rest of our day into Your able hands, praying for your peace to envelop each one of us.

In the name of Jesus Christ, Amen."

MAY 15
The cornerstone

In Matthew 21:23 onwards, Jesus narrates a parable about a vineyard. Its owner cultivated it and handed it over to gardeners, then departed on a journey. In due season, he sent his servants to collect his share of the harvest. However, the gardeners mistreated and killed the servants. In a final attempt, the owner sent his son, thinking, "Perhaps they will respect my son and give him my due." Yet upon seeing the son, the gardeners conspired, saying, "Let's kill him so that the inheritance will be ours." They murdered the son and discarded his body outside the vineyard.

Jesus then posed a question: "What do you think the owner of the vineyard will do?" The response was clear: he will destroy the wicked tenants and lease his vineyard to others who will give him his due. Jesus equated this to how the people and their ancestors treated God's messengers and would soon treat His Son, for their personal power and gain. He forewarned that the Kingdom of God would be taken from them and entrusted to others. Jesus then quoted Psalm 118, referencing the stone the builders rejected, which became the cornerstone. That very stone symbolizes Jesus, who, though rejected by many, became the foundational cornerstone of God's Kingdom.

This cornerstone, Jesus, is our God. Those who stumble upon Him are broken, but those on whom He falls are crushed to dust.

We have discovered this cornerstone, and we now belong to the Kingdom of God – a Kingdom reallocated from the unbelievers to those who have faith in Jesus Christ, the central pillar of our belief.

Thus, we pray: "Lord Jesus, we thank You for being the cornerstone of our faith, the path to righteousness, the true vine, and our singular route to the Father. We're eternally grateful for Your salvation. Lord, if there's any pride within us that hinders our humility toward You, we lay it at Your feet. If anything obstructs our journey with You today, or tempts us to betray or abandon You, remove it from our path. May the Holy Spirit guide us today, ensuring that our actions bring joy to You.

In the mighty name of Jesus Christ, King of kings, Amen."

MAY 16
Seven things that God hates

Proverbs 6:16-19

> [16] *These six things the* LORD *hates, Yes, seven are an abomination to Him:*
> [17] *A proud look,*
> *A lying tongue,*
> *Hands that shed innocent blood,*
> [18] *A heart that devises wicked plans,*
> *Feet that are swift in running to evil,*
> [19] *A false witness who speaks lies,*
> *And one who sows discord among brethren.*

There are seven things that God despises: a haughty look, a lying tongue, hands that shed innocent blood, a heart that devises wicked schemes, feet that are swift to run to evil, a false witness who pours out lies, and a person who stirs up discord among the brethren.

Let's take a moment to reflect upon ourselves to discern if any of these characteristics reside within us. If we identify any, let's humbly approach the feet of Jesus Christ, our King of kings, and earnestly pray:

"Lord, if any of these traits are present within us, or if we even harbor a desire for them, cleanse us today."

Holy Spirit, examine our hearts, and if any of these are found within us, purify, and remove them. Lord, refine us so that we do not act against your will, but rather, may our actions bring joy to You.

We commit this day into Your gracious hands, Jesus Christ. May You work within each of us. Holy Spirit, guide us, support us, and empower us, just as you do every day.

We place this day into Your blessed care, praying in the powerful name of Jesus Christ, King of kings. Amen.

MAY 17
Our rock of salvation

Psalm 18: 30

As for God, His way is perfect.
The word of the LORD is proven.
He is a shield to all who trust in Him.

God's actions are impeccable; His promises are pure and unshakable. He is a shield to all who seek refuge in Him. Who else can be called God other than our Lord? And who is the foundation of our salvation, if not Him? Amen. This is the deity we venerate.

Do you recall when we discussed the cornerstone? Another title for the Lord Jesus Christ is "The Rock." Upon this foundation, upon this unyielding truth, Christ said, "Upon this rock, I will build my church." Jesus Christ is the unwavering bedrock of our salvation. Who among the gods compares to our God? His actions are flawless; His promises are crystalline and steadfast. When God promises, He delivers, for Jesus Christ is unchanging, the same yesterday, today, and forever. With gratitude in our hearts, let us approach Him:

"Thank you, Father, for this day. Another day under Your merciful watch. You constantly reveal the depth and breadth of Your love and fidelity. Your unwavering commitment to Your promises has sheltered us, and Your protective embrace has been our haven. We are profoundly grateful. Lord Jesus, Your majesty knows no bounds; Your love is unparalleled. You are the Alpha and the Omega. Our hearts overflow with gratitude for Your saving grace, which ushered us from the shadows into Your marvelous light, transferring us from the dominion of darkness into Your radiant kingdom. More than that, You have adopted us into the divine family of God. As we end this day, we surrender the night into Your hands, O Lord. Bestow upon each one of us tranquility, love, and peace. We pray in the name of Jesus Christ, the King of kings. Amen."

MAY 18
Greatest commandment

Matthew 22:37

> *Jesus said to him, "'You shall love the LORD your God with all your heart, with all your soul, and with all your mind.'*

Once, a Pharisee approached Jesus Christ and inquired, "Which is the greatest commandment in God's Ten Commandments?" In response, Jesus shared, "Love the Lord your God with all your heart, with all your soul, with all your strength, and with all your mind. This is the foremost and paramount commandment.

And the second is equally vital: Love your neighbor as yourself." He further emphasized that all laws and commandments are anchored on these two foundational principles. What is Jesus conveying through this? As a God of love and compassion, He is asserting that love is the primary directive. Firstly, we are to love the Lord our God wholeheartedly, with every fiber of our being. Subsequently, we are to extend that same love towards our neighbors as we do towards ourselves.

Furthermore, Jesus reminds us that it is through genuine love that others will recognize us as His disciples. "Love one another as I have loved you, even to the extent of laying down my life for you," He says. Everything pivots on love. True love for God and our neighbors ensures we uphold His other commandments. We won't commit adultery, we won't murder, we won't steal, and we won't idolize other gods. The essence of all commandments is deeply rooted in love – a love exemplified by Jesus Christ, who sacrificed His life, even for those who opposed Him. So, as we reflect on this, let's offer a prayer of gratitude and commitment: "Thank You, Father, for this enlightening revelation. We seek Your guidance to love You with all our heart, soul, and mind. Grant us the strength to love our neighbors, even our adversaries, as we love ourselves. May this love elevate us closer to You, manifesting to the world that we are truly Your disciples. We pray in the cherished name of Jesus Christ, the King of kings. Amen."

MAY 19

Nothing is able to separate us from this love

Romans 8:38-39

> [38] *For I am persuaded that neither death nor life, nor angels nor principalities nor powers, nor things present nor things to come,*
> [39] *nor height nor depth, nor any other created thing, shall be able to separate us from the love of God which is in Christ Jesus our Lord.*

"For I am convinced that neither death nor life, neither angels nor principalities, neither the present nor the future, nor any powers, neither height nor depth, nor anything else in all creation, will be able to separate us from the love of God that is in Christ Jesus our Lord." Dear friends, truly, nothing in this world can ever separate us from the unwavering love and grace of the Lord Jesus Christ. Nothing at all.

However, the only exception is when we ourselves permit it. Only if we relent and let our barriers down. When we passionately love the Lord Jesus Christ with every fiber of our being — heart, soul, and spirit — there's absolutely nothing that can sever our connection with Him.

He remains eternally united with us, for He is the majestic Lord of lords, the supreme King of kings, and the divine Second Person of the Trinity. His love for us spans unimaginable depths and heights; it's so profound that even when we were at odds with Him, He sacrificially laid down His life for us. He relinquished the splendors of heaven to embrace humanity, manifesting in the humble form of a child born in a manger, epitomizing sheer humility.

Though He wielded unparalleled power and authority, capable of summoning divine forces at a mere gesture, He chose not to. Instead, He willingly subjected Himself to the agonizing and ignoble death on the cross, all for our redemption.

Jesus Christ is our beacon of hope, our fountain of love, and our ultimate purpose. He is the Alpha and the Omega. And what does this signify? It means He's our everything. Is He your everything? Truly, He's mine.

As Joshua proclaimed, "As for me and my house, we will serve the Lord." What's your declaration?

Let's come together in prayer: "Father, as we retire for the night, we lay our thoughts, actions, and gratitude at Your feet. We're profoundly thankful for the revelations You've granted us today, particularly the affirmation that nothing can ever distance us from the love of Christ Jesus, our Savior. Your promise is our anchor, offering trust and assurance. We beseech You to grant each one of us a peaceful night's rest. May our dreams be filled with visions of You, drawing us ever closer in worship and adoration.

In the revered name of Jesus Christ, we pray. Amen."

MAY 20
Taking sick friends to Jesus

One of our tasks as believers is to approach God collectively and pray in unison for our friends in our church who are suffering and in need of prayer. Jesus tells us that when two or three gather in His name, He is present among them. Furthermore, the more His children engage with Him, the more attuned God's ear becomes to our voices, amplifying the potency of our prayers.

I received a distressing message from Pastor Tim and Barbara Berends. Their daughter, Laura, who has been serving as a missionary on a remote island in Colombia with them for years and is notably the sole outsider among the natives, collapsed and was rendered unconscious. She was transported by boat to the primary city of Colombia and is currently in an intensive care unit.

We must unite in prayer for Laura. Pastor Tim highlighted a biblical passage in his message - Mark 2:2-12 - emphasizing the need to sometimes bear the weight of our fallen brethren and present them before Jesus Christ for healing. This passage recounts the tale of the paralyzed man, hindered by the crowd, who was lowered through a roof opening to be placed before Jesus. Witnessing the faith demonstrated by this act, Jesus proclaimed the man's sins forgiven and urged him to rise, take his bed, and depart.

Now, we are compelled to intercede for Laura in the same spirit of faith. I urge you to remember Laura in your prayers daily, and also to uplift Pastor Tim and Barbara. We have faith in God's transformative work in Laura's life and trust that He will bring to completion the healing He has initiated in her.

Let's pray in unity:

Heavenly Father, in the revered name of Jesus Christ, our King of kings, we present Laura Berends before You. You, Lord, are all-knowing, aware of her condition and location. Father, You are omnipotent, capable of all things. Jesus Christ, our healer, no ailment, or circumstance stands beyond Your reach. As You extended Your healing hand to heal multitudes two millennia ago, we believe You continue this divine work among us.

Lord, as we bring your servant, Laura, before You, we beseech You to lay Your restorative hand upon her. Elevate her from her affliction.

As Tim and Barbara journey to be by her side, guide and protect them, shielding them from any ailment, including Covid. With Laura in dire need of her parents' presence, assure their safe passage with Your steadfast hands.

We fervently pray for a miraculous turnaround in Laura's life and for her reunion with her family. In the authoritative name of Jesus Christ, King of Kings, we pray and receive by faith. Amen.

It is not just an occasional duty but a consistent responsibility for us to reflect and pray. I implore you to remember Laura in your prayers daily. We stand in solidarity with Pastor Tim and Barbara, lifting Laura up in faith, anticipating the joyous news of her recovery.

In the name of Jesus Christ, Amen.

MAY 21
Glory and greatness of God in this world

Psalms 19:1-2

> [1] *The heavens declare the glory of God;*
> *And the firmament shows His handiwork.*
> [2] *Day unto day utters speech, And night unto night reveals knowledge.*

The Scriptures tell us that the heavens declare the majesty and glory of God, bearing testament to His handiwork. Day unto day they pour forth speech, and night after night they display knowledge. Without a word, without sound, their message reverberates across the earth. The sun, emerging each day from the pavilion God ordained, exudes the joy of a groom on his wedding day or an athlete eager to sprint. It courses from one horizon to the other, casting its warmth universally.

Do we greet each morning with a similar zeal? With renewed fervor? Are we excited that God has gifted us a fresh day to journey across the expanse of our lives, spreading warmth, blessing others, sharing the Good News of Jesus Christ, or even offering just a word of encouragement to uplift someone's day?

The heavens, the earth, the cyclical dance of day and night, the relentless sun—all proclaim. As God's children, shouldn't our declaration be even louder? When we rise, we should be filled with the hope and jubilation of a bridegroom or a bride, for we trust in the God who holds our future. A God who is benevolent, desiring the very best for us. While we may covet certain things, some might be detrimental. They might appear beneficial momentarily, but God discerns our futures and knows the optimal path for us. If our desires align with His will, they will come to pass. We should aspire to the point where we proclaim, "Lord, I desire nothing but Your will." We should recognize that our wishes are often terrestrial, while His are celestial. He knows and does what's best. If He ever denies our requests, may He provide the wisdom for us to comprehend the reason, so we can grow in faith.

So, let's pray: Heavenly Father, in the esteemed name of Jesus Christ, our King of kings, we express our gratitude. The heavens, earth, sun, moon, and all of creation continuously proclaim Your sovereignty without uttering a word. Lord, let us extend to others the warmth of Your presence and the fragrance of the love of Jesus Christ.

May the aroma of Your presence envelop us, so others can partake. Endow us with words of encouragement and love for others today. Let our lives and those we interact with be enriched with Your blessings. We commit this day into Your sanctified hands.

In the name of Jesus Christ, the King of kings. Amen.

MAY 22
Praying always

Ephesians 6:18

> *praying always with all prayer and supplication in the Spirit, being watchful to this end with all perseverance and supplication for all the saints—*

The essence of this message is clear: always pray. The first time we prayed through Jesus Christ, it was to ask Him to absolve us of our sins. And He did. As time progressed, our prayers expanded. While our needs seem boundless, they are dwarfed by God's limitless storehouse of grace, blessings, and abundance. We should always keep the channels of prayer open.

Constant prayer signifies an uninterrupted relationship with God, akin to the bond between lovers. When we cherish someone, we yearn for ceaseless communication, just as someone in love desires endless conversations over the phone. Our adoration for God should echo this sentiment.

How splendid it is that we can approach God at any time, laying out our joys, worries, and desires, confident that He listens. God is ever faithful in His responses, but He yearns for worship that is genuine, rooted in truth and spirit.

Let's pray:

Father, our hearts overflow with gratitude for today, for the sustenance you've provided, and the countless ways you've displayed Your goodness.

May our hearts perpetually be inclined to converse with You, cherishing our relationship like that between the dearest of friends or the most passionate of lovers. As we rest tonight, we pray for a peaceful slumber, so that come morning, we rise rejuvenated, ready to honor and worship You anew.

In the name of Jesus Christ, Amen.

MAY 23

The Lord answers your prayer

Psalms 20:1-3

> [1]*May the* LORD *answer you in the day of trouble; May the name of the God of Jacob defend you;*
> [2]*May He send you help from the sanctuary, and strengthen you out of Zion;*
> [3] *May He remember all your offerings,*
> *And accept your burnt sacrifice. Selah*

May the Lord respond to your prayers in times of distress. May He extend help from His sanctuary and strengthen you from Mount Zion. May He recall all your offerings and accept your burnt sacrifices. May He grant the desires of your heart and bless all your endeavors with success. We eagerly await news of your triumph, and we shall proudly raise the banner of victory in the name of our God. May all your wishes align with His divine will. Amen.

Beloved, God is ever ready to respond to our calls. Scriptures remind us that He heeds our requests when they align with His divine purpose. "Ask, and it shall be given unto you; seek, and you shall find; knock, and the door shall be opened unto you." The Lord promises wisdom to those who ask for it and bestows an abundance of the Holy Spirit upon those whose requests align with His will.

The crux lies in our unity with the Lord. As we nurture our love for Him and walk alongside Him, our very essence starts to mirror that of Jesus Christ. Our desires begin to harmonize with His.

The Holy Spirit illuminates God's perfect will for us, guiding our prayers, teaching us the reasons behind our petitions, and instructing us on the appropriate responses.

Indeed, God fulfills every genuine request. However, my deepest yearning—and I believe yours too—is for our desires to resonate with God's will, not merely our own. If what I seek distances me from You, Lord, then I don't desire it. I only crave those blessings that draw me nearer to You, making me more like You, enabling me to radiate Your love. Grant me those things that help me grow and mature in You.

In gratitude, we say: Father, thank You for Your boundless love. Thank You for patiently awaiting our prayers, like a loving father awaiting his child's call. May Your will, the one that mirrors the goodness and beauty of Your Son Jesus Christ, prevail in our lives. In Jesus' name, Amen.

MAY 24
Foolish virgins

Matthew 25

In Matthew 25, Jesus narrates the parable of the ten virgins. Five of these virgins were prepared and brought oil for their lamps, while the other five, referred to as the foolish virgins, were unprepared without any oil. When the bridegroom arrived unexpectedly at midnight, the unprepared virgins were left scrambling, seeking oil from the others. However, the wise virgins could not share as they only had enough for themselves. They suggested the foolish virgins buy oil, but by the time they returned, the bridegroom and the prepared virgins had already entered the celebration, leaving the unprepared ones locked out.

This parable highlights the need for us to be always prepared for the unexpected return of the Son of God.

Jesus then delves into another parable about a master and his servants. Before embarking on a journey, the master entrusts varying amounts of coins to each servant: five, two, and one. Upon his return, he finds that the first two servants had been diligent, investing their coins and yielding more. However, the servant with one coin merely hid it away. This parable emphasizes the importance of wisely using the gifts or talents God bestows upon us in His service.

The core message is vigilance. Jesus encourages us to remain alert, not knowing when He might return. It's an urging to work earnestly, leveraging all our God-given gifts.

God's expectation is for us to grow, evolve, and bring forth abundant fruits from the seeds He plants within us. We are reminded to question ourselves: Have we fully surrendered our hearts to Him? Are we merely existing alongside Him or are we living in Him?

It's crucial to understand the difference between merely being with Him and living within Him. Living within Him brings growth and fruitfulness, while staying apart results in spiritual stagnation, making us like those foolish virgins.

Let us pray: Father, in the majestic name of Jesus Christ, we beseech you to mold us into diligent stewards. Grant us the grace to be like the wise virgins, ever prepared for Your glorious return. Purify our hearts, removing any hindrances that prevent spiritual growth, and align us closer to Your image. As we await Your coming, fortify us to bear abundant fruits with the talents You've endowed us with. In Jesus Christ's name, Amen. May the grace of the Lord be with you all.

MAY 25

You shall call Him Jesus

Matthew 1:21

> *And she will bring forth a Son, and you shall call His name JESUS, for He will save His people from their sins."*

You will call Him Jesus. The Lord Jesus Christ is known by many names. "Emmanuel" signifies "God with us." He is also known as "Jesus the Savior." "Joshua" means invigorating, and "Joshua Messiah" connects to our Lord as the anointed one. "Christ" means anointed with the Holy Spirit.

Our Lord Jesus Christ has the most endearing name as God's own Son. It is said that He was bestowed a name above all, such that everything on earth, beneath the earth, and in the heavens will bow and acknowledge Him as Lord.

The name of Jesus Christ surpasses any other name, whether on earth, below it, or in the skies above. When He appears, even the demons exclaim, "Have you come to condemn us to hell before the appointed time?" Everyone recognizes Him; both the righteous and the wicked are familiar with His presence. With a single command from God, they will vanish. He is the Creator who became flesh and dwelt among us. Another name for Him is "the Word." In the beginning, the Word was with God, and the Word was God Himself. The Lord Jesus Christ assures us, "Ask in my name, and you will receive."

We've previously discussed our desires: what we ought to seek and what we should refrain from desiring. It's also emphasized that blessings are granted according to God's will, and with it comes ever-increasing wisdom. However, in the name of Jesus Christ, every request is affirmed. His name stands unparalleled, more melodious, and delightful than any other.

Today, we express our gratitude to You, O Jesus Christ, for Your unbounded grace and love for each one of us. You redeemed us from the depths of darkness and brought us into Your marvelous light. By Your sacrifice, You have claimed us, marking us as members of Your family. We are ever thankful. We pray that God continually unravels the mysteries of Your magnificent names to every believer, so that in Your name, we find liberation wherever we go.

In the name of Jesus Christ, Amen.

MAY 26
Costly alabaster jar

Matthew 26:6-9

> [6] *And when Jesus was in Bethany at the house of Simon the leper,*
> [7] *a woman came to Him having an alabaster flask of very costly fragrant oil, and she poured it on His head as He sat at the table.*
> [8] *But when His disciples saw it, they were indignant, saying, "Why this waste?*
> [9] *For this fragrant oil might have been sold for much and given to the poor."*

And when Jesus was in Bethany at the house of Simon the leper, a woman approached Him with an alabaster flask of very costly fragrant oil. She poured it on His head as He sat at the table. His disciples, upon witnessing this, were indignant and questioned, "Why this waste? This fragrant oil could have been sold for much and given to the poor." Jesus, being aware of their sentiments, responded, "Why do you trouble the woman? She has performed a good deed for Me. You will always have the poor among you, but you will not always have Me. By pouring this fragrant oil on My body, she prepared Me for burial. I assure you, wherever this gospel is preached throughout the world, what this woman has done will be remembered as a testament to her."

Even after so many years, her deed is still revered. Have there been moments when someone offered something precious to God wholeheartedly, and we looked on thinking, "What a waste; they could have done this or that," without understanding their genuine intentions? We might only perceive the surface and not the deep-rooted love and devotion from which such actions stem.

Father, today we ask you to open the eyes of our spirit. Let us be sensitive to things that honor You, even if they seem contrary to worldly values. Bestow upon us the discernment to distinguish between what aligns with Your will and what doesn't. Guard our tongues, so we may not speak against Your divine intentions. May we always align our thoughts, words, and deeds with Your word. Today and every day, we seek to listen to and be guided by You wholeheartedly.

We surrender this day into Your blessed hands. Lord Jesus Christ, reign within us. Amen.

MAY 27
In hardship and sickness pray with the believers

James 5:13

> *Is anyone among you suffering? Let him pray. Is anyone cheerful? Let him sing psalms.*

Here's a proofread version of your devotional:

Is anyone among you suffering? Let him pray. Is anyone cheerful? Let him sing psalms. Is anyone among you sick? Let him call for the elders of the church to pray over him, anointing him with oil in the name of the Lord. The prayer of faith will save the sick, and if he has committed sins, they will be forgiven. Confess your sins and trespasses to one another and pray for each other, so that you may be healed. The earnest prayer of a righteous person has great power and produces wonderful results.

Something I've unfortunately observed in Iranian and Persian communities is the tendency to bring along elements of their old culture. In Christianity, when we face challenges or sickness, or when we're burdened, we are encouraged to share it with our Christian family. Why? Because the family of God, the body of Christ, the church that we belong to is our genuine family. We should gather according to the word and pray for one another.

Jesus Christ instructs us to love one another, and from this love, others will recognize that we are His disciples. Our unity and coming together signify that we should share everything. If we are in pain or facing challenges, we shouldn't hide. Instead, we should approach the elders of the church or fellow believers and let them pray for our healing. Sometimes in the church, when we learn that someone was ill or facing a problem, we should promptly reach out, talk, and present each other before God. Jesus said that where two or three gather in His name, He is there with them.

When facing issues, it's essential to come forward and pray collectively. The combined power of our prayers is formidable. It's like one child asking a favor of their father versus four children making a joint request. The latter is often more effective. Our heavenly Father is infinitely compassionate, but He desires our unity, understanding, and mutual support. This unity fosters humility and openness, making us more receptive to His blessings.

So, when dealing with challenges or illness, the best action is to call upon fellow believers or church elders and request their prayers.

Pray together and present your needs before God. After all, the fervent prayer of a righteous and faithful individual is powerful.

Father, we present our burdens to you. Lord, help us to share with one another, support each other, and communicate our struggles. When one rejoices, let us all celebrate; and when one weeps, let us all mourn. As we unite in prayer, we trust that You will answer us. Enlighten us with this truth.

In the name of Jesus Christ, Amen.

MAY 28

Lord Jesus, help us not to deny you today

Matthew 26:69-75

69 *Now Peter sat outside in the courtyard. And a servant girl came*
to him, saying, "You also were with Jesus of Galilee."
70 *But he denied it before them all, saying, "I do not know what you*
are saying."
71 *And when he had gone out to the gateway, another girl saw him*
and said to those who were there, "This fellow also was with Jesus
of Nazareth."
72 *But again he denied with an oath, "I do not know the Man!"*
73 *And a little later those who stood by came up and said to Peter,*
"Surely you also are one of them, for your speech betrays
you." 74 *Then he began to curse and swear, saying, "I do not know*
the Man! "Immediately a rooster crowded.
75 *And Peter remembered the word of Jesus who had said to*
him, "Before the rooster crows, you will deny Me three times." So,
he went out and wept bitterly.

In this scene, Jesus is taken to the high priest's house. Peter had followed to see what would happen to Jesus, and he sat outside in the courtyard. A servant girl approached him, saying, "You were with Jesus of Galilee." But Peter denied it, saying, "I do not know what you are talking about." Later, as he moved to the gateway, another girl recognized him and said, "This man was with Jesus of Nazareth." Again, Peter denied it vehemently, insisting, "I do not know the Man!" A bit later, bystanders confronted Peter, pointing out that his manner of speech revealed him to be one of Jesus' followers. In response, Peter began to curse and swear, reiterating, "I do not know the Man!" It was then that a rooster crowed, and Peter remembered Jesus' words, "Before the rooster crows, you will deny Me three times." Overwhelmed with guilt, Peter wept bitterly. As Luke notes, at that very moment, Jesus turned and looked directly at Peter, intensifying his anguish.

Let's offer a prayer to our Lord.

Thank You, God, for Your gift of salvation through Your Son. We are grateful, Jesus, for Your sacrifice that redeems us from sin. We praise You for welcoming us into Your kingdom and Your family. Lord Jesus, strengthen us so that we never deny You, neither in word nor in deed. Grant us the courage to share Your love and message with others.

Let us always stand firm in our faith. As it is written, if we acknowledge You before others, You will acknowledge us before the Father. Empower us to live in a way that not only honors You but also reflects our deep love for You. In the name of Jesus Christ, we pray, Amen.

May God's presence always be with you.

MAY 29
Bait of Satan

Yesterday we talked about offense and disappointment. Jesus Christ in Mathew 24.

It seems you've provided an incomplete sentence. Please continue with the passage from Matthew 24 or provide the section of the devotional book you'd like proofread, and I'll assist you further.

> 4 *And Jesus answered and said to them: "Take heed that no one deceives you.*
> 5 *For many will come in My name, saying, 'I am the Christ,' and will deceive many.*
> 6 *And you will hear of wars and rumors of wars. See that you are not troubled; for all these things must come to pass, but the end is not yet.*
> 7 *For nation will rise against nation, and kingdom against kingdom. And there will be famines, pestilences, and earthquakes in various places.*
> 8 *All these are the beginning of sorrows.*
> 9 *"Then they will deliver you up to tribulation and kill you, and you will be hated by all nations for My name's sake.*
> 10 *And then many will be offended, will betray one another, and will hate one another.*
> 11 *Then many false prophets will rise up and deceive many.*
> 12 *And because lawlessness will abound, the love of many will grow cold.*
> 13 *But he who endures to the end shall be saved.*
> 14 *And this gospel of the kingdom will be preached in all the world as a witness to all the nations, and then the end will come.*

The scriptures foretell that in the end times, many will take offense. Consequently, animosity will grow among individuals, and their love for God will wane.

One of Satan's greatest snares is to undermine the love that binds Christians together, subsequently jeopardizing our relationship with both fellow believers and God Himself. Should anyone cause us offense, it's essential—based on God's word and the teachings of Jesus Christ—that we approach that person directly. We should converse privately, seeking understanding and potentially forging a bond.

This principle is eloquently expounded upon in the Farsi translation of the book "Bait of Satan by John Bevere." It speaks to the covenant we ought to make, committing ourselves to Jesus Christ, vowing that if anyone offends us, we will promptly approach and address the issue with them. Similarly, if we are the offenders, we pledge to seek out the aggrieved and extend our heartfelt apologies. Above all, we strive to embody the forgiving nature that Christ showcased towards us.

Lord, we beseech You for wisdom and clarity, that our eyes may discern offenses, and the traps set by Satan. Let these trials augment our capacity for love, and instill in us patience, kindness, humility, optimism, and compassion. In the Holy Name of Jesus Christ, Amen.

When we establish such covenants with one another, it is our duty to uphold them. Should an individual's visage come to mind following this pact, perhaps it's the Holy Spirit's nudge, signaling us to initiate a conversation, offer an apology, or mend a strained relationship.

Lord, guide us to be proactive in honoring our covenants, ensuring that our relations—with You and with our fellow believers—remain pure, transparent, and rooted in goodness.

In the name of Jesus Christ, Amen.

MAY 30
Because of your name

Psalm 23

> [1]*The LORD is my shepherd; I shall not want.*
> [2] *He makes me to lie down in green pastures; He leads me beside the still waters.*
> [3] *He restores my soul; He leads me in the paths of righteousness For His name's sake.*
> [4] *Yea, though I walk through the valley of the shadow of death, I will fear no evil; for You are with me; Your rod and Your staff, they comfort me.*
> [5] *You prepare a table before me in the presence of my enemies; You anoint my head with oil; My cup runs over.*
> [6] *Surely goodness and mercy shall follow me All the days of my life; and I will dwell in the house of the LORD Forever.*

The Lord is my shepherd; I shall not want. He makes me lie down in green pastures; he leads me beside still waters; he restores my soul. He leads me in paths of righteousness for his name's sake. Even though I walk through the valley of the shadow of death, I will fear no evil, for you are with me; your rod and your staff, they comfort me. You prepare a table before me in the presence of my enemies.

Let's meditate on this promise. In this Psalm, David proclaims that God is our Shepherd. Jesus, too, identified Himself as the Good Shepherd. He desires only the best for His sheep. When we heed His voice and follow His lead, He safeguards us with His staff and confronts our adversaries. We can stand firm beside Him through life's trials and storms because He, who commanded the wind and waves, is our anchor. The one who shaped the heavens, and the earth has bestowed all authority in heaven and on earth upon Him. His love for us is boundless and steadfast. He acts on our behalf for the honor of His name, a name exalted above every name in heaven, on earth, and beneath the earth.

Consider the myriad names and titles ascribed to Jesus: Emmanuel, the Good Shepherd, the Savior. He embodies every one of these designations. Jesus declared, "I am the way, the truth, and the life. No one comes to the Father except through me."

Owing to His names, He promises to guide us along the righteous path. With the Creator of the universe on our side, fear is dispelled.

Today, we recognize and honor Jesus Christ, our Good Shepherd, Savior, Emmanuel ("God with us"), the Way, the Bread of Life, and the Fountain of Life. With open hearts, we turn to You, Lord, acknowledging Your deep desire for our well-being. Guide and bless us this day, all for the glory of Your name.

In Jesus Christ's name, Amen.

MAY 31

Who can stand in his holy position?

Psalms 24

> [1] *The earth is the LORD's, and all its fullness, The world and those who dwell therein.*
> [2] *For He has founded it upon the seas,*
> *And established it upon the waters.*
> [3] *Who may ascend into the hill of the LORD? Or who may stand in His holy place?*
> [4] *He who has clean hands and a pure heart,*
> *Who has not lifted up his soul to an idol,*
> *Nor sworn deceitfully.*
> [5] *He shall receive blessing from the LORD, And righteousness from the God of his salvation.*
> [6] *This is Jacob, the generation of those who seek Him,*
> *Who seek Your face. Selah*

The earth and everything in it belong to the Lord, the world and all who live in it. For He founded it upon the seas and established it upon the waters. Who may ascend the mountain of the Lord? Who may stand in His holy place? It is he who has clean hands and a pure heart, who does not trust in an idol or swear by a false god. They will receive blessing from the Lord and vindication from God their Savior. Such is the generation of those who seek Him, who seek the face of the God of Jacob.

The scripture poses the question: who can approach the mountain of the Lord? Who can stand in His sanctified presence? Thankfully, through the blood of Jesus Christ, both you and I have been purified, enabling us to stand in God's sacred space. It's this very blood that cleanses us, qualifying us to be in the presence of the holy and righteous God, for He sees the resurrected Jesus within us.

Yet, the scripture also speaks of purity and integrity, emphasizing the significance of clean hands. The Bible also mentions refraining from worshipping idols. But remember, idols aren't limited to mere statues or figures. Some elevate their spouses, children, homes, or even cars above God.

Let's ensure that nothing holds a higher place in our hearts than God. Elevating anything above Him makes it an idol in our lives. And regarding deceit, let's remember that in Christianity, there's no room for "white lies."

Our faith teaches us to be transparent and straightforward: let our 'yes' be 'yes', and our 'no' be 'no'.

Jesus once said that if anyone denies Him before men, He will also deny them before the Father. Christianity emphasizes truth, righteousness, and purity. With this in mind, let's draw near to God.

Father, we are grateful that through Jesus Christ, you have cleansed us with His blood, rendering us fit to approach You. May You continue to wash us with Christ's blood. Lord, prevent our pride or any earthly attachment from ever separating us from Your presence. As Christ taught, may our hearts remain as pure as children's, always fixed upon You.

In the name of Jesus Christ, Amen.

JUNE 1
The fear of the Lord is the first wisdom

Proverbs 9:10

> *The fear of the LORD is the beginning of wisdom, And the knowledge of the Holy One is understanding.*

This esteemed verse affirms that the foundation of wisdom lies in fearing God, while truly comprehending the Holy One grants understanding. Elsewhere in scripture, it's articulated that this godly fear is the commencement of faith.

Such reverence towards the Holy God augments life's wisdom. If one possesses wisdom, it propels them forward. Yet, neglecting it can lead to their detriment. But what truly is the "fear of God"? Is it merely trembling in His presence? Do we envision a God, aloft, ready to punish our missteps with wrathful retribution? Certainly not.

The fear we speak of stems from profound love and respect for God. It marries respect with reverence. To fear God means that when we deeply love Him, we are ever-mindful not to grieve Him. Given the immense power and holiness of our God, our utmost desire becomes to never offend or disappoint Him.

Such respect and godly fear aren't driven by the terror of punitive action but is rooted in love, esteem, and devotion. This fear prompts the introspection: "What would God feel if I act this way?" The underlying apprehension is not the dread of punishment but the sorrow of possibly disheartening our loving Father.

God, as we perceive Him, especially as believers, is a beacon of love and compassion. Our reverence for Him, consequently, arises from our heartfelt adoration and devotion. This is the true foundation of our faith.

Faith burgeons from this reverence—a reverence anchored in love and affection. By constantly keeping God at the forefront of our thoughts, we receive His guidance and the wisdom to navigate life's paths.

God encourages us to ask and promises answers in the name of Jesus Christ. Those who seek wisdom shall undoubtedly find it. Yet, at the heart of this wisdom is a godly fear—a fear birthed from love, respect, and deep-seated devotion.

Father, our gratitude for You knows no bounds. We are profoundly enamored by You.

May our reverence for You deepen, drawing us nearer to Your divine presence. Let our actions always resonate with Your pleasure, O Sacred One.

Today, Lord, guide us to tread upon Your destined paths, to walk hand in hand with You, and to witness Your benevolent hand upon our lives. We present before You all those ailing—may they find healing in Your embrace. Specifically, we pray for Laura; grant her complete health. We lay before You all other patients, and the challenge of the Covid virus—may Your healing touch transform their lives.

In the sacred name of Jesus Christ, Amen.

JUNE 2
Healing of the leper

Mark 1:40

> *Now a leper came to Him, imploring Him, kneeling down to Him and saying to Him, "If You are willing, You can make me clean."*

In the scriptures, we read about a leper who approached Jesus, humbly knelt before Him, and earnestly said, "If you are willing, you can make me clean." Overwhelmed with compassion, Jesus reached out and touched the man, an act contrary to societal norms. People were terrified of leprosy, avoiding those afflicted and even resorting to casting stones to keep them at bay, fearing contagion. But in Jesus, we see a divine love that fearlessly touches the untouchable.

Can we pause and imagine the depth of that touch? Perhaps it had been years since anyone had come close to this man, let alone touched him. Yet, with a single touch and word from Jesus, the leprosy vanished.

After the miracle, Jesus gave the healed man a clear directive: "Don't tell anyone about this. Instead, go to the priest and let him examine you. Take along the offering required in the law of Moses for those who have been healed of leprosy. This will be a public testimony that you have been cleansed."

The purpose? The priest, who once declared the man unclean, would now bear witness to the transformative power of Jesus. However, rather than adhering to Jesus' instruction, the man broadcasted his healing everywhere. Such that, due to the ensuing attention, Jesus could no longer enter towns openly.

From this account, we glean a few pivotal lessons. When God accomplishes a significant work in our lives, it's vital to bear testimony as He directs, not as our emotions or impulses dictate. God's instructions, whether they entail action or restraint, are steeped in divine wisdom. We should heed them, even if we don't immediately grasp the reasons.

Father, in Jesus' name, we seek your grace today to discern your handiwork in our lives and, when called upon, to be faithful witnesses of your mighty acts. Help us to follow your directives, recognizing that your wisdom far exceeds our understanding. In all things, may we elevate your name, aligning our lives with your perfect will. We entrust our lives to you, knowing you desire the very best for us. We pray in the magnificent name of Jesus Christ, our King of kings. Amen.

JUNE 3
Your sins are forgiven

Mark 2:6-7

> [6] *And some of the scribes were sitting there and reasoning in their hearts,*
> [7] *"Why does this Man speak blasphemies like this? Who can forgive sins but God alone?"*

In one notable account from the Gospels, Jesus is at home, and four men, determined to bring their paralyzed friend to Him, ingeniously lower him through the roof due to the crowded entrance. Witnessing their faith, Jesus proclaims to the paralyzed man, "Your sins are forgiven."

However, some religious leaders present took offense, thinking, "Why does this man speak like that? Only God can forgive sins." Jesus, discerning their thoughts, challenged them: "Which is easier, to say to the paralytic, 'Your sins are forgiven,' or to say, 'Rise, take up your bed and walk'?"

To prove His divine authority on earth, Jesus commands the paralyzed man to get up and walk, which he does, astounding all present.

The profound lesson from this event is twofold: First, Jesus, with His divine knowledge, sees the spiritual root of our issues. In this instance, the underlying cause of the man's paralysis was sin. By addressing and forgiving the sin, Jesus healed the man both spiritually and physically.

Secondly, this narrative demonstrates Jesus' divine nature. By asserting His authority to forgive sins—a prerogative exclusive to God—He tacitly claims His divinity.

The Lord Jesus always peers into our hearts, responding not just to our spoken words but our innermost thoughts and intents. In His compassion and mercy, He provides answers that sometimes go deeper than our immediate concerns, addressing the core of our being.

Father, we are grateful for this new day. Thank you, Lord Jesus, for perceiving our hearts' depths and responding with love and wisdom. May we approach You sincerely, knowing You will always answer. We recognize Your sovereign hand in everything, trusting in Your capabilities. May our actions, thoughts, and responses today reflect love, unity, and harmony, bringing joy to Your heart.

In the precious name of Jesus Christ, Amen.

JUNE 4

Who Is my mother, or my brother?

Mark 3:31-32

> [31] *Then His brothers and His mother came, and standing outside they sent to Him, calling Him.*
> [32] *And a multitude was sitting around Him; and they said to Him, "Look, Your mother and Your brothers are outside seeking You."*

As Jesus Christ was speaking, His mother and brothers came and stood outside where He was. They called out to Him, and the people sitting around said, "Look, Your mother and brothers are outside, seeking You."

Jesus looked around and asked, "Who are my mother and brothers?" He then gestured to those seated around Him and declared, "Here are my mother and my brothers! For whoever does the will of God is my brother, sister, and mother."

Through this, the Lord reveals the defining mark of a true disciple and who earns the honor of being called the brother, sister, or mother of Jesus Christ. It's when we align ourselves with God's will, when we remain in His presence, and when we foster an intimate relationship with Him, that we discern His divine will.

We come to understand God's intentions by immersing ourselves in His Word, and He continually guides us through His Holy Spirit. There might be times when we feel estranged from our own families, but our fervent prayer remains that our siblings, parents, and extended family come to know Christ. Our utmost petition for our loved ones is for their salvation and the gift of eternal life. We stand firm on the promise God has extended to us: "Believe on the Lord Jesus Christ, and you will be saved, you and your household."

Thus, when we pray, we remind God of His promise, asking Him to draw our families to His heart. Let's always remember that the genuine disciples of God, as Jesus emphasized, are those who act according to God's will.

Heavenly Father, in the mighty name of Jesus Christ, we express our gratitude for Your Word. Lord Jesus, thank You for elucidating who truly belongs to You. God, we implore Your presence daily. May we continually seek Your face, comprehend Your desires, and execute them in our lives. Father, with the Holy Spirit indwelling us, guide our steps to exemplify faithful and devout discipleship. In the precious name of Jesus Christ, Amen.

JUNE 5
The mysteries of kingdom of God

Jesus continued to elucidate parables to the multitudes. Later, in solitude with the twelve disciples, He expounded the Parable of the Sower.

He said to the twelve and those with them, "To you has been given the privilege of understanding the mysteries of the Kingdom of God. But to outsiders, these truths are conveyed in parables."

Who were these individuals with Him? They were the ones close to Jesus, those who had cultivated an intimate bond with Him. They walked with Him and were consistently in His presence.

Jesus clarified, "To you and those who remain close to me, who have fostered a relationship with me, these mysteries will be unveiled. However, to those outside, they will be shared in parables." When questioned why, He replied, "For they may indeed look, but not perceive; they may hear, but not grasp the depth of the message. If they were to understand, their transgressions would be pardoned."

Today, let us approach God and proclaim:

"Lord, we are grateful for Your grace that brought us from obscurity to illumination. Jesus Christ, empower us to consistently remain in proximity to You, to perpetually keep You at the heart of our focus. Let us never deviate our gaze from You. You've promised to reveal these divine truths to us. As we receive these revelations, empower us not to hoard them but to share, liberating others. We are deeply honored to be regarded as Your friends, for You said, 'I have called you friends, for I have shared with you everything I've learned from my Father.' May we prove worthy of this profound friendship and merit Your confidences, love, and communion."

Father, fortify our faith today and steer us towards seeking You in all facets of our lives.

In the majestic name of Jesus Christ, the King of kings, Amen.

JUNE 6

The Lord is my life and salvation. Whom should I be afraid of?

Psalms 27

> [1]*The* LORD *is my light and my salvation; Whom shall I fear? The* LORD *is the strength of my life; Of whom shall I be afraid?*
> [2] *When the wicked came against me To eat up my flesh, My enemies and foes, They stumbled and fell.*
> [3] *Though an army may encamp against me, My heart shall not fear; Though war may rise against me, In this I will be confident.*

The Lord is my light and my salvation; whom shall I fear? God is the stronghold of my life; of whom shall I be afraid? When the wicked advance against me to devour me, it is my enemies and my foes who will stumble and fall.

Even if an army besieges me, my heart will not fear. Even if war breaks out against me, I remain confident. As stated in the book of Romans, "If God is for us, who can be against us?"

The Lord is both my light and my salvation. Jesus Christ is the light of the world and the Savior of humanity. This Sunday, we reflected upon the various names attributed to the Lord Jesus Christ. The Lord is the refuge of my soul. In Him alone can we find true safety, for He supports and aids us in every circumstance.

He declares, "I am the good shepherd. The good shepherd lays down His life for the sheep." So, if challenges arise, if we feel overwhelmed, surrounded by adversaries or swamped by life's storms, remember this: God is on our side.

In the profoundest darkness, He is our beacon. He is our rescuer, the holder of all power and authority. Possessing Him, the Creator of the universe, whose might surpass all, whose name is exalted above every name both on earth and in the heavens.

He reassures us, "I have not given you a spirit of fear but of power, love, and self-discipline." Our eternal Father, the enduring Father, the benevolent Father desires the best for His children.

Holding onto these promises and recognizing the immense love and care of our Lord Jesus Christ, we march forward, honoring God the Father, God the Son, and God the Holy Spirit, unified in essence.

We express our deepest gratitude, Lord Jesus Christ, for being our compassionate Lord who always desires our well-being, never abandoning us, and eternally accompanying us. May the brilliance of Your life and salvation radiate ever brighter upon each of us. Wherever we are, may we never forget that You, and only You, are our light, salvation, and sanctuary. With You by our side, we have nothing to fear. In the name of Jesus Christ, Amen.

JUNE 7
Go and tell your friends

Mark 5:18

> [18] *And when He got into the boat, he who had been demon-possessed begged Him that he might be with Him.*

Jesus cast out a legion of demons from a man who was uncontrollable. As Jesus was about to depart by boat, the man, freed from the demons, begged to accompany Him. However, Jesus declined, instructing him instead to return home and recount to his friends and community the wonders God had done for him and the compassion he had received.

The man heeded Jesus' command, journeying through Decapolis, sharing the miracles Jesus had performed on him, and all who heard him were astonished.

There are times when the Lord might say "no" to us. We may have a particular direction or purpose in mind, but He might redirect us elsewhere. It is for a greater plan – God's vision of where we can be most impactful for His kingdom. Like the man once tormented by demons, who yearned to follow Jesus after being healed, God sometimes has other designs for us. He saw a purpose for the man among his own people, to bear witness to the transformative power of Christ.

Wouldn't it be wondrous if we could heed and obey God's directions as the man did, sharing His goodness with others? Such obedience can result in a bountiful harvest for the Kingdom.

So, Heavenly Father, in the name of Jesus Christ, our King of Kings, we express our gratitude for today. We thank You for the incredible works You perform in each of our lives. Grant us the courage and strength to share Your deeds with others. May our testimonies yield an abundant harvest for Your eternal kingdom. In the name of Jesus Christ, we dedicate today and all our days into Your gracious care. Amen.

JUNE 8
Wait on the Lord

Psalms 27:11-14

[11] Teach me thy way, O LORD, and lead me in a plain path, because of mine enemies.
[12] Deliver me not over unto the will of mine enemies: for false witnesses are risen up against me, and such as breathe out cruelty.
[13] I had fainted, unless I had believed to see the goodness of the LORD in the land of the living.
[14] Wait on the LORD: be of good courage, and he shall strengthen thine heart: wait, I say, on the LORD.

The scripture says, "God, teach me Your ways and guide me along a smooth path in the face of my enemies." The Persian translation might express, "Lead me to the right path." However, the emphasis should be on a "smooth path." It continues, "Do not surrender me to the desires of my adversaries, for false witnesses have risen against me." It portrays a scene where rage emanates from their very breath. A pivotal moment of despair is captured in the line, "I would have lost heart had I not believed in seeing the goodness of God in the land of the living." While the Persian version translates this to a call to trust in God, the original text emphasizes the act of waiting on the Lord. It's about patiently witnessing His work, especially when surrounded by seemingly insurmountable challenges.

We are reminded that in situations where everything appears impossible, with Lord Jesus Christ, all becomes possible. The scripture illustrates this by saying, "I would've lost heart," signifying a loss of courage, if not for the unwavering belief in God's providence right here in the land of the living. While many speak of judgment in the afterlife, the scripture asserts that God's justice and miracles are at work even now, here among us.

Take, for instance, Mark 5, where Jairus, a synagogue leader, approaches Jesus, seeking healing for his ailing daughter. As they make their way to Jairus's home, messengers arrive with grim news that the daughter has passed away. They suggest there's no longer a need for Jesus. Yet, Jesus's response is steadfast, "Do not be afraid; only believe."

Today, the message we extract from these scriptures is clear: Do not be consumed by fear. Instead, anchor yourself in faith, trusting that God's divine intervention will manifest even in our present circumstances. Therefore, friends, let us wait on the Lord. Stay courageous, for He will fortify our hearts. I reiterate, wait upon the Lord. Amen.

JUNE 9

Miracles belong to those who are ready to believe

Mark 6:2

> [2] *And when the sabbath day was come, he began to teach in the synagogue: and many hearing him were astonished, saying, From whence hath this man these things? and what wisdom is this which is given unto him, that even such mighty works are wrought by his hands?*

Upon Jesus Christ's return to His hometown, Nazareth, He visited the synagogue to speak. As He addressed the assembly, many were astounded. They wondered aloud, "From where did He gain such knowledge? And what divine wisdom empowers Him to perform these miracles? Is He not the carpenter, the son of Mary, and brother to James, Joseph, Juda, and Simon? Aren't His sisters among us?"

Instead of marveling at His teachings and miracles, they became skeptical. The scripture says they took offense at Him. Why were they offended? Because Jesus was perceived as one from the lower echelons of society, lacking formal religious education and stature. This made it hard for them to reconcile His divine capabilities with their limited perception of Him.

In response to their skepticism, Jesus said, "A prophet is honored everywhere except in his own hometown and among his relatives." Consequently, He couldn't perform many miracles there, save for healing a few individuals. Was it because Jesus's power was limited? Certainly not.

John MacArthur offers a perspective suggesting that Jesus's limited miracles in Nazareth could be attributed to two reasons: Firstly, many didn't approach Him, unlike in other towns. Thus, fewer miracles were witnessed. Secondly, out of His immense love and grace, Jesus might have refrained from performing more miracles to prevent hardening their hearts further, which would have increased their judgment on the final day. Most astonishingly, Jesus was amazed at their lack of faith. Despite their familiarity with Him, they dismissed His deeds and miracles.

Miracles truly manifest where there is genuine faith. So today, let's declare:

"Lord Jesus Christ, we wholeheartedly embrace You. We recognize You as the healer, the almighty. We cherish Your words as they are filled with love and wisdom. May Your presence transform any remnants of our disbelief into unwavering faith.

In the name of Jesus Christ, King of Kings, Amen."

JUNE 10

Looking for fault or good

Mark 7

> [1]*Then came together unto him the Pharisees, and certain of the scribes, which came from Jerusalem.*
> [2]*And when they saw some of his disciples eat bread with defiled, that is to say, with unwashen, hands, they found fault.*

When the Pharisees traveled from Jerusalem, they brought with them not just their physical presence but also their preconceptions and judgments. They witnessed Jesus's disciples eating without ceremonially washing their hands and immediately took issue. Despite witnessing the miracles and teachings of Jesus, they were intent on finding fault. What's worth noting is that their criticisms were based not on divine principles but on human customs and rituals.

This serves as a reminder for all of us. Are we constantly looking for faults in others? Do we focus only on what's wrong, ignoring the vastness of goodness around us? If we actively seek flaws, we'll surely find them – justified or not – but often through a lens clouded by our biases.

Jesus's words ring true: "The eye is the lamp of the body. If your eyes are healthy, your whole body will be full of light. But if your eyes are unhealthy, your whole body will be full of darkness." Let's strive to be beacons of light, seeing the good in others and uplifting them, rather than casting them into the shadows of our judgments.

Joining in prayer, we say:

"Gracious Father, we're grateful for Your teachings that guide our vision and hearts. Today, we pray for clarity in sight, that we may focus on the light and goodness in others. Banish any darkness within us, allowing only light, truth, and love to permeate our being. Empower us with a spirit that seeks to uplift, encourage, and love. We are thankful for Your ever-present guidance, and in the mighty name of Jesus Christ, we pray. Amen.

JUNE 11
What defies us?

Mark 7:14

> [14] *When He had called all the multitude to Himself, He said to them, "Hear Me, everyone, and understand:*

It is written that the Lord gathered the people around Himself and proclaimed, "Let all of you understand this: Anything that enters the human body from outside does not make a person impure or defiled. Instead, it is the things that emerge from within that defile a person."

Upon hearing this, His disciples sought clarification, and He explained that what enters the body eventually leaves it through natural processes. Thus, He was emphasizing that external things do not defile one's spirit or character. It's the innermost thoughts and intentions, such as malice, adultery, murder, theft, envy, deceit, and arrogance, that truly corrupt a person.

So, let us approach the Lord today and pray,

O Lord, reveal to me anything within that does not reflect You. Remove these impurities and fill me anew with Your Holy Spirit. If I harbor malicious thoughts, transform them into thoughts that honor You. If I view the world with a judgmental eye, let me see through Your lens of love. I lay down my pride and every ounce of negativity that resides in my heart. Purify me, so that my vision is clear, my spirit is aligned with Yours, and my heart becomes a sanctified dwelling place for the Holy Spirit.

Thank You, Father, for hearing our pleas. Search our hearts, refine us, and let us be vessels for Your kingdom's work.

We pray this in the name of Jesus Christ, Amen.

JUNE 12

Do you remember when the Lord saved you from the depth of darkness?

psalm 30

> [1] *I will extol You, O LORD, for You have lifted me up, And have not let my foes rejoice over me.*
> [2] *O LORD my God, I cried out to You, And You healed me.*
> [3] *O LORD, You brought my soul up from the grave; You have kept me alive, that I should not go down to the pit.*
> [4] *Sing praise to the LORD, you saints of His, And give thanks at the remembrance of His holy name.*

Psalm 30 declares, "O God, I extol You. Why? For You have lifted me up and have not let my foes triumph over me. O Lord my God, I called out to You, and You healed me. O God, You raised my soul from the grave, preserving me from those descending into the abyss."

Do we recall the moments when God raised us from the depths? Can we remember those instances when, with tears in our eyes and desperation in our hearts, we invoked His name and He responded? When He mended our illnesses, restored our spirits, and resolved our tribulations?

Do we remember the times God pulled us from the chasm of death? Let's take a moment today to reminisce about the countless times God manifested His mighty works in us and in those around us. Reflecting on these moments empowers us to exalt God wholeheartedly, to express our gratitude sincerely, and to profess our undying love for Him.

God, You are magnificent and peerless, and Your unwavering presence is our constant assurance. Yours is the name above all names; whenever we summon You, we are confident of Your reply. Today, we offer our profound thanks. When affliction struck, we reached out, and You brought healing. Through the sacrifice of Your Son, You redeemed us from the throes of death, liberating us from profound darkness and ushering us into the luminance of Your realm. You transitioned us from bondage to sonship. Today, we stand as members of Your divine family. From the core of our being, we offer our gratitude and sing Your praises. Amen.

JUNE 13

The cost of Christ's discipleship

Mark 8:34

> [34] *When He had called the people to Himself, with His disciples also, He said to them, "Whoever desires to come after Me, let him deny himself, and take up his cross, and follow Me.*

Scripture reminds us that Jesus gathered His disciples and declared, "If anyone wishes to follow Me, he must deny himself, take up his cross, and follow Me. For whoever wants to save his life will lose it, but whoever loses his life for My sake and the Gospel's will find it. What benefit is it for someone to gain the whole world, yet forfeit their soul? Or what can a person give in exchange for their soul?"

Friends, have we ever pondered the cost of discipleship? What does Jesus truly mean when He insists on self-denial as a prerequisite for following Him? It signifies that our own deeds, no matter how noble, cannot bring about our salvation. Our redemption isn't a result of our virtuous acts but solely through the grace and sacrifice of Jesus Christ.

His immeasurable grace, the blood He shed on the cross, was the ultimate price for our sins. To be His disciples, we must understand our complete reliance on Him. When we acknowledge our inadequacies and confess that without Christ we are nothing, we are truly embracing our cross. This means setting aside our pride and ambitions, and earnestly seeking His will.

When Jesus mentions losing life to find it, He emphasizes surrendering our will to His divine plan. Holding onto our life, our desires, and our worldly ambitions will lead us astray. However, surrendering all, placing our trust in Him, and recognizing our utter dependence on His grace is the path to eternal life.

Choosing to prioritize worldly gains could jeopardize our eternal souls. However, if we ardently follow Christ, take up our cross daily, and offer all we have to Him, then the core, the very soul within us, finds its true purpose and life.

Today, let's lift our voices in gratitude. "Father, we are deeply grateful for Your words and the immense love You've shown us. Strengthen us, Lord, to forsake our self-centered desires, to bear our cross daily, and to faithfully follow You, acknowledging that only You can grant us salvation. We pray all this in the powerful name of Jesus Christ, Amen."

JUNE 14
Greatest person in the kingdom of heaven

Mark 9:30

> 30 *Then they departed from there and passed through Galilee, and He did not want anyone to know it.*

In Capernaum, Jesus returned to His disciples with a foreboding message. He confided in them, "When I go to Jerusalem, they will end my life. Yet, on the third day, I will rise again." His words perplexed them, and out of fear, they refrained from seeking clarity. Their focus soon shifted to a trivial debate amongst themselves: Who among them would be the most esteemed in God's kingdom?

Upon realizing their discussion, Jesus inquired about its nature. But they remained silent, perhaps aware of the triviality of their debate in light of Christ's profound revelations. Despite their silence, Jesus discerned their thoughts and addressed their internal struggle for prominence.

He elucidated, "The Kingdom of God isn't akin to earthly dominions. Here, authority and servitude are juxtaposed. In worldly realms, the leader dictates, but in God's Kingdom, true greatness stems from servitude."

To drive home His message, Jesus beckoned a toddler to His side. In Greek, the term translates to a two-year-old child. Using this child as a metaphor, He elaborated on the nature of faith required to enter God's Kingdom: complete dependence and unwavering trust, akin to a child's reliance on their parents.

Consequently, the true measure of greatness in God's sight isn't determined by dominance or status but by humility, service, and an unwavering, childlike faith.

Today, let's extend our gratitude: "Lord Jesus, thank you for your everlasting presence and your life-giving word. As you have taught us, guide us to embody humility, to serve selflessly, and to place our undivided trust in You, akin to a child's unyielding faith in their parents. We seek to live by your teachings daily.

In Jesus' name, Amen."

JUNE 15
First ask Jesus

Mark 10:46

> 46 *Now they came to Jericho. As He went out of Jericho with His disciples and a great multitude, blind Bartimaeus, the son of Timaeus, sat by the road begging.*

As Jesus departed from Jericho, throngs of people trailed behind Him. Amidst the crowd sat Bartimaeus, a blind beggar. Sensing the commotion, he inquired about the source. Upon hearing it was Jesus of Nazareth, he began fervently shouting, "Jesus, Son of David, have mercy on me!" Despite being chastised and told to silence his cries, his pleas grew even louder.

Recognizing the man's persistent faith, Jesus summoned him. While Jesus was undoubtedly aware of Bartimaeus's desires, He still asked, "What do you want me to do for you?" Bartimaeus's response was clear: "I want to regain my sight."

This account teaches us several lessons. Often, we remain silent, thinking we can handle everything on our own. Like Bartimaeus, we must recognize our helplessness and call out to Jesus. He already knows our needs, but do we? And are we vocalizing them to Him?

I've found myself overlooking the need to consult God, thinking I can manage alone. But reality often reminds me that turning to God first, rather than as a last resort, is paramount. He assures us: "Ask in my name, and you shall receive; seek, and you shall find."

Starting today, let's prioritize seeking God's guidance. Let us consistently turn to Him, asking, "Lord Jesus, illuminate our path, provide solutions, and make clear your will for us." Jesus is ever-willing and always available. His embrace is ever-present, His ears are always attentive, and He stands ready to respond.

Today, we place our trust in Your loving hands.

In Jesus' name, Amen.

JUNE 16
The fruitless fig tree

Mark 11:12

> [12] *Now the next day, when they had come out from Bethany, He was hungry.*

Scripture recounts Jesus's final days in Bethany. One morning, feeling hunger, He glanced afar and noticed a fig tree lush with leaves. Drawing closer, Jesus found the tree barren of fruit despite it being a time when it should have borne some, even if it wasn't the primary season. In response, Jesus declared that no fruit would ever grow on it again – a pronouncement His disciples witnessed. By the next day, the tree had withered away.

One might wonder, why did Jesus curse this fig tree? Was it a mere outburst of hunger-driven frustration? The tree, after all, was not in its primary fruit-bearing season. But here's a nuance: a fig tree laden with leaves, particularly in that region, signals the presence of fruit. But Jesus found none.

The tree, in essence, was deceptive. Its verdant leaves promised fruitfulness but delivered emptiness. Thus, Jesus cursed it, so it would no longer mislead with its facade. Historically, in the Old Testament, the fig tree symbolized Israel. Through this act, Jesus was also delivering a profound message to the Israelites: while they might look the part, they lacked spiritual fruit. This lack of genuine faith would manifest when they would soon turn against Jesus.

A barren tree is destined to wither and be fuel for fire. Let this be a reminder for us to bear genuine fruits of faith, love, and righteousness.

Lord, let us not be content with mere appearances. Let our inner beings — our hearts, minds, and souls — be fruitful and pleasing to You. May we not just look good on the outside but be truly righteous in our core. Let every aspect of our being reflect Your glory. May we always remain in Your grace, bearing fruits that are worthy of Your kingdom. Today, and every day, we place our trust in Your hands.

In Jesus's name, Amen.

JUNE 17

Full faith and trust in God

Mark 11:22

[22] So Jesus answered and said to them, "Have faith in God.

When Peter witnessed the withered fig tree that Jesus had cursed, he exclaimed in surprise. Jesus responded, urging Peter and the others to have faith in God's power. His declaration about moving mountains wasn't a literal directive but rather an invitation to believe in the seemingly impossible when faith is genuine.

The phrase about commanding a mountain to be uprooted and cast into the sea was a Jewish idiom during Jesus's time. John McCarter elucidates that this was an expression used for great teachers and rabbis who could solve complex problems, implying a mastery over challenging situations. Jesus wasn't advocating for actual displacement of mountains but emphasizing unwavering faith in God's might.

True believers, as they grow in their relationship with God, come to understand His will more profoundly. Jesus teaches that prayers aligned with God's will, when said with faith, will be answered. It's not about making arbitrary requests but about syncing our desires with the heart of God. When our prayers are led by the Holy Spirit, they resonate with God's intentions, and such prayers, when uttered with faith, never go unanswered.

Jesus consistently taught about genuine faith, not about seeking signs and wonders. It's about believing in God's capability to fulfill what He has promised and recognizing that His will is always what's best for us.

Today, we express our gratitude, Lord, for the remarkable power of faith you've imparted to us. We earnestly desire that our wishes mirror Your will, knowing that Your plans are always for our good and the advancement of Your kingdom. We humbly lay our aspirations before You, seeking alignment in purpose and direction.

In the precious name of Jesus Christ, Amen.

JUNE 18

Praise the Lord with a loud noise

Psalm 33

> *Rejoice in the LORD, O you righteous! For praise from the upright is beautiful. [2] Praise the LORD with the harp; Make melody to Him with an instrument of ten strings. [3] Sing to Him a new song; Play skillfully with a shout of joy.*

"It says, 'Righteous people, rejoice in the Lord, for He praises the righteous.' Praise the Lord with the harp. Sing unto Him with an instrument of ten strings. Sing Him a new song; play skillfully with a loud noise. For the word of the Lord is right, and all His works are done in truth. He loves righteousness and judgment; the earth is full of the goodness of the Lord. By the word of the Lord, the heavens were made, and all their hosts by the breath of His mouth. He gathered the waters of the sea together as a heap; He stored up the depths in storehouses.

Let all the people of the earth fear the Lord, and let all the inhabitants of the world honor Him. For He spoke, and it was done; He commanded, and it stood fast. Amen. Our Lord is the Lord of love and power, the God who created the entire earth and the sky, the God who decreed with His word and it came to pass. In the beginning, the Word was with God, and the Word was God. And everything that God created, He decreed, and it came into existence. God remains sovereign, reigning over all things on earth, underground, and in heaven. Everything is in the hands of God. When we contemplate the majesty of God, the glory of this God who created the whole earth, the sky, and all that is in them, we recognize His profound love for us. He loved us so much that He left His kingdom in heaven, donned a human body, and lived humbly among us, even to the point of the cruel death on a cross. Yet, death could not hold the Lord. On the third day, He arose, washing away all our sins and trespasses with His glorious and eternal blood.

So today, we express our gratitude to you, Lord Jesus Christ. We thank you for all your great deeds: for loving us so profoundly that you laid down your life for us on the cross, for saving us from darkness and bringing us into your marvelous light. Because you have made us the light and salt of this world, let us go forth and proclaim the great things God has accomplished and continues to perform in each of our lives.

Everything is in His hands, and all will work out for good for those who love Him and are called according to His purpose. For God is not like man to forget His promises. His promises are eternal and steadfast. Amen.

Thank you, Lord. We entrust today into your blessed hands, praying that we may witness your majesty, glory, love, and goodness in all things. We give thanks in the name of Jesus Christ. Amen.

JUNE 19
Do we have to pay our taxes?

Mark 12:13

> 13 *Then they sent to Him some of the Pharisees and the Herodians, to catch Him in His words.*

It's noted that some Pharisees, who were followers of Herod, sought to ensnare Jesus with their questions. They approached Him and said, "Master, we know that you are truthful and impartial, for you do not regard the appearance of people but truly teach God's way. Is it lawful to pay taxes to the Roman emperor or not? Should we pay them or shouldn't we?" Aware of their duplicity, Jesus responded, "Why are you trying to trap me? Show me a denarius." When they handed Him the coin, He asked, "Whose image and inscription is this?" They replied, "Caesar's." Jesus then proclaimed, "Render to Caesar the things that are Caesar's, and to God the things that are God's." They were astounded by His reply.

Why highlight such an account today? As Christians, we are exhorted to maintain integrity in all our endeavors, especially in matters of taxation. Jesus's teaching here is unequivocal: we are obligated to fulfill our tax responsibilities to any governing authority we fall under. While employing an accountant to help manage our finances is entirely acceptable, our goal should always be to identify lawful means of tax reduction, not to engage in deceit.

If presented with an opportunity to sidestep taxes by paying in cash, our Christian duty dictates that we decline. It's essential to remember that evading taxes is not a display of honesty and uprightness.

There is no concept of "white lies" in Christianity. As Jesus instructs, our "yes" should mean "yes," and our "no" should mean "no."

Father, we thank you for your guidance and your teachings. Lord Jesus, we are grateful for the lessons on integrity and honesty you provide, especially concerning taxation. We place everything into your blessed hands.

In the name of Jesus Christ, Amen.

JUNE 20

The word of the Lord would not return void

Isaiah 55:11

> *So shall My word be that goes forth from My mouth; It shall not return to Me void, But it shall accomplish what I please, And it shall prosper in the thing for which I sent it.*

The scripture states, "My words shall not return to me void but will accomplish what I desire and achieve the purpose for which I sent them." Often, many friends or church members mention that numerous newcomers are primarily motivated by securing immigration documentation. Once their objective is achieved, they depart. Responding to this, a Persian-speaking female pastor said to her church leaders, "In whose name do these individuals find favor in the courts? By whom do they obtain their permanent residency, status, or asylum?" The answer is Jesus Christ. Even in those courtrooms, it is solely through faith in Him that they secure asylum and residence. However, the veracity of their claims is a matter between them and God. God does not share His glory with anyone. Our role is to disseminate the word of God. As the prophet Isaiah conveyed, the Lord's words, when spoken, do not return void. Instead, they achieve His intent and manifest His will. The word of God has its purpose. It plants seeds in the hearts and minds of all. If today, some exploit it for personal gain, I am confident that the truth of the seed sown in their hearts will, in due time, guide them to salvation. But the line between deception and truthfulness is a matter between the individual and God. In every corner, the name of the Lord Jesus Christ is uplifted. Every knee shall bow and every tongue confess that Jesus Christ is the Lord, and through His name, all shall find salvation.

So, if any among you have utilized faith for personal gain, know that it's not too late. God embodies truth, and the door to repentance is always open. Those who walk with Him daily recognize the joy of His presence. His blessings surpass worldly treasures. To walk alongside Him, to cultivate a relationship with Him, is more rewarding than anything else.

Reflect on this today and elevate His name, Amen.

JUNE 21
Come and taste the Lord

Psalm 34:8

> *Oh, taste and see that the LORD is good; blessed is the man who trusts in Him!*

The scripture tells us, "Taste and see that the Lord is good." Let's experience the Lord's goodness for ourselves.

He is the singular deity across all religions who boldly declares, "Come, taste and experience me. Discover the depth of my goodness." This is our God, the one and only.

The Lord who is unafraid of being questioned, the Lord whose very essence is love and kindness, beckons us.

Jesus Christ calls out, "All who are weary and burdened, come to me. Take up my yoke, for it is easy and light."

Let us, together, immerse ourselves in the Lord's presence today. Let's feel His goodness, His grandeur, and His warmth. Let us delve deeper into His love with each passing moment and give thanks for His ultimate sacrifice on the cross.

For He epitomizes goodness. In His humility, He gave up Jesus. Through Jesus' crucifixion—a most agonizing death—He demonstrated His profound love for us. Come, let's experience His goodness.

Father, we approach You today with gratitude in our hearts, recognizing Your sweetness, gentleness, and boundless love. Thank you, Jesus Christ, for Your enduring love demonstrated on the cross. A love that is ceaseless, with arms forever open to embrace us.

Today, we lay down our burdens at Your feet, O Jesus Christ, gladly taking up Your light yoke, which is simply to believe in You as our Savior. May You walk beside us.

In the name of Jesus Christ, Amen.

JUNE 22

The lord protects the righteous

Psalm 34:15-19

> [15] *The eyes of the LORD are on the righteous, And His ears are open to their cry.*
> [16] *The face of the LORD is against those who do evil, To cut off the remembrance of them from the earth.*
> [17] *The righteous cry out, and the LORD hears, And delivers them out of all their troubles.*
> [18] *The LORD is near to those who have a broken heart, And saves such as have a contrite spirit.*
> [19] *Many are the afflictions of the righteous, But the LORD delivers him out of them all.*

The scripture reminds us that God is attentive to the virtuous, heeding their pleas. Yet, He stands against those who do wrong, ensuring their presence will ultimately fade from the earth. When the righteous cry out, God hears them and liberates them from their afflictions.

God draws near to those with broken spirits, offering salvation and consolation to those who might have lost hope. A virtuous person might face numerous challenges, but God rescues him from every predicament. Amen.

God stands with the upright, the virtuous, and the faithful. He remains steadfastly by our side, never abandoning us. Jesus Christ assures, "I am always with you and will never forsake you." His Holy Spirit continuously supports and guides us.

Thus, when we face adversities or heartbreak, let us present our concerns to God today. Let's lay them at the feet of Jesus Christ, for He assures us that He not only hears our laments and supplications but responds to them, freeing us from every distress.

True goodness and righteousness come from placing our faith in Jesus Christ as our Lord and Savior. When He speaks of righteousness, He refers to those who believe. Those who have faith are deemed righteous and upright in the name of Jesus Christ.

Today, let's approach God with gratitude, saying: "Thank you, Lord, for through Your sacrifice and resurrection, you've deemed us righteous.

You bore the cost for our transgressions. For the sins that required our lives as payment, You paid with Your life, once and for all.

Lord, our sole responsibility is to believe in You, acknowledging You as God, our Savior, the way, and the truth. May we lay everything at Your feet.

So today, may we not retreat from Your presence. Instead, let's present every concern, every detail at Your feet, striving to be magnanimous and righteous. Direct us in our daily endeavors with Your Holy Spirit.

In the name of Jesus Christ, Amen.

JUNE 23

Christ sits at the right hand of the power and coming with the clouds

Mark 14:60-63.

> [60] *And the high priest stood up in the midst and asked Jesus, saying, "Do You answer nothing? What is it these men testify against You?"* [61] *But He kept silent and answered nothing. Again, the high priest asked Him, saying to Him, "Are You the Christ, the Son of the Blessed?"*
> [62] *Jesus said, "I am. And you will see the Son of Man sitting at the right hand of the Power, and coming with the clouds of heaven."*
> [63] *Then the high priest tore his clothes and said, "What further need do we have of witnesses?*

On that fateful night, Jesus Christ was at the high priest's house. False witnesses took turns testifying against Him. Rising amidst the chaos, the high priest questioned Jesus, "Won't you defend yourself? How do you respond to these accusations?" Yet, Jesus remained silent, offering no rebuttal. Pressing further, the high priest inquired, "Are you the Messiah, the Son of God?" To this, Jesus replied directly and unambiguously, "I am, and you will see the Son of Man seated at the right hand of Power and coming with the clouds of heaven."

In shock, the high priest tore his robes, exclaiming, "Why do we need any more witnesses? You've heard the blasphemy. What's your verdict?"

Now, when Jesus said, "you will see," did the high priest indeed witness it? I believe he did. For when Jesus yielded His spirit on the cross, the Bible recounts that the temple curtain, a substantial fabric of 10 centimeters thickness, was split from top to bottom. This was no ordinary tear; it symbolized the barrier between God and His people being eradicated by Jesus's sacrifice. And as the high priest had torn his clothes in a symbolic gesture of witnessing blasphemy, God showed him, through the tearing of the temple curtain, that what Jesus said was not blasphemous, but the undeniable truth.

Traditionally, only the high priest was permitted into the temple's most sacred space. Given this, it's likely that the high priest was among the first to witness this divine act - the curtain being torn.

Similarly, each one of us must recognize Jesus Christ for who He truly is, understand His purpose, and acknowledge the role He plays in our lives. We will witness Jesus, seated at the right hand of the Father, and anticipate His glorious return. Holding onto this hope, let our faith in Jesus Christ, the Alpha and Omega, the exalted name above all names in heaven and on earth, remain unshaken. Amen.

JUNE 24
Who is like our God?

Psalm 35:9-11

> 9 *And my soul shall be joyful in the* L*ORD; It shall rejoice in His salvation.*
> 10 *All my bones shall say, "*L*ORD, who is like You, Delivering the poor from him who is too strong for him, Yes, the poor and the needy from him who plunders him?"*
> 11 *Fierce witnesses rise up; They ask me things that I do not know.*

The scripture reminds us: our souls should find joy in the Lord, taking delight in His salvation. "All my bones shall declare: Lord, who compares to You? You free the oppressed from overpowering foes, and rescue the downtrodden and needy from those who would exploit them." Amen.

God's presence is a constant, always available for each of us, especially the vulnerable and impoverished. Poverty isn't just material; it can be a state of the soul, a condition of the mind, or even an emotional void. Regardless of its form, God extends His hand to uplift every downtrodden spirit, ensuring protection against those who might wish us harm.

The Lord is our rescuer, our beacon of hope. Today, let us raise our voices in gratitude and praise, acknowledging Him as our savior in all circumstances. Every joy, every moment of happiness, springs from the love of Jesus Christ, who redeemed us with His sacrifice. He remains ever-vigilant, safeguarding us from afflictions and shielding us from those who might oppose or oppress us. In obedience to His teachings, we pray not just for ourselves but for our adversaries too.

Rather than meeting malice with malice, we heed Christ's call to combat evil with kindness. We intercede for those who wrong us, praying for their enlightenment. We beseech the Lord to pull them from the shadows of their transgressions so they, too, may join in singing His praises.

In the sacred name of Jesus Christ, Amen.

JUNE 25

Come down from the cross, so that we may believe in you

Mark 15:27-33

> [27] *With Him they also crucified two robbers, one on His right and the other on His left.*
> [28] *So the Scripture was fulfilled which says, "And He was numbered with the transgressors."*
> [29] *And those who passed by blasphemed Him, wagging their heads and saying, "Aha! You who destroy the temple and build it in three days,*
> [30] *save Yourself, and come down from the cross!"*
> [31] *Likewise the chief priests also, mocking among themselves with the scribes, said, "He saved others; Himself He cannot save.*
> [32] *Let the Christ, the King of Israel, descend now from the cross, that we may see and believe." Even those who were crucified with Him reviled Him. Jesus Dies on the Cross*
> [33] *Now when the sixth hour had come, there was darkness over the whole land until the ninth hour.*

The scriptures tell us of that solemn moment when Christ was crucified between two thieves, one on his right and the other on his left. Bystanders jeered, shaking their heads and blaspheming, taunting Him with His words, "You who said you'd tear down this temple and rebuild it in three days, save yourself. Come down from the cross." The high priests too joined in the mockery, challenging, "He saved others but can't save Himself. If He truly is the King of Israel, let Him descend now from the cross for all to see and believe."

In our moments of doubt, we too might wonder: If He truly was the Messiah, why didn't He display His power then? Why didn't He come down and make believers of them all?

But to grasp the profoundness of this, we must ask: Why did Jesus come to this world? His very purpose, His mission, was the cross. The Messiah, possessing the power to avoid the cross, chose it. He humbled Himself, bearing it for our sakes, for our salvation.

In that moment, it's as though the devil sought to tempt Jesus once more, using those around Him to challenge:

"If you truly are who you claim, come down. Prove yourself." But Christ's mission was not about proving or demonstrating might but about sacrifice and redemption.

He came to bear the cross, to die for humanity's sins, and to rise on the third day, triumphing over Satan and death. In doing so, He paid our ransom, once and for all. Amen.

When doubt whispers, let's lay our uncertainties at Christ's feet and ask, "Lord, reveal the truth to us." The entire ministry of Jesus, all His teachings and miracles, culminate in the cross and resurrection. Without these, as Paul reminds us, our faith would be in vain. We give thanks to Jesus for willingly embracing the cross, cleansing us of our sins. We entrust our lives to His care and ask Him to guide and reign in each of our hearts.

In the name of Jesus Christ, Amen.

JUNE 26
Whom do we thank?

Daniel 2:19-20

> [19] *Then the secret was revealed to Daniel in a night vision. So Daniel blessed the God of heaven.*
> [20] *Daniel answered and said: "Blessed be the name of God forever and ever, For wisdom and might are His.*

James 1:17

> [17] *Every good gift and every perfect gift is from above, and comes down from the Father of lights, with whom there is no variation or shadow of turning.*

When we draw near to God, it is fitting to extol Him for His wondrous deeds and the blessings He showers upon us. Let our praises ascend and our worship magnify the God who bestows upon us every good gift.

In those intimate moments with God, we find the perfect opportunity to express our awe at His goodness, to thank Him for His endless mercies, and to articulate the reverence and love we hold for Him in our hearts.

Let our words, springing from our innermost feelings, declare God's grandeur and His mighty works in our lives. Remember those heartfelt words we were taught as children? "I thank you, Jesus" and "I appreciate You." Expressing gratitude not only strengthens our human relationships but profoundly deepens our bond with God. By thanking Him, we recognize and affirm the immeasurable gifts and blessings He has poured into our lives.

In prayer, some of the most profound words, the most impactful phrases, are "thank you" and "I appreciate it."

O Lord, we lift our praise and adoration for all the bounties and graces You have graciously granted us.

In the name of Jesus Christ, Amen.

JUNE 27
Do not be offended by evildoers and villains

Psalm 37

This Psalm reminds us: Do not be consumed by worry because of evildoers, and do not envy those who do wrong. Like grass, they will soon wither and fade.

Place your trust in the Lord and continue to do good, and you will dwell in safety in the land. Find your joy in the Lord, for He will grant you the desires of your heart. Commit your ways to Him, lean on Him, and He will come to your aid. He will make your righteousness shine like the dawn. Amen? Amen.

We should fix our gaze upon Jesus Christ. When faced with evildoers, recognize their actions as evil, but understand that it's God's place to address it. Hand them over to God in prayer, hoping that they might turn back, repent, and embrace the love of Jesus Christ.

This Psalm advises against envying those who seem prosperous in their wrongdoings. Rather than letting jealousy cloud our judgment, we should focus on what? Trusting in God and doing good where we are, ensuring our security and peace. God's presence is a constant in our lives; He never abandons us. Being His children, we are assured of His unwavering support. Our greatest advocate, comforter, friend, and companion is Jesus Christ.

And He stands up for us. Our Savior, Jesus Christ, at the right hand of the Father, intercedes on our behalf and makes our righteousness evident for all to see. We are called to be the world's light, and our light should shine so brightly that people, through our good deeds, see our Heavenly Father and glorify Him. Amen?

Those of us who have accepted Jesus Christ as our Lord are the salt and light of the world.

Dear Father, we are grateful for your word today. Guide us to not take offense at those who do wrong but to lift them up in prayer. Keep us from envy and teach us to lean solely on you, Jesus Christ. May we walk hand in hand with you, today and always. We lay today, with all its intricacies, in your loving hands.

In the name of Jesus Christ, Amen.

JUNE 28
Mary herself needed a savior

Luke 1:40-56

Your message provides a perspective on the biblical account of Mary and Elizabeth, emphasizing the importance of Jesus Christ as the sole mediator and Savior. Here's a revised version of your devotional for better clarity and flow:

When Mary visited Elizabeth, the moment was profoundly spiritual. As Mary arrived, Elizabeth, filled with the Holy Spirit, felt John leap with joy in her womb. Elizabeth exclaimed in wonder, "Why am I so favored that the mother of my Lord should come to me?"

In response, Mary, also filled with the Holy Spirit, proclaimed her famous Magnificat: "My soul glorifies the Lord and my spirit rejoices in God my Savior; for He has looked with favor on His lowly servant." Mary recognized the greatness of the Lord and His works, noting His mercy that extends from generation to generation, His mighty deeds, and His fulfillment of the promises made to Abraham and his descendants.

Mary did not see herself as divine or a figure of worship. She described herself as "lowly" and recognized her need for a Savior. This magnifies the essence of her message: it's not about her but about God and His great work.

Mary's humility stands as a stark reminder to us all. While many honor and respect her as the mother of Jesus, she herself recognized the distinction between her role and that of her Son. Jesus Christ, who was both fully God and fully man, is the one who died and rose for our sins.

The Scriptures make it clear: Jesus is the one mediator between God and humanity. While figures like Mary, Peter, Paul, and John play significant roles in the biblical narrative, they are not to be idolized or equated with Christ. There's only one path to God the Father, and that's through Jesus Christ, empowered by the Holy Spirit. So, as we reflect on the biblical account and its lessons, let us turn our hearts to prayer:

Lord Jesus Christ, King of Kings, our Savior, we thank you for your unparalleled sacrifice on the cross. You, who left the splendors of heaven to dwell among us, humbled yourself to die a brutal death, only to conquer it three days later. Death could not hold you. In your resurrection, you declared victory for all who believe in you. We honor and exalt you alone, along with God the Father and the Holy Spirit.

In your holy name, we pray, Amen.

JUNE 29

Let us think about good and pure things

Philippians 4:8

> [8] *Finally, brethren, whatever things are true, whatever things are noble, whatever things are just, whatever things are pure, whatever things are lovely, whatever things are of good report, if there is any virtue and if there is anything praiseworthy—meditate on these things.*

Paul writes, "Finally, brothers and sisters, whatever is true, whatever is honorable, whatever is right, whatever is pure, whatever is lovely, whatever is commendable, if there is any excellence and if anything worthy of praise, think about these things. Whatever you have learned and received from me, and heard from me, put these into practice, and the God of peace will be with you." Amen.

Friends, today, let's channel our minds towards these good things: the truth, the honorable, the righteous, the pure, the lovely, and the commendable. In doing so, we can rejuvenate our minds and shift our worldview. And what is Paul's promise? When we live by these principles, the very source of peace, God Himself, will accompany us.

Just today, I had a conversation with Pastor Tim who reminded me of this powerful verse. How timely it is for our current situation! When the weight of the world bears down on us or when adversity strikes, let's recalibrate our focus. Let's immerse ourselves in the truth, the honorable, the pure, the lovely, and all things praiseworthy. By doing so, we open our hearts to receive God's peace. Shouldn't we all aim to dwell on the good rather than the negative? Amen?

Our Lord Jesus Christ teaches us, "Do not repay evil with evil, but overcome evil with good." So, whenever a negative thought tries to overshadow us, let's counter it with a positive one, redirecting our minds to what's noble, beautiful, pure, and virtuous.

Today, let us diligently work towards this mindset, welcoming the divine peace of God and the serenity from Jesus Christ into our lives. The Lord assures us, "I do not give you peace as the world gives. Instead, I grant you My own peace." May we embrace and cherish this unique peace from Christ. Amen. May God be with you always.

JUNE 30

The Lord will not forget the righteous

Psalm 37:23-27

> [23]*The steps of a good man are ordered by the LORD,*
> *And He delights in his way.*
> [24]*Though he falls, he shall not be utterly cast down; For the LORD upholds him with His hand.*
> [25]*I have been young, and now am old;*
> *Yet I have not seen the righteous forsaken, nor his descendants begging bread.*
> [26]*He is ever merciful, and lends;*
> *And his descendants are blessed.*
> [27]*Depart from evil, and do good;*
> *And dwell forevermore.*

The Scriptures tell us that God stands by those He delights in and guides them in the paths they should tread. Even if they stumble, they won't fall, for the Lord holds them by the hand.

From my early years to this day, as I've grown older, I've never witnessed the righteous being abandoned or their children seeking bread in vain. They are ever giving, lending generously, and their offspring are a blessing. To find lasting stability, shun evil and embrace goodness. God cherishes the truth and never forsakes the faithful. He stands by them steadfastly, while the offspring of the wicked face ruin. The righteous shall inherit the land and dwell upon it forever. Amen.

Whom does God pledge His support to? Those He takes pleasure in. We, who have welcomed Jesus Christ as our Lord and affirm the Holy Spirit's presence within us, are the very ones in whom God delights. Remember, our salvation isn't earned by our good deeds; it's granted solely by the grace of our Lord Jesus Christ. By accepting Him as our Savior, who bore our sins on the cross and triumphed over death, we receive this unmerited favor.

Grace is a gift we never earned. Indeed, by our actions, we merited a fate far from His grace. But we weren't saved by deeds. Our salvation came only through Jesus Christ's grace and our faith in Him. As we walk in faith, the fruits of the Spirit manifest in our lives as good deeds. Thus, when God observes these deeds – the outcome of the Spirit's work in us – He supports us.

How were we recognized as righteous? Through Jesus Christ's sacrifice and resurrection and our faith in Him. Yet, this faith must yield fruit. The fruits of our faith materialize as our good deeds.

They're not a list of tasks we've been told to do, but rather, they arise naturally from the Spirit of God working within us. As we live this truth, Jesus assures us of His constant presence. And this Psalm echoes that sentiment.

Father, we express our deepest gratitude for the indwelling of the Holy Spirit, for bringing us from the realm of darkness into Your marvelous light, and for Your Son, Jesus Christ, who bore our sins on the cross. May the fruits of our faith – our deeds – shine brilliantly, leading others to extol Your glorious name.

In the name of Jesus Christ, Amen.

JULY 1
Our best for Jesus

Tomorrow marks Palm Sunday, just five days before the crucifixion of Jesus Christ and His triumphant entry into Jerusalem. On this very day, Saturday, Jesus and His disciples, while en route to Jerusalem, visited the house of Martha and Mary. There, Lazarus, who once was dead, was present—the same Lazarus whom Jesus had resurrected.

This day, nearly 1900 years ago, is referenced in John 12:1: "Then, six days before the Passover, Jesus came to Bethany, where Lazarus was, who had been dead, whom He had raised from the dead."

The scripture recounts that six days before the Passover, Jesus arrived in Bethany, the home of Lazarus, whom He had brought back to life. During His stay, they had supper, with Martha taking the role of server. Lazarus was among those seated with Jesus. Mary, in a poignant moment, took a precious vial of pure spikenard oil, anointed Jesus' feet, and then wiped them with her hair. The fragrance from the oil permeated the entire house. In another account, it's mentioned that she broke the alabaster box, pouring all its contents on Jesus' feet and using her hair to dry them. Judas Iscariot, the disciple set to betray Jesus, remarked, "Why wasn't this perfume sold for three hundred denarii and the money given to the poor?" Yet his concern wasn't for the needy. He harbored ulterior motives, for he was a thief who managed the disciples' money bag and often pilfered from it.

Jesus, addressing Judas' comment, said, "Leave her alone. She has done this in preparation for my burial." In another account, He mentions, "She has done a good thing for me in anticipation of my death. Wherever the gospel is proclaimed, what she has done will also be spoken of, in memory of her. The poor you will always have with you, but you will not always have me." This poignant moment occurred just a night before Jesus' glorious entry into Jerusalem on Palm Sunday. This brings forth the question for all of us: Are we offering our best, our most cherished possessions, at the feet of Jesus? Are our love and reverence for Him so profound that we'd humble ourselves to cleanse His dusty feet with our own hair and hands?

Let's approach Him today with this prayer: “Lord Jesus Christ, we love You. Help us offer our best to You today and every subsequent day. Let our devotion be so unwavering that at any given moment, we can witness Your presence and lift You higher. May we forever be at Your feet, humbling ourselves in Your honor. In the precious name of Jesus Christ, Amen."

JULY 2
Why Jesus rebuked the demon confessing to His deity?

Luke 4:33

> [33] *Now in the synagogue there was a man who had a spirit of an unclean demon. And he cried out with a loud voice,*

In a synagogue, a man possessed by an unclean spirit cried out, "What do you want with us, Jesus of Nazareth? Have you come to destroy us? I recognize you — the Holy One of God!" Jesus rebuked the spirit, commanding it, "Be silent and come out of him!" And the demon obeyed.

In another instance, as recorded in verse 41, demons were expelled from many, exclaiming, "You are the Messiah, the Son of God." I've often pondered why Jesus, upon hearing such affirmations of His divinity, silenced these spirits. Would it not have benefited Him for others to hear these testimonies of His Messiahship? The Scriptures hint that His time had not yet come. By allowing these spirits to declare His identity, it might have prompted the masses to forcibly make Him their king. This would have disrupted Christ's divine mission — to offer Himself as the singular, ultimate sacrifice for humanity's sins.

The people of that time anticipated a Messiah who would rise as a political leader, freeing the Jews from their oppressors, the Romans. They were not privy to the profound truth that Christ's kingship was of a different nature — He reigns within the hearts of believers. Every instance where these spirits recognized Him as the Christ, the Son of God, Jesus promptly silenced them. Yet, these episodes serve as undeniable evidence of Christ's divinity. These spirits were acutely aware of Him, anticipating the judgment awaiting them, even questioning, "Have you come to torment us before the appointed time?"

Their recognition of Jesus contrasts with their refusal to submit to Him. We, in contrast, have not only recognized Jesus but have also welcomed Him as our Lord and Savior. This acceptance signifies our faith and the indwelling of the Holy Spirit, guiding us towards the truth.

Father, as we reflect on this week, we are reminded that nearly 1990 years ago, Lord Jesus, You willingly endured the cross, taking upon Yourself our sins. We are deeply grateful. Today, empower us to declare You as our Lord, the Holy One of God, the Son, and the Savior of the world.

In the name of Jesus Christ, Amen.

JULY 3
The power of prayer

James 5:16

> *Confess your trespasses to one another, and pray for one another, that you may be healed. The effective, fervent prayer of a righteous man avails much.*

The earnest prayer of a righteous person is powerfully effective. Over the past couple of days, Sunday and Monday, the Holy Spirit moved my heart to intercede for a friend I hadn't communicated with in some time. Tears flowed as prayers rose.

Yesterday, I promptly reached out via email to my priest friends and other dear ones in Christ, inviting them to unite with me in this prayer. Together, we lifted our voices to God, affirming that when two or three gather in His name, the strength of their collective prayer multiplies. Remarkably, even before the emails were fully delivered, I received a message from that very friend. After weeks of silence, he reached out, and our hearts overflowed with gratitude.

Though we have been praying daily for his spiritual well-being, it was in these particular two days that I felt an intensified urging from the Holy Spirit. God, in His faithfulness, hears and responds. As James instructs, when faced with challenges, gather and pray. He further encourages believers to confess their sins to one another, assuring that fervent prayer from a righteous heart avails much. Just consider Elijah — a man with emotions like ours. He fervently prayed for a drought, and for 3 years and 6 months, the heavens closed. Yet, upon his subsequent prayer, rain drenched the parched land, and it yielded its produce.

The transformative power of prayer is undeniable. Jesus invites those burdened and wearied to approach Him, promising rest and relief. The cares and concerns we bear daily — for our families, friends, livelihoods, and other responsibilities — Jesus beckons us to lay them at His feet. In exchange, He offers His light and easy yoke: faith, trust, and communion with Him.

Father, we come before You today with hearts full of gratitude. We recognize that even before we speak, You are attuned to the cries of our hearts. May we never hesitate to seek the prayerful support of our fellow believers in times of need, for together, our voices resonate more powerfully in Your ears. Today, we present all our petitions, confident in Your ability to work all things together for our good. Fulfill your perfect will in us. In the name of Jesus Christ, Amen.

JULY 4
I have come for the sinners

Luke 5:29

Then Levi gave Him a great feast in his own house. And there were a great number of tax collectors and others who sat down with them.

On that day, Jesus Christ encountered Matthew, also known as Levi. With a simple command, "Follow me," Matthew left everything behind to follow Jesus. In gratitude, Levi hosted a grand feast for Jesus at his house. Among the attendees were many tax collectors and some labeled as 'sinners.' The sight of Jesus dining with them ruffled the Pharisees and religious leaders. "Why do you eat and drink with tax collectors and sinners?" they challenged. Jesus, in His profound wisdom, responded, "It is not the healthy or the righteous who need a doctor, but the sick. I have not come to call the righteous, but sinners to repentance."

This scenario mirrors the critiques some levy against the church today. When a 'sinner' or someone deemed 'unworthy' comes to the church, or when the church doesn't align with personal expectations, the same disdain is expressed. However, the church is precisely where those aware of their brokenness and sin should be. It is a sanctuary for those in spiritual turmoil, for those seeking redemption.

There is no flawless church. Some search endlessly for perfection, hopping from one congregation to another, noting what each lacks. But no church is immune to imperfection. We are encouraged to remain in the church where we feel called, striving to address and rectify its shortcomings through the love of Christ. For the church is meant to be a haven where those in spiritual need can encounter Jesus.

"I have come not for the healthy, but for the sick." The church serves as a hospital for the spiritually wounded, offering both spiritual and, at times, physical healing. Remember, no church is perfect. If we feel drawn to a particular congregation, it's our duty to serve within it with genuine love and kindness. Not by being judgmental or indulging in gossip, but by emulating the unconditional love and grace of Jesus.

It was through love and compassion that our Lord Jesus Christ triumphed over the world, not by condemnation or slander. So, let's remind ourselves that the church is a sanctuary for all, especially for repentant sinners like you and me. Even as we falter and sin, we continually turn to Jesus for forgiveness and renewal. Amen.

JULY 5
Do we get angry of healing and saving the sick?

Luke 6:6

> *Now it happened on another Sabbath, also, that He entered the synagogue and taught. And a man was there whose right hand was withered.*

One day, as Jesus was teaching in the synagogue on the Sabbath, He encountered a man with a paralyzed right arm. The Jewish and Pharisee priests were present, keenly observing Jesus to see if He would heal on the Sabbath – they hoped to find something to accuse Him of.

Aware of their intent, Jesus addressed the man with the withered arm, "Stand up and come to the center." As the man obeyed, Jesus turned to the onlookers, challenging their mindset: "I pose a question to you. On the Sabbath, is it right to do good or to do harm? To save a life or destroy it?" After a pause, He told the man, "Stretch out your arm." Miraculously, the man's arm was restored.

However, rather than celebrating this incredible act of healing, the religious leaders were filled with fury. They began whispering amongst themselves, plotting their next move against Jesus.

The Jews held the belief that no work should be done on the Sabbath. While God had instructed them to rest, their interpretation had evolved into a strict doctrine that prohibited any form of action. God never meant for it to be this way. This is why Jesus posed the question about doing good on the Sabbath. It was a challenge to their rigid beliefs.

And when faced with an undeniable miracle—a man healed after years of affliction—instead of expressing gratitude and awe, these leaders were consumed by anger. It's a somber reflection for all of us. How tragic it would be if, instead of celebrating someone's healing or salvation, we were filled with resentment or sought to discredit the one who performed the act!

May we never fall into such a trap. Let's pray that we never grow cold or indifferent to the wonders of God's love and power. If we ever reach a point where we resent God's goodness, it would indeed be our downfall.

So, Father, open our eyes to Your work in the world. May we always recognize and applaud Your miracles and Your grace, even if they occur at times or in ways we might not expect.

Let us remember that the Sabbath was made for man's rest and not as a burden. Let's strive to do good at all times, to offer thanks, and to uplift Your name.

Today and always, guide our steps and our thoughts. May we always witness Your goodness and respond with gratitude and joy. In the name of Jesus Christ, we offer our thanks and praise. Amen.

JULY 6
Do not judge so you will not be judged

Luke 6:37

> *"Judge not, and you shall not be judged. Condemn not, and you shall not be condemned. Forgive, and you will be forgiven.*

Before delving into this, Jesus Christ teaches about loving our enemies. When we lend something to someone, we shouldn't expect its return. Yet, in Luke 6:37, He advises, "Do not judge, and you will not be judged. Do not condemn, and you will not be condemned. Forgive, and you will be forgiven. Give, and it will be given to you. A good measure, pressed down, shaken together, and running over, will be poured into your lap. For with the measure you use, it will be measured to you."

The Lord Jesus Christ outlines the principles of God's Kingdom. In this divine realm, merely loving our friends isn't enough. Even non-believers do that. He emphasizes that we shouldn't lend only to our friends and family with the expectation of getting our money back. Instead, He instructs us to lend to anyone who asks. He further challenges us to love and show kindness to our enemies. Moreover, He warns against judging or condemning others, lest we face the same fate.

To be forgiven, we must first forgive others. This is a sentiment echoed in the Lord's Prayer: "Father, forgive us our trespasses, as we forgive those who trespass against us." We're called to be generous, to lend and give, assuring that it will be returned to us in greater measure: full, pressed down, shaken together, and overflowing.

Every act of kindness we extend returns to us in equal or greater measure. With this understanding, let's express our gratitude to the Father for His boundless love and goodness. As the Apostle John noted, even books innumerable couldn't capture the extent of His deeds.

Father, we thank You for Your immeasurable love, goodness, and the blessings showered upon us. We're most grateful for Your redemptive grace, which brought us from darkness into Your marvelous light. Jesus, we remember with gratitude Your sacrifice on the cross 2000 years ago. You took upon our sins, the very things that separated us from the Father, and erased them, asking only for our faith in return.

With deep appreciation, we recognize our forgiven transgressions. May we carry this grace with us, reflecting Your love daily.

As we forgive, give to others, and bless those around us, may we abstain from condemnation, proceeding always with love.

Holy Spirit, fill our hearts and guide our steps. Wherever we find ourselves, may we serve as living testimonies of Jesus Christ, spreading the sweet fragrance of His love. We offer our thanks and praises in the mighty name of Jesus Christ, Amen.

JULY 7

Is our faith stronger than that of the roman centurion?

Luke 7:1-11

During Jesus Christ's journey to Capernaum, a Roman centurion sought Him out due to his dearly loved servant's grave illness. In an act of profound faith, the centurion sent Jewish elders to fetch Jesus for healing.

As described in verse 6, upon hearing this, Jesus began to approach the centurion's house. But before He arrived, the centurion sent friends with a message: "Lord, don't trouble Yourself, for I do not deserve to have You come under my roof. That's why I did not even consider myself worthy to come to You. But say the word, and my servant will be healed. For I myself am a man under authority, with soldiers under me. I tell one to go, and he goes; and another to come, and he comes. I say to my servant, 'Do this,' and he does it."

Jesus was astounded upon hearing this. He exclaimed to the crowd around Him, "Truly, I tell you, I have not found such great faith even in Israel." Soon after, the messengers discovered the servant in perfect health.

The centurion's cultural awareness shines through this narrative. He knew that, according to Jewish customs, entering a Gentile's home or even a mere touch could render a Jew ceremonially unclean. By not allowing Jesus to enter his house or approach him, the centurion was respecting these customs.

Yet, the most captivating part of this story is the centurion's exceptional faith. Even Jesus testified that He hadn't seen such faith throughout Israel. The centurion recognized Jesus's authority, equating it to his own command over his soldiers. This realization led him to believe that just a word from Jesus would suffice for healing.

As believers, we should reflect: Is our faith as strong as the centurion's? Do we trust Jesus's words as this Roman officer did? Given that we acknowledge Jesus as Lord and have the Holy Spirit within us, our faith should be unwavering. If doubt lingers, we ought to pray for strengthened faith.

Father, today, we stand in awe of the centurion's profound faith. May our trust in You eclipse even his deep conviction. Strengthen the areas of our faith that waver and transform our doubt into unwavering belief. We're confident in Your abilities, Lord Jesus, knowing that nothing is beyond Your reach. We surrender our lives to You, praying for Your perfect will to be done in every facet. In the precious name of Jesus Christ, Amen.

JULY 8

Why Jesus allowed the demons to enter the swine?

Luke 8:26-40

In the Gospels, we find an account where Jesus traveled across the lake to the region of the Gadarenes, an area inhabited predominantly by non-Jews. Upon His arrival, He encountered a man possessed by numerous demons, so many that they named themselves "Legion." This man did not live in a conventional home, nor did he wear clothing. Instead, he resided amongst tombs, displaying superhuman strength by breaking any chains that bound him.

When the demons within the man saw Jesus, they instantly recognized His divine authority. They fell prostrate, exclaiming, "Jesus Christ, Son of the Most High God, have you come here to torment us before the time?" They begged Jesus not to send them into the abyss but instead into a nearby herd of pigs. Scripture notes that this herd was vast, numbering around two thousand. Jesus permitted their request. Immediately, the demons left the man and entered the pigs, causing the entire herd to rush down a steep bank into the lake where they drowned.

Those tending to the pigs were witnesses to this supernatural event. They fled to the city, recounting everything, especially about the man's miraculous deliverance. The town's residents came to see the spectacle for themselves. They found the once-demoniac, now clothed and in his right mind, sitting peacefully at Jesus' feet. The sight filled them with a mix of awe and fear. They begged Jesus to depart from their region.

One might wonder why Jesus allowed the demons to enter the pigs, leading to their demise. God revealed an insight: through this act, Jesus demonstrated the destructive nature of evil. Whether in humans or animals, demons bring only chaos and destruction. Moreover, Jesus highlighted His unmatched power over such malevolent forces. The townspeople's fear likely stemmed from a sudden recognition of their own sinful nature, thinking, "If this is the fate of possessed pigs, what awaits us?" Instead of seeking redemption, they asked Jesus to leave.

The formerly possessed man, however, had a different plea. He yearned to follow Jesus. But Jesus had a mission for him: "Return home and declare how much God has done for you." The man obeyed, evangelizing throughout the Decapolis. Paul's later journeys hint that a church had been established there, possibly through the testimony of this very man.

Life often presents us with baffling situations. While we might not always grasp their meaning, seeking God's guidance reveals their purpose. Every experience, good or bad, molds our journey.

Father, we come before You with gratitude for Your infinite wisdom. You work in mysterious ways, turning even adversity into blessings. Through every storm, we are comforted by Your promise: "I will never leave you nor forsake you." We rest in this assurance, knowing all things work together for our good. We praise and thank You, in the name of Jesus Christ, Amen.

JULY 9

As the deer pants for streams of water

Psalm 42

Psalm 42 is among the most poignant in the Book of Psalms. In it, the psalmist likens his soul's yearning for God to a deer's intense thirst for flowing streams. The English rendition describes this thirst with the phrase, "as the deer pants," emphasizing not just an ordinary thirst but a profound and desperate craving.

This profound yearning is for the living God, an intense desire to experience God's presence and be revitalized by His life-giving waters. It's this thirst that the psalmist compares to his yearning to appear before God.

For Christians, this sentiment has added depth. We believe that both Jesus Christ and the Holy Spirit reside within us. This divine presence isn't confined to temples or sacred spaces; our very hearts are the temples where God dwells. Thus, the access to this life-giving water is always within our reach.

Do our souls pant for God with the same intensity? Do we long for the living waters that Jesus promises? For He said, "I am the water of life. Whoever is thirsty, let them come to me and drink, and they will never thirst again."

Jesus embodies all that we need — He is the way, the truth, the life, the light of the world. May our souls ever yearn for Him, mirroring the desperate thirst depicted in Psalm 42.

Father, we are profoundly grateful that Your Spirit dwells within us, making our hearts Your temple. May our yearning for You amplify each day, making us as desperate for Your presence as the deer panting for streams of water. As we turn to You in prayer and immerse ourselves in Your Word, may our souls be continuously refreshed and quenched by Your everlasting love. We give You thanks and praise, in the mighty name of Jesus Christ, our King of kings. Amen.

JULY 10
Hope in God

Psalm 42:11

"Why are you downcast, O my soul?" the psalmist laments. In another passage, he asks, *"Why are you so disquieted within me?"* These are cries of a heart familiar with pain, a soul acquainted with depths of sorrow.

But even in these valleys of despair, the psalmist finds a glimmer of hope: "Put your hope in God," he urges himself, "for I will yet praise Him, my Savior and my God." Do you resonate with this cry today? Are the weight and worries of the world threatening to drown you? Is despair gnawing at your spirit?

Yet, in the midst of this desolation, Scripture offers a balm: "My soul, why are you downcast?" Remember the steadfast love of the Lord. For Christians, Jesus Christ embodies this unwavering hope — He is the beacon of salvation, the very embodiment of love, light, life, and every good thing.

Our hope is not just for the here and now but transcends our earthly existence. Jesus promises us eternal communion with Him, a hope that surpasses all understanding. The Holy Spirit, God's indelible mark upon our hearts, is a testament to this promise.

So, even when despair seems unending, cling to the hope that is in Jesus Christ. Remember His sacrificial love, His boundless grace. Today, let us lay down our burdens, fears, and sorrows at His feet. For He has promised, "Come to me, all who are weary and burdened, and I will give you rest."

Lord, we present our anxieties, struggles, and despairs to You. We trust in Your promise to make our burdens light. Fill our hearts with Your love, joy, and peace. May our lives reflect Your grace and bring a smile to Your face. In the mighty name of Jesus Christ, Amen.

JULY 11
What kind of spirit is within us?

Luke 9:50-56

In the book of Luke, we learn that Jesus Christ is on His journey to Jerusalem and chooses to pass through a Samaritan village. It's important to note that the Samaritans and Jews had a tense relationship, primarily because the Samaritans built their own temple and blended idolatry with Judaism.

I refer to an older translation for this passage, as the Amplified and Mojdeh translations omit key portions of verses 55 and 56. As the narrative goes, as Jesus' days of ascension drew near, He set His face resolutely towards Jerusalem. He sent His apostles ahead of Him. They entered the Samaritan territory to make preparations for His arrival. However, the people did not receive Him, simply because His destination was Jerusalem.

When His disciples James and John witnessed this rejection, they asked, "O Lord, do you want us to command fire to come down from heaven and consume them, just as Elias did?" This crucial detail is missing in some translations.

Jesus responded to them, "Do you not know what kind of spirit you are of?" For the Son of Man did not come to destroy lives but to save them. Instead of retaliating, He simply chose to journey to another village. While some translations only mention this departure, the emphasis on the disciples' spirit is vital.

This interaction offers a profound lesson for all Christians. Jesus asks us to reflect on the nature of the spirit within us. The Holy Spirit in us embodies love, forgiveness, kindness, and grace. We observe that Jesus not only refrains from harmful actions but also withholds rebuke.

Thus, we must internalize this lesson. When faced with opposition, our spirit should not retaliate with curses, harmful words, or negative actions. We shouldn't resort to speaking ill of them behind their backs either.

Our spirit, the one imparted to us by God, is that of love and grace. It's a spirit that seeks to save, not destroy. It's a spirit that embodies salvation, love, self-sacrifice, and grace.

May God grant us the wisdom and strength to resist the urge to retaliate or demean others. And when we're tested, may we draw strength from the Holy Spirit within us to pray for their well-being, salvation, and love.

Today, let us place our trust in God's benevolent hands with this earnest prayer.

In the name of Jesus Christ, the King of kings, Amen.

JULY 12
Do you give God's glory to someone else?

Luke 11:16-23

In the Gospels, we read about a profound incident where Jesus Christ casts out an evil spirit from a mute person, and immediately, the man begins to speak. However, as noted in verse 15, some skeptics argued that Jesus' power to expel these spirits stemmed from the devil himself, the chief of evil spirits. They even claimed He did so with the help of Beelzebub, the prince of demons.

In response, Jesus used a compelling analogy: any government divided against itself cannot stand. Similarly, if the devil was at odds with himself, he would fall. Christ then pronounced, "But if I drive out demons by the finger of God, then the kingdom of God has come upon you."

During a recent talk at my church, I emphasized the burdens we carry to Jesus. Everyone bears burdens, but for us Persian speakers, we also shoulder the legacies of both Persian and Islamic civilizations.

One significant burden I've observed in our community is superstition. I've encountered numerous Christians who, despite their faith, still cling to amulets like the "evil eye" stone, believing it protects them from harm. By relying on these symbols, we inadvertently credit them with the protective power and grace that rightfully belongs to the Holy Spirit. Such actions tread dangerously close to blaspheming against the Holy Spirit, a sin that the Bible warns is unforgivable.

When we attribute the blessings, protection, and favor in our lives to mere objects or superstitions, we're essentially sidelining Jesus Christ and His sacrifice. Therefore, I urge you to examine your surroundings. If there are items or beliefs in your life that detract from the glory of Christ, it's time for a spiritual cleanup.

Remember, the only path to God the Father is through Jesus Christ, the King of kings and Lord of Lords. There's no room for alternate saviors or mediators.

Let us pray together: "Heavenly Father, reveal to us any objects or beliefs that steal Your glory. Empower us to eliminate them from our lives so we can wholeheartedly elevate You. Guide us, Lord, and let Your Holy Spirit be our sole protector and guide.

In the precious name of Jesus Christ, we pray. Amen."

JULY 13
With what kind of eyes do you look at the world?

Luke 11:33

Jesus teaches an illuminating lesson: no one lights a lamp only to hide it or place it under a basket. Instead, they set it on a lampstand, allowing its light to brighten the room for all who enter. He parallels this with a profound insight: the eyes are the lamp of the body. If our eyes—our perspective—are clear and pure, our entire being is filled with light. Conversely, if our vision is clouded with negativity or prejudice, our whole essence is shrouded in darkness. He poses a question: if our internal light source is tainted with darkness, how profound will that darkness become?

In essence, our eyes are like a lens, shaping how we perceive the world around us. When this lens is untainted, it reflects and radiates the pure light it captures. We must introspect: Do we gaze upon the world with God's perspective of love and grace, or do our eyes betray malice and suspicion?

Jesus notes the skepticism of His generation, labeling them wicked for demanding a sign. And so, He prompts us to reflect on our perspective: How do we view Him? The world? Our neighbors? If we view with compassion and kindness, our inner light shines brighter. However, if our gaze harbors negativity and mistrust, we plunge deeper into the shadows.

So, we approach our Heavenly Father, praying: "Lord, dispel the shadows within us. Holy Spirit, illuminate our hearts and minds. Grant us eyes that see with clarity and purity, mirroring Your divine perspective. May the light within us stand as a beacon, guiding others towards Your eternal love. We pray this in the name of Jesus Christ, Amen."

JULY 14
Why worry when we can pray

Luke 12:22-27

Jesus imparted a vital lesson to his disciples: "Do not be anxious about your life—what you'll eat or wear. Life is far more than just sustenance, and the body more than attire." He pointed to the crows as an example. Despite not sowing or reaping, nor possessing storage spaces, they are cared for by God. If such birds are nurtured by the Divine, aren't we of far greater value?

He posed a thought-provoking question: "Can any of you, by worrying, add an hour to your life or increase your height?" If we're powerless over such minor aspects, why be consumed with anxiety about the rest? Jesus culminates his teaching with a call to prioritize: "Seek first the kingdom of God, and all your necessities will be met."

The message is not an admonishment against planning or considering our needs, but rather a warning against becoming ensnared in needless worry. Pondering on what to prepare for dinner is different from being consumed by anxiety about it. When worry becomes our default, it often indicates a lack of trust in God's provision.

A common saying encapsulates this sentiment: "Why worry when you can pray?" And what does it mean to seek God's kingdom? It is to continually pursue a relationship with Him, seeking His guidance in all things. This communion with God is realized through prayer.

So, rather than succumbing to worry about life's necessities, let's recognize the abundance around us. God doesn't instruct us to be passive, but to act without the paralyzing weight of anxiety. His encouragement is to prioritize seeking His guidance and presence.

Today, let's lay our worries at His feet, trusting in His promise of peace—a peace distinct from the fleeting solace the world offers. "Lord, we surrender our anxieties and concerns to you, seeking the enduring peace only you can provide.

In the name of Jesus Christ, Amen.

JULY 15
The Lord immediately answers our cries

Psalm 46:1-3

God is our refuge and strength. Scripture also describes God as our shelter and refuge. In times of difficulty, He is our helper, always ready to come to our aid. Therefore, we shall not fear.

Even if the earthquakes, causing mountains to plummet into the depths of the oceans, or if the seas churn in a fury, and mountains tremble, we remain steadfast. Despite such calamities, our faith remains unshaken because God is our refuge, our strength, and the rock upon which we stand.

When adversities arise, when tempests roar, when earthquakes shake the very ground beneath our feet or tsunamis threaten, our hearts remain calm. Why? Because God is our immediate helper in times of distress. He hears our cries and responds without delay.

God has assured us, "I did not give you a spirit of fear, but a spirit of adoption." We can, therefore, call Him 'Father' or even 'Dad'. This familial bond we share with God makes Him even closer to us. This relationship is made possible by the sacrificial work of Jesus Christ, His grace, His blood shed on the cross, and His triumphant resurrection on the third day. Through Him, we not only gain eternal life and entrance into the Kingdom of God but also become part of God's family.

The privilege of being called God's children is only attainable through the acceptance of Jesus Christ's sacrifice and resurrection. When we truly accept Jesus as our Lord, Savior, and Messiah, we're reminded that we've been given not a spirit of fear but one of adoption, enabling us to call upon God as 'Father'.

Imagine a child calling out to their father after a fall. Doesn't the father rush to the child's side upon hearing the cry for help? In the same way, God is our ever-present helper, always attentive to our calls.

In the face of trials and storms, our focus should remain on Jesus Christ and God, the Creator of all things. Recall the account when Jesus was asleep on a boat during a fierce storm. The disciples, in panic, awoke Him, saying, "Master, don't you see we are perishing?" Jesus arose and rebuked the storm, asking His disciples, "Why is your faith so small?" Such is the power of God who guides us through life's tumults. When we call on Him, He is ever ready to help.

The Lord Jesus promises, "I will never leave you nor forsake you." We are deeply grateful, Lord, for Your unwavering presence, for always standing by our side, and for Your timely help in our moments of need.

As we move forward, we commit this day into Your blessed hands. In the name of Jesus Christ, Amen.

JULY 16
Small but mighty able to transform all things

Luke 13:18-21

Jesus once said, *"What is the Kingdom of God like? To what shall I compare it?"* It's like a mustard seed that a person plants in his garden. Despite being one of the smallest seeds, it grows and becomes a tree, offering shelter to birds that nest in its branches.

He continued, "The Kingdom of God is also like leaven. A woman mixes a small amount with three cups of flour until the whole batch of dough rises." This tiny bit of leaven, seemingly insignificant, possesses the power to transform the entire batch of dough.

Similarly, the mustard seed, though minuscule, when sown in fertile soil, grows into a massive tree. Not only does it bear fruit for the gardener, but it also becomes a sanctuary for others, with birds finding refuge in its branches.

When God emphasizes something more than once, it's an indication of its profound importance. Both the mustard seed and leaven might appear inconsequential, but they carry immense power. A power that's transformative. They are small yet mighty, influencing and transforming everything they touch.

In the same way, the seed of the Kingdom of God, our faith in Jesus Christ—who died for us and rose again, now seated at the right hand of God—though it might start as a tiny seed in our hearts, has the potential to grow exponentially. When nurtured, this faith becomes a beacon for others, turning the mundane into the miraculous.

Father, we thank You for this mustard seed of faith. We're grateful for the transformative power of Your Kingdom and for Jesus Christ, who, through His sacrifice, has not only granted us entry into Your Kingdom but has also adopted us into Your family. No longer are we mere servants, but we're Your children, co-heirs with Christ.

Lord, as we commit this day into Your hands, may the seed of faith within us grow, providing shelter and refuge for many. In Jesus' name, we pray, Amen.

JULY 17

The price of Christ discipleship

Luke 14:26

Jesus once said to the crowd around Him, "If anyone comes to me and does not prioritize me above his father, mother, wife, children, brothers, sisters, and even his own life, he cannot be my disciple. Whoever does not bear his own cross and follow me cannot be my disciple. For who, wanting to build a tower, doesn't first sit down and calculate the cost to see if he has enough to complete it?" And concluding in verse 33, He says that unless you're willing to surrender all, you cannot be my disciple.

What then is the cost of discipleship with the Lord Jesus Christ? Some translations may use the term "hate" in reference to family, but the essence of the message is about love prioritization.

The pivotal question is: how can one prioritize Jesus above all else?

The first commandment instructs us to "love the Lord your God with all your heart, soul, strength, and mind." When we truly love someone with every fiber of our being, everything else becomes secondary. Such love means Jesus becomes our foremost priority – our Alpha and Omega, the beginning and the end. Nothing else, not even our closest kin or worldly treasures, can rival His place in our lives.

Reflect on this: Do we reciprocate the love Jesus showed us? His love surpasses that of parents, siblings, and the world. He, the King of kings, sacrificed Himself on the cross for us. He asserts that if we're not prepared to place everything secondary to Him, we can't be His disciples. This level of dedication is only achievable when our love for Jesus overshadows all else.

So, we must introspect: Do we love Jesus more than our familial ties and worldly possessions? If the answer is affirmative, we are on the path to becoming His devoted disciple. Otherwise, we must re-evaluate our commitment before taking further steps.

In Revelation, Jesus declares that we should either be fervent in our faith or entirely cold, for a lukewarm stance is distasteful to Him.

Lord, today we implore You: fan the flames of our devotion. May our love for Jesus, the Holy Spirit, and You, Father, surpass all else. Help us to be exemplary disciples of Christ. We entrust this day to Your divine care. In the name of Jesus Christ, the King of kings, Amen.

JULY 18
The lost sheep, coin and son

Luke 15

Luke 15 conveys the profound message of God's boundless love for the lost through parables of the lost sheep, the lost coin, and the prodigal son.

The Pharisees and scholars criticized Jesus for associating with sinners, tax collectors, and prostitutes. In response, Jesus shared these parables. He asked, if someone had a hundred sheep and lost one, wouldn't he leave the ninety-nine to find the missing one? When found, he'd rejoice and celebrate with friends. Similarly, there's greater joy in heaven for one sinner who repents than for ninety-nine righteous who don't need to.

The story of a woman who, despite having ten silver coins, searches diligently for one she lost emphasizes the same. When she finds it, she rejoices with her neighbors. This reflects the joy among the angels when one sinner repents.

The prodigal son's tale epitomizes God's grace. A son squanders his inheritance but, upon realization, returns to his father. The father, representing God, celebrates his return, symbolizing God's unfailing love and forgiveness.

From the Gospel of John, we learn that a crucial role of the Holy Spirit and Jesus is to redeem sinners. When a sinner acknowledges Jesus as the Savior who shed His blood for our purification and proclaims His resurrection, heaven rejoices.

In many churches, when someone accepts Jesus, the congregation echoes the heavenly celebration by singing praises. This act mirrors the celestial joy and underscores our role: to share the Gospel, the good news of Christ's redemptive work.

In essence, God's love is such that He seeks out each lost soul. It is He who calls, redeems, and rejoices. We, in turn, are called to share this news, leading others towards eternal life.

Thank you, Lord, for Your relentless love and grace that saves us. May we faithfully share Your good news with others. In Jesus Christ's name, Amen. Blessings to all.

JULY 19

Faithful in small things

Luke 16:9-14

In a parable, a landlord hears of his accountant's wrongdoing and dismisses him. But before leaving, the accountant shrewdly reduces the debts of his master's debtors to win their favor. The landlord acknowledges the man's cleverness.

Jesus then instructs us: Use worldly wealth to gain friends so that when it's gone, you'll be welcomed into eternal dwellings. Faithfulness in little things leads to faithfulness in much, and dishonesty in small things predicts dishonesty in greater things. If you can't be trusted with worldly wealth, who'll trust you with true riches? If you're unfaithful with someone else's property, who'll give you your own?

He emphasizes, "No servant can serve two masters." One cannot serve both God and money.

The parable warns against making money our god, for when we do, it competes with our devotion to the Divine. It isn't money itself that's evil but our attitude towards it. When we prioritize God, using our resources for His Kingdom, we inherit true riches – eternal life.

Jesus then narrates about Lazarus (Eliezer) and a rich man. While the rich man lived lavishly, Lazarus languished in poverty at his doorstep. In death, their fortunes reverse: Lazarus finds comfort, and the rich man faces torment. The rich man's wealth, which he failed to share, became his downfall.

Let's pray:

Thank you, Father. Guide us to prioritize You above all. May our lives reflect our devotion to Jesus Christ, using all you've blessed us with for Your Kingdom. Every gift, protection, and blessing come from You. May we steward them for Your glory and for the benefit of others. In Jesus' name, Amen.

JULY 20
The real gift

Psalm 50:7-16

God speaks to His chosen people in the scriptures, declaring, "Hear me, O Israel, for I am your God. I won't chastise you for your offerings, as they are consistently presented before me. But do you think I require your bulls or goats? Remember, every creature on the earth and in the sky is already mine. If I were to hunger, would I look to you for sustenance? Would I feast on the meat of bulls or savor the blood of goats?"

The deeper message here is that God doesn't just desire our physical offerings; He yearns for our heart's genuine gratitude. As Psalm 50 elucidates, everything in this world belongs to God. So, when we bring our gifts to the altar in church, it's essential to grasp that it's not the material value that matters. Instead, our offerings should echo a sentiment: "Thank you, Lord, for the blessings you've showered upon me. Here's a token of my profound gratitude."

What God treasures above all is our authentic praise. He seeks individuals who worship Him wholeheartedly and in truth. Every gift we present should emanate from a heart bursting with gratitude, not from a sense of mere duty. As we offer with genuine appreciation, God assures us, "In your moments of despair, cry out to me, and I shall be your refuge, ensuring you have reasons to glorify me."

Let's bow our heads in prayer:

Father, in the precious name of Jesus Christ, we extend our deepest gratitude. We are eternally thankful for guiding us from life's shadows into your illuminating light and for the redemption we find in Christ. We recognize and value the daily provisions you lay before us. In moments of turbulence, we are confident that you stand as our protector. Lord may our offerings always be a reflection of our genuine thanks. May our lives continually exemplify your endless grace and love. In the unmatched name of Jesus Christ, we pray. Amen.

May your day be filled with divine blessings.

JULY 21
Repenting heart

Psalm 51

Psalm 51 captures the deep remorse of King David, penned after the prophet Nathan confronts him about his transgressions with Bathsheba. Recall how David, instead of leading his army, witnesses a captivating woman, Bathsheba, from his rooftop. Despite learning she's the wife of one of his valiant soldiers, Uriah, David yields to temptation, an act that spirals into deception and ends in Uriah's orchestrated death. Following Uriah's demise and Bathsheba's period of mourning, David takes her as his wife.

Nathan's revelation of God's displeasure propels David into a profound state of repentance. Rather than justifying his kingly stature, David humbles himself, recognizing the gravity of his sins not just against Bathsheba and Uriah but, fundamentally, against God. He abused the divine power and authority vested in him, taking away Uriah's most cherished possession and life.

In his heartfelt plea, David implores, "Create in me a pure heart, O God, and renew a steadfast spirit within me. Do not cast me from your presence or take your Holy Spirit from me." This poignant moment underscores David's unwavering pursuit of God. It prompts us to introspect: Do our hearts yearn for God as David's did? When confronted with our wrongs, do we promptly repent, seeking God's grace and mercy? It is paramount to acknowledge our sins and recognize that, in essence, we've sinned against God.

Our journey of faith will have moments of falter, but the key lies in swift repentance. We must echo David's plea, seeking purification and the continued presence of the Holy Spirit in our lives. God, in His boundless mercy, awaits our return, arms wide open.

Let us pray:

Heavenly Father, we're eternally grateful for Your unfailing love and open arms. Instill in us a heart quick to repent and turn back to You. Should temptation encroach upon us, illuminate our path, Lord, showing us the way out, ensuring we don't translate sinful thoughts into actions. We commit this day, and every day, into Your gracious hands, always counting on Your abundant mercy.

In the name of Jesus Christ, Amen.

JULY 22
Today salvation has come to this house

Luke 19:1-11

In the town of Jericho, Jesus Christ encountered Zacchaeus, a chief tax collector renowned for his immense wealth. Despite his prominence, Zacchaeus, being of short stature, couldn't see Jesus due to the crowd. Demonstrating his earnest desire to see the Savior, he humbly climbed a sycamore tree.

As Jesus approached, He looked up and said, "Zacchaeus, come down quickly, for I must stay at your home today." This divine acknowledgment led to murmurs among the onlookers, who were displeased to see Jesus associating with someone they deemed a sinner.

Zacchaeus, standing tall amidst the judgments, declared his intent to give half of his wealth to the poor and to repay fourfold anyone he had cheated. Jesus, recognizing Zacchaeus's genuine repentance, proclaimed, "Today salvation has come to this house, because this man, too, is a son of Abraham. For the Son of Man came to seek and to save the lost."

This account underscores Zacchaeus's profound transformation. His actions resonate with a profound message: true devotion to Christ transcends status, wealth, and societal judgments. Zacchaeus's willingness to part with his wealth was not the cause of his salvation but an outward sign of his internal change of heart.

More than a narrative of redemption, this tale illustrates the relentless pursuit of Jesus to save the lost. Unlike other religions where followers seek divine favor, in Christianity, it is Christ who seeks and saves. He identifies the lost, calls them by name, and lovingly brings them back into the fold.

Reflecting on our journeys, we realize it's not us who found Jesus, but rather He who found us. Each of us is a testament to His unyielding love and grace.

Let's pray:

Heavenly Father, we're immensely grateful for Your Son, Jesus Christ, who relentlessly seeks and saves the lost. Thank you for the sacrifice on the cross and the redeeming blood that washes away our sins. Through Your resurrection, we are justified. May Your Holy Spirit, dwelling within us, guide our steps and open our eyes to Your divine work. Empower us to partner with You and not obstruct Your divine mission. In the name of Jesus Christ, Amen.

JULY 23

What is our motive for questioning God?

Luke 20:1-19

In the temple, as Jesus Christ taught, priests and Jewish scholars questioned Him, asking, "By what authority do you perform these acts?" Just the previous day, Jesus had driven traders from the temple, declaring, "This must be a house of prayer, but you have turned it into a den of thieves." Recognizing their hidden motives, Jesus posed a question of His own: "Was the baptism of John the Baptist of divine or human origin?" They deliberated among themselves, fearing the repercussions of their response, eventually admitting, "We don't know." Jesus replied, "Then I won't reveal by what authority I do these things."

However, Jesus immediately presents the parable of the vineyard and its tenants. In the story, a landowner establishes a vineyard, entrusts it to tenants, and departs. When he sends servants to collect his share of the produce, the tenants mistreat and reject them. Eventually, the landowner dispatches his son, thinking he would be respected. Yet, the tenants, seeking to seize his inheritance, murder the son outside the vineyard. Jesus then poses another question, "What will the landowner do?" His implication was clear: He is the Son, and they are the ones who will reject and kill Him.

In life, when we pose questions to God, we must introspect. Are our inquiries genuine, seeking His guidance? Or are they driven by hidden agendas, aiming to challenge Him? Often, Jesus answers our questions with questions of His own, urging us to confront the truths within our hearts.

Lord, as we seek answers, let our questions spring from genuine hearts, desiring to understand Your will. When You respond, grant us the discernment to comprehend and the fortitude to act. Let us not selfishly seek answers we desire, but let Your responses guide our path. Entrusting this day into Your benevolent hands, may we always exalt Your name, recognizing Your sovereignty over all.

In Jesus Christ's name, Amen.

JULY 24

Did God's signs and miracles stop with the death of apostles?

Matthew 17:20

"If you have faith as small as a mustard seed, you can say to this mountain, 'Move from here to there,' and it will move. Nothing will be impossible for you."

There are some Christians who hold the belief that all divine signs and miracles ceased with the demise of the apostles. They argue that the Bible did not exist before this, and afterward, it stands as the sole holy guidebook. However, this viewpoint is not supported by the Word of God itself. The Scriptures continuously affirm that with faith, all things are possible. So, what exactly is faith? Our faith is deeply rooted in God's grace, a grace exemplified by the sacrificial act of the Lord Jesus Christ, who shed His blood on the cross for our redemption. Accepting this profound truth instills faith within us.

By embracing Jesus Christ as our Savior, acknowledging His sacrifice on the cross for our sake, and recognizing His resurrection that paved our way to the Kingdom of God, we are reborn as children of God. This is the essence of our faith: our unyielding belief that Jesus Christ is our only path to the Father, our Savior, and the embodiment of Truth.

Comprehending this foundational belief enables us to perform wonders through faith and grace. Each one of us, regardless of our cultural or personal backgrounds, was led to Jesus Christ through various signs, visions, dreams, and miracles. It wasn't our pursuit of Him, but His pursuit of us. Much like the parable of the lost sheep, He seeks us out, and when He finds us and we respond to His call, He dwells within us.

The miraculous works of God didn't conclude with the apostles. Jesus Himself proclaimed that His followers would perform even greater wonders than He had. And history attests to this. Throughout the ages, Christians have been vessels of God's miraculous signs and wonders.

Interestingly, as persecutions intensify, God's grace and His miraculous interventions also multiply. Every believer in Jesus Christ becomes a testament to His power and might. Just recently, I witnessed yet another of His miracles. Faced with a seemingly insurmountable challenge, where all avenues seemed closed, we turned to God, knowing that no circumstance could bind His hands. To our astonishment, a breakthrough came the very next morning – an event so unlikely on a public holiday, a day of quarantine. But with God, all things are possible.

God assures us that when we ask in His name, our petitions are granted. When we seek Him, we find Him, and when we call upon His name, doors open. His wonders and signs will perpetually manifest in the lives of believers.

We offer our profound gratitude to God, the living deity who anticipates our prayers and acts in alignment with His divine will. Lord, we're eternally grateful for Your attentive ear and Your unwavering presence. We beseech You to constantly remind us to seek You in all circumstances, knowing You desire only the best for Your children. May we always remain under Your protective embrace.

In the precious name of Jesus Christ, Amen.

JULY 25
When you're called to court use it to testify to Christ

Luke 21, and especially Luke 21:12-16

In the Scriptures, the disciples seek to understand the end times, but a particular segment stands out, emphasizing, "You will be brought before kings and rulers for my name's sake. But this will turn out for you as an occasion for testimony." We're reminded that preparation isn't necessary because God grants the wisdom and eloquence that none can refute. Amen?

I've often reminded our church members: When you face trials, in whose name do you seek refuge as a Christian? By whose name are you granted asylum or residency? It's in the revered name of Jesus Christ.

Indeed, many followers of Christ may find themselves in court because of their Christian faith. Some might leverage this very faith to secure residency in nations like Canada or European countries. And all this happens in whose name? In the magnificent name of Jesus Christ.

Christ forewarned us that, owing to His name, we would stand before authorities and rulers. But He advises us not to view these moments with dread but as divine opportunities to bear witness to His glory. These moments become platforms to testify about the Truth. And who is this Truth? It is Jesus Christ, the King of kings, the divine Son, who came for our redemption, died on the cross, resurrected on the third day, and ushered us into the Kingdom of God. He is both our eternal Father and God.

Moreover, He assures us that we don't need rehearsed answers because He bestows upon us the eloquence and discernment which no one can contest, a gift from the Holy Spirit. When we wholeheartedly embrace Jesus Christ, and when we steep ourselves in the Word of God, the Holy Spirit empowers our speech. This divine wisdom is undeniable and irrefutable.

Therefore, when we're questioned by any authority, be it judges or kings, we should perceive it as an opportunity to share the transformative power of God's love and His mighty deeds in our lives. He assures us He will provide the wisdom they cannot refute.

It's vital to remember that these judges are discerning, having encountered numerous cases. They can see through pretense. But always hold onto the truth of the name by which you're shielded everywhere: the name of Jesus Christ. Even in legal settings or other challenging situations, it's by His name we find salvation. Amen? Amen.

Lord, we're immensely grateful for Your exalted name that reigns above all. Thank you for teaching us not to be paralyzed by fear or anxiety.

Instead, you've shown us to use these moments to testify about Your love and the salvation You've granted. Instill in us the bravery to elevate Your name in every situation. In the powerful name of Jesus Christ, Amen.

JULY 26

A small piece of bread with love is better than kingly dinner

Proverbs 15:16-17

Scripture teaches us the value of contentment and reverence. It suggests that it's far better to possess little, if that little is coupled with respect and fear of God, than to have vast treasures accompanied by troubles and anxiety. It tells us that a modest meal, enjoyed in an atmosphere of love and affection, is preferable to a grand feast tainted with enmity.

When we speak of fearing God, it's not about trembling in terror but a reverent awe of God's magnificent character—a concept we've delved into previously. This fear is the beginning of wisdom. It's not an apprehension that God might punish us arbitrarily; rather, it's a profound respect stemming from deep love. It's about revering a God who, despite holding the power over heavens and the earth, cherishes us so dearly that He didn't even spare His own Son for our sake.

Such reverence translates to a fear of disappointing Him, not a dread of retribution. It's an aversion born out of sheer love, a desire not to hurt Him in any way.

True wealth lies not in material abundance but in having even a modest share suffused with God's love and reverence. A simple meal shared in love is more nourishing than a banquet marred by hatred. An old adage goes, "Your demeanor has soured my meal." It underscores that the environment in which we partake is as important as the food itself.

In spaces filled with love, respect, and godly fear, even scant resources flourish, while vast riches seem trivial without these virtues. Today, let us progress with hearts full of love, reverence, and gratitude. Let's utter a heartfelt thanks to our Heavenly Father.

Thank you, Lord Jesus, for being our all. For demonstrating Your boundless love by sacrificing Yourself on the cross. You epitomize love and affection. With You, even our humble means are magnified, while immense treasures without You hold no value.

Let us always bear this truth in our hearts.

We commit today into Your blessed hands, O God. Grant us contentment in what we have. Let us continually express gratitude for every small blessing You bestow upon us and for Your constant presence. We pray that today, and always, we live enveloped in Your love, reverence, and awe. In the precious name of Jesus Christ, Amen.

JULY 27
Servant leadership

Luke 22:24-25

After the Last Supper, as Jesus and His disciples walked, a dispute arose among them: who among them was the greatest? In response, Jesus shared profound wisdom. In this world, rulers and leaders exert authority over their subjects, who obey without question. But in the Kingdom of Heaven, true greatness is defined by one's willingness to serve others.

In worldly settings, the master sits while servants attend to him. But Jesus said, "I am among you as one who serves." He showcased the very essence of servant leadership—a leadership model grounded in love, sacrifice, and humility.

Entrance into God's Kingdom hinges on love and devotion. It starts with Jesus' unmatched love—He left His heavenly abode, became flesh, endured a brutal crucifixion for our sins, and conquered death itself.

Jesus said, "Greater love has no one than this, to lay down one's life for one's friends." This encapsulates the ethos of servant leadership. In God's Kingdom, paradoxically, the first becomes the last and the last, the first.

To be exalted in God's sight, we must humble ourselves, placing others' needs above our own. The mark of genuine love is the desire to serve, uplift, and assist those around us. Therefore, in God's realm, the most revered leader is the one who serves most selflessly.

Father, we thank You for revealing the mysteries of Your Kingdom. Knowledge without application is futile, and if we fail to live these truths, our accountability increases. Lord, grant us the grace to serve others daily, to love unconditionally, and to manifest Christ-like love and humility in all we do.

May we strive, every day, to be pleasing in Your eyes so that at life's end, we might hear You say, "Well done." We entrust this day and all our days into Your loving hands.

In the name of Jesus Christ, Amen.

JULY 28
Do we deny Jesus?

Luke 22:56-63

This is the location where Jesus Christ was arrested, and Peter followed Him from a distance. Verse 56 describes a scenario where a maid noticed Peter as he sat in the glow of the fire. She intently looked at him and claimed, "This man was with Jesus."

Peter refuted this, asserting, "Woman, I do not know Him." Shortly thereafter, another bystander recognized him, suggesting that Peter was one of Jesus' followers. Yet, Peter reiterated, "Man, I am not." As time passed, a third person, with greater conviction, declared that Peter was indeed with Jesus, especially given his Galilean origins.

Peter responded, "Man, I don't know what you're talking about." And while he spoke, a rooster crowed. The Lord Jesus Christ turned and fixed His gaze on Peter. In that moment, Peter recalled Jesus' prophecy: "Before the rooster crows today, you will deny me three times." Overwhelmed with guilt, Peter left the scene in tears.

This very Peter, just hours before—perhaps 8 or 10, had, during supper, assured Jesus, "I will never deny You. I will die with You, even go to prison, but will never deny You." Yet Jesus had prophetically responded, "Peter, before the rooster crows today, you will deny me three times."

Intriguingly, it wasn't soldiers or religious leaders who cornered Peter. It was merely a maid and a few bystanders. Fearful of sharing Jesus' fate, Peter, usually so steadfast, denied His Lord.

For those of us who have embraced Jesus Christ as our Lord and Savior, we're called to unwavering honesty. God mandates that we always speak the truth, irrespective of circumstances. This explains why, in Christianity, even "white lies" find no refuge.

Peter's denial stemmed from his lack of trust in God's protective power. When we lie, we essentially demonstrate a lack of faith in God's omnipotence. In trying to evade trouble through deceit, we indirectly convey our skepticism of His providence.

Yet, God reassures us: "Always place your trust in Me. Even in the bleakest moments, I will rescue you." He ensures that even dire situations can culminate in blessings for those who love Him and are chosen by Him.

Jesus Himself instructed us to be straightforward: Let our affirmation be genuine and our negations, sincere. He warned, "If anyone denies Me before men, I will also deny him before My Father in heaven."

We thank You, Father, for Your boundless love, for Your unwavering truth, and for teaching us the virtues of honesty and integrity. Help us to stand strong in our convictions, recognize Your reigning power, and witness how You can transform every adversity into a blessing for Your glory. Lord, strengthen our resolve to be truthful today and always.

In the name of Jesus Christ, Amen.

JULY 29

Obedience is better than sacrifice

1 Samuel 15:20-25

> [20] *And Saul said to Samuel, "But I have obeyed the voice of the LORD, and gone on the mission on which the LORD sent me, and brought back Agag king of Amalek; I have utterly destroyed the Amalekites.*
> [21] *But the people took of the plunder, sheep and oxen, the best of the things which should have been utterly destroyed, to sacrifice to the LORD your God in Gilgal."*
> [22] *So Samuel said: "Has the LORD as great delight in burnt offerings and sacrifices, As in obeying the voice of the LORD? Behold, to obey is better than sacrifice, And to heed than the fat of rams.*
> [23] *For rebellion is as the sin of witchcraft, And stubbornness is as iniquity and idolatry. Because you have rejected the word of the LORD, He also has rejected you from being king."*
> [24] *Then Saul said to Samuel, "I have sinned, for I have transgressed the commandment of the LORD and your words, because I feared the people and obeyed their voice.*
> [25] *Now therefore, please pardon my sin, and return with me, that I may worship the LORD."*

The story of Saul's war with the Amalekites presents a lesson in obedience. God instructed Saul to obliterate everything: the Amalekites, their livestock, and all their possessions. Yet Saul, after the battle, spared King Agag, the finest sheep and cattle, and even kept some valuable treasures.

Samuel confronted Saul, questioning his disobedience to God's command. In verse 20, Saul defended himself, "I did obey the LORD's command. I went on the mission the LORD assigned me. I completely destroyed the Amalekites and brought back Agag their king. The soldiers took sheep and cattle from the plunder, the best of what was devoted to God, in order to sacrifice them to the LORD at Gilgal."

Here, Saul's partial obedience is evident. Not only did he refrain from killing King Agag and sparing some livestock and treasures, but he also displayed no remorse. Unlike David, who promptly repented upon realizing his sin, Saul remained unyielding, placing the blame on his soldiers.

Although Saul might've executed a majority of God's instruction, his incomplete obedience didn't reflect the actions of a king truly devoted to God. Samuel, articulating God's sentiments, posed a poignant question: Does the LORD delight in burnt offerings and sacrifices as much as in obeying the LORD? Obedience, as Samuel pointed out, is more esteemed than sacrifices. He equated disobedience to grave sins like witchcraft and idolatry. Due to Saul's defiance, God decided to strip him of his kingship.

Obedience surpasses superficial sacrifices. God doesn't merely desire our offerings; He seeks a heart that is undividedly devoted to Him. A heart that trusts Him, knowing His intentions are always for our welfare. Saul's incomplete obedience cost him his kingdom. If only he had wholly obeyed God, he would've enjoyed God's favor indefinitely. Yet, God found another, one whose heart was wholly committed to Him.

In reflection, let us offer our prayer: "Dear Father, grant us the strength and wisdom to follow Your commands entirely, not out of obligation but out of genuine love and trust. Even when we can't comprehend Your ways, empower us to obey with our whole being. Let us always remember that You, in all Your magnificence, orchestrate everything for our benefit. We place this day, and all our days, in Your nurturing hands.

In the name of Jesus Christ, Amen."

JULY 30
Satan the father of liars

John 8:44

> *You are of your father the devil, and the desires of your father you want to do. He was a murderer from the beginning, and does not stand in the truth, because there is no truth in him. When he speaks a lie, he speaks from his own resources, for he is a liar and the father of it.*

In the Scriptures, Jesus addresses the malicious nature of the devil. He describes him as "a murderer from the beginning, having no truth within him. When he lies, it is consistent with his character; for he is a liar and the father of lies."

During my time in prayer today, God granted me a revelation that ties into this profound truth. The root of everything that opposes God in our lives stems from this spirit of deceit. The inception of lies traces back to the Garden of Eden when Satan deceived Eve, saying, "You will not certainly die... for when you eat from it, you will be like God," which was a falsehood.

Every lie begins subtly, luring us with its façade. "Go ahead and sin. After all, God is forgiving," the enemy whispers. While God is indeed merciful and forgiving, it doesn't mean we should take His grace for granted by intentionally sinning or lying.

The mastermind behind all deception is Satan, the father of lies. He plants seeds of doubt in our minds: "You're still the same sinner. How can the blood of Jesus cleanse you? Such beliefs are ludicrous."

He fuels our anxieties with lies, making us question God's promises. "Why trust in prayer when you can worry about the outcome?"

Our call is to combat these falsehoods. How? By wielding the truth found in the Word of God. Ephesians describes it as a double-edged sword. Remember how Jesus responded to Satan's temptations with Scripture, proving that despite being tempted, He did not succumb to sin.

It's time for introspection. Let's discern the lies we've unknowingly entertained. Let our prayer today be: "Heavenly Father, in the mighty name of Jesus, the King of kings, we approach Your throne. Holy Spirit, we ask that You purge us of the spirit of lies and any misconceived beliefs. Illuminate our hearts with Your truth, dispelling every shade of deceit. We thank You and praise You.

In the precious name of Jesus Christ, Amen."

JULY 31
Marriage in Christianity is a covenant

Matthew 19:3-12

In a compelling passage, the Pharisees confront Jesus with a question about divorce: "Is it permissible for a man to divorce his wife for just any reason?"

Jesus' response hearkens back to the very foundation of creation: "Haven't you read that at the beginning, God 'made them male and female,' and decreed that a man will leave his parents to unite with his wife, and the two will become one flesh? They're no longer two separate entities but one united being. Thus, what God has yoked together, let no man separate." The Pharisees then counter with, "Why then did Moses sanction divorce?" Jesus elucidates that while Moses permitted it due to their hardened hearts, His own decree is more stringent: anyone who divorces, except on the grounds of infidelity, and marries another, is committing adultery.

This year, I celebrate the 30th anniversary of my union with Insook. Three decades ago, we vowed to be life partners. Many wonders about the secret to our lasting bond. It's rooted in understanding that, within Christianity, marriage is a sacred covenant. It signifies that my spouse becomes the sole focus of my romantic affection. Regardless of life's ups and downs, we remain together. On our wedding day, we pledged to each other and before God, promising to cherish and uphold our bond "till death do us part." It's not conditional on fluctuating emotions but a lifelong commitment.

In Christianity, the sanctity of marriage, both in its commitment and physical intimacy, is reserved solely for a husband and wife. As Jesus highlighted, "they are no longer two but one." Our faith upholds the sanctity of the marital bed, emphasizing purity and fidelity.

In our marriage, God is the central pillar. As we both grow closer to Him, we inevitably grow closer to each other. That's the foundational secret to a successful Christian marriage. I'll delve deeper into these insights in future discussions. May God's grace envelop each one of you.

Gracious Father, thank You for the gift of marriage and the wisdom You impart. We pray for all couples to honor their marital vows and for those yet to marry to comprehend the depth of this commitment in Christianity. Lord, we entrust this day and our futures into Your loving hands. Amen.

AUGUST 1

Husbands love your wives as Christ loved the church

Ephesians 5:25

> *Husbands, love your wives, just as Christ also loved the church and gave Himself for her.*

The scripture speaks clearly to husbands: "Love your wives as Christ loved the church and gave Himself up for her." Christ exemplified this love by purifying the church through His sacrifice, washing it with water through the Word, making it spotless and free of blemish. He presents it in all its glory, without any flaw, to Himself.

Men, therefore, should love their wives with the same depth of feeling they naturally hold for their own bodies. He who loves his wife truly loves himself. After all, no one ever despised his own body but looks after it with care, mirroring how Christ nurtures the church.

Drawing from my own three-decade-long marriage journey, I've come to understand that pride has no room in this sacred bond. And why do I say this? If I'm called to cherish my wife with the same profound love Christ demonstrated for the church, even to the point of laying down His life, then what could be of greater significance than that? Certainly not pride. It is pride that sows discord, leading one to believe they're right while their spouse is in the wrong.

Men, our calling is to love our wives with the depth and selflessness that Christ showed. What follows is an essential practice: immersing our marriages in prayer and the Word. This divine triangle – God at the pinnacle, husband and wife at its base – becomes closer knit as both spouses draw nearer to God.

Let's make it a habit: couples should start and end their day with joint prayer. Such unity in seeking God's face can only cleanse and uplift the marital bond. Men, while praying with your wife is crucial, praying for her is equally vital. One of my daily petitions goes, "Lord, please shower Insook with joy, wisdom, discernment, peace, and employ her in the service of Your Kingdom."

If ever there's friction or disagreement with our wives, let's approach them openly, earnestly seeking their perspective. Yet, even before that, take these grievances to God. Ask Him, "Lord, is this pride leading me astray or is this a genuine prompting from Your Spirit? Enlighten me."

Before voicing out concerns which might cause strife, commit them to God. Let Him, who's also the Lord of our spouses, intervene and provide clarity.

From today, let's be proactive in lifting our wives in prayer. In forthcoming sessions, we'll also discuss the role of women in this sacred equation. May God bless each one of you. Amen.

AUGUST 2
Wives honor your husbands

Ephesians 5:21-25

> [21] *submitting to one another in the fear of God. Marriage—Christ and the Church*
> [22] *Wives, submit to your own husbands, as to the Lord.*
> [23] *For the husband is head of the wife, as also Christ is head of the church; and He is the Savior of the body.*
> [24] *Therefore, just as the church is subject to Christ, so let the wives be to their own husbands in everything.*
> [25] *Husbands, love your wives, just as Christ also loved the church and gave Himself for her.*

Yesterday, we explored verses emphasizing the role and responsibility of husbands. Today, let's delve into understanding women's roles in the marital bond.

Scripture urges mutual submission due to our reverence for Christ. Wives, you are encouraged to submit to your husbands as unto the Lord. Just as Christ is the head of the church - His body, and its Savior, so too are husbands the head of their wives. The church submits to Christ, and in a similar vein, wives should submit to their husbands in everything.

Upon reading this, some might perceive it as perpetuating a patriarchal stance. But let's delve deeper. Why do we revere Christ? Why is He our head? It's His unparalleled love and the sacrifice of His life that draws our obedience and submission. In the same light, husbands are exhorted to love their wives as they do their own bodies, mirroring Christ's love for the church.

If a husband genuinely embodies this Christ-like love, sacrificially placing his wife before himself, then the instruction for wives to respect and submit to their husbands becomes more about mutual love and understanding than mere patriarchy. In verse 33, it clearly mentions that while husbands should love their wives, the wives should respect their husbands. The relationship between Abraham and Sarah in Genesis serves as an exemplar. Sarah revered Abraham as her "Lord," while Abraham viewed Sarah with deep respect, referring to her as a distinguished lady.

Love and respect are two sides of the same coin. If wives disregard this mutual love and respect, can they genuinely expect their husbands to reciprocate in kind?

Christianity emphasizes the union of one man and one woman. This marital covenant represents the spiritual oneness between Christ and the church. In the same way, a husband and wife become a singular entity, reflecting the unity of Christ with His believers.

In conclusion, let's pray: Father, we thank You for illuminating this truth. May it guide our daily lives and fortify Christian marriages. Let couples unite in love and respect, weathering all seasons together, for they are unified with You, as You are with them.

In the name of Jesus Christ, Amen.

AUGUST 3

Husbands don't be harsh towards your wives

Today we want to continue our discussion about marriage in Christianity, first we talked about husbands. Husbands love your wives the way Jesus Christ loved the church. Yesterday we talked about women, That the word of God in Ephesians tells women to respect your husbands and be respectable to them, now how do we respect them?

Colossians 3:19

Husbands, love your wives and do not be bitter toward them.

Scripture implores husbands to love their wives and refrain from treating them harshly. One of the hallmarks of a Christian is the mastery over one's own temper and bitterness. A salient fruit of the Holy Spirit is meekness, symbolizing the strength to regulate our anger.

Recall Jesus' words, as mentioned in Matthew, about the divine design of man and woman. God fashioned them to come together in matrimony, where a man leaves his parents to unite with his wife, and they become one flesh. If we perceive our spouses through the lens of this divine unity, seeing them with the same love and reverence as we do Jesus, it's evident that love is reciprocal. Recognizing our shared oneness with Christ, it becomes second nature to treat each other with gentleness.

By actively listening and seeking to understand the motives behind each other's actions, we cultivate compassion and unity. Central to a Christian marriage is the foundational love that binds two individuals as one. Consequently, if we act harshly towards our spouse, we're essentially doing the same to ourselves. Such behavior indicates a lack of the Holy Spirit's fruit in our lives.

While we are all encouraged to love one another as Christ loves the church, husbands bear a special mandate. They are likened to the head of the family, called to love their wives and lay down their lives for them, mirroring Christ's love for His church. Embracing gentleness and casting aside severity is paramount.

Approaching each situation in love, acting with compassion, and quelling our anger when provoked are essential Christian virtues.

At the heart of this is humility - the cornerstone of marital success and unity in Christian teachings. Do we seek humility in prayer? Do we intercede for our spouses?

One of the most pivotal aspects of a Christian marriage is not just the collective prayers we offer each morning and night but also the individual prayers we say for each other. From this day forward, may we be diligent in praying for our spouses, offering heartfelt petitions, and shedding any traces of resentment or skepticism towards them. Amen.

AUGUST 4
The pure and holy sexual relationships

Today I want to talk about single people in addition to married people.

Hebrews 13:4

> *Marriage is honorable among all, and the bed undefiled; but fornicators and adulterers God will judge.*

Scripture is unambiguous: we must honor and uphold the sanctity of marriage. It explicitly states that everyone should respect the marriage bed, ensuring its sanctity is untouched by impurity. Those who defy this, committing adultery whether within or outside marriage, will not escape God's judgment.

The call for purity and holiness is clear in the Bible. Jesus Himself proclaimed that even casting a lustful glance at another amounts to adultery in the heart. While the commandment says "Do not commit adultery," Jesus magnifies its gravity, emphasizing that even a lustful gaze is adulterous in nature.

In Christianity, the paradigm of marriage consists of one man and one woman. The marital bond is not only pure but also holy. We are not called to be promiscuous or to engage in sexual relationships outside of this sacred bond. A prevalent question among the youth today is: Is it permissible for a boyfriend and girlfriend to cohabit and engage in sexual relations prior to marriage? The answer, according to Christian doctrine, is a resounding no. Sex is reserved for the confines of matrimony. We are beckoned to maintain our purity, preserving our virginity until that commitment. For those who may have faltered before embracing Christianity, the redemption and forgiveness offered by Jesus Christ call you now to a life of purity and sanctity.

Should you find that special someone, discern through prayer that they are the one God intends for your life journey, it is then appropriate to solemnize that relationship through marriage. Sex is strictly reserved for this committed relationship.

Furthermore, Christianity acknowledges only unions between a man and a woman, dismissing same-sex marriages. The scriptures are unequivocal on this matter. To all the singles navigating relationships, I urge you to present your love and desires to God.

Preserve your purity through the strength and guidance of the Holy Spirit. God differentiates sexual sin as it binds two souls, making them one. Illicit relations, which contradict Biblical teachings, inflict profound repercussions on individuals, both physically and mentally.

As your spiritual guide, it is incumbent upon me to clarify that, within Christianity, sexual relations are exclusively reserved for the bounds of marriage.

Father, we are endlessly grateful for Your teachings and the path You illuminate for us. I pray fervently that You embolden each one of us with the Holy Spirit, guiding us to live within the realms of Your holiness and purity.

In the precious name of Jesus Christ, Amen.

AUGUST 5
Who is your role model?

1 John 2:6

> *He who says he abides in Him ought himself also to walk just as He walked.*

Scripture clearly declares: walk as Jesus Christ walked. In our world today, there are countless role models: from the fields of sports, where figures like Messi stand out in football and Muhammad Ali in boxing, to other sectors where people have established themselves as icons and figures of admiration. They often become our heroes and the individuals we aspire to emulate.

However, for us as Christians, who is our true role model? Who should be our hero, our guiding light? For you and me, the answer is singular and clear: Jesus Christ. Scripture urges us to tread the path that He walked. By imitating Jesus Christ in thought, word, and deed, we are following the example of the one who perfected our faith, our Savior who lived among us, facing our trials and tribulations, and the one who, in His infinite love and humility, chose the path of profound sacrifice. He is the model we should emulate, not any other.

And to guide us in this journey of emulation, Jesus Christ blessed us with the Holy Spirit, the Spirit of God, to reside within each of us. The more we live in accordance with His teachings, the more we become like Him. As 2 Corinthians articulates, we are the living letters penned by Christ, visible and readable for all to see.

When Jesus Christ becomes our benchmark, when our love for others mirrors His boundless affection, and when we passionately spread the good news just as He did, we truly embody His teachings. By loving our enemies, our neighbors, and aiding those in need, we not only imitate Jesus Christ but grow increasingly to resemble Him. By immersing ourselves in His teachings, cultivating a relationship with Him through prayer, and focusing solely on Him, we embody His spirit.

If anyone were to ask me about my hero or role model, my response would be unwavering: Jesus Christ, and no one else. Who is your role model?

A poignant reflection, especially in moments of dilemma, is to ponder: What would Jesus Christ have done in this situation?

There was once a popular bracelet inscribed with the acronym "WWJD", meaning "What Would Jesus Do?" This simple reminder prompts us to think of how Jesus would act in our place.

Our calling, dear brethren, is to emulate Jesus Christ in every facet of our lives.

Father, we are profoundly grateful for today. We beseech You to assist us in making Jesus Christ our role model each day. Grant us the strength to mirror His ways continually, recognizing that through Your Holy Spirit, we can strive to embody His likeness in every moment. We offer our deepest gratitude.

In the precious name of Jesus Christ, Amen.

AUGUST 6
The boy with 5 loafs of bread and a few fish

John 6:8-9

> [8] *One of His disciples, Andrew, Simon Peter's brother, said to Him,*
> [9] *"There is a lad here who has five barley loaves and two small fish, but what are they among so many?"*

On a particular day, Jesus ascended a mountain, drawing crowds to Himself. Seeing the multitudes, He posed a question to Philip: "How can we feed these people?" Philip, overwhelmed by the sheer number, replied that even 200 dinars would not suffice to provide each one with even a small morsel of bread. But then, Andrew, Peter's brother, introduced a young boy to Jesus. This boy had five loaves of bread and a few fish. Yet, as Andrew stated, "How far will they go among so many?"

Here's where the divine unfolds. Jesus instructs the crowd to sit. Though there were 5,000 men recorded here, other accounts indicate that, including women and children, the number ranged from 15,000 to 20,000. With a prayer and a blessing, He multiplied the boy's modest offering. Through His disciples, He distributed the miraculously increased food, and every single person was nourished.

Later, He instructed the disciples to gather up the leftovers, emphasizing no waste. To their astonishment, they filled twelve baskets with the remaining fragments. The crowd, witnessing this miracle, believed Him to be the awaited prophet.

However, the central lesson of this narrative lies not just in the miracle but in the boy's act. This boy, amidst a vast crowd in a remote location, possessed a meager meal. Yet, when presented with an opportunity to give, he did not cling to his security. There is no record of reluctance, no expression of fear of hunger. This boy willingly handed over his sustenance, understanding perhaps that in the hands of Jesus, even the smallest gift could yield abundance.

We must introspect: Do we hold onto our 'five loaves and two fish' out of fear? Do we trust God enough to believe that when we give, even if it seems like it's our last, He can multiply it and meet not just our needs but also bless many others through it?

Today, let us approach our Heavenly Father with a renewed heart of trust and say,

"Lord, all that we have is from You. If there's anything in our possession that can bless another, please illuminate our hearts and guide our hands. Let us give willingly, joyfully, trusting that You will multiply our offerings for the benefit of many."

We thank You, Father, for this profound lesson of faith and generosity.

In Your blessed name, Amen.

AUGUST 7

Wisdom and encouragement words

Proverbs 16:22-24

> [22] *Understanding is a wellspring of life to him who has it. But the correction of fools is folly.*
> [23] *The heart of the wise teaches his mouth, And adds learning to his lips.*
> [24] *Pleasant words are like a honeycomb, Sweetness to the soul and health to the bones.*

In Proverbs, chapters 22 to 24, King Solomon, a man renowned for his wisdom, teaches us a profound truth: Wisdom is the fountain of life for its possessor, while ignorance invites folly's punishment. A wise person's heart not only influences their actions but also their words. "The heart of the wise instructs his mouth, and adds persuasiveness to his lips."

Solomon compares kind and loving words to the sweetness of honey. Such words have the power to heal, rejuvenate, and uplift a weary soul. Think of the times when a single word of encouragement or a heartfelt compliment changed the trajectory of your day. How powerful is the spoken word when used with wisdom and love!

The Apostle James, in his epistle, echoes Solomon's sentiments. If you lack wisdom, he writes, ask God, who gives generously to all without finding fault, and it will be given to you. Jesus Christ, our Savior, also advised us to speak from the abundance of our hearts. A wise heart, therefore, guides its speech. The words of the wise are not just empty phrases; they are infused with understanding, encouragement, and love. They discern the good in people and uplift them, and even their admonitions come draped in hope and encouragement.

What a beautiful lesson for us to imbibe in our daily interactions. Today, let us bring two sincere petitions before our Heavenly Father:

Dear Lord, we humbly ask for an increase in wisdom. May we grow in discernment and understanding, recognizing the value of every individual we meet. Additionally, Father, let every word we utter today be a source of encouragement and hope. Let our speech be seasoned with grace, lifting the spirits of those around us, reflecting Your love and compassion.

In the precious name of Jesus Christ, we pray, Amen.

AUGUST 8
Human way ends in death

Proverbs 16:25-26

> [25] *There is a way that seems right to a man, But its end is the way of death.*
> [26] *The person who labors, labors for himself, For his hungry mouth drives him on.*

Scripture admonishes us: "There is a way that seems right to a man, but its end is the way to death." There's wisdom in these words, a reminder that our human perspective is limited, and we can easily be led astray by our desires or perceptions.

When one labors, they labor for themselves. The driving force? Their own hunger and needs. But as believers, are we letting our immediate needs dictate our paths, or are we bringing our aspirations and desires before God?

Proverbs also tells us to commit our actions to the Lord and trust in Him to guide our paths. How many times have we embarked on a journey, confident in its rightness, only to discover later that we should've sought God's counsel first? Just because a path seems right doesn't mean it leads to life. God, in His omniscience, knows the end from the beginning.

Christ beckons us with open arms, saying, "Come to me, all you who are weary and burdened, and I will give you rest." He invites us to lay down our burdens, our worries, and our plans at His feet, seeking His perfect will.

Today, let's challenge ourselves. Before embarking on any venture, let's pause and pray: "Father, in the name of Jesus, this seems right to me, but You know its end. If it's not Your will, reveal it to me. I desire only what brings glory to Your name and furthers Your kingdom."

It's easy to be driven by our immediate needs or desires. But are these desires aligned with God's will? Are we surrendering our hunger and thirst to Jesus, trusting Him to provide?

Christ assures us, "Your Heavenly Father knows what you need. But seek first His kingdom, and all these things will be added to you."

Let our primary focus be on God's kingdom, trusting that as we commit our ways to Him, He will direct our paths.

Today, Heavenly Father, we surrender our plans, desires, and decisions to You. Let us always remember to seek Your counsel first. May Your Spirit remind us to constantly check our intentions against Your word and wisdom. Thank you for always guiding us and being our refuge.

In the precious name of Jesus Christ, we pray, Amen.

AUGUST 9
Jesus the light of life

John 8:3-13

[3] *Then the scribes and Pharisees brought to Him a woman caught in adultery. And when they had set her in the midst,*
[4] *they said to Him, "Teacher, this woman was caught in adultery, in the very act.*
[5] *Now Moses, in the law, commanded us that such should be stoned. But what do You say?"*
[6] *This they said, testing Him, that they might have something of which to accuse Him. But Jesus stooped down and wrote on the ground with His finger, as though He did not hear.*
[7] *So when they continued asking Him, He raised Himself up and said to them, "He who is without sin among you, let him throw a stone at her first."*
[8] *And again He stooped down and wrote on the ground.*
[9] *Then those who heard it, being convicted by their conscience, went out one by one, beginning with the oldest even to the last. And Jesus was left alone, and the woman standing in the midst.*
[10] *When Jesus had raised Himself up and saw no one but the woman, He said to her, "Woman, where are those accusers of yours? Has no one condemned you?"*
[11] *She said, "No one, Lord."*
And Jesus said to her, "Neither do I condemn you; go and sin no more."
[12] *Then Jesus spoke to them again, saying, "I am the light of the world. He who follows Me shall not walk in darkness, but have the light of life." Jesus Defends His Self-Witness*
[13] *The Pharisees therefore said to Him, "You bear witness of Yourself; Your witness is not true."*

In the Scriptures, we encounter a profound moment in Jerusalem where Jesus was teaching in the temple. The Pharisees and priests, ever eager to challenge Jesus, brought forth a woman caught in the act of adultery. They presented her before Christ, stating that according to Moses' law, she should be stoned. They posed the question, "What do you say?"

Interestingly, the man with whom the woman was caught was conspicuously absent. Why was only the woman brought forth? It's a question that lingers, hinting at the double standards of the time.

In response to their accusatory query, Jesus, in His timeless wisdom, bent down and began writing on the ground. The content of His writing remains a mystery. Some speculate He listed the sins of the Pharisees or even named their own secret wrongdoings. But Jesus remained silent, offering no verbal response.

Growing impatient, they pressed Him further. Rising, Jesus spoke the immortal words, "Let him who is without sin among you be the first to throw a stone at her." Confronted by their own shortcomings, the crowd dispersed, from the eldest to the youngest. When Jesus looked up, only the woman remained.

"Woman, where are they? Has no one condemned you?" Jesus asked. To which she replied, "No one, Lord." And Jesus, embodying mercy and grace, told her, "Neither do I condemn you; go, and from now on sin no more."

But the narrative doesn't end there. Jesus, always teaching, immediately followed this event by declaring, "I am the light of the world. Whoever follows me will not walk in darkness but will have the light of life." In this, He not only pardoned the woman but provided her, and all of us, with a way forward. By acknowledging Him as the light, we can escape the darkness of sin.

In Jesus, we find the solution to our failings. He offers not just forgiveness but a path to righteousness. When we walk in His light, the darkness of sin is dispelled, replaced by the illuminating guidance of the Savior.

Let's pray:

Lord Jesus, the Living Water and the Light of the World, You are the Alpha and the Omega. We are forever grateful for Your endless mercy and guidance. In our weaknesses, may we always turn to You, laying our transgressions at Your feet, seeking Your cleansing and redemption. Grant us the strength to follow You ardently, that we may never stray from Your radiant path. Today and always. Amen.

AUGUST 10
Abide in my words

John 8:31

[31] *Then Jesus said to those Jews who believed Him, "If you abide in My word, you are My disciples indeed.*
[32] *And you shall know the truth, and the truth shall make you free."*

In the scriptures, Jesus Christ spoke profoundly to those Jews who believed in Him, saying, "If you abide in my word, you are truly my disciples, and you will know the truth, and the truth will set you free." This proclamation is not just for them but for us as well.

My dear friends, it's not enough to merely hear or read the Word of God; we must immerse ourselves in it and let it shape our lives. But how do we achieve this? Firstly, by dedicating time daily to delve into God's Word, and secondly, by inviting the Holy Spirit, who dwells within us, to illuminate its truths and reveal its mysteries. When we internalize and live by the Word, we don't just speak of the gospel – our very lives become a testament to the love and grace of Jesus Christ.

True freedom springs forth when we are grounded in the truth of God's Word. This freedom liberates us from the chains of despair, envy, bitterness, and every form of negativity. What is this transformative truth? It's the revelation that Jesus Christ is the Son of God, who sacrificed Himself for our sins and triumphed over death through His resurrection. The beautiful reality is that Jesus, the Father, and the Holy Spirit, in their unified love, desire nothing but the best for each one of us.

I urge you, let's make it a daily ritual. Begin each morning in communion with God through His Word and end each night in the same manner. Before you read, pray for discernment and understanding, and after, pause and listen, allowing God to minister to your heart.

Let's pray:

Heavenly Father, thank You for Your living Word that brings life, guidance, and freedom. Strengthen our resolve to remain rooted in Your Word, that through it, we might reflect Your love and truth in all we do.

In the precious name of Jesus Christ, we pray. Amen.

AUGUST 11
And Jesus found him

John 9

Here is the story of the man born blind. The Lord Jesus Christ made mud using His saliva, applied it to the man's eyes, and instructed him to go wash at the Pool of Siloam. After doing so, the man's sight was restored.

The disciples questioned Jesus about the cause of the man's blindness, wondering if it was due to the man's sins or his parents'. Jesus responded, "Neither this man nor his parents sinned, but this happened so that the works of God might be displayed in him." After his miraculous healing, the man, now 30 years old, was brought to the synagogue. There, he faced questions because Jesus had healed him on the Sabbath. The religious leaders argued that Jesus was a sinner for doing such work on the Sabbath. However, the healed man defended Jesus, stating he had never heard of anyone opening the eyes of a person born blind.

Interestingly, because of his testimony, he was cast out of the synagogue. The Bible records in verse 35 that when Jesus learned of this, He sought out the man and asked him, "Do you believe in the Son of Man?" The man replied, "Lord, who is he, so that I may believe in him?" Jesus said, "You have seen him, and it is he who is speaking to you." The man responded with faith, saying, "Lord, I believe," and he worshiped Jesus.

Jesus used this moment to teach an important lesson: "I came into this world for judgment, so that those who do not see may see, and those who see may become blind." The profound truth is that in Christianity, it isn't about our seeking God; rather, God seeks us. He always takes the first step toward us. He knocks on the door of our hearts, and if we open it, He promises to come in and commune with us.

When the man was questioned about his healer, he admitted he hadn't seen Him but believed His name was Jesus. When Jesus heard this, He took the initiative to find the man, proving that it is God who searches for us, longing for a relationship.

Do we open our spiritual eyes, especially when faced with challenges, societal norms, or cultural pressures? Do we allow our hearts to .perceive the true nature of God?

Today, we pray:

O God, thank You for seeking us out. We are grateful for the gift of faith, enabling us to open our hearts to You, recognizing You as our Lord, Savior, and the promised Messiah.

May our spiritual eyes always be attuned to Your divine light, and not just the illumination of our understanding. Grant us the grace to view the world through Your perspective and to remain receptive to Your love, mercy, and presence. In the name of Jesus Christ, Amen.

AUGUST 12
I am the gate

John 10:9-11

> [9] *I am the door. If anyone enters by Me, he will be saved, and will go in and out and find pasture.* [10] *The thief does not come except to steal, and to kill, and to destroy. I have come that they may have life, and that they may have it more abundantly.*
>
> [11] *"I am the good shepherd. The good shepherd gives His life for the sheep.*

This marks the third "I am" proclamation of Jesus Christ. He declares, "I am the gate; whoever enters through me will be saved. They will come in and go out, and find pasture. The thief comes only to steal and kill and destroy; I have come that they may have life, and have it to the full. Amen."

What Jesus Christ imparts in this message mirrors what He conveyed in chapter 9. The pathway to God the Father is exclusively through Jesus. He is the singular door; by entering through Him, we gain access to the Father.

Jesus proclaims, "I have come so that they may have life, and have it abundantly." Only through Him do we discover a life imbued with profound meaning and purpose.

I must reiterate: the notion that all paths lead to God is fundamentally flawed. The one true way is through Jesus Christ, the Son of God, our Lord. He, who assumed a human form, discerned that our salvation lay in His self-sacrifice, culminating in the shedding of His blood. By rising on the third day, He vanquished death and Satan, bestowing eternal life upon those who place their faith in Him, transforming them into children of God.

Do any other religions or philosophies make such a claim? Have any of their leaders willingly laid down their lives for our sake? Solely through Jesus Christ - the Lamb of God, the Lion of the tribe of Judah, the preeminent Son of God - do we attain eternal life, drawing close to God the Father and experiencing His profound love.

Our hearts overflow with gratitude for God's call, drawing us closer to Him, for He is the Good Shepherd. He assures, "My sheep listen to my voice; I know them, and they follow me."

Today, we extend our thanks to God for the revelation that the sole pathway to Him is through our Lord Jesus Christ, the sacrificial Lamb of God, the Son of God, and our Lord.

O God, may we perpetually turn to You, entrusting our every concern into Your capable hands. We dedicate this day to Your divine oversight, for You are the Alpha and Omega, the Gate and the Good Shepherd. Amen.

AUGUST 13
Do we walk in the light or darkness?

John 11:9

> 9 *Jesus answered, "Are there not twelve hours in the day? If anyone walks in the day, he does not stumble, because he sees the light of this world.*

In the Scriptures, we find Jesus desiring to visit the home of Martha and Mary due to the passing of Lazarus. He rhetorically asks, "Aren't there twelve hours of daylight?" emphasizing that one who walks in daylight won't stumble because they are guided by the world's light. But at night, in the absence of light, they are prone to falter.

This profound reflection came as a response to His disciples' concerns. They had cautioned Him about going to Jerusalem, where the Jews sought to harm Him. Through this, Jesus presents us with a soul-searching question: Do we walk in the world's light, in the radiant glow of Jesus Christ?

When we let His light permeate our hearts and souls, when we draw strength from His Word and trust in His ways, we remain steadfast. Our path is clear, and our feet do not waver. However, if we choose to tread the path of darkness, conceal our actions, and give in to sin, we risk faltering. This stumbling isn't merely due to the absence of the world's light but, more crucially, because there is no inner light – the absence of Jesus within.

By welcoming Jesus Christ as our Savior, His luminous presence illuminates our very being. His light is our guide, ensuring our path remains clear. Yet, when we stray, when we reject His brilliance and His teachings, darkness engulfs us. The absence of His light within predisposes us to stumble.

Let's bow in gratitude. Thank you, Father, and profound thanks for Your Son, Jesus Christ, the true Light of the world. Your guiding presence, through the Holy Spirit, resides within us. Lord, help us never to obscure this divine light, to never snuff it out. If there's anything within us that seeks to extinguish this light, we pray that in Jesus' name, You would dispel it. Instead, fill us anew with Your radiant presence. Amen.

AUGUST 14

May we not close our eyes to your miracles

John 12:37-40

> [37] *But although He had done so many signs before them, they did not believe in Him,*
> [38] *that the word of Isaiah the prophet might be fulfilled, which he spoke: "Lord, who has believed our report? And to whom has the arm of the* L*ORD been revealed?"*
> [39] *Therefore they could not believe, because Isaiah said again:*
> [40] *"He has blinded their eyes and hardened their hearts, Lest they should see with their eyes, Lest they should understand with their hearts and turn, So that I should heal them."*

In the Scriptures, we're shown that many witnessed Jesus perform a multitude of miracles and signs, yet they still did not believe in Him. This unbelief fulfilled the prophecy of Isaiah who had lamented, "Lord, who has believed our message? And to whom has the arm of the Lord been revealed?" Isaiah further foretold their stubbornness, revealing that their eyes would be blinded and hearts hardened. Thus, they would not truly see, understand, or turn to God for healing.

My earnest prayer for each of us is that we don't become so enveloped in spiritual darkness and denial that God perceives our hearts as permanently shut off. There's a profound tragedy in becoming so steeped in darkness that all avenues to perceive and understand God's wonders are closed. The most grievous fate is when God lets one go, leaving them to their own devices due to the consistent hardening of their heart.

Repeatedly turning away from God's miracles, signs, and teachings, risks leading us to such a state. So, let's approach God with a humble heart, praying:

"O Lord, may we never shut our eyes or harden our hearts to Your wondrous deeds. Illuminate our eyes and attune our ears, so we might recognize Your mighty acts at every juncture in our lives, in the lives of those around us, and in the majesty of Your creation. Allow us to hear Your gentle voice in all things, drawing our hearts ever closer to You. We pray for healing – a profound, transformative healing – and that we remain in communion with Your Son, Jesus Christ, with You as our Father, and with the Holy Spirit. All this we pray in the name of Jesus Christ. Amen."

AUGUST 15
May I not cause you shame

Psalm 69:5-7

> *5 That Your beloved may be delivered, Save with Your right hand, and hear me.*
> *6 God has spoken in His holiness: "I will rejoice; I will divide Shechem And measure out the Valley of Succoth.*
> *7 Gilead is Mine, and Manasseh is Mine; Ephraim also is the helmet for My head; Judah is My lawgiver.*

In the Psalms, David, the man after God's own heart, opens up with a profound transparency, "O God, my sins are not hidden from you; you see even my foolishness. And, Almighty God, may those who have placed their trust in you never be put to shame because of my missteps." Such depth in his words! David acknowledges his imperfections and pleads that his failings don't deter others in their faith journey.

Isn't that a sentiment many of us can resonate with? We're all imperfect, possessing weaknesses and lapses that perhaps only God is fully aware of. David's prayer is profound and can be the plea of each of our hearts. "Lord, because of my own failings and inadequacies, let not those who look to you, those who love and serve you, be disheartened or stumble."

It's painful to think of Christian leaders and mentors who have faltered in their journey. Their missteps have sometimes led many believers to doubt, lose heart, and even drift away from their faith. Such instances underscore David's earnest plea - that our personal failings shouldn't disillusion others in their spiritual pursuits.

Jesus's words about the significance of leading the little ones come to mind. He stressed that causing any believer, especially newcomers in faith, to stumble would carry grave consequences. Let that weight help us reflect and pray with David's urgency.

So, our collective prayer today can be:

"Lord Jesus Christ, you are fully aware of our flaws and the depth of our failings. Illuminate us to recognize our shortcomings and grant us the humility to acknowledge them. Forgive our transgressions, our lapses in judgment, and our moments of foolishness. Steady our steps and help us to never be the cause of disillusionment or despair for those who have entrusted their lives to you. May we always point others to you, the unchanging rock and firm foundation. In the mighty name of Jesus Christ, Amen.

AUGUST 16
Whoever rewards evil with good, evil will not depart from him

Proverbs 17:13 and 15

> [13] *Whoever rewards evil for good, Evil will not depart from his house.*
> [15] *He who justifies the wicked, and he who condemns the just, Both of them alike are an abomination to the LORD.*

This teaches us that if we repay good with evil, evil will never leave our house. Verse 15 further clarifies that God despises those who wrongfully accuse the innocent and exonerate the guilty.

Regrettably, contemporary societies, both in the West and the East, have morphed to a point where good is perceived as evil and vice versa. Morality is now determined by what's popularly accepted. If the majority favors something, it's deemed good; if not, it's labeled as bad.

However, in God's perspective, what He declares as good remains good, and what He condemns as evil is unequivocally evil. The Spirit He instilled within us differentiates between right and wrong. When we eradicate God, specifically God the Father, from our society and His Word—the Bible—is deemed irrelevant or forbidden, it leads to moral chaos. If a society or country begins to dictate that prayer is not allowed, reading the Bible in schools is prohibited, or any such decrees, it's as though God says, "I'll leave the decisions to you."

It's under such conditions that morality gets inverted. But those who repay good with evil, who exonerate the guilty and falsely accuse the innocent, believing they're invincible, forget that the omnipotent God, who crafted every eye and ear, observes and hears all. Such individuals will face divine retribution.

We must always measure our actions against the yardstick of the Bible. We are admonished not to repay good with evil. Instead, we're encouraged to counter evil with goodness, exemplifying Christ's teaching to love even our enemies. If one strikes you, turn the other cheek. If someone demands your coat, offer your shirt as well. Our call is to repay evil with good, for by doing so, blessings, love, and the Holy Spirit will forever grace our homes.

May God empower us to always respond to evil with goodness, to uphold righteousness, and in every circumstance, to question, "What would Jesus have done?" We give thanks and praise to You, Lord.

In the name of Jesus Christ, Amen.

AUGUST 17
Wash my feet

John 13:7-11

> 7 *Jesus answered and said to him, "What I am doing you do not understand now, but you will know after this."*
> 8 *Peter said to Him, "You shall never wash my feet!" Jesus answered him, "If I do not wash you, you have no part with Me."*
> 9 *Simon Peter said to Him, "Lord, not my feet only, but also my hands and my head!"*
> 10 *Jesus said to him, "He who is bathed needs only to wash his feet, but is completely clean; and you are clean, but not all of you."*
> 11 *For He knew who would betray Him; therefore He said, "You are not all clean."*

On the final night, Jesus set aside His garments, took up a towel, and began washing His disciples' feet with water. When He reached Peter, Peter asked, "Do you intend to wash my feet?" Jesus replied, "What I'm doing now might seem puzzling, but you will understand later."

Peter insisted, "You shall never wash my feet." Jesus retorted, "Unless I wash you, you have no part with me." This prompted Peter to exclaim, "Then, Lord, wash not only my feet but also my hands and my head!" Jesus explained, "Someone who has bathed only needs his feet washed to be completely clean. You are clean, but not all of you."

Upon embracing Jesus Christ as our Lord and Savior, all our sins are nailed to the cross. Not only are they forgiven, but they're also forgotten. This transformation takes place when we accept Him as our Savior and Lord. Yet, we remain flawed, continuing to sin.

However, the indwelling Holy Spirit quickly convicts us when we err. Once God reveals our missteps, our immediate response should be repentance. It's like returning to Him for a foot washing. While our essence remains cleansed, we need to regularly approach Him, confessing, "Lord, you know all things. If there's any wrongdoing within me, reveal it, grant me the time to repent, and fortify me to cast it away."

God promises that we'll never face temptation beyond our capacity. While Satan might lure us, God always provides an exit. Temptation will persistently challenge us, but our reaction is pivotal.

Do we entertain these temptations, allowing them to blossom into desires that preoccupy our thoughts and hearts? This is often the genesis of sin. Therefore, at the first hint of temptation, we should present it at Jesus' feet, praying, "Lord, cleanse me and keep me from succumbing to this temptation, preventing it from birthing sin."

Daily, we require Jesus to wash our feet and, through the Holy Spirit, direct our steps in His righteous path. Amen.

AUGUST 18
That you may have peace in Me

John 16:33

> *These things I have spoken to you, that in Me you may have peace. In the world you will have tribulation; but be of good cheer, I have overcome the world."*

After the Last Supper, Jesus spoke to His disciples, revealing, "I must depart and return to the Father." He continued, "I've shared these truths so you may find peace in union with me." In other contexts, it reads, "Find peace in me. You will face trials in this world, but take heart." In some translations, He assures, "Do not be afraid, for I have overcome the world." Despite His foreknowledge that they would desert Him, Jesus queried in verse 31, "Do you truly believe?" He proclaimed, "Soon, you will scatter, leaving me isolated. Yet, I am never truly alone for the Father is always with me."

Jesus's message for us resonates: "When memories flood back, find solace in my words and trust that I am the genuine Savior. In this world, you will face challenges." He reminds us, "If I, your Master, suffered, won't you, my followers, experience hardships too?" He cautioned that persecution would come in His name, yet reiterated the purpose of His revelations was to grant us peace in Him.

In moments of adversity and strife, our singular focus should be Jesus. Draw near, anchor in Him, and experience a profound peace that transcends comprehension. This peace arises from the intimate union between Jesus and the Father and between us and Jesus, facilitated by the Holy Spirit.

This union floods us with His tranquility. Jesus encourages, "Despite the world's turmoil, remain courageous. As I have often said, 'God has not endowed you with a spirit of fear, but with a spirit of adoption, compelling you to cry out, Abba, Father.'" What's the significance? Every time we call out, He draws near.

Stay emboldened. Why? Because Jesus triumphed over the world, evil, and even death. Through Him, we share in this victory. Amen?

Today, let's express our gratitude. "Thank you, Lord, for your sacrificial love, for vanquishing Satan, the world, and death itself. Through faith in you, we are more than conquerors."

In the midst of life's storms and the adversary's onslaughts, may we stand firm, declaring, "I am victorious in Jesus. I am enveloped in His peace. God hasn't bequeathed me a spirit of fear, despair, or gloom, but one of adoption, hope, joy, and serenity." Can I get an Amen? Amen.

AUGUST 19

Father, I pray for those you have given Me

John 17:9-11

> [9] *"I pray for them. I do not pray for the world but for those whom You have given Me, for they are Yours.*
> [10] *And all Mine are Yours, and Yours are Mine, and I am glorified in them.*
> [11] *Now I am no longer in the world, but these are in the world, and I come to You. Holy Father, keep through Your name those whom You have given Me, that they may be one as We are.*

In these verses, we observe Jesus Christ in deep communion with God, fervently praying. He says, "I intercede not for the world, but for those you have entrusted to me, for they are yours." He emphasizes the profound unity between the Father and Himself: "All that is mine is yours, and all that is yours is mine." Through these chosen individuals, Christ's glory is magnificently revealed.

It's crucial to understand the focus of Jesus' prayer. He prays specifically for those entrusted to Him by the Father, distinguishing them from the world. This special group is none other than us – the beloved children of God who have accepted Jesus as our Savior, Guide, and Lord.

Many proclaim that God does not show favoritism. Indeed, He showers the earth with rain and bestows blessings upon all. However, when it comes to His children, there's a unique protective and intercessory fervor. Jesus doesn't intercede for the entire world in the same manner; His emphasis is on His own – those called into His family.

God's heart yearns for all to come into salvation, prompting our divine mandate to evangelize. We're entrusted with spreading the Good News, so more can join the family of God and experience these blessings. But until that fruition, God demonstrates a special care for His children. Scripture doesn't say He sends angels to guard the entire world but specifically to watch over those who place their faith in Him.

We can navigate life's most treacherous valleys confidently, knowing we're never abandoned. Jesus assures His beloved that He remains perpetually by their side. It's astounding to fathom the privileged position we hold in God's eyes.

As believers, we're cradled in the arms of the Creator of all things. The One we adore as Lord, Friend, and Father continuously intercedes for us.

Our faith dispels fear and doubt, especially when we fix our gaze upon Jesus. The profound unity - Jesus in the Father, and us in Jesus – underlines our collective identity as one family, sheltered under God's eternal canopy.

With this empowering realization, let's stride forth today, proclaiming, "Lord, we're profoundly grateful for your election, for incorporating us into your divine family. Thank you for your unwavering presence, your ceaseless intercession. Grant us the grace to fulfill our divine commission, to share the Good News and magnify your illustrious name among the nations." Amen.

AUGUST 20
The name of the Lord our strong tower

Proverbs 18:10

> *The name of the LORD is a strong tower; The righteous run to it and are safe.*

Solomon, in his wisdom, declared that the name of God is a potent fortress where the righteous find refuge and security. In his era, God was known by the name Jehovah.

Fast forward to our times, having embraced Jesus Christ as our Savior and Lord, we have come to recognize more intimate appellations of God. We've been introduced to the Holy Trinity: God the Father, the Son, and the Holy Spirit. These three distinct personas represent the unity of one God. We've come to understand and appreciate each facet of this triune deity.

Jesus Christ, putting on the garb of humanity, descended to our realm, offered himself on the cross, vanquished death, and sanctified us through His redeeming blood and powerful name. Most crucially, He unveiled the Father to us, engrafting us into the divine family. Thus, we're now privileged to address God as our Father.

But when do we realize the potency of God's name as an impenetrable fortress?

Scripture declares that Jesus was endowed with a name that towers above all other names – whether in heaven, on earth, or beneath the earth. This name, Jesus Christ, surpasses all, making it the mightiest bastion in the universe. And when we, the righteous – sanctified by Jesus' blood and professing unwavering faith in Him as the sole Savior and Lord – take shelter in His name, we find unparalleled safety.

This is the name emblematic of the one whose spiritual residence we inhabit. He's not only invited us into His dwelling but has also established His abode within our hearts. Amidst life's tempests and uncertainties, invoking this powerful name offers us unfailing protection and peace.

So, if you find yourself in dire straits, longing for refuge today, draw near to the exalted name of Jesus Christ. Take shelter beneath His protective mantle and experience the profound peace and security only He can provide. Amen.

AUGUST 21
Are you the king?

John 18:37

> *Pilate therefore said to Him,*
> *"Are You a king then?"*

When Jesus stood before Pilate, the Roman governor posed a poignant question: "Are you the King of the Jews?" Jesus' reply was profound. "You say rightly that I am a king. But my kingdom is not of this world." He proclaimed that His mission was to bear witness to the truth. Those attuned to the truth, He said, would recognize and heed His voice.

Pilate, perhaps perplexed by this notion of truth, posed another question: "What is truth?" Yet he walked away before hearing an answer. We, however, have the privilege of knowing the truth as revealed in the scriptures. The truth is that God, the Eternal Father, sent His only begotten Son, Jesus Christ, into the world as the embodiment of His love and grace.

The King of all kings, Lord of all lords, and the very Son of God came to this earthly realm to unveil a divine truth. Those who are receptive to this truth hear His voice, yield to His call, and embrace Him as their Savior. They recognize the significance of His sacrifice on the cross, where He bore the weight of our sins and our curses. His resurrection is the emblem of His triumph over death and Satan.

His transformative power, driven by His boundless grace, lifts us from the abyss of darkness into His marvelous light. Through the Holy Spirit's workings, we transition from sinfulness to righteousness.

Jesus beckons us into God's kingdom, where we're destined not merely as subjects but as kings, leaders, and His beloved children. This is the liberating truth: that God sent Jesus Christ, the singular path to salvation for humanity. To embrace this truth is to find true freedom.

Let us pray:

Thank you, Lord Jesus, for leaving the splendors of heaven to don the mantle of humanity. In your humility, you bore the cross, overcame the clutches of death and the adversary, and paved the way for our salvation. Draw us ever closer to your heart and help us dwell in this truth for eternity. Amen.

AUGUST 22
The king

James 5:16

> *Confess your trespasses to one another, and pray for one another, that you may be healed. The effective, fervent prayer of a righteous man avails much.*

It is said that the earnest prayer of a righteous and good person is very powerful and effective. In the past few days, God placed the Holy Spirit in my heart, prompting me to pray for a friend whom I haven't heard from in a while. We were in deep prayer and weeping. Immediately, I emailed my pastor friends, my longstanding friends in Jesus Christ, so they too could participate in this prayer. We all prayed together, experiencing the profound power of collective prayer. The power of prayer multiplies when two or three, or more, gather together and approach God in unity. Those emails were still en route when the person, whom we had not heard from for weeks, responded, and we thanked God.

Indeed, we pray daily for this individual, seeking his salvation and his return to God. But those two days, the Holy Spirit had touched my heart with such intensity that I could not resist. We acted, and God listens to each and every one of us.

But if calamity strikes, James instructs us to gather and pray collectively for healing. He also advises, if you are guilty, confess to one another. Admit your sins to each other and pray for one another so that you may be healed. James emphasizes that the fervent prayer of a righteous person is very effective. Elijah, who was emotionally like us, prayed earnestly that it would not rain, and for three and a half years, there was no rain in the land. He prayed again, and it rained, and the earth produced its fruit. The power of prayer, friends, is extraordinary.

Jesus Christ says, "All of you who are burdened, come to me and take up my yoke, for my yoke is easy and I am gentle and humble in heart." We carry our burdens, our myriad problems, our daily concerns for family, friends, work, life, and everything. Jesus Christ invites, "come and lay them at my feet, and take my yoke for it is light." What is His yoke? It is faith in Him, trust in Him, dialogue, and communion with Him.

So, Father, today we step forward and say: Thank you, O God, that you hear us when we raise our voices. Before we speak, You have answered.

Allow each one of us, O God, not to isolate ourselves when we are in trouble, but to reach out to fellow Christians and, based on what You have taught us, ask them to pray for us. Let us pray together because You hear, and You answer, O Father. Today, we bring all our desires and all our needs to You, O Jesus Christ. You can do everything well and according to Your will, which is the best will for us. So do it, Father,

In the name of Jesus Christ, Amen.

AUGUST 23
Mother, at the last moments

John 19:25

Now there stood by the cross of Jesus His mother, and His mother's sister, Mary the wife of Clopas, and Mary Magdalene.

Here is where Jesus Christ finds Himself in the final moments on the cross. Near the cross where Jesus was affixed, His mother stood alongside her sister, Mary the wife of Cleophas, and Mary Magdalene.

Seeing His mother and the beloved disciple John standing together, Jesus said to His mother, "Woman, behold your son," and to the disciple, "Behold your mother." From that moment, the disciple took her into his own home. Even in His last moments, Jesus, as the eldest son, did not forsake His responsibility towards His mother.

During those times, the eldest son assumed the role of the father. By then, there was no mention of Joseph, Jesus Christ's earthly father and Mary's husband. It seemed he had passed away, leaving all the responsibility for His mother on Jesus Christ.

Even in His final moments, although Jesus, knowing the transcendence of His mission, did not need to address such matters, He did not neglect His responsibility. He entrusted His mother to the care of the disciple He loved the most, the disciple who was invariably by His side, resting his head on Jesus's chest.

John, whom Jesus loved dearly, immediately complied and took Mary into his home, despite Jesus having other siblings. This teaches us that we too have responsibilities to our families; God commands us to execute all our tasks with utmost diligence and integrity, to do our job with all our might and virtue.

Let's examine our hearts today, scrutinize our actions. Have we overlooked any responsibilities? Have we neglected duties to family members that we ought to have fulfilled? Jesus did not forget His mother and His family even in His last moments.

Intriguingly, it's documented that His own brothers and sisters initially didn't believe in Him. Yet, post His resurrection, He appeared to His younger brother James—the first child of Mary and Joseph after Him—and James became the leader of the Church in Jerusalem.

Let us, therefore, remember to scrutinize our hearts, to uphold all familial responsibilities as dictated by God, and to execute them with the promptitude of John.

In the name of Jesus Christ, Amen.

AUGUST 24
Your will be done

We have arrived at a segment in the Lord's Prayer where we say, "Our Father in heaven, hallowed be Your name. Your kingdom come." We have deliberated on the concept of the kingdom, and then it proceeds, "Your will be done, on earth as it is in heaven."

What is it that we are conveying to God? His will is executed on earth, His intentions are manifested here, and we are expressing to God, "Lord, we desire Your will and Your desire to prevail everywhere. In heaven, on earth, within us. Primarily, let Your will be done on this earth, in this heart, within us."

May our will, our desires align with Yours. Nonetheless, I emphasize, let Your will, not ours, Your desires, not ours, prevail on this earth. This is our abode; in all our situations, through our dilemmas and our virtues, we seek the realization of Your will here on this earth, as it is in heaven. Thus, we declare to God, "O Lord, manifest Your will in us, around us, and we are content solely with Your will and desire."

Jesus Christ proclaimed, "I came to fulfill the will of God and to execute what God commanded me to do. I do whatever the Father instructs." And on His last night, He prayed, "O Father, if it is possible, let this cup pass from Me; yet not as I will, but as You will," acquiescing even to His impending death.

For we comprehend that the will of God, God's aspiration for those who adore Him and are summoned in His name, invariably concludes in goodness. Romans 8:28 assures us that everything, not merely some things, will work together for good for those who love God and are called according to His purpose. Everything, even the seemingly insurmountable and the apparently irresolvable. If it aligns with God's will, it will transpire. Everything will culminate in goodness for us who acknowledge Jesus Christ as Lord, encompassing our ultimate fate.

We are reminded that God has not endowed us with a spirit of trepidation but a spirit of adoption. He urges, "Cry out, Abba, Father!" Therefore, Christians should not harbor fear of death. Corinthians elucidates that to be absent from the body is to be present with the Lord. The moment we depart from this terrestrial realm, we are united with Lord Jesus Christ for eternity. Hence, death is not the cessation; it is the inception of everlasting life and should not be viewed with fear. Thus, we pray, "O Lord, our Father, let Your will, Your desires be fulfilled in each one of us, on this earth, around us, and we are content with Your will." Amen.

AUGUST 25
Give us this day our daily bread

The Lord's Prayer (continued).

In our last discussion on the Lord's Prayer, we reflected on "Your will be done, on earth as it is in heaven," and now we proceed with, "Give us this day our daily bread." The Lord Jesus Christ advises, "Therefore do not be anxious, saying, 'What shall we eat?' or 'What shall we wear?'"

If you, being earthly fathers, have a child who asks for bread, would you offer him a stone? Or if he asks for a fish, would you present him with a serpent? How much more will your heavenly Father provide for you?

"Seek first the kingdom of God and His righteousness, and all these things will be added to you."

We begin with, "Our Father in heaven, hallowed be Your name. Your kingdom come; Your will be done, on earth as it is in heaven. Give us this day our daily bread." Priority is given to the kingdom; we are to seek the kingdom of God foremost. Let all things be for God; let us pursue Him with all our heart, with all our being, and with all our mind.

God is cognizant of our necessities. When we ask, "God, grant us our daily bread," He not only provides but does so abundantly. The cup He offers overflows; it's not half-empty. The plate He provides is bountiful; it's not half-filled. He blesses our sustenance generously.

The fundamental prerequisite, however, is our prioritization of the kingdom of God, the love of God, the will of God, and all that pertains to God, Jesus Christ, and the Father. Then, all other things will be accorded to us.

Therefore, we extend our gratitude to the Father. Thank You for esteeming us above all else, particularly when we receive Jesus Christ as our Savior, the King of kings, the Sovereign of our hearts. Then, we are Your children, and You nurture us more meticulously than any earthly father, fulfilling our needs and supplying our daily bread.

For this, we are truly thankful. Amen.

AUGUST 26
Forgive our debts as we forgive our debtors

The Lord's Prayer (continued)

This portion of the Lord's prayer is expanded and explained by our Lord. Is this prayer for nonbelievers? No, a nonbeliever cannot call God, Father. The only persons that can call God, Father, are those that have surrendered their lives and hearts to Jesus Christ and following Him. Hence, this is the prayer of the believers, and we are telling God to forgive our sins and our everyday errors as we forgive those who do wring to us.

Later Jesus expands on this: If your brother sins against you and then comes to you and ask for forgiveness, forgive him. Peter asks: Should forgive my brother seven times? Jesus responded: No, not seven times but seventy times seven. He meant that we need to forgive as long as that person is asking for forgiveness. Later He gives us more parables. The parable of the servant who owed the king billions of dollars brought before the king and was sentenced to sell all he had along with his wife and children to pay back his debt. He fell on his knees before the king and ask for his mercy and patience and time to pay back. The king felt compassion and actually forgave all his debts. As he goes out of the court, he sees one of his coworkers that owed him $100. He grabs the fellow by the throat and ask him to pay up. The fellow fell on his knees and ask for mercy and time, but he would not and put the man in the prison to pay. The other servants who saw what happened reported it to the king. King got very angry and bring the wicked servant and ask him: Oh, wicked servant, I have forgiven you billions of dollars should you have done the same to your fellow servant?

Our debt to the Lord for our sins are Billions and billions which He forgave when we repented and accepted the Lord Jesus as our Lord and Savior. The Lord continues to forgive us on daily basis. What He expect of us is do the same to those who sins against us and demonstrate His forgiveness to our family, friends, people around us. We are called to love and love everyone even our enemies and feed them if they are hungry and give them drink if they are thirsty, to give them our shirt in addition to our jacket to cover them. Christian love has forgiveness in its heart. So, if you and I who call ourselves Christians would not forgive and close our heart to forgiveness, our Father in heaven would not forgive us either. Jesus in His parables tells us to have a forgiving heart.

So, today let us bring those that we have not forgiven before the Lord and say: Lord I bring before you this person (name) who wronged me, who offended me, who belittled me, who abused me, who accused me, who betrayed me, who, who, who; I forgive them in your name and please forgive me for my unforgiving heart. Lord, bless them and bring them to know you.

In name of Jesus, Amen.

AUGUST 27
Lead us not into temptation but deliver us from evil

The Lord's Prayer (Continued)

We've delved into the following parts of the Lord's Prayer: "Our Father which art in heaven, Hallowed be thy name. Thy kingdom come. Thy will be done in earth, as it is in heaven. Give us this day our daily bread, and forgive us our debts, as we forgive our debtors. And lead us not into temptation, but deliver us from evil."

Today, our focus is on the segment: "lead us not into temptation, but deliver us from evil." The Bible articulates several times that God does not tempt anyone; temptation emanates from the desires of the heart, our thoughts, and is the work of the devil.

For a believer who embraces Lord Jesus Christ as Savior, God does not tempt but may allow temptations to strengthen our faith. The Bible assures us that God never allows temptations beyond our capacity to resist or overcome.

So, what does it mean to ask God, "do not tempt us, but deliver us from evil"? The Bible implies that God provides an escape, a deliverance, every time temptation approaches. We need to recognize and decide upon the escape path provided.

Consider Joseph and his encounter with Pharaoh's commander's wife. She persistently tempted him, but Joseph resisted, asking, "How can I commit such a sin against God and against your husband?" Eventually, Joseph fled, leaving his clothes in her hand, illustrating that God provides an escape route for each of us.

Temptation precedes sin; it is the thought that lures us into sinning. We might trivialize this thought initially, deeming it harmless. However, such thoughts imagine actions and reactions that eventually lead us to sin. The optimum time to escape is when temptation surfaces. When it comes, we should implore, "O God, deliver us from the temptation of Satan." God, being ever-listening, will save us.

Hence, we ask God to prevent temptations from even beginning and to liberate us from Satan's temptations. Jesus Christ taught that harboring adulterous thoughts is akin to committing adultery.

Thus, we must promptly reject such thoughts, recognizing they are not from God, who is pure and holy. In Jesus' name, we should pray to be taken away from temptation and progress with this divine shield.

Thank you, God, for always providing a way out for us. In the name of Jesus Christ, Amen.

AUGUST 28
For yours is the kingdom, the power and the glory

The Lord's Prayer (Continued)

This segment concludes our reflection on the Lord's Prayer. We have traversed through its initial phrases: "Our Father which art in heaven, Hallowed be thy name. Thy kingdom come. Thy will be done in earth, as it is in heaven. Give us this day our daily bread, and forgive us our debts, as we forgive our debtors. And lead us not into temptation, but deliver us from evil."

The concluding part proclaims, "for thine is the kingdom, and the power, and the glory, forever."

O God, it is You who are capable of all things, for You wield all the power. You are the sovereign King to whom all glory belongs. You alone can accomplish all things, executing them in the supreme manner.

You are our King, our Master, and our Glory. By uttering these words, we confess and profess, O God, O Father, that You are the singular living and true God. You are the Lord, the repository of all the world's power.

The entirety of the kingdom rests in Your hands; You are the supreme ruler and proprietor of all. Glory is exclusively Yours; thus, we exalt no one else. We appoint no one else as the king and master of our hearts.

No one else wields power over us; it is solely You, only You, Father. You merit all praise; all these attributes are embodied in You. Thus, You can perform all things within us, through us, for us, and for everyone.

So, this is our confession to our God the Father, recognizing Him as the most potent of all, the King of kings, with everything within His grasp. The glory and majesty are solely His. And how does it conclude? With "Amen."

What does "Amen" signify? It means complete agreement with what has been said, a plea to God to let it be so. So, friends, today let us align ourselves with the power, kingdom, glory, and majesty of God the Father, Amen.

AUGUST 29
Obey the governors and pray for them

Everyone must obey the governing authorities, as there is no power except from God, and the existing authorities have been appointed by Him. Therefore, whoever resists them resists the ordinance of God, and those who resist will bring judgment on themselves. Rulers are not a terror to good works, but to evil. Do you want to be unafraid of the authority? Do what is good, and you will have praise from the same.

He is God's minister to you for good. But if you do evil, be afraid; for he does not bear the sword in vain. He is God's minister, an avenger to execute wrath on him who practices evil. Consequently, you must be subject, not only because of wrath but also for conscience' sake. This is also why you pay taxes, for they are God's ministers attending continually to this very thing. Render therefore to all their due: taxes to whom taxes are due, customs to whom customs, fear to whom fear, honor to whom honor.

Sometimes, because leaders, governors, prime ministers, and presidents act wrongly, we tend to disrespect the position and authority God has granted them. Regardless of their conduct, God has designated them for His purposes. If we truly believe that all rulers are ordained by God, obedience is our duty. The Bible instructs disobedience only when authorities command actions contrary to God's word. In such cases, like Shadrach, Meshach, and Abednego in Nebuchadnezzar's time, refusal is essential.

Nevertheless, respect, tax payment, and avoiding complaints are incumbent upon us. We are the bearers of Christ's love, peace, purity, and tranquility, and we should exhibit these through our good deeds, tax payments, and tithes. And most importantly, we are called to pray for our leaders, especially when they err, instead of speaking against them.

Let us henceforth bring our concerns to God in prayer, seeking His intervention that our leaders might acknowledge Jesus Christ as Lord and serve in alignment with His will. May we, undiscouraged, continue in peace and tranquility, fulfilling our responsibilities in the best way possible. Amen.

AUGUST 30

Fear of the Lord leads to life

Proverbs 19:22-24

[22] *What is desired in a man is kindness, And a poor man is better than a liar.*

[23] *The fear of the LORD leads to life, And he who has it will abide in satisfaction; He will not be visited with evil.*

[24] *A lazy man buries his hand in the bowl, And will not so much as bring it to his mouth again.*

Love is the true adornment of man; it is better to be impoverished yet truthful than to be affluent and dishonest. For to fear God breathes life into man, ensuring his prosperity and shielding him from calamity, shielding him from the wickedness of the devil. Today, we contemplate verses 22 and 23 and reflect on the message that to love is to adorn oneself in righteousness.

It is an undisputed truth that lying is a manifestation of evil, foreign to the nature of God. In Christianity, we have reiterated that there is no room for so-called "white lies." Christ teaches us to let our affirmatives be affirmatives, and our negatives, negatives. To deny Christ before men is to be denied before the Father. Hence, we are beckoned to uphold truthfulness unreservedly. To be impoverished yet maintain integrity is far more commendable than acquiring wealth through deceit, for God values honesty, love, unity, and truth above all.

The author further imparts that to fear God is to imbue oneself with life, to be endowed with success, and to be cloaked in protection against calamities. To fear God is not to tremble and shrink, but to harbor a profound respect— a respect stemming from love and reverence for our Creator, who sculpted the heavens and the earth and holds sway over all creation. It is a fear born of respect, a mindful caution not to tarnish His love or cause Him offense.

To live in Godly fear is to act in constant awareness, ensuring that our actions don't displease God. By perennially aligning our intentions with His will, we attune ourselves to His divine whispers, His words woven in the sacred scriptures. To discern the origin of the voices we hear—be it divine, self-driven, or diabolical—we must juxtapose them against God's Word. If we live in perpetual respect, cautious not to offend our beloved Creator, this reverence nurtures our spiritual life. A heart in union with God is impervious to evil, unseverable from the divine embrace. Amen.

AUGUST 31
The benefits of attending church in person (1)

Hebrews 10:25 exhorts us not to forsake the assembling of ourselves together, a habit to which some have accustomed themselves. Instead, we should be encouraging one another, and even more so as we see the Day approaching. Christians are called to gather, to immerse ourselves in the Word, and to collectively worship the Lord Jesus Christ, as highlighted by the practices of the early church in the New Testament, found in Acts, 1 Corinthians, and Colossians.

It's imperative, especially now as we emerge from a period of isolation due to the pandemic, that we reconnect and rekindle our communal bonds through face-to-face gatherings and church attendance. This practice is not merely about adhering to tradition; it's about building and maintaining our connection to God and to each other.

When we step into the church, we feel a sense of holiness, a sense of divine presence that connects us to God and to each other. It allows us to cultivate a sense of gratitude, focusing on what we have rather than lamenting what we lack. This gathering offers us an opportunity to establish and strengthen our social and familial relationships, particularly our bonds with our spouses and fiancés, centering these relationships around our common belief.

Entering the sanctuary of the church, we imbibe a sense of respect, peace, and tranquility. It provides opportunities to serve, to understand and learn from tribulations, and to learn forgiveness. It fills our hearts with hymns of praise to God and allows us the chance to explore and understand the deeper meanings of life.

The Church is a place where we encourage each other, growing in our spiritual lives and learning to forgive and understand one another better. Our collective worship helps us to navigate through our problems, learning the lessons that tribulations teach us.

So, I hope this conversation serves as encouragement and inspiration to all of us to make a commitment to gather again. Let's plan to be together next week, with everyone arriving at 1:20 pm for a 1:30 pm start, and for those who wish to join in prayer, let's gather at 1:00 pm. I look forward to seeing all of you there, experiencing the blessings of communal worship. May God be with each and every one of us. Amen.

SEPTEMBER 1
3 benefits of coming to church (2)

In today's devotional, we delve deeper into the significance of attending church and explore the benefits it confers. I previously outlined ten points briefly; today, we shall revisit a few, emphasizing their importance in fostering unity and spiritual growth.

Firstly, I emphasized that the church nurtures our relationship with God. When we accept Jesus Christ as our Savior, we are imbued with the Holy Spirit, fostering an intimate connection with God. This profound relationship is deepened within the church's sanctity, where the presence of God, the Holy Spirit, and Jesus Christ is palpably felt, allowing us to worship in truth and spirit. Many attest to the alleviation of anxiety and the dispelling of negative thoughts upon entering the church, highlighting the transformative power of divine presence. Thus, physically attending church facilitates a more personal relationship with God, enriching our spiritual life.

Secondly, the church offers a space to contemplate God's blessings and goodness. Approaching the divine with gratitude and reflection diminishes our sorrows, trials, and tribulations, allowing us to focus on Christ's nature. In such a collective atmosphere, our spiritual alignment and connection with God are enhanced, serving as a reminder of our faith's resilience and depth.

The third point revolves around mutual edification; believers refine one another through shared experiences and insights. The communal aspect of the church enables us to realize we are not isolated in our struggles, offering solace and understanding through shared experiences. Mutual support and shared wisdom underscore the collective strength found within our congregation, reaffirming our faith and resilience in Christ.

Attending church goes beyond mere presence within a building; it's a proclamation of our unity with God and His emissaries, a living testament to our faith and commitment. I earnestly hope to see many of you in church this week, enriching our collective worship and unity.

Let's remember, our gathering for prayer begins at 1 pm, with the main program commencing at 1:30 pm. I encourage everyone to arrive by 1:20 pm. Our forthcoming sermon will explore the teachings within Galatians. May God bless you all. Amen.

SEPTEMBER 2

Attending church in person improves our relationship with our spouse (3)

Let's delve further into the multitude of benefits that emanate from attending church in person. We previously discussed the strengthening of our relationship with God, how being in a church amplifies our gratitude, and how the reverence and peace experienced there enhance our interpersonal relations, allowing believers to uplift each other.

Another aspect we touched upon is the positive influence it has on our relationships, specifically with our spouses. The church's focal point fortifies the common beliefs and the faith we share in Jesus Christ. It places emphasis on our shared values, diminishing lesser disagreements. The closer we move towards God, the closer we become as a couple, fostering mutual respect and love. Jesus Christ urges men to love and respect their wives and women to love their husbands, establishing equality among genders in Christ. Thus, attending church collectively centers our focus on Jesus Christ and our shared faith, forging stronger bonds under God's word.

Moreover, attending church imbues us with a sense of respect, calmness, peace, and tranquility. Many, including notable individuals like Henry Ford, have sought solace and solutions within the church's sanctity during tumultuous times. The presence of the Holy Spirit and God within the church soothes our spirits and realigns our focus on the Lord.

In conclusion, the church is a haven of peace and spiritual enrichment, open to all seeking solace and divine connection. This week, we will gather in the hall at 1:00 PM for prayer, followed by the main program at 1:30 PM, including the Last Supper ceremony, symbolizing unity and collective worship. I hope to witness the presence of each one of you there.

May God be with you all.

SEPTEMBER 3

Attending Church helps us to find the lessons for our trials (4)

In our devotional today, we proceed with our reflections on the myriad benefits of attending church in person. We previously emphasized how attending church fortifies our relationship with God, particularly in holy places infused with His presence. The sanctity we feel within those holy walls enhances our connection with the Divine.

Moreover, it provides us a focused environment to deepen our gratitude towards God and foster our relationships with fellow believers, uplifting each other in faith. When we attend church collectively, it strengthens the bonds within our families and couples, promoting mutual respect, calm, and peace.

Now, I'd like to expound on some additional aspects of attending church in person. It grants us the opportunity to reciprocate the boundless love and grace bestowed upon us by God. As we interact with fellow believers, we partake in this divine exchange, contributing not just financially but also through prayers and sharing the wonders of His gifts.

Moreover, attending church illuminates the lessons hidden within our tribulations through the words of the pastor, elders, and fellow believers. It guides us on navigating these hardships with gratitude and understanding, seeking God's presence in every situation.

Remember, the Bible underscores the significance of communal worship and unity in Christ. It is within the church that we can elevate each other in faith. So, I fervently hope to see each one of you in church this week. Our gathering begins with prayer at 1 o'clock, followed by the main program at 1:30, conducted in adherence to health protocols.

Please, make it a point to attend. I eagerly anticipate seeing all of you and encourage you to stay safe. May the Lord Jesus Christ be with you all, may the grace and love of the Father surround you, and may you experience the fellowship of the Holy Spirit.

SEPTEMBER 4
Church fills our hearts with songs of praise (5)

Continuing our discourse on the manifold benefits of attending church in person, we've repeatedly emphasized how stepping into a church facilitates enhanced communion with God, granting us a focused environment to reflect upon His boundless blessings. This communal experience fosters interconnectedness among us and augments familial bonds, imbuing us with respect, peace, and tranquility inherent in the sacred ambiance of the church.

It is within these holy walls that we find opportunities to extend our gratitude to God, reciprocating His blessings by contributing to the church and learning invaluable lessons from hardships and trials.

Today, I want to underscore the transformative power of forgiveness learned within the church—a foundational virtue of faith in Jesus Christ. Our Savior, in the Lord's Prayer, stressed the significance of mutual forgiveness, encapsulating its essence in parables that delineate the boundless mercy of God in contrast to human reciprocation of mercy.

Forgiveness is the cornerstone of Christianity. We are called to emulate God's boundless forgiveness, absolving those who wrong us and interceding for them through prayers. The act of forgiveness mirrors God's infinite love and mercy, extending His divine grace to fellow beings.

Moreover, attending church imbues our hearts with hymns and divine melodies, allowing us to worship God with instrumental and vocal praises, for He, Jesus Christ, is the sole worthy recipient of adoration. God cherishes worshippers who exalt Him wholeheartedly, a form of worship that emanates naturally from those who profoundly love the Lord Jesus Christ.

Lastly, the church serves as the platform where we discern the true essence of life. We are profoundly thankful to God for bestowing upon us a sanctuary where we can congregate to uplift, forgive, mature, and fortify each other's faith. It is through our collective presence and unity in the church that our relationships with God and fellow believers are deepened, allowing us to truly live the teachings of Christ. Amen.

SEPTEMBER 5
The lips of knowledge are a precious jewel

Proverbs 20:15

> *A wise son makes a father glad, but a foolish man despises his mother.*

I read it from the King James Version because I believe it articulates it best. It states, "There is gold, and a multitude of rubies: but the lips of knowledge are a precious jewel." The Hermeneutics Version asserts that wise words are more precious than gold and rarer than jewelry. Solomon is communicating here that while there is much gold and many jewels that are precious, the lips that part with knowledge, with wisdom, and the wisdom that emanates from such a mouth, is more valuable than any jewel. What is this wisdom, this knowledge, and this understanding that he is discussing? What wisdom and knowledge are we referencing? Are we discussing human wisdom and knowledge? It is about attaining the knowledge and wisdom of God when we study the Word of God, when we dedicate time to converse with God, when we prioritize God in everything, and place the Lord Jesus Christ above all else, and we don't depend on our own knowledge and comprehension. Elsewhere, Solomon advises not to depend on your own knowledge and wisdom, but to entrust everything to God. And to seek His knowledge and wisdom. Thus, when the mouth opens and speaks of this knowledge and wisdom, it draws from the knowledge and wisdom of God conveyed through His words. When we read His word, He asks us, do you desire knowledge? Do you crave wisdom? Ask for it. James declares that if you desire knowledge and wisdom, ask God, and He will grant wisdom abundantly. So, let us approach God and declare, O God, we don't rely on our own knowledge, on our own wisdom, on our own understanding. Because our knowledge and comprehension are insignificant compared to Yours. O God, bestow upon us Your knowledge, understanding, and wisdom through Your Holy Spirit. To utilize it for Your kingdom, and to enact Your will on this earth as it is in heaven. Thank You, Father, for this wisdom. Grant each one of us the wisdom, understanding, and knowledge we need to progress. Thank you. Amen.

SEPTEMBER 6
Bring our doctrinal disputes to the leaders

Acts 15

This discussion speaks of the first church council, a pivotal moment when a man from Jerusalem met Paul and Barnabas and proclaimed that salvation is not attainable until one is circumcised and adheres to the law of Moses. This sparked intense disagreement, leading to the decision to address this dispute at the church council in Jerusalem. This instance serves as a prime example for Christians, illustrating that when discrepancies arise regarding beliefs, doctrines, or unfamiliar matters, it's prudent to refer them to church leaders for resolution.

This first and paramount council emphasized that salvation is exclusively through grace and faith in Jesus Christ, not by our deeds. We delved into this last week in church; we receive salvation only through the grace of Jesus Christ, a gift we are undeserving of. Instead of meting out the death we merited, the Lord, in his love, donned human flesh and endured death for our salvation. This is the essence of grace. This council marked the inception of many; subsequent ones convened in 300 AD, 400 AD, to discuss fundamental Christian beliefs. The essence of my message is, when confronted with disagreements or uncertainties, we are beckoned to seek counsel from our leaders. If discrepancies persist, higher councils become the reference point, and often, God reveals His truth through these leaders. James advises seeking the leaders for prayers of healing and support, emphasizing that the presence of Jesus Christ is affirmed when two or three gather in His name. Let's hope we continue to bring our incomprehensions and our concerns to God and our leaders.

Stay blessed, and may God be with you.

SEPTEMBER 7

Faith, justified, peace and reconciliation, standing in grace

Romans 5:1-2

> [1]*Therefore, having been justified by faith, we have peace with God through our Lord Jesus Christ,*
> [2] *through whom also we have access by faith into this grace in which we stand, and rejoice in hope of the glory of God.*

Therefore, having been justified by faith, we stand in the presence of God with peace, a peace that was procured by our Lord Jesus Christ. It is through faith in Christ that we have been enveloped in the grace of God—a grace in which we stand firm. We rejoice not only in the hope of sharing in the glory of God but also in our tribulations.

These verses are potent and echo what we have reiterated before: it is by faith. Faith comes when we believe in our hearts and declare with our mouths that Jesus Christ is Lord. This confession is an outpouring of faith, a bubbling over of the love and adoration within us that cannot be contained.

Just as our conversations are laden with mentions of our loved ones, our hearts brim over with the love of Jesus Christ and God—a love far superior. We have been deemed righteous by faith in the sight of God, how? Because Jesus Christ, having paid the price with His blood, has justified us and reconciled us to God.

We now savor the peace with God, established by our Lord Jesus Christ. We have been reconciled and are at peace with God, entering into God's grace through faith in Christ.

Grace is a gift we did not deserve; we merited quite the opposite. God's grace is paramount when the consequence of sin is death. But Jesus Christ, having donned human flesh, experienced death in our stead. By our belief in Him, we received the antithesis of death—eternal life. Amen?

This grace is not transient; we are steadfast in it, harboring not only the hope of partaking in God's glory but also finding joy in our tribulations. When we have faith and are enveloped in grace, we inherit God's kingdom alongside Jesus Christ, sharing in the divine glory.

Why are we happy in our efforts? Because we know that we are working hard for the glory of God, Amen?

So, today let us go forward with the same power, with these two verses that open us to all matters of life, in faith and grace, and say with faith in Jesus Christ, through Jesus Christ, through His grace we became known as righteous, and in peace with God. And now we inherit God's glory, and all that we do is for His glory. Amen? Amen.

SEPTEMBER 8
Lord why are you silent and sitting

Psalm 83

[1]O God, do not be silent, do not hold your peace,
[2]because your enemies have revolted and those who hate you have become arrogant and rebellious,
[3]secretly plotting against your people. And they conspire against those who seek refuge in You.

There will come a time, perhaps even now, when you pray and feel as though you're receiving no answers, as if God is silent. It may seem like He's sitting calm and quiet, leaving us feeling alone, as though we're the only ones facing these adversaries and challenges. When we pray, it can sometimes feel as if our prayers simply hit the sky and bounce back without an answer. But is this truly the case? The Lord Jesus Christ assures us, "I will never leave you alone."

There's a beautifully written poem called "Footprints."

The poem illustrates two sets of footprints walking side by side. At some points, there's only one set of footprints, and later, two sets appear again. The narrator reflects that during challenging times, only one set of footprints is visible. "Lord, we walked together, but during hardships, I saw only one set." Upon closer examination, the narrator realizes that the single set of footprints belongs not to them, but to the Lord. In those moments of difficulty, it is He who carries and guides us through.

He doesn't always promise to take away our hardships, but He assures us, "I am always with you. I will never leave you, whether in good times, hardships, or storms." Looking back, we can see God's constant presence. We realize that even when He appears silent, He's always at work. And when our understanding becomes clearer, we often discover that even when we thought He was inactive, God was orchestrating things behind the scenes.

So, let's not lose hope. Even if it feels like God is silent or distant, we must press forward with the belief that He always remains true to His word and will never abandon us. He always acts for our ultimate good.

Sometimes, when we deeply desire something that seems unattainable, we pray and work hard for it. If the outcome isn't what we hoped for, it's an invitation to reflect.

We can think, "I love the Lord Jesus Christ, and He is my savior who wants the best for me. Perhaps what I desire isn't what's best in God's eyes, but He has something even better in store." In those moments, we can declare,

"God, let Your will, not mine, be done. I trust that You always know what's best for me." Amen.

SEPTEMBER 9
The Lord knows the motivations

Proverbs 21:2

> *Every way of a man is right in his own eyes,*
> *But the LORD weighs the hearts.*

Scripture tells us that all human actions seem right in their own eyes, but God discerns the motives. In another translation, it's conveyed that God tests hearts. Justice and judgment are more precious to the Lord than sacrifice. To God, acts of justice and judgment are more pleasing than mere ritualistic sacrifice. Often, the things we desire to do seem righteous and without fault to us.

However, every action should be evaluated against God's divine will. Does our desired action bring glory to the Kingdom of God? Does it exalt the name of Jesus Christ? Is it a blessing to others? Will it enhance the lives of those around us? God scrutinizes what's in our hearts.

What drives our actions? Are we motivated by self-interest, even if it comes at the detriment of others? Do our actions diminish the name of Jesus Christ or do they glorify Him instead of ourselves?

These are crucial reflections we must engage in before embarking on any endeavor. It's imperative to present our intentions to God and inquire, "Lord, this is my plan, but what is Yours? What delights You?"

In every aspect of life, big or small, we should approach God with our decisions, expressing, "Lord, I desire all my actions to be for Your pleasure, for the magnification of Your name, and for the glory of Your kingdom. If this aligns with Your will, let it be so. Otherwise, redirect me and show me the right path."

God is always there to guide us. He examines hearts and assesses motives. This is why the scripture emphasizes that justice and judgment are more esteemed than sacrifice. If our deeds are carried out with justice, fairness, love, and compassion, they are more significant than any ritualistic offering to God. Our actions should reflect God's love and glory.

So, Father, we present all our actions and motivations before You, Lord Jesus Christ. May You work within us, empowering us to fulfill Your purpose. Grant us wisdom and peace in our undertakings. Lord, steer us away from paths that don't align with Your will, and reveal Your divine purpose to us. In the name of Jesus Christ, Amen.

SEPTEMBER 10
Baptism, the seal and testimony to faith

Acts chapter 19

In Acts 19, Paul arrives in Ephesus. Upon encountering the Ephesians, he asks, "Did you receive the Holy Spirit when you believed?" They respond, "We didn't even know there was a Holy Spirit." Surprised, he then inquires, "Into what then were you baptized?" They reply, "Into John's baptism." Paul then explains to them about Jesus Christ. While the baptism of John the Baptist was for the repentance of sins, preparing them to accept Jesus Christ, upon hearing the full message of Christ, they are baptized in His name.

This raises a question: Is baptism merely a symbol of faith? Or must one be baptized to truly be a believer? The answer is no. As Ephesians declares, if one believes in their heart and confesses with their mouth, they are saved. Salvation is a matter of faith and God's grace; it's only through the grace of our Lord Jesus Christ that we're saved, not by our deeds.

Acknowledging our sins, we repent and proclaim, "Jesus Christ, only through You can we be saved." And with genuine faith, we recognize Him as our Savior, Master, and Lord.

So, what role does baptism play? Baptism serves as a public affirmation of our salvation. Through baptism, we outwardly confess our inward faith, symbolizing our unity with Jesus Christ in His death, burial, and resurrection. Baptism is a testament to our commitment because we believe in our hearts and proclaim with our mouths. While faith originates in the heart and doesn't necessitate baptism for its inception, baptism holds significance as an outward demonstration of our inner convictions. And in whose name are we baptized? In the name of the Father, the Son, and the Holy Spirit.

In Matthew 28, Jesus Christ instructs, "Go therefore and make disciples of all nations, baptizing them in the name of the Father and of the Son and of the Holy Spirit." Faith is initiated by God's grace and an accepting heart. Through repentance, we come to understand that Jesus Christ is the sole path to salvation. By His grace, we are redeemed, and upon belief, we undergo baptism as a seal of God's work.

In some contexts, it's mentioned that the Holy Spirit descends upon the baptized, making a dwelling within them. However, more often, when we come to faith, the Holy Spirit already indwells us, and baptism serves as a testimony to our faith. Amen.

SEPTEMBER 11

The will of the Lord be done

Acts 21

In the scriptures, we find Paul journeying towards Jerusalem for the last time. He reaches Caesarea, where Philip resides with his four virgin daughters, all prophets. A man named Agabus, also a prophet from Judah, approaches Paul. Taking Paul's belt, Agabus binds his own hands and feet, declaring, "Thus says the Lord: The Jews at Jerusalem will bind the owner of this belt in the same way and will hand him over to the Romans." Upon hearing this, the disciples are distraught, pleading with Paul not to proceed to Jerusalem. But Paul responds, "Why are you weeping and breaking my heart? I am ready not only to be bound but also to die in Jerusalem for the name of the Lord Jesus." Recognizing the depth of Paul's conviction, they resign themselves, saying, "The Lord's will be done."

This journey to Jerusalem was revealed to Paul by the Holy Spirit and Jesus Christ. It was intended for Paul to bear witness to kings and rulers, sharing the gospel with them. It wasn't that the Holy Spirit dissuaded Paul, but rather, He disclosed to the disciples the challenges Paul would face. Out of love for Paul, they wished to shield him from harm.

Paul, however, was acutely aware of his divine mandate to journey to Jerusalem and fulfill his mission in the name of Jesus Christ. As Jesus Himself stated, "Whoever does not carry their cross and follow me cannot be my disciple." This leads us to a pivotal question: Are we prepared to bear our crosses and follow Him?

Indeed, if we bear our crosses with self-centered intentions, the journey becomes exceedingly arduous. However, when we walk with Jesus leading the way, focusing solely on Him — our Lord, Savior, friend, and guide — all adversities fade into the background. Our gaze isn't fixated on challenges, but on the Lord of love and compassion. We are anchored by His promises that He will never forsake us and will always accompany us. Our hope is fortified by the assurance of eternal communion with Him.

Understanding God's will might entail embracing suffering. Yet, knowing it's for the advancement of God's kingdom and His glory makes every challenge worthwhile. By keeping our eyes on Jesus Christ, all else pales in comparison.

May God's will manifest in both your life and mine. Amen.

SEPTEMBER 12
Pentecost

Today, in our devotional, we delve into the significance of Pentecost. Most Christians are familiar with the events of this day. However, before its Christian connotation, Pentecost was a Jewish festival celebrating the first harvest. It marked the joyous occasion of the first fruits being reaped from the fields.

Furthermore, on this same day, the Ten Commandments were given to Moses. By the time of Christ, this Jewish festival had evolved to commemorate the reception of God's commandments through Moses.

Intriguingly, the sequence of celebrations transitioned from acknowledging the first fruit harvest, to the giving of the commandments, and ultimately, to God anointing His church with the Holy Spirit. On this day, God poured His Spirit onto those gathered in prayer, fulfilling the promise Jesus Christ had made: "It is to your advantage that I go away, for if I do not go away, the Helper will not come to you. But if I depart, I will send Him to you."

Isn't the symbolism profound? Pentecost became the celebration of the church's "first fruits", as the Holy Spirit descended upon believers, invigorating them. It's no wonder that, when Peter preached, three thousand souls were added to the church. With the outpouring of the Holy Spirit, the rigid laws were transcended, replaced by the law of love and compassion.

Pentecost stands as a remarkable day, not just historically but spiritually. It is a day of celebration for all Christians, marking the moment when the Holy Spirit first cascaded onto believers, filling them with divine presence and purpose. From the first fruit harvest to the emancipation from the rigidity of the law, Pentecost symbolizes growth, freedom, and spiritual transformation.

Father, we express our profound gratitude for the gift of the Holy Spirit. To the Holy Spirit, our guide and mentor residing within us, we offer our thanks. May You continuously fill and guide us, showing us the path of righteousness in every step.

SEPTEMBER 13
Our testimony the most effective weapon

Acts 22:21-22

In Chapter 21, we find Paul journeying to Jerusalem. Upon entering the temple, he is recognized by certain Jews from Asia who had encountered him previously. They incite the crowd, falsely accusing Paul of speaking against Moses, stirring up communities, and defiling the temple by bringing in a non-Jew. Although these claims were untrue, an agitated mob seizes Paul, dragging him out of the temple to assault him. When Roman soldiers become aware of the commotion, they intervene, separating Paul from the mob and taking him into custody. As they approach the barracks, Paul requests permission to address the crowd and begins speaking to them in Hebrew.

Notably, Paul does not delve into theological debates or defend his actions concerning the law. Instead, he shares his personal testimony. He recounts his life prior to encountering Christ, highlighting his zealous commitment to Judaism, his role as a Pharisee, and his relentless persecution of Christians. He narrates the transformative moment on the road to Damascus when a blinding light, brighter than the noonday sun, enveloped him, and the Lord Jesus Christ spoke to him. He continues, describing his temporary blindness and the subsequent healing he received through one of Jesus's disciples in Damascus.

The Bible underscores the paramount significance of two elements: the redemptive blood of Jesus Christ and the power of personal testimony. Our testimonies stand as formidable tools in the life of a believer. They represent our unique encounters with Christ, the transformative experiences that can't be denied or refuted. By sharing our testimonies, we present irrefutable evidence of God's work in our lives.

The blood of Jesus and our personal testimonies are instrumental in leading others to salvation. Thus, it's imperative for us to remember and share our testimonies. When called upon, they serve as our most genuine and relatable tools for evangelism.

Engaging in debates isn't our primary mission; sharing our testimonies is. Our tales of encountering the Lord Jesus Christ, surrendering our hearts to Him, and witnessing His transformative power in our lives serve as living testimonies. Scripture encourages us to live in such a manner that others see Christ through our actions.

Both our words and our deeds should resonate with the love and teachings of Jesus, serving as a living testament to His grace.

We thank our Heavenly Father and strive to reflect Him, not only through our words but also through our conduct. Our lives should exemplify the living testimony of Jesus Christ. Amen.

SEPTEMBER 14
The Lord protects his children

Acts 23

In Acts 23, we find Paul detained within a Roman garrison. Forty Jews conspire against him, swearing an oath neither to eat nor drink until they've succeeded in killing Paul. They plot to have Paul brought before the high priest, intending to ambush and murder him en route. However, Paul's nephew discovers their scheme and informs Paul, who subsequently relays the intelligence to the Roman commander. In response, the Romans clandestinely transport Paul with a sizeable detachment of soldiers to the governor of Caesarea during the night.

So, what's the significance of these events? What unfolds here is a testament to God's divine orchestration, ensuring the safety of those chosen for His purposes.

Romans 8:28 assures us, "And we know that in all things God works for the good of those who love him, who have been called according to his purpose." Paul's relocation from Jerusalem to Caesarea heralded the commencement of God's promise—that Paul would bear witness for Him before influential leaders. As we continue reading, we see Paul testifying before Governor Felix, then before King Herod, and ultimately standing before Caesar in Rome, proclaiming the gospel at every juncture.

What began as a sinister plot was repurposed for divine good. God can work through individuals regardless of their allegiance to Him. This is a timeless truth we must hold close: regardless of circumstances, God will ensure our welfare because we've surrendered our lives to Jesus Christ as our Lord, Savior, and Master.

Even when death looms large, all will be well. Romans assures us that no weapon forged against us shall prosper. Indeed, God harnesses every challenge, turning it to our advantage.

With this hope and promise, let's boldly navigate each day. Facing trials, tempests, or illnesses, we declare: "Lord, You reign supreme. You desire the very best for us, and You can transform even the gravest situations into blessings for us and Your kingdom." Amen.

SEPTEMBER 15
Paul mission and ours

Acts 26

In the scriptures, we find Paul in Caesarea, preparing to defend himself before King Agrippa. Agrippa, a descendant of the Herodian line, was well-versed in Jewish matters.

Intriguingly, in verse 12, we see Paul once again recounting his testimony in defense. He shares his life before Christ, his transformative encounter with Jesus in the wilderness, and the radical change that ensued. While other parts of the Bible provide glimpses into Paul's life before and after his conversion, verses 16 through 18 offer a comprehensive account of the mission that Jesus personally entrusted to Paul. It's perhaps the only place that presents a full narrative of what Jesus communicated to Paul during their encounter in the desert. Jesus says to him, "I am the same Jesus whom you are persecuting. Rise and stand on your feet, for I have appointed you as a minister. You must testify about what you've witnessed today and what I'll reveal to you in the future."

Jesus elaborates on Paul's mission, declaring he would be delivered from the Jews and sent to the Gentiles with a specific purpose: to open their eyes, lead them from darkness to light, and from the power of Satan to God. Through faith in Jesus, they would receive forgiveness of sins and a place among the sanctified.

This mirrors Jesus' Great Commission in Matthew 28, where He instructs, "Go and make disciples of all nations, baptizing them in the name of the Father, and of the Son, and of the Holy Spirit." The goal is discipleship, enabling others to partake in the Kingdom of God. And as Jesus emphasizes here, the only path to forgiveness and salvation is through faith in Him.

Each of us is called to share our testimony, to proclaim what God has done in our lives. It's our duty to share our transformative experiences, shedding light on God's redemptive power. In doing so, we offer others the chance to move from darkness to light, from captivity to freedom in Christ.

May we wholeheartedly embrace this mission, ensuring that others too can experience the joy and eternal promise of life with God. Amen.

SEPTEMBER 16

Lord saves us and our co-travelers

Acts 27

In Acts 27, we find Paul en route to Rome, journeying by sea. When they reach a port, Paul warns them of impending danger should they continue their voyage. However, his caution goes unheeded, and they press on. Sure enough, a storm ensues, and hope dwindles as days pass without the sight of the sun, and sustenance becomes scarce. Amidst the despair, Paul addresses them, "Friends, you should have taken my advice not to sail from Crete; then you would have spared yourselves this damage and loss. But now I urge you to keep up your courage because not one of you will be lost; only the ship will be destroyed. Last night an angel of the God to whom I belong and whom I serve stood beside me and said, 'Do not be afraid, Paul. You must stand trial before Caesar; and God has graciously given you the lives of all who sail with you.'"

What we witness here is the manifestation of God's unyielding plan. Even amidst tumultuous storms and seemingly inevitable doom, God safeguards not only His chosen servant but also those accompanying him. And what's Paul's response? Not one of arrogance, but one of faith. He reassures them, emphasizing his unwavering trust in God's promises. True to God's word, the ship is wrecked, but every soul on board is spared.

If we find ourselves amidst life's storms and tribulations, and if we are sincerely seeking God and walking in His path, we must remain steadfast in our faith. God doesn't just ensure our well-being, but He also extends His protection to those around us. And the pivotal question that emerges is: how many of those sailors, prisoners, and fellow travelers turned to God because of Paul's faith and testimony? Indeed, all heeded Paul's advice and were saved.

We may never fully grasp the extent of our influence in this world, but someday, in heaven, we might be approached by souls who proclaim, "I am here because of your words. I am here because of your deeds. I am here because you played a part in my salvation." Amen.

SEPTEMBER 17
Prayer for Iran and Afghanestan (1)

1 Timothy 2:1

> [1]*Urge, then, first of all, that petitions, prayers, intercession and thanksgiving be made for all people—*
> [2]*for kings and all those in authority, that we may live peaceful and quiet lives in all godliness and holiness.*
> [3]*This is good, and pleases God our Savior,*
> [4]*who wants all people to be saved and to come to a knowledge of the truth.*

You may ask why we are reading these verses today. Pastor Gregory Yousefian requested all the Persian Christians to pray and fast for Iran. We have decided not only to pray for Iran and Iranians in Iran but also pray for Afghanistan and Afghan people. We have read in Bible to pray for the kings, rullers and governors of all places and nations despite of their character. We have not been called to curse them but to pray for them because the Lord has chosen them and gave them the power and is using them for His purposes. As the Lord says about Pharo in Exodus: I have raised you up to glorify my name and my ways through you in Egypt. In Proverbs 21we read: The hearts of the kings are in the hands of the Lord and He will move them like the waterways. Everything is in the hands of the Lord and He reigns. We are called to pray for the governors, presidents, prime ministers, kings and queens to come to know the truth and be empowered by His wisdom to help people accordingly.

So today let us start this prayer: Father in name of Jesus Christ, the Lord of lords and king of kings, we bring before you all the chiefs and governors of Iran. Father, we bring to you the situation of drinking water in Khozestan, you know who is responsible and what has happened there, and you also know how to fix this problem. Oh Father, in name of Jesus Christ, give wisdom to those who are in charge of this situation how to restore the drinking water to people and the farms. Oh Lord, please be with the people, lift them up, bless them and provide for them. Lord, we pray for the sick and afflicted, you are the healer, and you are able to heal them and restore them. So, Lord please open the doors of heaven and heal this people.

Lord, we pray for Afghanistan and their situation with Taleban. Oh Father, in name of Jesus please be with this people, protect them and bring them to know you. Lord, we bring the leaders of Taleban before you, who need you more than anyone else. Oh Lord Jesus Christ, please change their hearts and return them to you and put your love and mercy in them. Thank you Lord. In name of Jesus Christ, Amen.

SEPTEMBER 18
Healing prayer for Iran and Afghanistan (2)

Rev. Edward Yousefian has issued a call to all Persian-speaking Christians to unite in prayer for Iran on the three days of August 18, 19, and 20. In light of the current situation, Pastor Tim and I suggest we also include Afghanistan in our prayers and fast on their behalf. As previously explained, fasting in Christianity can take various forms, whether it's abstaining from food, water, television, coffee, or other indulgences. It signifies setting aside worldly pleasures to intensify our prayers and connection with God.

Today, our hearts are with the people of Iran and Afghanistan. A prophetic word in Jeremiah 49:38 speaks of Elam, the ancient name for Iran. The LORD declares, "I will set my throne in Elam." In recent times, we have witnessed large groups of Iranians turning to the Lord Jesus Christ. Where once, around 1900, it took the life of a missionary to bring one Muslim to Jesus Christ, we now see a vast number of Iranian Muslims embracing the Lord Jesus Christ as their Savior every day. This prophecy for the Iranians has been, and continues to be, fulfilled.

Let us join in prayer. I'll start, and I invite you to continue praying and fasting in the coming days.

Father, in the mighty name of Jesus Christ, our King of kings, we approach Your throne. You reign supreme, holding everything within Your control. In Timothy, You instruct us to pray for leaders and officials, that they might come to know You and govern their people justly. We lift up the leaders of Iran: the president, the ministers, and all in authority. May they too find salvation in You. Grant them wisdom to govern righteously, to alleviate hunger, to combat this pandemic, and to restore water to Khuzestan. As we pray for the people of Iran, may Your healing hand touch them physically and spiritually, bringing both health and salvation.

Furthermore, we bring before You the situation in Afghanistan, where 23 Christian missionaries face the threat of execution. You, O Lord, have the power to intervene and shield them. May the hearts of the Afghan rulers, including the Taliban, be turned towards You. Transform them, Lord, and lead them to recognize the Lord Jesus Christ as their Savior.

We entrust both nations into Your capable hands, confident in Your sovereignty and love.

In the name of Jesus Christ, Amen.

SEPTEMBER 19
Prayer for Iran and Afghanistan (3)

Today, we again lift our hearts in prayer for the people of Iran and Afghanistan. As you go about your day, especially if you're observing any form of fasting, remember them and intercede on their behalf in the mighty name of Jesus Christ.

Let us unite our hearts in fervent prayer for our Iranian and Afghan brothers and sisters.

Father, in the majestic name of Jesus Christ, our King of kings, we come before You. We thank You for Your endless bounty, Your boundless love, and the countless blessings that flow from Your throne. From the earth to the heavens, from the east to the west, Your love and compassion know no bounds.

We thank You, Father, for the gift of Your Son, whom You did not withhold from us. We're grateful, Jesus, for the blood You shed on the cross, bearing our sins and curses. And we celebrate Your victorious resurrection on the third day when You triumphed over death, sin, and all curses. Thank You for sending the Holy Spirit and for Your unwavering promises – that all things work together for the good of those who love You and are called according to Your purpose.

Father, as we intercede for Iran, we ask for Your mercy. In the midst of the havoc that Covid wreaks, we pray for healing. Touch the nation of Iran with Your healing hand, Lord. Let their physical healing pave the way for spiritual revelation, leading many to recognize and accept You as their Savior, Messiah, and Lord.

We pray for wisdom for the leaders of Iran. Transform their hearts, Lord. Instill in them a desire to act in the best interest of their people. Grant them insight to effectively combat the pandemic and to restore the water to Khuzestan. Your word in Jeremiah speaks of setting a throne in Elam, ancient Iran. Even now, we see the fulfillment as numerous Iranians turn to You. Let this number multiply, Father.

For Afghanistan, we ask for Your mercy and grace. We bring the Taliban regime before Your throne. Change their hearts, Lord, and guide them towards Your paths of righteousness. May the land of Afghanistan experience liberation in Your mighty name.

In faith and unity, we present these petitions, believing that You hear and answer. In the matchless name of Jesus Christ, our King of kings, we pray. Amen.

SEPTEMBER 20
Prayer for Iran and Afghanistan (4)

Today's devotional marks the third and final day of prayer for Iran and Afghanistan, and we gather together in unity. We pray that the Holy Spirit, who purifies the world from sin, brings justice to the people of Iran and Afghanistan. In the name of Jesus Christ, King of kings, we express our gratitude for all Your blessings, for Your boundless greatness, and for Your love that stretches from the earth to the heavens, O Lord. We thank You, Father, and we thank You, Lord, for Your son, Jesus Christ. We are profoundly grateful for the blood He shed for us on the cross. He rose from the dead on the third day, conquering death and sin, and through His sacrifice and resurrection, we are recognized as righteous. We exalt You, Lord. Your name is holy; You are the embodiment of holiness and grandeur. O God, as we stand in Your presence, we uplift the people of Iran. Holy Spirit, our guide and our mentor, we beseech You to pour out upon the Iranian populace. Liberate each soul from their sins. Illuminate the path to salvation for them. The sole way to salvation is through our Lord Jesus Christ. As 1 Corinthians 1 informs us, Jesus Christ embodies the power and wisdom of God. May You, Jesus Christ, establish Your throne in both Iran and Afghanistan, reigning supreme, for You are the divine power and wisdom. Beloved Holy Spirit, bestow Your blessings upon the people and rulers of Iran and Afghanistan. Redeem them, drawing them closer to Your embrace. O Jesus Christ, lead them to recognize You as the singular path to the Father, the ultimate God and Savior. We implore You, God, to heal every individual in Iran, especially from the ravages of this Corona. Softens the hearts of leaders and rulers, endowing them with compassion and benevolence, ensuring their actions and intentions align with the welfare of their people. Father, bestow Your mercy upon all Iranians and Afghans, shielding them from harm. Enlighten their hearts to discern the truth, that this truth may bring them salvation. We present our earnest prayers for Khuzestan and its water crisis. You possess the knowledge and means to restore its water in the most effective and swift manner. Act, O Father. O God, preserve these lands from drought, famine, and the tragic loss of fauna and flora. Grant discernment to the authorities, enabling them to address these challenges in the most effective manner. May Your glorious name be revered throughout. We offer this prayer in the mighty name of Jesus Christ, King of kings. Amen.

SEPTEMBER 21
Your body is the temple of Holy Spirit

1 Corinthians 6:19

"Do you not know that your body is the temple of the Holy Spirit who is in you, whom you have from God, and you are not your own?"

This verse reminds us that our bodies are the dwelling place of the Holy Spirit, a gift from God. Furthermore, we no longer possess sole ownership over our bodies, for they were acquired at a significant price; therefore, we should use them to glorify God.

In this passage, Paul addresses the Corinthians, discussing sexual immorality, dietary habits, and overall conduct. His central message is that upon accepting Jesus Christ and being indwelt by the Holy Spirit, our bodies are sanctified. They transform into temples. Why temples? Because they house the Divine. Recognizing that, as Christians, our bodies serve as holy vessels for the Holy Spirit can profoundly influence our decisions, guiding us away from sin and wrongdoing.

Always bearing in mind that God is not just with us but within us is pivotal. The Holy Spirit consistently nudges our conscience, pointing out our missteps. Remember, our bodies are current residences of God, not merely potential ones. This awareness should make us think twice: each time we sin, we inadvertently drag God into it. How then can we ensure reverence?

We must treat our bodies with utmost respect. This involves a balanced diet, regular exercise, and overall health maintenance. Avoiding detrimental habits like smoking and drug use is essential.

Today, let's internalize this truth: our bodies are the sanctuaries of God and the Holy Spirit's dwelling place. May this realization fortify us against temptations and guide our actions, ensuring they align with God's will.

Amen. May God be with you.

SEPTEMBER 22
Not to slander our neighbors secretly

Psalm 101, verse 5 states, "Whoever secretly slanders his neighbor, Him I will destroy; The one who has a haughty look and a proud heart, Him I will not endure." This can be understood as, "I will bring to ruin anyone who slanders their neighbor in secret. And I will not tolerate those with arrogant eyes and a haughty heart."

Do we find ourselves gossiping behind the backs of our neighbors, friends, family, or church members? Do we denigrate others in private? The verse makes it clear: God opposes those who secretly slander their neighbors and those with prideful hearts and arrogant eyes. Such behaviors indicate a superiority complex and a departure from humility.

We are reminded of Jesus' teachings: "Blessed are the meek, for they shall inherit the earth." Subsequently, Psalm 101:6 notes, "My eyes will be on the faithful in the land, that they may dwell with me; the one whose walk is blameless will minister to me." God cherishes a humble spirit and a kind heart.

Christ's core message to us is love. He instructed, "Love one another. The greatest commandment is to love God with all your heart, soul, and mind. And the second is like it: Love your neighbor as yourself." These two commandments are inseparable.

Today, let's introspect. If we find ourselves harboring negative thoughts or speaking ill of someone, let's immediately turn to God in repentance. Begin praying for those individuals—even if they're adversaries. We're called to pray for their well-being, not their downfall. As Christ declared from the cross, "Father, forgive them, for they do not know what they do." Likewise, we should echo this sentiment.

Let's be vigilant about our words and thoughts, always examining them in light of the Holy Spirit. May the Spirit alert us whenever we stray from His path. Let our hearts overflow with prayer and kindness, forsaking slander and malice. Amen.

SEPTEMBER 23
Let us not envy the evil person

Proverbs 24:1-2

> *"Do not be envious of evil men, nor desire to be with them; for their heart devises violence, and their lips talk of troublemaking." Another interpretation reads, "Be not thou envious against evil men, neither desire to be with them. For their heart studieth destruction, and their lips talk of mischief."*

It's a caution against being attracted to or envying those who might seem prosperous but lack righteousness. God reminds us elsewhere: The wicked face eventual ruin, but the righteous shall thrive eternally.

God distances Himself from those who harbor jealousy, engage in gossip, or perpetrate harm. He warns of the perils of association with such individuals. Thus, we must exercise discernment in our associations, resisting the temptation to envy those who may seem successful yet are morally astray. For their hearts are rife with malicious intent, their speech replete with harm.

The tongue is a formidable weapon, its wounds often invisible yet deeply scarring. Physical bruises might fade, but the internal marks left by harmful words can persist, becoming lasting internal wounds that skew our morals and thoughts.

Yet, with God's grace and the Holy Spirit's guidance, we find the strength to forgive, echoing Christ's plea: "Father, forgive them, for they know not what they do." In doing so, we find healing for the soul-deep wounds inflicted by others.

Today, let's pray against the lure of envy and the pitfalls of negative association. Let's ask God to equip us with discernment to recognize and evade evil and grant us the compassion to pray for those ensnared by it.

In surrendering this day and our hearts, we declare, "Father, in the name of Jesus Christ, guide us." Amen.

SEPTEMBER 24
There is only one God

1 Corinthians 8:2-5

In 1 Corinthians 8:2-5, Paul addresses the matter of eating food offered to idols, stating: "So, concerning food sacrificed to idols: we know that 'an idol is nothing at all in the world' and that 'there is no God but one.' Indeed, even if there are so-called gods, whether in heaven or on earth—as there are many gods and many lords—yet for us, there is but one God, the Father, from whom all things came and for whom we live; and there is but one Lord, Jesus Christ, through whom all things came and through whom we live."

Paul continues by discussing the nature of this understanding and the sensitivity required when dealing with fellow believers who might not share the same strength in this conviction. However, the core message remains: there is only one God, our Father. While other entities might be termed as 'gods', they are merely spirits of deceit.

Jesus Himself professed, "I am the way, the truth, and the life. No one comes to the Father except through me." In a world with diverse belief systems and many entities hailed as gods, we must recognize and hold firm to the truth that God is singular, our Heavenly Father. And the sole path to Him is through Lord Jesus Christ.

He emphasizes that everything came into existence through Jesus, and our very existence is through Him. Through Jesus' sacrificial death on the cross and His triumphant resurrection on the third day, He defeated sin and death. And it is through faith in this act that we receive grace, becoming children of God, and heirs to the promise of eternal life.

So, amid the myriad voices and beliefs of the world, let's anchor our faith in this truth: Our God is one, the Father. And our Lord Jesus Christ is the bridge that connects us to Him, ensuring eternal life. Amen.

SEPTEMBER 25
Who do we imitate?

1 Corinthians 11:1

"Imitate me, just as I also imitate Christ."

Paul urges the Corinthians: "Follow my lead as I emulate Lord Jesus Christ." This prompts a crucial question for us today: Who do we regard as our ultimate role model? For Christians, that epitome of life, the benchmark of character, the individual we esteem above all and ardently seek to emulate is Jesus Christ, the Son of God.

Upon accepting Jesus, when the Holy Spirit dwells within us, the ultimate purpose is our transformation to be more Christ-like. As believers, our objective should always be to resonate increasingly with Jesus' nature and character. He should be our gold standard, superseding any contemporary icons or celebrities.

Indeed, while some might admire sports stars or other public figures for their specific achievements, for Christians, the ultimate role model is Jesus.

The Holy Spirit actively works within us, daily refining and removing attributes not in alignment with Christ's nature, sculpting us progressively into His likeness. Our aspiration as Christians is to ultimately embody the love, compassion, and character of Jesus.

Paul's call to the Corinthians, who had never personally witnessed Christ, was clear: "Look at me. Emulate my actions, for they reflect the teachings of Jesus." In essence, Paul was a living testimony of Christ's teachings.

Today, let's anchor ourselves in Christ, turning to Him in every circumstance, seeking His guidance and direction. There was a popular trend where believers wore bracelets inscribed with WWJD - "What Would Jesus Do?" It was a tangible reminder to always consider Christ's perspective in every situation.

Let's continue to view Jesus Christ as our ultimate role model, consistently striving to mirror His love, wisdom, and righteousness in our lives. Amen.

SEPTEMBER 26
Bless the Lord oh my soul

Psalm 103:1-5

> *"Bless the LORD, O my soul; And all that is within me, bless His holy name! 2 Bless the LORD, O my soul, and forget not all His benefits: 3 Who forgives all your iniquities, who heals all your diseases, 4 Who redeems your life from destruction, who crowns you with lovingkindness and tender mercies, 5 Who satisfies your mouth with good things, So that your youth is renewed like the eagle's."* Amen.

Today, let's approach God with gratitude, reverence, and love, acknowledging and celebrating all that He continually does for us. Let's sanctify His name and remember the multitude of His blessings every moment. By recalling the vastness of His kindness, we draw nearer to Him, fortifying our connection and moving forward with hearts brimming with thankfulness. This appreciation only enhances the quality of our days.

Among His countless gifts, foremost is the sacrifice of Jesus Christ, who died for our sins, offering forgiveness and healing. By His wounds, we find healing. He redeems us from destruction, granting us salvation and eternal life through His selfless act on the cross. For those who embrace Jesus Christ, who repent and walk beside Him, a promise awaits. We're not only redeemed but also crowned with His ceaseless love and mercy.

Such profound love fills our souls with goodness, rejuvenating our spirit and vigor, much like an eagle soaring high. Isn't that wonderful?

So, let's perpetually express our gratitude for every blessing and kindness bestowed upon us. May we always cherish His deeds and walk hand in hand with Him, every step of the way. Amen.

SEPTEMBER 27
Not to partake in the communion unworthily

1 Corinthians 11:27

> *Therefore, whoever eats this bread or drinks this cup of the Lord in an unworthy manner will be guilty of the body and blood of the Lord.*

Paul discusses the significance of the Lord's Supper, the Last Supper, and communion. He cautions the Corinthians, stating, "Whosoever shall eat this bread, and drink this cup of the Lord, unworthily, shall be guilty of the body and blood of the Lord. But let a man examine himself, and so let him eat of that bread, and drink of that cup. For he that eateth and drinketh unworthily, eateth and drinketh damnation to himself, not discerning the Lord's body."

The Last Supper is a symbolic act. While some churches commemorate it every Sunday, others do so on the first Sunday of the month. This act of breaking the bread and drinking the wine is a commandment from Christ, reminding us of His sacrifice. He asks us to remember His body, which was broken for us, and His blood, which was poured out for us.

However, it's vital to note that the Last Supper is intended for believers. It serves as a moment of reflection, to commemorate the body and blood of the Lord. Before participating, Paul emphasizes the importance of self-examination.

This introspection is to evaluate our actions, to discern if we have sinned, and if so, to repent and seek God's forgiveness. It's a time to cleanse our souls, to address feelings of jealousy, grudges, or any other misgivings. If we have wronged someone, it's the moment to seek reconciliation.

The Supper serves as a profound reminder of the love and sacrifice of Jesus Christ. Before partaking, taking a moment of silence to self-reflect, acknowledging our missteps and seeking forgiveness, ensures we honor the true essence of this sacred act.

Thus, when we come together for the Lord's Supper, it's essential to pause, introspect, and address any feelings of guilt or resentment. By doing so, we can partake in the bread and wine, truly remembering and honoring the sacrifices of Lord Jesus Christ. Amen.

SEPTEMBER 28
We are the members of one body

1 Corinthians 12

This passage speaks about the gifts of the spirit and the body. I share with you from verse 12: "For as the body is one and has many members, and all the members of that one body, being many, are one body: so also is Christ. For by one Spirit we are all baptized into one body, whether Jews or Gentiles, whether slave or free; and we were all given one Spirit to drink. For the body is not one member, but many."

Imagine if the foot would say, "Because I am not the hand, I do not belong to the body," would it make it any less a part of the body? And if the ear were to say, "Because I am not the eye, I do not belong to the body," is it then not a part of the body? If the entire body were an eye, where would the sense of hearing be? God has placed each of the parts in the body just as He wanted.

This echoes the words of Saadi, who stated that if one part suffers, every part suffers with it. Interestingly, years before Saadi wrote this, it was mentioned in Corinthians, emphasizing the interconnectedness of all members.

The church, being the body of Christ, comprises different members, each endowed with unique gifts. These gifts, be it healing, wisdom, teaching, prophecy, miracles, or others, are granted by the Holy Spirit. They are not meant to elevate one above another, but to work harmoniously to edify the church.

Paul further states that the parts we think are less honorable are indispensable. Thus, we must recognize and appreciate every gift, for they are given for the upliftment and strengthening of God's church.

Today, let us seek God's guidance, asking Him to reveal the gifts of the Spirit in us, grant us wisdom, and enable us to use our gifts effectively for the betterment of His body and for His glory.

In the name of Jesus Christ, Amen.

SEPTEMBER 29
Without Love none of our spiritual gifts worth anything

1 Corinthians 13:1-3

> [1]*Though I speak with the tongues of men and of angels, but have not love, I have become sounding brass or a clanging cymbal.*
> [2]*And though I have the gift of prophecy, and understand all mysteries and all knowledge, and though I have all faith, so that I could remove mountains, but have not love, I am nothing.*
> [3]*And though I bestow all my goods to feed the poor, and though I give my body to be burned, but have not love, it profits me nothing.*

Though we may speak with the tongues of men and even angels, without love, it's but an empty sound, like a hollow drum. If our words and actions are not grounded in genuine love, they lack the essence and divine glory that God intended.

Jesus Christ emphasized the importance of love, instructing us to love one another just as He loved us. He underscored that our love for one another is a testimony to the world of His presence in our lives. Even if we were to speak in the most eloquent languages of men or the heavenly tongue of angels, without love, our words would be empty.

The same goes for wisdom. No matter how profound our understanding or how vast our knowledge, if it's not utilized with love at its core, it becomes hollow. Such wisdom, when not used to foster love, tends to elevate oneself rather than glorifying God.

Furthermore, even acts of charity, when done without genuine love, can end up causing more harm than good. Paul's words serve as a reminder that every act, no matter how noble it might appear, if devoid of love, is futile.

In essence, love should be the foundation of all our actions, words, and thoughts. It's the very essence that gives meaning to our existence and our relationship with God and fellow human beings.

Today, let's pray to God, asking Him to guide our every action and thought, ensuring they are rooted in love. May every gift and blessing we receive be used to spread love, today and always.

In the name of Jesus Christ, Amen.

SEPTEMBER 30
Our labor is not in vain in the Lord

1 Corinthians 15:56

> *The sting of death is sin, and the strength of sin is the law.* [57] *But thanks be to God, who gives us the victory through our Lord Jesus Christ.*

Paul, in his preceding verses, dwells on the subject of the resurrection of the dead. He addresses a debate where some argued against the reality of resurrection. Paul emphasizes that if there was no resurrection, if Christ Himself hadn't been resurrected, then our faith and hope would be rendered meaningless.

However, Christ's death and subsequent resurrection signify the defeat of the sting of death, which is sin, and the strength of sin, the law. Through His sacrifice and victory over death, Christ has offered us a share in this triumph. By accepting Jesus Christ as Lord, we not only acknowledge His victory but become partakers in it because His Spirit now dwells within us. Amen.

Paul thus urges us, in light of this glorious victory, to persevere in our faith and endeavors. We must understand that with the triumph of Christ comes an empowered assurance in everything we do. Knowing that Christ bore all our sins and transgressions on the cross, we are now liberated to serve God in spirit and truth, with the Holy Spirit guiding our path.

Whatever our calling might be – be it street cleaning, working in a store, academic pursuits, or service – we should undertake it with utmost dedication. Our actions should reflect the love and grace of God, so that others, upon witnessing our dedication, may give thanks to our Heavenly Father.

Let us then march forward, fortified by the knowledge that our efforts are never in vain in the eyes of God. We are His treasured children, precious in His sight, thanks to the sacrifice and victory of our Lord Jesus Christ.

In every trial and in every triumph, let us remember that through Him, we are victors in all things. Amen.

OCTOBER 1
Let all that we do be done in love

1 Corinthians 16:13

Watch, stand fast in the faith, be brave, be strong.

Always remain vigilant and firmly rooted in your faith. Display courage and strength in all circumstances. Let all your actions be driven by love and executed in love.

God often instructs us to be as wise as serpents while maintaining the innocence and purity of doves. We should be shrewd when navigating the deceitful snares of the devil, temptations, and sins. Yet, in our interactions, it is vital to remain genuine and compassionate, viewing the world through loving eyes and consistently acting out of love and kindness.

Paul, in his concluding remarks to the Corinthians, emphasizes the need for vigilance and unwavering faith. Jesus Christ assures us that all we need to do is stand resolutely in our beliefs, anchored in Him, and God will manage the rest. When we stand, it should be with an unwavering spirit and an empowered heart.

Such courage and strength emanate from profound faith – a faith rooted in the knowledge of Christ's sacrifice for us on the cross, ensuring our sins are forgiven. With His triumphant resurrection, He conquered death, granting us victory in Him. With Jesus Christ enveloping us and the Holy Spirit guiding us, what or who should we fear?

"If God is for us, who can be against us?" This profound truth invigorates our faith, granting us the courage and strength to persevere. Yet, it's imperative that our faith isn't merely a statement, but an actionable principle. Love and kindness should not merely be words we utter; they should reflect in our deeds.

Today, and every day, let us resolve to stay alert, unwavering in our faith, and embody bravery and strength. May all our endeavors be drenched in love and kindness. Amen.

OCTOBER 2
The fragrance of Christ in us

2 Corinthians 2:14-15

> [14] *Now thanks be to God who always leads us in triumph in Christ, and through us diffuses the fragrance of His knowledge in every place.*
> [15] *For we are to God the fragrance of Christ among those who are being saved and among those who are perishing.*

Praise be to God who, in His infinite wisdom and grace, continually holds us within the embrace of Christ's victorious procession. Through us, He disperses the captivating aroma of His divine knowledge everywhere we go.

To God, we are the essence of Christ's fragrance, perceptible among both the saved and the lost. To some, our very presence may resonate as a stark reminder of mortality, leading them further down a path of destruction. Yet, for others, we exude the invigorating scent of life, leading them towards eternal salvation.

With the Holy Spirit dwelling within us, manifesting the spirit of Christ, we inherently bear His attributes, including His unmistakable fragrance. This divine aroma radiates from our speech, our conduct, our acts of love, our fervent prayers, and simply by our presence among others.

However, this Christlike essence may bear contrasting connotations. To those who remain distant from Christ's embrace, our aura might signify impending doom, for without Christ, they are destined for eternal separation. But to those drawn towards Christ's light, our presence signifies hope, salvation, freedom from the shackles of sin, and the embodiment of divine love.

So, today, let us introspect, ensuring every facet of our existence aligns with God's purpose. Let's pray, "Lord, guide our actions, words, and deeds, ensuring that those around us perceive only the pure essence of Christ within us." May our presence breathe life into their spirits and not signify impending doom. May we carry this divine fragrance everywhere, making every space a testament to God's love. Amen.

OCTOBER 3

We are the ambassadors of the message of reconciliation with God

2 Corinthians 5:17-20

> [17] *Therefore, if anyone is in Christ, the new creation has come: The old has gone, the new is here!*
> [18] *All this is from God, who reconciled us to himself through Christ and gave us the ministry of reconciliation:*
> [19] *that God was reconciling the world to himself in Christ, not counting people's sins against them. And he has committed to us the message of reconciliation.*
> [20] *We are therefore Christ's ambassadors, as though God were making his appeal through us. We implore you on Christ's behalf: Be reconciled to God.*

If we are in Christ, we are made anew. Our past is washed away; everything is transformed. All is from God, who brought us back to Himself through Christ. He has now entrusted us with this message of reconciliation. It is as if God Himself is making His appeal through us, urging the world to find their way back to Him through Christ.

When we embrace Jesus Christ, our past sins are left at the foot of the cross. As we are immersed in Him through baptism, we are reborn, our past sins washed away. And with the Holy Spirit dwelling within, we are no longer bound by our former selves. Every time we're tempted to revert to our old ways, we must remember that we are now a new creation in Christ. God has mended our relationship, once fractured by sin, through the sacrifice of Jesus.

God desires no one to be lost but yearns for all to find their way back to Him. Having experienced this beautiful reconciliation ourselves, we are now tasked as God's representatives. We bear the honor and responsibility of sharing this message of reconciliation with those yet to hear it. We are called to be ambassadors of love, unity, and grace.

In Him, we find unity and a deep connection with others. So, let us share this immense blessing we've received: the gift of reconciliation with God. The greatest treasure we can possess is a deep and intimate relationship with Him. Let's spread the word, sharing the incredible power of reconciliation made possible only through Jesus Christ. Amen.

OCTOBER 4
Do not go under unequal yoke with unbelievers

2 Corinthians 6:14

> *Do not be yoked together with unbelievers. For what do righteousness and wickedness have in common? Or what fellowship can light have with darkness?*

Paul's admonition against being unequally yoked with unbelievers is a call to ensure that our core values, beliefs, and principles aren't compromised. It's a reminder that righteousness and wickedness, light and darkness, Christ and Satan have no fellowship together. When we embrace Christ and His teachings, the Holy Spirit dwells within us, making us living temples of God.

As such, we must be wary of reverting to old habits, especially those that conflict with our Christian values. This doesn't mean we should isolate ourselves from all non-believers. On the contrary, we are called to be the light in the midst of darkness, to be the salt of the earth, and to share the Gospel.

However, Paul's words caution us against forming partnerships (whether in business, marriage, or otherwise) where our foundational beliefs could be jeopardized. While it's vital to interact, share, and spread the message of Christ, we should do so without compromising our faith.

In essence, while we live in the world and engage with it, we shouldn't let the world dictate our values or draw us away from our faith. We should radiate the love of Christ, embody truth and integrity, and ensure that our interactions always honor Him. Amen.

OCTOBER 5
Those Who Have Been Redeemed of God Say So

Psalm 107:1-3

> *Give thanks to the LORD, for he is good; his love endures forever. Let the redeemed of the LORD tell their story— those he redeemed from the hand of the foe, those he gathered from the lands, from east and west, from north and south.*

O give thanks unto the LORD, for He is good: for His mercy endureth forever. Let the redeemed of the LORD say so, whom He hath redeemed from the hand of the enemy and gathered them out of the lands, from the east, and from the west, from the north, and from the south. This is one of the Christian hymns, "Let the redeemed of the Lord say so." "Redeemed" means those whom God has delivered. Who are they? These redeemed ones are you and I. Jesus Christ, with His blood and His own sacrifice, redeemed and delivered us. From where? From different places. And why did He pay this ransom? Because His love is everlasting. The love of God is forever in Christ. We, the redeemed ones, must say, "Thank God, thank God and glory to Him," because He is good, and His love is eternal. He has redeemed us from all tribulations; He saved us from all our sins and from all curses with His blood on the cross. He gathered us from the different lands where we were scattered.

And where did He take us? To His own kingdom — the kingdom of heaven and the kingdom of God. Although we may be citizens of different cities and countries, we are, in fact, citizens of heaven and the kingdom of God. We are the ones who were redeemed, the ones who accepted Jesus Christ as Lord and Savior. We, who confessed that He redeemed us with His blood on the cross and that with His death and resurrection, overcame death, sin, and the devil. Through Him, because He lives in us, we are set free and redeemed. We have returned to the kingdom of God, and we are the family of God. You and I, who accepted Jesus Christ as Lord and Savior, are these redeemed ones, redeemed by the Lord. So today, let all the redeemed ones say together, "Thank God the Merciful, whose love and affection are forever." Amen.

OCTOBER 6
Prayer for the governors

1 Timothy 2:1-4

> [1] *I urge, then, first of all, that petitions, prayers, intercession and thanksgiving be made for all people—*
> [2] *for kings and all those in authority, that we may live peaceful and quiet lives in all godliness and holiness.*
> [3] *This is good, and pleases God our Savior,*
> [4] *who wants all people to be saved and to come to a knowledge of the truth.*

As we know, the government under Canadian Prime Minister Justin Trudeau has been re-elected. We, as Christians, have a duty to pray for all rulers, statesmen, leaders, and officials as guided by 1 Timothy 2: "I exhort therefore, that, first of all, supplications, prayers, intercessions, and giving of thanks be made for all men; For kings, and for all that are in authority; that we may lead a quiet and peaceable life in all godliness and honesty." This is good and acceptable in the sight of our God and Saviour, who desires all men to be saved and

to come to the knowledge of the truth. Today, let's offer our prayers for the incumbents, the rulers, the prime ministers, and all those newly elected to the Canadian government.

Father, in the name of Jesus Christ, the King of Kings, we thank you for Prime Minister Justin Trudeau, his government, and the opposition party. We lift them up before you, praying that they come to know Jesus Christ as their Lord and Saviour. Grant them wisdom, enlighten them to act in the best interests of Canadians. We ask for hearts within them that seek the good of the people, discerning righteousness from wrong according to your Word, the Bible. While not everything that appears good to us may be righteous, instill in their hearts that which is pleasing to You. Guide these leaders, both in Canada and globally, with Your Holy Spirit, showing them how to best serve their people, uplifting them in knowledge and well-being, without persecuting your name.

May Your will be manifested in and through these leaders. Your Word states that the hearts of kings are in Your hands, and like rivers, You guide them. Recognizing Your sovereignty, we acknowledge that it's by Your will that these leaders have been appointed. You have shown time and again, through figures like Nebuchadnezzar and Darius, that You give and take away power.

So, with the same wisdom that You place someone in a position of leadership, may You work in them and through them, and in their families. We commit this day and every other day into Your blessed hands. When we are aggrieved or in dispute, help us to lift our concerns to Your feet and intercede for these leaders.

We entrust our days into Your loving hands, in the name of Jesus Christ. Amen.

OCTOBER 7
My grace is sufficient

2 Corinthians 12:7

or because of these surpassingly great revelations. Therefore, in order to keep me from becoming conceited, I was given a thorn in my flesh, a messenger of Satan, to torment me.

Here, Paul states: "And lest I should be exalted above measure through the abundance of the revelations, there was given to me a thorn in the flesh, the messenger of Satan to buffet me, lest I should be exalted above measure. For this thing I besought the Lord thrice, that it might depart from me. And He said unto me, 'My grace is sufficient for thee: for my strength is made perfect in weakness.' Most gladly, therefore, will I rather glory in my infirmities, that the power of Christ may rest upon me. Therefore, I take pleasure in infirmities, in reproaches, in necessities, in persecutions, in distresses for Christ's sake: for when I am weak, then am I strong."

Some suggest the thorn Paul refers to is a physical ailment, while others believe it might be a demonic torment. Regardless of its nature, Paul fervently asks God on three occasions to remove it. This recalls how Jesus, on the eve of His crucifixion, prayed in the garden, asking if the impending suffering might be taken from Him. Yet, in His surrender, He sought God's will above His own. Similarly, God responds to Paul, not by removing the affliction, but by reassuring him, "My grace is sufficient for you." God's grace becomes evident, especially in our challenges. Such trials are essential for character development, ensuring we remain humble and reliant on His strength.

Understanding this, Paul embraces his infirmities. He recognizes that God's grace shines most brightly in our moments of weakness. The more vulnerable or powerless one feels, the more God's grace and might become evident in one's life.

When Paul grasps this truth, he no longer laments his affliction. Instead, he sees how this "thorn" amplifies God's grace in him. "For when I am weak," Paul realizes, "then I am strong."

So, if today we find ourselves beset by a "thorn," or we've prayed for God to remove a particular burden and He hasn't, let us seek understanding. If this trial refines our character in Christ, let us embrace it. Let's pray, "O Lord, if this challenge makes me more like You, let it remain. Bestow upon me Your grace, and may I be a testament to Your enduring love." Amen.

OCTOBER 8
A Gift to the Lord wholeheartedly and generously

2 Corinthians 8:1

And now, brothers and sisters, we want you to know about the grace that God has given the Macedonian churches.

Here, Paul extols the virtues of the churches in Macedonia – those in Philippi, Thessalonica, and Berea. These communities were beset with challenges due to wars and economic hardships, further exacerbated by Roman oppression. Yet, despite their deep poverty, they displayed extraordinary generosity, contributing gifts to support other churches.

Intriguingly, their foremost act was to surrender themselves to God, and subsequently, to the apostles. Their commitment wasn't merely a show of faith but a profound expression of selflessness and devotion. They didn't merely give out of obligation but from a genuine overflow of their love for Christ and His church. Their actions, underlined by their complete submission to the Lord's will, showcased the transformative power of Christ working within them.

This serves as a potent reminder to us all. Our offerings to God should emanate from the depths of our hearts. Giving shouldn't be viewed as a duty but as a heartfelt expression of our love for Him. God desires willing and joyous givers, not those who give begrudgingly or out of obligation.

So, when we feel prompted to contribute to the church or any charitable cause, let us pause and ask: "Lord, what would you have me give?" We must ensure our gifts are given wholeheartedly and generously, without any compulsion.

Remember, God's desire is to mold us into His image – generous, loving, and sacrificial. May we emulate His spirit of giving: selflessly, lovingly, and freely. Amen.

OCTOBER 9
Let's go forward with Lord's grace and peace

Galatians 1:3

> *Grace be to you and peace from God the Father, and from our Lord Jesus Christ, Who gave himself for our sins, that he might deliver us from this present evil world, according to the will of God and our Father: To whom be glory forever and ever. Amen.*

Let us pray with these words in our hearts:

Father, we thank You for Your immeasurable grace and peace, granted to us through our Lord Jesus Christ, the King of kings. He bore our sins, enduring the weight of our transgressions upon the cross, cleansing and sanctifying us. Through His sacrifice, we find healing and redemption.

We are humbled by this gift of grace, a gift we did not earn. In exchange for our deserving judgement, You offered us mercy, salvation, and eternal life with You. Through Christ's sacrifice, Your Holy Spirit dwells within us, a constant reminder of Your love and mercy.

Lord, in these challenging times, we find solace in Your grace and peace. All glory and honor belong to You, forever and ever.

Today, we lift up Iran before You. We pray for healing and protection over those afflicted with the virus. Grant wisdom and guidance to the nation's leaders, that they may act with compassion and fairness. May they come to know You and dedicate their hearts to serving the greater good.

Bless the wealth of the nation, that it may be used for the welfare of its people. Establish Your righteous reign in both Iran and Afghanistan.

We also remember our Afghan brothers and sisters. Protect them, Lord, and lead them to You. Guide the Taliban, that they might find Your light and turn from their ways. Your desire is salvation and redemption for all.

Empower each of us to share Your gospel, to be instruments of Your peace. We thank You for Your enduring blessings.

We offer this prayer in the mighty name of Jesus Christ, the King of kings. Amen.

OCTOBER 10
His work is honorable and glorious

Psalm 111

> *"Praise ye the LORD. I will praise the LORD with my whole heart, in the assembly of the upright, and in the congregation. The works of the LORD are great, sought out of all them that have pleasure therein. His work is honorable and glorious: and his righteousness endureth forever. He hath made his wonderful works to be remembered: the LORD is gracious and full of compassion."* Amen.

Wouldn't you rejoice in praising God with all your heart, voice, and strength amidst the congregation and the righteous? There are moments during church gatherings when God's spirit uplifts us to the point where we spontaneously exclaim, "Hallelujah! God, how magnificent and powerful You are! We thank You for all Your marvelous deeds."

We give thanks to God, elevating us, the ones who delight in Him. We recognize God's astounding works, His magnificent creations, and His enduring righteousness. Yet, remember that verse 3 emphasizes "His work" and not "His works." Singular in its significance, full of glory, it is a work that culminates in eternal righteousness.

What could this singular "work" be? It appears to be salvation—accomplished through the blood of His Son, Jesus Christ. A work bursting with glory, leading to everlasting righteousness. Upon recognizing this profound act of God in Jesus Christ, who cleansed us from our sins and overcame the constraints of death, we perceive God's primary work, filled with splendor and majesty.

While anyone with open eyes can discern God's incredible acts in nature, in every individual, and even within the intricacies of every atom and cell, it's paramount to remember that our God is steeped in grace and mercy. Even when we were distanced from Him, He did not withhold His Son, Jesus Christ. Out of sheer love and compassion, He descended from His heavenly abode, taking human form to endure our trials and tribulations. Thus, ensuring that we can never claim God's aloofness from our struggles. He bore every hardship, even the most agonizing ones, succumbing to the harshest of deaths.

However, can death truly restrain the Lord? Absolutely not. By rising again, He triumphed over death and evil. This spectacular act underscores God's lasting righteousness, especially for those of us who embrace Jesus Christ as our Savior. Let us, therefore, rise in unison and proclaim our heartfelt "Hallelujahs" to God, appreciating His immeasurable grandeur. Amen.

OCTOBER 11
Bear one another's burdens

Galatians 6:1

> *Brothers and sisters, if someone is caught in a sin, you who live by the Spirit should restore that person gently. But watch yourselves, or you also may be tempted.*

It is written, "Brethren, if a man be overtaken in a fault, ye which are spiritual, restore such a one in the spirit of meekness." And then it continues, "considering thyself, lest thou also be tempted. Bear ye one another's burdens, and so fulfil the law of Christ." When one of our Christian brethren errs or falls into sin, it is our duty to approach him and lift him up with kindness and understanding. We are not to be judgmental, pointing fingers and exclaiming, "You sinned! Repent!" Instead, we should approach with a compassionate heart, asking, "What happened? How did it come to this?"

"Bear ye one another's burdens, and so fulfil the law of Christ." But what is the law of Christ? He declares a new covenant, saying, "Love each other as I have loved you, so that the world may see your love for one another and give praise to your Father."

The essence of Christ's law is love. It's love that shoulders the burdens of others, love that acts with gentle care, love that remains steadfast, love that practices patience, and love that embraces humility. When a member of our congregation stumbles, it's our responsibility to approach that individual with love and care, extending a helping hand. It doesn't mean we avoid addressing the truth. We should, but always with love and understanding, taking the time to listen.

For if a fellow Christian, especially a genuine believer, has erred and you are aware, it becomes your duty to shed light on the situation. At times, they might be oblivious, ensnared in the web of their actions and failing to recognize the gravity of their sins. Our responsibility extends to bringing this awareness, but always with tenderness and a heart full of compassion, without any accusatory tone. It's crucial to remember this lest we fall into the trap of pride, considering ourselves superior.

So, let us carry this message and practice it in our lives.

In the name of Jesus Christ, Amen.

OCTOBER 12
All things are gathered together in Christ

Ephesians 1:9-10

> [9] *he made known to us the mystery of his will according to his good pleasure, which he purposed in Christ,*
> [10] *to be put into effect when the times reach their fulfillment—to bring unity to all things in heaven and on earth under Christ.*

In the initial chapter of Ephesians, Paul's words are so profound that one can't help but realize this writing flows through the inspiration of the Holy Spirit, transcending mere human articulation.

Paul delves into the once-hidden mystery of God's will, which has since been unveiled to us. He states, "Having made known unto us the mystery of his will, according to his good pleasure which he hath purposed in himself." God has unraveled His divine purpose, manifesting it through Christ Jesus, the second person of the Holy Trinity. This purpose sees God taking the form of flesh, walking among us.

But what exactly is this divine will? It is an intent that consolidates everything—whether in the heavens or on earth—under one umbrella, that is, in Jesus Christ. The Scriptures affirm that all goodness stems from Jesus Christ. John attests that all creation exists for Him and through Him.

Thus, every earthly and heavenly entity, every manifestation of goodness, greatness, power, and all that we perceive as supreme, find their ultimate essence in Jesus Christ. His all-encompassing grace envelopes us. Attributes like love, compassion, humility, healing, selflessness—all converge in the person of Jesus Christ.

Reiterating His unparalleled stature, Scriptures declare that His name towers above any other, whether in the heavens, on earth, or beneath. Revelation prophesies that every knee shall bow, and every tongue will affirm that Jesus Christ is Lord. Everything we seek—be it forgiveness or deliverance from life's tribulations—is embodied in Jesus Christ, our Lord, our Savior, the Son of God.

Today, let us march forward, bearing in our hearts this profound truth: all culminates in Him, and unparalleled power resides in His name. Amen.

OCTOBER 13
God made us alive with Christ

Ephesians 2:4-8

> 4 *But because of his great love for us, God, who is rich in mercy,*
> 5 *made us alive with Christ even when we were dead in transgressions—it is by grace you have been saved.*
> 6 *And God raised us up with Christ and seated us with him in the heavenly realms in Christ Jesus,*
> 7 *in order that in the coming ages he might show the incomparable riches of his grace, expressed in his kindness to us in Christ Jesus.*
> 8 *For it is by grace you have been saved, through faith—and this is not from yourselves, it is the gift of God—*

But God, in His infinite mercy and due to His immense love for us, even when we were engulfed by our sins, breathed life into us alongside Christ. As Jesus Himself proclaims in John: The Father's love for the world is so profound that He didn't withhold even His only begotten Son from it. Even when our sins rendered us spiritually lifeless, even when we ambled, oblivious like spiritual zombies, He still loved us.

Paul emphasizes elsewhere how Christ sacrificed Himself on the cross even when we were adversarial towards Him. By embracing Jesus and His redeeming act, God elevates us, bestowing upon us new life. As Jesus was resurrected from the dead on the third day by the Father, in the same spirit, we too are uplifted through Jesus' blood.

Upon accepting Him, we are elevated, purely by God's grace and His love, independent of our deeds. And as Jesus was ascended to sit beside the Father, so are we positioned alongside Him in heavenly realms.

At this moment, we are seated with Jesus. Why? Because His Spirit dwells within us. Jesus Christ's Spirit resides in us, enabling direct communion with God, needing no intermediaries. We stand where Jesus stands, empowered by the Holy Spirit within, drawing us nearer.

This overwhelming grace of our unparalleled God is evident through Jesus Christ, reflected in His kindness across future generations, within us, and all around us. He reiterates: Our salvation stems from grace through faith in Him, not attributed to our own actions.

Father, we express our gratitude today for this boundless grace and Your profound love for us. We thank You for welcoming us into Your kingdom. We are grateful for the sacrificial act of Jesus Christ on the cross and His resurrection. We cherish the transformations You bring about within us through the Holy Spirit. Lord, bring Your work in us to fruition, enabling us to disseminate this love and compassion to others. We offer our thanks, Father, in the name of Jesus Christ, Amen.

OCTOBER 14
Praise the name of the Lord

Psalm 113:1-4

> [1]*Praise the* LORD. *Praise the* LORD, *you his servants; praise the name of the* LORD.
> [2] *Let the name of the* LORD *be praised, both now and forevermore.*
> [3] *From the rising of the sun to the place where it sets, the name of the* LORD *is to be praised.*
> [4] *The* LORD *is exalted over all the nations, his glory above the heavens.*

Praise ye the LORD. Praise, O ye servants of the LORD, praise the name of the LORD. Blessed be the name of the LORD from this time forth and forevermore. From the rising of the sun unto its setting, the LORD's name is to be praised. The LORD is exalted above all nations, and His glory towers above the heavens. Amen.

We acknowledge the name of the Lord. The Lord Jesus Christ, God the Father, and the Holy Spirit — they are One.

The Psalmist conveys a powerful message: to continually praise the name of the Lord. For how long? Eternally. From dawn till dusk. No matter where we are, we should lift our voices, proclaiming our gratitude to God repeatedly. "Blessed be Your name."

O Jesus Christ, Your name stands supreme, surpassing any other on earth, in heaven, and beyond. The Lord reigns majestically above all nations; His splendor is unparalleled in the heavens. He is the Sovereign Lord of all – of every individual and every nation. God the Father, the Son, and the Holy Spirit, together they reign supreme.

Many of us, hearing the divine call, walk hand in hand with the Lord, embracing Him as our Savior. He, who purified us with His blood, vanquishing our sins and curses. Through His resurrection, He justified us, and through His Spirit within us, He has elevated us to celestial realms beside Him.

Such a magnificent Lord truly deserves our deepest adoration and reverence. As Jesus Christ once revealed, God seeks those who worship Him with their entire being — heart and soul.

True love has an unmistakable quality; it compels us to speak of the beloved constantly. If we feel such intensity for earthly affections, imagine the depth of our feelings for the Creator who molded us, loves us unconditionally, and even sacrificed Himself for us. Let's carry this sentiment today, elevating His name from sunrise to sunset.

Wherever we find ourselves, let us elevate our voices in gratitude, saying, "Thank you, God. Thank you, Jesus Christ." Blessed be His name, for it shines brighter than any other. Today, and every day, let's celebrate His name, allowing it to shine gloriously through us. Amen.

OCTOBER 15
Married life in Christ

Ephesians 5:22-27

> [22] *Wives, submit yourselves to your own husbands as you do to the Lord.*
> [23] *For the husband is the head of the wife as Christ is the head of the church, his body, of which he is the Savior.*
> [24] *Now as the church submits to Christ, so also wives should submit to their husbands in everything.*
> [25] *Husbands, love your wives, just as Christ loved the church and gave himself up for her*
> [26] *to make her holy, cleansing her by the washing with water through the word,*
> [27] *and to present her to himself as a radiant church, without stain or wrinkle or any other blemish, but holy and blameless.*

Marriage, as portrayed in Scripture, highlights a profound unity: "Wives, submit yourselves unto your own husbands, as unto the Lord. For the husband is the head of the wife, even as Christ is the head of the church: and he is the Savior of the body. Therefore, as the church is subject unto Christ, so let the wives be to their own husbands in everything."

However, this directive isn't rooted in patriarchy, as the following guidance clarifies: "Husbands, love your wives, even as Christ also loved the church, and gave himself for it." This signifies the profound commitment and self-sacrifice expected of husbands.

Christianity views marriage as a sanctified bond where two individuals merge into one entity. It's beautifully summarized: "That is why men and women separate from their parents and join each other, and both become one."

This sacred union calls for mutual love, respect, and understanding. While wives are encouraged to respect their husbands akin to their reverence for Christ, husbands are reminded to exhibit the selfless love Christ bore for the church. Can one truly claim to love selflessly and yet act with arrogance or domineering pride? Certainly not!

True love, as described in 1 Corinthians 13, is patient, kind, and devoid of envy or resentment. Such love is the bedrock of a successful marriage. It paves the way for mutual respect, understanding, and the ability to see past each other's imperfections.

Hence, it's this caliber of love that couples are beckoned to imbue in their marital bonds. By centering Christ in our lives and letting His Spirit guide our hearts and actions, couples draw nearer to Him. And in this journey toward Christ, they invariably find themselves drawing closer to each other, reflecting Christ's love in their union.

May this understanding enrich our relationships and strengthen our bonds. May God bless and guide us in our journeys together. Amen.

OCTOBER 16

The fruits of spirit (1): Joy

Galatians 5:22-24

> [22] *But the fruit of the Spirit is love, joy, peace, forbearance, kindness, goodness, faithfulness,*
> [23] *gentleness and self-control. Against such things there is no law.*
> [24] *Those who belong to Christ Jesus have crucified the flesh with its passions and desires.*

The fruits of the Spirit, as Scripture tells us, include love, joy, peace, longsuffering, gentleness, goodness, faith, meekness, and temperance. And against such virtues, there stands no law. Amen?

In our forthcoming discussions, we aim to delve deeper into these fruits, shedding light on their significance in our lives.

Among them, the joy mentioned is distinct from fleeting happiness. This joy emanates from the steadfast and unalterable promises of God. It isn't a momentary elation derived from material gains, like a new home or a financial windfall. Such transient pleasures pale in comparison to the profound, soulful joy that believers experience—a joy that's deeply rooted in God's immutable promises.

This explains why, even amidst adversity, Christians can remain buoyant. Recall the unwavering spirits of Paul and Barnabas: when imprisoned and battered, they chose to sing hymns to the Lord rather than bemoan their fate. Their joy stemmed not from circumstances but from an unwavering faith in God's promises. It's the same joy that reminds us, "Though I walk through the valley of the shadow of death, I will fear no evil: for thou art with me; thy rod and thy staff they comfort me."

It's the joy in the knowledge that even in death, our souls transition to the comforting presence of Jesus Christ. This profound joy rests on the assurance that by surrendering our lives to God, we are eternally saved.

The world is in constant pursuit of this profound joy, yet it remains elusive to many. But for those who have embraced Jesus Christ as their Savior, Lord, and Guide, this joy is palpable and enduring.

May this divine joy, anchored in God's unchangeable promises, continue to fill our hearts and souls. Amen.

OCTOBER 17
The fruits of spirit (2): Love

In Galatians 5, the fruits of the Spirit are enumerated as love, joy, peace, longsuffering, gentleness, goodness, faith, meekness, and temperance. Having discussed joy previously, let us now delve into the profound theme of love.

The love spoken of here transcends mere emotional affection. It's not the romantic love shared between two individuals, which often hinges on reciprocity. This divine love is not contingent on conditions or circumstances; it's a deep-seated, genuine respect and acknowledgment of another being.

It's a love characterized by the willingness to lay down one's life for another, much like Jesus did for us. As Jesus Himself stated, there's no greater love than to lay down one's life for a friend. What's even more remarkable is that Christ's love extended beyond this. He gave His life for us when we were still estranged from Him, showcasing the true nature of agape love.

Agape, in essence, embodies the unadulterated, unconditional love that exists between God and man. It's love without expectations, love that sacrificially dedicates itself to others, and its constancy is unwavering. It's not the fickle love of today which might wane tomorrow based on trivial disagreements or unmet expectations. This love is enduring, unchangeable, steadfast like a rock.

This agape love, a fruit of the Spirit, is cultivated within us by the Holy Spirit. As we draw closer to Jesus, engage in conversations with Him, and immerse ourselves in His teachings, we find ourselves transformed, increasingly reflecting Christ's boundless love and compassion.

Let's journey forward, fortified by this everlasting love. Amen.

OCTOBER 18
The fruits of spirit (3): Peace

Galatians 5:22 tells us, "But the fruit of the Spirit is love, joy, peace, longsuffering, gentleness, goodness, faith, meekness, temperance." We've previously delved into joy and love. Today, let's explore the profound theme of peace.

This peace isn't merely an absence of external conflict; it's a deep, inner tranquility grounded in our relationship with Jesus Christ and the assurance of our salvation. Unlike fleeting moments of calm we experience in the world, this divine peace remains steadfast even amidst life's most raging storms.

Derived from the work of the Holy Spirit within us, this peace is a gift from Christ. He said, "My peace I give unto you: not as the world giveth." What kind of peace does He bestow? The assurance that He's perpetually by our side, that all things work together for good to those who love God, and that no weapon forged against us shall prevail.

The term "peace" in the Greek language, when used as a verb, alludes to the act of joining or binding together. It's about unity and connection. This peace, then, is a divine bond with Jesus Christ, an unbreakable connection that remains intact regardless of our external circumstances.

So even when we find ourselves amidst life's tempests, as believers, we can be anchored in serenity, rooted in the work Christ has accomplished within us and the unwavering love He has for us. No trial or tribulation can rob us of this divine peace.

Today, and every day, let's move forward enveloped in God's peace, growing ever deeper in His love and grace. Amen.

OCTOBER 19
The fruits of spirit (4): Long suffering patience

Galatians 5:22

> *"But the fruit of the Spirit is love, joy, peace, longsuffering, gentleness, goodness, faith, meekness, temperance."*

We have discussed joy, love, and peace. Today, we delve into patience, also described as long-suffering.

What exactly is this type of patience? How can we define it? It's the patience that equips us with the strength and resilience to bear the pain inflicted upon us, both past and present. Sometimes, it even compels us to endure accusations and stand resilient against these emotional assaults.

But why? It is because of the hope and faith we hold.

This isn't the patience that emerges from helplessness, where one might think, "I'm out of options in this situation, so I'll just wait. I'll endure with anxiety, wait for it to pass, and hope that someone comes to my aid." No.

This patience is a gift from the Holy Spirit. It is rooted in our hope and the assurance that everything will turn out well for those who are chosen by God and love Him. Even when we find ourselves amidst storms, witnessing our worlds crumble, we are confident that no matter the circumstance, God remains by our side.

The Lord bestows this patience upon us, a gift of the Holy Spirit, enabling us to persevere. We believe that by enduring challenges, hardships, and storms, the eventual outcome will be to our benefit. Such is the nature of this patience.

This patience stands firmly on hope and on God's unchanging promises. It's the patience a parent exhibits for a child who has renounced his family and forsaken his beliefs. It's a patience that's been tried and tested over a prolonged period. But within this prolonged suffering lies steadfast patience, because we are cognizant of God's greater plan. We entrust our tribulations to God, confident in His ability and willingness to work for the best interests of His children.

In essence, this patience is anchored in hope, faith, and love. Amen.

OCTOBER 20
The fruits of spirit (5): Kindness

Galatians 5:22.

> *"But the fruit of the Spirit is love, joy, peace, longsuffering, gentleness, goodness, faith, meekness, temperance."*

We've already discussed joy, love, peace, and longsuffering. Today, our focus is on kindness.

So, what type of kindness are we referring to? It's the kindness that manifests as gentleness and goodness towards others, mirroring the kindness that the Lord Jesus Christ showed — His gentle, tender, and loving demeanor towards all.

How can we cultivate and express such kindness and gentleness? The answer lies in immersing ourselves deeper in the love and teachings of the Lord Jesus Christ. The closer we align ourselves with Jesus, the more our capacity for kindness and love towards others grows. He taught us a new covenant, urging us to "love one another as I have loved you and given my life for you." We are beckoned to exhibit kindness, regardless of the circumstances.

Let us view every situation through the lens of Jesus Christ's love and compassion. Let's remind ourselves that even when we were in opposition to Him, He chose to sacrifice Himself for us, showcasing unparalleled love. In every interaction, we should ponder, "If Jesus were present, how would He have reacted? How would He have shown love and kindness?"

Let's pray: O God, guide us to love as You do. Help us exhibit kindness akin to Yours, to uplift and cherish others in the same way You do. May the fruit of kindness, a gift of the Holy Spirit, flourish within each of us. Use us as vessels to demonstrate the fruit of kindness to others and enhance our spirit of gentleness and goodness.

In the name of Jesus Christ, Amen.

OCTOBER 21
The fruits of spirit (6): Goodness

Galatians 5:22

> *"But the fruit of the Spirit is love, joy, peace, longsuffering, gentleness, goodness, faith, meekness, temperance."*

We've discussed love, joy, peace, patience, and kindness. Now, let's talk about goodness. What is the basis for this goodness? This goodness is the kind we show to others, driven by the love and affection within us and influenced by the work of the Holy Spirit. We were called to demonstrate goodness and kindness. Our goodness emanates from God's love and kindness. We must always set a good example for those around us. So, what does goodness mean? Goodness involves prioritizing the well-being of others. It means acting with honesty and basing our decisions on love, kindness, and genuine goodness. Goodness is when we don’t elevate ourselves unduly. It is a type of goodness that stems from love for others. We are called to be exemplars of love and kindness in every setting: in our communities, workplaces, churches, and everywhere we go. However, this kind of goodness emerges solely from the Holy Spirit's work within each of us. It is a goodness that emanates from God's love, the Holy Spirit's influence, and God's loving work in each of us. This represents the goodness of Jesus Christ. In His ultimate act of goodness, He even sacrificed His life for His enemies, so we too must strive for such goodness. Even when someone lacked faith in Him, whether they sought healing for a daughter or a servant, He provided that healing. That's true goodness. I hope that today, both you and I can radiate this goodness to all around us, leading them to embrace the love, warmth, and the presence of Jesus Christ as their Savior and Lord. Amen.

OCTOBER 22
The fruits of spirit (7): Faithfulness

Galatians 5:22

> *"But the fruit of the Spirit is love, joy, peace, longsuffering, gentleness, goodness, faithfulness, meekness, temperance."*

We've discussed love, joy, peace, patience, kindness, and goodness. Today, we delve into faithfulness.

What does faithfulness entail? Being faithful to God is paramount. God's unwavering faithfulness to us compels our reciprocal loyalty and dedication to His love and grace. Yet, our commitment extends beyond our relationship with God. We are called to demonstrate faithfulness to fellow Christians, ensuring not only loyalty but also reliability. Being true to our commitments and to those who place their trust in us is essential. This is echoed in Jesus Christ's teaching: "Let your yes be yes, and your no be no." When we make promises, we must honor them. Others should be able to trust in our consistency, honesty, and faithfulness. When we exhibit faithfulness and integrity in our interactions, conversations, professional endeavors, material dealings, and spiritual journey, we establish trust. We must be honest in our financial obligations, including taxes. We owe it to each other not to engage in deceit. At work, dedicating our time earnestly ensures employers can rely on our commitment and diligence. Should a friend or acquaintance seek our assistance or commitment, once we affirm our willingness, we must adhere to it. No one should have to question our motives or actions repeatedly. In essence, our "yes" should always mean "yes," and our "no" should unequivocally mean "no." Such a stance cultivates faithfulness, honesty, and trustworthiness within us. It's all a manifestation of the Holy Spirit working within us, refining our character to emulate Jesus Christ more closely. May this spirit of faithfulness, this fruit of integrity, reliability, and honesty, shine brightly in each one of us. Amen.

OCTOBER 23
The fruits of spirit (8): Gentleness/Meekness

Galatians 5:22

> *"The fruit of the Spirit is love, joy, peace, longsuffering, gentleness, goodness, faithfulness, meekness, temperance."*

Today, let's explore meekness and humility. What does Christian scripture teach us about this form of humility? It speaks of a humility that is not just about being humble but also remaining calm and simple. It's a calmness, simplicity, and humility that refrains from seeking revenge for wrongs done to us. Gentleness and meekness imply an enduring spirit, one that is not easily offended.

A truly humble person, as portrayed in the Bible, possesses three distinct traits:

1. He consistently submits to the will of God, desiring to align his actions and intentions with God's plan and purpose.
2. He possesses a willingness to learn, an open heart ready to absorb lessons, always being teachable. While some may resist guidance or correction, a humble person gratefully accepts it, integrating the wisdom into his life and adapting accordingly.
3. He consistently places others' needs and interests above his own.

So, what defines this unique humility, gentleness, and meekness? It's a humility that doesn't resort to revenge; instead, it seeks to elevate others. It's a humility anchored in discerning and following God's will in every situation, yielding to His guidance. It's a humility that graciously accepts constructive criticism, always ready to evolve because of the recognition that no one stands above the rest. Moreover, it's a humility that is deeply considerate, always valuing the well-being and interests of others.

All of these virtues manifest in our lives through the transformative work of the Holy Spirit within each of us. Amen.

OCTOBER 24
The fruits of spirit (9): Self-control

Galatians 5:22

> *"The fruit of the Spirit is love, joy, peace, longsuffering, gentleness, goodness, faithfulness, meekness, temperance."*

Today, let's delve into the concept of self-control. What does self-control signify in this context? Self-control empowers us to regulate our body's desires and our responses in various situations. Importantly, this control isn't superficial, driven by a fear of looking bad. Rather, this self-control stems from love, kindness, and the patience bestowed upon us by God. It is the self-control that prompts us to pray for someone who offends us, rather than retaliating in anger. When driving, if someone recklessly cuts us off, self-control guides us to pray for that individual, hoping they won't endanger others with their actions. If family, friends, or acquaintances speak ill of us, self-control ensures that we don't reciprocate with negative words about them, even if those words hold some truth. True self-control encourages open communication; it might lead us to pull someone aside and say, "What you mentioned earlier hurt me. Can we talk about it?" It's not merely about refraining from impulsive reactions, but also about not retaliating when wronged. As God teaches, we should counteract evil with goodness and offer kindness even to those who persecute us. In this light, self-control is intertwined with love, patience, forbearance, goodness, and humility. We thank you, Father, for bestowing upon us the fruits of your Holy Spirit. Lord, please remove any obstacles within us that hinder these fruits and fill us with your Holy Spirit. May we always bear abundant fruit in your name.

We pray this in the mighty name of Jesus Christ, the King of kings. Amen.

OCTOBER 25
Thanksgiving prayer

Psalm 100

Today, as Canada celebrates Thanksgiving, a day dedicated to expressing gratitude, let us approach God with heartfelt thanks. Psalm 100 verses 4 and 5 state, "Enter into His gates with thanksgiving, and into His courts with praise: be thankful unto Him, and bless His name. For the Lord is good; His mercy is everlasting; and His truth endures to all generations."

Dear friends, let's take a moment today: grab a sheet of paper, your phone, iPad, or tablet, and begin crafting a list of blessings to thank God for. Recall that everything we possess and cherish originates from Him. Every good thing is a gift from above, bestowed upon us by His gracious hands.

Let us approach Him, let us pass through the gates of His love, acknowledging our boundless affection for Him. Let's elevate His name in gratitude, recognizing that all we are and all we have is because of Him. We extend our deepest thanks, acknowledging that His love spans from the earth to the heavens. We're grateful for the unparalleled gift He granted us: His son, Jesus Christ.

Thank you, Jesus, our Lord and Savior, for the blood you spilled on the cross to absolve us of our sins and burdens. We appreciate your resurrection on the third day, marking your victory over death, Satan, and ensuring our place within God's family, His kingdom.

Lord, we're profoundly thankful for the Holy Spirit, our guiding light and mentor, who resides within us. Your gifts to us, Lord, are immeasurable. We're grateful for your protective shield, as your Word promises the angels' guardianship over us.

The Psalm declares, "If it weren't for You, O Lord, we would be lost." It is solely due to Your benevolence, protection, and love that we thrive.

Our gratitude knows no bounds. We thank You for our health, for the provisions You've blessed us with. We are grateful that You are ever-present, allowing us to sing Your praises. Your might knows no limit; Your presence is unending.

We are endlessly grateful for Your companionship, even during our most challenging times, for it is Your presence that fortifies our spirit. Every obstacle we face is surmountable because of Your promise to work everything for the good of those who love You.

Thank you for the assurance that no weapon formed against us shall prosper. Our heartfelt gratitude is for the closeness we share with You, for everything You've done, and continue to do. We lift our praises to the Father, the Son, Jesus Christ, and the Holy Spirit. Amen.

OCTOBER 26
Let us pray for our pastors and elders everyday

2 Thessalonians 3:1-2

> *"As for other matters, brothers and sisters, pray for us that the message of the Lord may spread rapidly and be honored, just as it was with you. And pray that we may be delivered from wicked and evil people, for not everyone has faith."*

In this passage, as in his other epistles, Paul entreats: "Finally, brethren, pray for us, that the word of the Lord may have free course and be glorified, even as it is with you: And that we may be delivered from unreasonable and wicked men: for all men have not faith." In many of his letters, Paul not only intercedes for the church members but also urges them to pray for him and other leaders.

Each of us is summoned to consistently pray for our pastors, church leaders, and ministers. What should our prayers encompass? We should pray for their health and, as Paul emphasizes, the efficacy of their words and teachings, for God's glory to shine through their ministry, and for blessings upon them. We should also pray for their protection from unreason and malice, given that not everyone embraces faith. We must seek wisdom for them, guiding their speech with grace, love, and compassion.

Always bear in mind that there are devoted individuals in our church community who continually keep us in their prayers. They invest their time studying the Word, seeking fresh revelations, and sharing God's message with us. As such, it becomes our sacred responsibility as church members to uplift our pastors, leaders, and ministers daily in prayer, expressing our gratitude for them. We should intercede for their health, families, protection, financial well-being, and all aspects of their lives, imploring God to abundantly bless and especially safeguard them.

Today, let us initiate this commitment: to daily uphold our pastors, church leaders, and ministers in prayer. Father, we come before You, placing our priests and church leaders in Your hands. You know them intimately. Bestow upon them wisdom and blessings. Elevate them, Lord, ensuring their protection. Maintain their health and infuse them more profoundly with the Holy Spirit. Keep them at arm's length from malicious individuals, allowing them to be the shining lights and the salt of the earth in our church. Bless their families, their endeavors, and every facet of their lives. In the name of Jesus Christ, Amen.

OCTOBER 27
Man's heart reflects the man's personality

Proverbs 27:19

"As water reflects the face, so one's life reflects the heart."

Just as a face is mirrored by water, so the heart mirrors the person.

While the Bible frequently alludes to the heart as the repository of all emotions and intentions, we understand physiologically that it's not the heart but the brain that serves this function. However, when emotions surge, causing our hearts to palpitate, it's often described in terms of the heart. What truly transpires in my heart and yours? Our inner thoughts and feelings inevitably manifest in our expressions and overall demeanor.

Much like how our reflection is captured in a mirror or water, our hearts reveal our true personalities. We, as Christians, are divinely favored. Why? Because the Spirit of God resides within our hearts. This emphasizes the importance of maturing in Christ to resemble His image more closely.

The content of our hearts inevitably shines through. The Holy Spirit's transformative work within us, as evident through the fruits of the Spirit, becomes discernible in our character. Whatever resides in our heart finds a way out, reflecting in our actions, work, and even facial expressions. Doesn't anger or sadness clearly register on our faces?

Regardless of our attempts to conceal or suppress our true feelings, they eventually surface, influencing our personalities. If one harbors vengeance, slander, jealousy, or resentment, it will become evident. Conversely, if one's heart is filled with goodness, patience, kindness, and humility, these too will radiate outward.

As we journey forward, with the Holy Spirit actively working within our hearts, may we become living reflections of Jesus Christ, so that everyone who encounters us sees His likeness in us. Amen.

OCTOBER 28

Do you tell your friends about the good news of Bible?

Matthew 28

When Jesus Christ ascended to heaven, He commanded, "Go ye therefore, and teach all nations, baptizing them in the name of the Father, and of the Son, and of the Holy Ghost."

This prompts a crucial inquiry: Do we share with our neighbors, friends, relatives, and acquaintances the immense blessing and grace we've received through Jesus Christ? Do we share the good news that God, taking on human form, lived among us, sacrificed Himself on the cross for our sins, and rose on the third day? By acknowledging and accepting Him in our hearts, we gain eternal life and salvation. While the world relentlessly seeks peace, have we proclaimed that we've found it in Him? Do we extend this message to others?

Do we encourage them to join us in church, to hear and witness God's Word? Do we intercede for them in prayer? The significance of church attendance cannot be understated. It's within the church that we edify and bolster one another. As Proverbs aptly states: "Iron sharpens iron."

We should actively invite, guide, and journey with others to the church. Paul proclaims, "I have become all things to all people," adapting his methods to ensure the Gospel reaches every heart. His mission was to ensure everyone had the opportunity for salvation through Jesus Christ, to discover eternal life and true peace.

So, I pose this question to you: Are you actively disseminating this good news? Do you welcome others to your church to hear God's transformative Word? Do you make it a priority to attend church yourself? Today's reflection invites introspection and consideration.

May God empower us to broadcast this good news far and wide. Lord, instill in us a deep commitment to your church and motivate us to bring others along.

May they hear your comforting words, attain salvation, and bask in your boundless grace. Amen.

OCTOBER 29
Benefits of going to Church

Matthew 16:18

"And I tell you that you are Peter, and on this rock I will build my church, and the gates of Hades will not overcome it."

On this foundation, the Lord pledges to establish His church, ensuring that the powers of darkness will never prevail against it. He beckons us to be part of His congregation, to unite in fellowship, and to uplift one another.

I've touched on this theme in previous devotionals, possibly last year. But its importance merits reiteration: We were designed for community, not isolation. In unity, we can recount God's mercies and grace in our lives.

Our personal testimonies are potent tools. They fortify fellow believers and imbue them with hope. It's within the church walls that we immerse ourselves in God's Word. The Lord assures that when two or three gather in His name, He is present among them.

However, obstacles often arise to deter us from attending church. Frequent deterrents include disputes, feelings of exhaustion, or health complaints like headaches. These challenges aren't unique to just a few; many of God's devoted servants have chronicled similar experiences in their writings. Such hurdles can be perceived as the enemy's tactics to keep us away from collective worship.

In these moments, we must firmly recognize and declare that such hindrances aren't God-ordained. God's desire is for us to convene in His house, to edify one another. If we stay away from the church, whom are we pleasing? Certainly not God but the adversary.

Every hindrance keeping us from the church isn't of divine origin. God's call is clear: He wants us to assemble, celebrate His name, bolster our faith, share in collective joy, and bear each other's burdens. Church attendance is paramount, and the adversary persistently tries to deter us.

Now that we're privy to his schemes, when temptations arise—be it fatigue, health concerns, or mere reluctance—we must identify them as the enemy's snares. It's imperative to stand firm, reject these impediments, and assert our intention to worship. Instantly, you'll sense the Holy Spirit's empowerment propelling you forward. In such times, let's beseech God, asking Him to thwart these barriers and guide us to His sanctuary. Amen.

OCTOBER 30

Pray and praise continually and consistently

In today's devotional, I want us to unite in prayer. Last week, during my personal devotional time with God, He impressed upon my heart an urging for intensified prayer, emphasizing the need to direct our petitions towards His body, in love, especially for Persian-speaking Christians. As some among us are currently grappling with illnesses, we wish to intercede for them, presenting their needs before God's throne.

The scripture reminds us, "Is anyone among you sick? Let them call the elders of the church to pray over them and anoint them with oil in the name of the Lord." This counsel is what James shared with us. We are exhorted to pray continually and unceasingly, as reiterated in Thessalonians. The fervent prayer of a righteous person is powerful and effective. If anyone among us requires prayer, please voice it so we can collectively intercede. To uplift the church and one another, we should approach God earnestly in prayer.

God desires us to ardently stand in the gap for His body. Observing our dwindling numbers, we desperately need God to revitalize everyone, instilling and magnifying His love in all our hearts. May He reignite our passion and original love for Jesus Christ and undertake mighty deeds within His body, in Mohabat church, and amongst other Persian speakers.

Now, let's jointly pray, particularly for those who are unwell.

Father, in the name of Jesus Christ, we present Afshin, Arash, and Shiva before you. Lord, lay your healing hand upon them, bestowing complete restoration. Just as you healed Peter's mother-in-law, enabling her to rise and serve, we pray these dear ones also rise, dedicating themselves wholly to Your service. For Darius, who battles cancer, touch him, heal him, and make him a testament to Your miraculous works.

We thank you for the healing bestowed upon Laura and for her complete recovery. Gracious Father, we lift up Nika, praying for her healing touch. As we present the sick amongst us, we affirm our trust in Your healing virtue. We thank You for our church community, the freedom to congregate, and the venue you've provided. Strengthen our churches and fortify our faith.

Father, we stand against the enemy's schemes that seek to sow discord and separation among us.

Whenever the adversary tempts us away from church fellowship, reminding us of fleeting ailments or worldly distractions, let us recognize these as ploys to draw us away from You. Anything that alienates us from You is not divine. Thus, we resist the enemy's efforts against Your church and its members.

May we be incessantly immersed in prayer and worship, ensuring that our days are punctuated with moments of communion with You. Lord, empower us to remain steadfast in prayer and praise.

In Jesus' name, we pray. Amen.

OCTOBER 31

Do we pant with all our soul for the word of Christ?

Psalm 119:129-136

Your testimonies are wonderful; Therefore my soul keeps them.
130 The entrance of Your words gives light; It gives understanding to the simple.
131 I opened my mouth and panted, For I longed for Your commandments.
132 Look upon me and be merciful to me, As Your custom is toward those who love Your name.
133 Direct my steps by Your word, And let no iniquity have dominion over me.
134 Redeem me from the oppression of man, That I may keep Your precepts.
135 Make Your face shine upon Your servant, And teach me Your statutes.
136 Rivers of water run down from my eyes, Because men do not keep Your law.

Do our hearts yearn deeply for the Word of God? Is our passion for our Lord of love and affection, Jesus Christ, so fervent that witnessing others diminish His name, malign His Word, or scorn His divinity brings tears to our eyes? Do we cherish His words and testimonies, longing to preserve them in the core of our being? The opening of Your word enlightens the soul. "In the beginning was the Word, and the Word was with God, and the Word was God. In Him was life; and this life brought light to humanity. Yet, the light shines in the darkness, and the darkness has not overcome it." - Jesus Christ.

The Word of God, the light of the world, the fountain of life, the eternal bread – how eagerly do we seek His Word, desiring to hear His teachings and commandments? While He showers us with His grace unceasingly, do we genuinely strive to walk in His ways? Invoking His name, which stands exalted above all names in the heavens and on earth, we are reminded of His promise: "I am always with you and will never forsake you." He continually guides us through His Holy Spirit.

Today, let's truly comprehend the immense treasure we possess. Let's acknowledge the profound grace bestowed upon us when we embraced Jesus Christ as our Savior, Lord, and King of kings. May we perpetually advance with this fervor, with this sense of awe, and with hearts and souls that hunger insatiably for His words and His presence. Amen.

NOVEMBER 1
Let us not forget the works of Christ in our lives

Titus 3:1-3

> [1]*Remind them to be subject to rulers and authorities, to obey, to be ready for every good work,*
> [2]*to speak evil of no one, to be peaceable, gentle, showing all humility to all men.*
> [3]*For we ourselves were also once foolish, disobedient, deceived, serving various lusts and pleasures, living in malice and envy, hateful and hating one another.*

Here, Paul is reminding Titus of his responsibilities towards the members of the church. He says: "Put them in mind to be subject to principalities and powers, to obey magistrates, to be ready for every good work. To speak evil of no man, to be no brawlers, but gentle, showing all meekness unto all men. For we ourselves also were sometimes foolish, disobedient, deceived, serving diverse lusts and pleasures, living in malice and envy, hateful, and hating one another." We must remember who we were before finding Jesus Christ as the Lord. Before His grace saved us from death and damnation, and before He brought us out of darkness into light. We were sinful, envious, hateful towards others, and selfish. But when the Lord Jesus Christ saved us by His grace, making us a new creation, all this changed. Now, we must demonstrate the fruit of Jesus Christ's work in our actions. We should be obedient to rulers and officials, pray for them, and be genuinely prepared for every good deed. We ought to be peacemakers, not fighters, and always be considerate and humble. Here's an idea: When we faced challenges and problems, when we prayed and God responded, let's make it a point to jot those moments down. Keep a notebook to record what God has done for you — how He answered your prayers and lifted you up during tough times. Many of us, when everything is going well, tend to forget the Lord and all that He has done for us. It's during these times that the devil tries to pull us back into our old ways. This is why regularly reading the Word, maintaining relationships with church members, fellow Christians, and attending church are so crucial. "Lest we forget Gethsemane, lest I forget Thy agony; Lest I forget Thy love for me, lead me to Calvary." This old hymn reminds us not to forget the tremendous sacrifice Christ made for us. So today, let's move forward, remembering the works of the Lord Jesus Christ, approaching life with immense gratitude, humility, and kindness, fulfilling all the good works He has set before us. Amen.

NOVEMBER 2

If you hear his voice today, do not harden your heart

Hebrews 3:7-8

> [7]*Therefore, as the Holy Spirit says: "Today, if you will hear His voice,* [8] *Do not harden your hearts as in the rebellion, In the day of trial in the wilderness.*

Here it says, "Wherefore as the Holy Ghost saith, today if ye will hear His voice, Harden not your hearts." Everything that the Lord Jesus Christ tells us usually emphasizes that yesterday is gone, so we shouldn't dwell on it, and tomorrow isn't promised, so we shouldn't worry about it. But today, today has its own tasks. Do you recall what He says in the Lord's Prayer? "Give us this day our daily bread." Today is crucial. Today is the day we must decide, the day we might hear the voice of the Holy Spirit reminding us of a misdeed, pointing out a sin we've committed. If He warns us that we haven't forgiven someone or whispers that our actions are misguided, or if a thought we entertain isn't right— if the thought stems from our pride or selfishness— If we hear His voice today, let's not harden our hearts. Just as Jesus Christ knelt in the garden on the night He was betrayed and said to God, "not as I will, but as Thou wilt," let us attune our ears to the voice of the Holy Spirit today. Let's not resist or defy what He communicates to us but instead, with open hearts, say, "O God, may Your will be done." Help us to act according to Your desires. Forgive us for the sins we've committed, for the errors in our thinking. Forgive us for failing to forgive others. You replaced our stony hearts with Your Holy Spirit and granted us new, compassionate hearts. Preserve these hearts as tender, pliable, peaceful, adaptable, and soft. Amen.

NOVEMBER 3

So, let us freely approach the throne of grace

Hebrews 4:16

> *Let us therefore come boldly to the throne of grace, that we may obtain mercy and find grace to help in time of need.*

When we accepted the Lord Jesus Christ as our Savior, Lord, and Master, surrendering our hearts, minds, and lives to Him, we entered into His grace. It's by this grace that we were saved. When He died on the cross, the Bible describes how the Holy Curtain, which separated the holiest part of the temple from the rest, was torn from top to bottom. This act symbolized the removal of the barrier between God and His people. Because the ultimate mediator, Jesus Christ, presented Himself and bore our sins. And after three days, He resurrected, bestowing the Holy Spirit upon each of us. It's by His grace, and not our deeds, that we are saved. Now, there's no veil separating us from God. We can approach the Father freely, entering the Holiest of Holies, because the Spirit of Christ within us sanctifies and justifies us. So, when we find ourselves weakened by distress, sin, or other trials, we mustn't let these hurdles discourage us. Instead, let's confidently approach the throne of grace. Let's turn to God and say, "Father, here I am, with all my flaws, all my transgressions, presenting my entirety to You." For we are not only saved by grace but are sustained daily by that grace and faith. It's by this grace and our faith that we find the strength to face each day, not merely through our efforts alone. This daily infusion of grace is essential, and what does He instruct us to do? Approach the throne of grace, embrace God's boundless mercy, and seek His grace. Why? To fortify us in times of need. God's grace and mercy are ever-present, ready to aid and uplift us in every circumstance we encounter. So today, let us boldly draw near to God's throne of grace, secure in His mercy, and receive that grace to aid us, ensuring all we do brings glory to God. Amen.

NOVEMBER 4

Inner joy caused by going to God's house

Psalm 122:1

> *I was glad when they said to me, "Let us go into the house of the LORD."*

David speaks here of the profound joy and elation he felt when invited to go to God's temple. Each of us must reflect and ask: Do we experience the same excitement when someone suggests, "Let's attend church together?" Do we eagerly await Sundays? Is there an inner jubilation that prompts us to think, "Ah, today is the day for church!" or "How many more days until I can go to church again?" Is that passion present within us? That eagerness for God's house, to be with our church community, to engage with our spiritual family, to uplift one another - do we feel it? If such joy is missing, we need to ask why. What or who diminishes this longing and joy for the house of God in our hearts? Scripture warns us that the devil prowls around like a roaring lion, seeking to accuse and deter believers. We must remain vigilant, recognizing the devil's schemes. God instructs us to be as innocent as doves but as shrewd as serpents. We're called to have a pure heart, with childlike faith in Him, trusting that His words are true. Yet, we must also be astute, guarding against falling into the devil's snares. What are these snares? When we plan to attend church, he might whisper, "You're exhausted, just rest at home today," or "You've had a long week, relax and watch TV," or even, "Your friend invited you out; it'll be fun!" But we know that the inner joy and spiritual elevation we gain from attending church, from partaking in worship, and from hearing His word is incomparable to worldly pleasures. Paul emphatically declares, "What can separate me from the love of God, from the love of Jesus Christ?" Indeed, nothing worldly can sever this bond. So, when conflicting thoughts arise or when distractions beckon, stand firm. Recognize that the joy and zeal for God's house, and the blessings awaiting there, surpass all else. And we shouldn't forsake them for anything. Amen.

NOVEMBER 5

I Look to God for help

Psalm 121

> *I will lift up mine eyes unto the hills, from whence cometh my help.*
> *My help cometh from the LORD, which made heaven and earth.*
> *He will not suffer thy foot to be moved: he that keepeth thee will not slumber.*
> *Behold, he that keepeth Israel shall neither slumber nor sleep.*

The LORD is your keeper; the LORD is your shade at your right hand. Neither the sun shall harm you by day, nor the moon by night.

The LORD shall preserve you from all evil; He shall safeguard your soul.

The LORD shall watch over your departure and your arrival, from this moment onward and for all eternity.

When we look to God, it's not just about placing our hope and faith in Him, or seeking His aid. Since we have accepted Jesus Christ as our Lord, Savior, and Master, God constantly serves as our protector, in every circumstance and at every place. This assurance stands as long as our focus remains solely on Him.

May our gaze be set on Him, our hope anchored in Him, and may He be the primary source from whom we anticipate assistance. Scripture emphasizes, "Should I look to man for help? No." God is our shepherd and our Father. He should be our first point of contact in times of need. He desires the best for us, consistently accompanying and caring for us.

So, from this day forward, whenever we require support, guidance, or anything else, let's first turn and reach out to our heavenly Father and Jesus Christ. Amen.

NOVEMBER 6

I seek the goodness of the Lord's house

Psalm 122:8-9

For the sake of my brethren and companions, I will now say, "Peace be within you." [9] Because of the house of the LORD our God I will seek your good.

Here, David prays for Jerusalem, stating: "For my brethren and companions' sakes, I will now say, 'Peace be with thee.' Because of the house of the Lord our God, I will seek thy good."

The word "seek" signifies that I am actively pursuing it, striving for its welfare to the best of my ability.

This should be our perspective towards the house of the Lord, towards His Church. The Church, being God's house, is where believers congregate. It's where they worship God collectively, extol His name, recite His teachings in unity, and uplift one another. They intercede on behalf of each other.

Daily, we should approach God and entreat, "O God, bless Your church, bestow peace and health upon it." Especially for the specific church we feel called to, considering it our spiritual home. This church, this spiritual haven, beckons us. We are implored to pray daily for its peace, its prosperity, its welfare, its safety, and its divine protection. Yet our responsibility extends beyond mere words – our actions should echo our prayers. We should desire the best for our church and act to ensure its well-being.

Let's advance today with this perspective, with this enlightenment. "O God, fortify our church, safeguard it, shield it, instill peace and harmony within its walls, elevate it. And if there's a role I must play, a task I must undertake, guide me. Endow me with the vigor to serve, for the sake of the church and for the benefit of my fellow believers." Amen.

NOVEMBER 7
If the Lord was not with us

Psalm 124

If it had not been for the LORD on our side, when men rose up against us, then they would have swallowed us up alive when their anger was kindled against us. The waters would have overwhelmed us, and the torrent would have swept over us; the raging waters would have swept us away. Blessed be the LORD, who has not let us be torn by their teeth. We have escaped like a bird from the snare of the fowlers; the snare has been broken, and we have escaped. Our help is in the name of the LORD, the Maker of heaven and earth. Amen?

Were it not for the Lord, each of us would have been consumed by our sins, misdeeds, and curses; we would have met our demise.

Had it not been for the Lord, we would remain shrouded in darkness. But due to Lord Jesus Christ, who sacrificed His life on the cross for our sake, and who triumphed over death, rising on the third day, we have been saved by His mighty name.

In church yesterday, we discussed how Jesus Christ surpasses all beings and angels in stature.

Jesus Christ, the Son of God, reigns supreme, transcending all. He is the divine essence. When we embrace Him as our Lord, Guide, Redeemer, and King, and when He bestows His Holy Spirit upon us, angels are then assigned to guard and protect believers like you and me.

If it had not been for the Lord, those of us who have put our faith in Jesus Christ would have been vanquished. We would have been consumed by our adversaries, and the turbulent waters of life's tempests would have drowned us. It is by God's providence that we are shielded every moment, regardless of our awareness or feelings to the contrary. With God beside us, we are empowered to confront all challenges, knowing that He never abandons us. For when God is with us, who can stand against us?

Let us move forward today with gratitude in our hearts, expressing our thanks to the Lord. O Jesus, we extol Your name, which is exalted above all names in heaven, on earth, and beneath the earth. We are alive and able to praise You freely today because of Your boundless kindness, love, and blessings. We give thanks to You, Lord. In the name of Jesus Christ. Amen.

NOVEMBER 8
When we only trust God

Psalm 125

They that trust in the LORD shall be as Mount Zion, which cannot be removed, but abides forever. As the mountains surround Jerusalem, so the LORD surrounds His people from this time forth and forever. Who are the people of God? Paul declares: We, who have accepted Jesus Christ as our Lord and Savior, are the genuine people of God. Jesus Christ, the eternal Son of the eternal God, is the eternal priest akin to King Melchizedek. It is Jesus Christ who sacrificed Himself once and for all, so we no longer need to offer animals such as cows, sheep, and camels as atonements for our sins. We are the authentic children and people of God. God assures us that if we are His people and place our trust solely in Him, we will be unshakeable like Mount Zion. Despite facing winds, rains, storms, and snow, the mountain remains steadfast. Even during earthquakes, it holds its ground. On what foundation? It stands on the bedrock of our faith in Jesus Christ, our eternal hope of dwelling with Him eternally. It remains unwavering due to God's promises that never waver. When we entrust ourselves to Lord Jesus Christ, our stability is eternal. God declares that just as mountains encompass and shield Jerusalem, He encompasses His people. This protection isn't fleeting; it's everlasting. When we give our hearts to Jesus Christ, recognizing Him as our Lord, Master, and Savior, we reside in God and He in us, creating a unity. When a few of us gather in His name, He is amidst us, reinforcing the significance of communal worship. The same protection applies to His church, where His followers congregate. Today, may we increasingly witness God's protection, His guidance, and our unwavering trust in Him through our actions and demeanor. Amen.

NOVEMBER 9

When the Lord brought us back from captivity to His house

Psalm 126

When the LORD restored the fortunes of Zion, we were like those who dream. Our mouths were filled with laughter, our tongues with songs of joy. Then it was said among the nations, "The LORD has done great things for them." Indeed, the LORD has done great things for us, and we are filled with joy. Restore our fortunes, O LORD, like the streams in the Negev. Those who sow with tears will reap with songs of joy. He who goes out weeping, carrying seed to sow, will return with songs of joy, carrying sheaves with him.

When I read this psalm, I'm reminded of those ensnared by the world, trapped by desires, having forgotten the love and compassion of Lord Jesus Christ. Much like the Israelites who were exiled and enslaved by the Babylonians, they too are held captive by life's worldly desires.

But this prayer is as much for them as it is for us. "O God, seek and free us from the chains that bind us to this world. Guide us back to your house, where we reside beside You, Jesus Christ." We pray for those who once walked with You but have since strayed.

Lord, extend Your mercy to them. Another translation suggests that the captives return in groups, banding together in their journey back to You.

Our heartfelt plea is for the upliftment of those who have stumbled or turned away, those who have forgotten You and Your Holy Spirit. Rekindle their memories, elevate their spirits, and guide them home. Reignite their faith and draw them closer to Your embrace, so they may also reap a bountiful harvest in You.

We recognize the tears shed by their friends, family, and church members, pleading for their return. In exchange for their tears, grant them the joy of witnessing this harvest and the joy of seeing loved ones freed from bondage.

May even the unbelievers witness this miraculous transformation and proclaim, "Look at the marvelous deeds the Lord has performed for them." Amen.

NOVEMBER 10
Faith is the substance of things not seen

Hebrews 11:1- 3

> [1]*Now faith is the substance of things hoped for, the evidence of things not seen.*
> [2] *For by it the elders obtained a good testimony.*
> [3] *By faith we understand that the worlds were framed by the word of God, so that the things which are seen were not made of things which are visible.*

This chapter is about faith. "Now faith is the substance of things hoped for, the evidence of things not seen. For by it the elders obtained a good report." By faith, we understand that the universe was formed at God's command, so that what is seen was not made out of what was visible.

The chapter then speaks about the people of the Old Testament. It references Abel and Cain, Noah, Enoch, Abraham, and others. It highlights how they moved forward with faith, and even when their circumstances seemed contrary to God's promises, they remained steadfast in their belief.

The scripture states that faith is the foundation of our hopes. Hope is birthed from promises, and we trust the promises of those we believe in. Therefore, if we believe in God, we trust His promises, which give rise to our hope. This faith becomes the assurance for what we do not yet see.

Consider Abraham. When he was 100 years old and his wife Sarah was 90, God promised them a son. Despite the seemingly impossible nature of this promise, given their ages, they held onto their faith. And in time, the promise was fulfilled when Sarah bore Isaac.

It is by faith that we understand the universe was created by God's word, not through theories like evolution. What is visible today came into existence by the power of what was then invisible.

At the core of our beliefs, faith in God and His grace forms the foundation of our hope and salvation. May we place our complete trust in the promises of the Lord Jesus Christ, embracing them wholeheartedly.

Today, even if circumstances appear to be against us or what we observe seems contrary to our beliefs, let's remember that our faith undergirds our hopes. Amen.

NOVEMBER 11

Pride, the cause of strife and sin

Proverbs 28:25

> *He who is of a proud heart stirs up strife, but he who trusts in the LORD will be prospered.*

The New Millennium version says a greedy man provokes strife. However, the English version states: "He that is of a proud heart stirs up strife: but he that puts his trust in the LORD shall be made prosperous."

I believe we've discussed this before: the root of all sins is pride. It's pride that convinces me I am superior to you, or suggests to you that you are above me. Pride declares, "This is my right, and I'm superior to that individual." Pride proclaims, "You are mighty and dominant, and you can attain anything regardless of the means." It's pride that fosters racism, breeds discrimination, and instigates sin. Indeed, pride is the source of all wrongdoing. Satan, once among the most radiant of angels and the luminary of God, was reduced to the most deceptive and basest of angels because of pride. One of the most cherished and transformative fruits of the Holy Spirit working within us is humility, which stands in stark contrast to pride. Thus, let's examine our own pride daily. When pride surfaces, suggesting our superiority, God reminds us not to view ourselves as better than others. Esteem others, placing them before yourself. This is humility.

So, Father, we approach You today and ask: Lord, rid us of any pride within us. When pride seeks to dominate, remind us of the need for humility in Your presence. Grant us humility and eradicate pride from our hearts, assisting us in placing our trust in You always. Not in ourselves or our own ego, but in You, Lord. In doing so, we will be blessed with abundance and kindness from Your generous hands. Amen.

NOVEMBER 12
Lord's Prayer (1)
Our Heavenly Father

Today, our devotional is drawn from the Lord's Prayer. When the disciples asked Jesus Christ how they should pray, much like John had taught his own disciples, Jesus gave them one of the most profound prayers – the Lord's Prayer, which is cited in two of the Gospels. The prayer starts with, "Our Father who art in heaven, Hallowed be thy name." Over the next few days or possibly this week, we aim to delve into different sections of this prayer.

The reason being, God has beckoned us to the act of prayer. Currently, our prayers are needed for the church, for each other, and for ourselves. However, prayer signifies a direct connection with God. As believers in Jesus Christ, with the Holy Spirit residing within us, it's crucial for us to strengthen and clarify this bond. Recently, guided by God, Pastor Tim and I initiated group prayers. We will explore this in the upcoming days.

The prayer commences with: "Our Father who art in heaven, Hallowed be thy name." Often, our primary act in prayer is to approach God and acknowledge His significance to us, to declare His essence. By saying "our Father", we proclaim: "Oh God, You are our Heavenly Father." We embrace and confess this truth. Why? Because upon accepting Jesus Christ as Lord, we became a part of God's lineage. Not everyone can call God their Heavenly Father. Only those who've accepted Jesus Christ as their Lord and Savior have the privilege to refer to Him with this title. Our initial step? To acknowledge Him as our Father. A father epitomizes someone who cherishes his offspring deeply, often sacrificing immensely for their well-being. Similarly, our Heavenly Father spared no expense for us, even giving up His own Son. It's pivotal to remember that the Father, the Son, and the Holy Spirit are one entity. He desires the very best for His children. When one of His children addresses Him as "Heavenly Father", God responds with tenderness, saying "Yes, my dear?"

Merely addressing Him as "Heavenly Father" and confessing that God is our father affirms our belief in Jesus Christ. It is a testament to His sacrifice on the cross for our sins and His subsequent resurrection. Because of this acceptance, the acknowledgement of Jesus Christ's death and resurrection, and His identity as the Son of God and Lord, we are permitted to address God as our Father. Isn't that so? Thus, let's direct our prayers henceforth and invoke Him as our "Father", not just as God. Amen.

NOVEMBER 13
Lord's Prayer (2)
Hallowed be Thy name, Your kingdom come

We will continue discussing the Lord's Prayer.

"Our Father who art in heaven." We've delved into the significance of acknowledging our Heavenly Father.

"Hallowed be thy name. Thy kingdom come." When we profess that Your name is holy, we affirm its sanctity and yearn for its reverence in every aspect and everywhere.

O God, Your name stands supreme and sacred. We recognize its divinity and desire its reverence at every juncture of our lives. Let us never tarnish Your holy name. Let us never disrespect it or use it casually or inappropriately.

May Your name be revered in all facets of our existence and throughout the world. May others also recognize, understand, and hold Your name in high esteem. May they too sanctify Your name upon witnessing Your wondrous acts.

Blessed be Your name across all corners of the earth, in every language, nation, and culture. Your name transcends all others. So, when we say, "Hallowed be thy name," we commit to upholding the sanctity of Your name. Just as we would defend the honor of our earthly father if it were questioned, we vow to do the same, if not more, for Your esteemed name. May Your name remain revered universally.

"Thy kingdom come." O Lord, we yearn for Your kingdom and Your divine rule. We seek its eternal presence as it governs every being and entity.

May Your kingdom establish its dominion on this earth, manifesting its influence in everything and everyone. While You reign supreme over the world, may the eyes of the people be unveiled to perceive this kingdom.

We belong to Your kingdom; we are its valiant soldiers and its rightful heirs. Our hearts constantly seek Your kingdom, day in and day out. We aspire for its influence in our lives.

Guide us in every moment, preside over our triumphs and tribulations, and reign even when we falter.

O Lord, You are our sovereign, and we ardently desire Your kingdom. Amen.

NOVEMBER 14

Lord's Prayer (3)

Thy will be done in earth, as it is in heaven

We will continue reflecting on the Lord's Prayer.

"Our Father which art in heaven, Hallowed be thy name. Thy kingdom come. Thy will be done on earth, as it is in heaven."

We have acknowledged God as our Father and expressed our reverence for His sacred name. We have yearned for His kingdom and aspired for its influence everywhere. We recognize Him as the reigning force, ensuring that His salvific message touches every corner of the earth and every heart. By affirming our place in His kingdom, we are declaring our membership in His divine family.

Now, Jesus teaches us to pray, "Thy will be done on earth, as it is in heaven."

God assures us, "I desire the best for you, blessings beyond your imagination." He pledges that His will is always for the good of those who love Him and are called according to His purpose.

As believers, God's will represents the epitome of blessings and promises for us. He desires prosperity, peace, and spiritual abundance for our lives. Whether in times of joy or sorrow, comfort or challenges, when we align with His will, we are essentially saying, "O God, let Your will prevail, not mine, on earth as it is constantly realized in heaven."

In heaven, God's will is unquestionably done, always. By praying for His will on earth, we are inviting His divine purpose into our lives, saying, "Lord, I seek Your will, no matter the circumstances, because I trust that Your intentions for me are of love and grace."

Although the future may be unknown to us, we have the blessed assurance that it's securely held in the hands of our loving Father, who desires only the best for His children.

"May Your will be manifest on this earth, just as it is eternally actualized in heaven." Amen.

NOVEMBER 15
Lord's Prayer (4)
Give us this day our daily bread

Continuing our journey through the Lord's Prayer, we find solace in the words:

"Give us this day our daily bread."

It's a profound acknowledgment that our Father in Heaven is the ultimate Provider. When we speak these words, we are expressing our dependency on God for our physical sustenance as well as our spiritual nourishment. It's a heartfelt cry, an admittance that every morsel of bread, every breath of air, every moment of grace, comes from His benevolence.

Although we might work and earn, although we might sow and reap, behind it all stands our Heavenly Father, orchestrating, providing, and ensuring our needs are met. By asking for our daily bread, we don't just ask for food, but for wisdom, strength, guidance, and all that we need for the day.

Jesus, in His teachings, highlighted the generous nature of the Father. If earthly parents, with all their imperfections, strive to give good things to their children, how much more will our perfect Heavenly Father provide for us? Every good and perfect gift does indeed come from above.

Yet, the daily bread isn't merely about provision, it's about trust. Trust that God knows what we need even before we voice it. Trust that even in times of lack, His grace is sufficient. Trust that He has our best interests at heart, always.

In praying for our daily bread, there's an element of surrender too. We are laying down our desires, our plans, and asking for God's perfect will to be done in our lives. "Thy will be done" is not just a phrase; it's a lifestyle, a daily decision to prioritize God's plan over ours.

So, as we come before our Father today, let's approach with a heart full of gratitude, knowing that He who feeds the birds of the air and clothes the lilies of the field will surely take care of us. With a heart of faith, let's trust in His unfailing love and provision.

Father, today, and every day, we rely on You for our daily bread. Provide for us, guide us, and may Your will be done in our lives. Amen.

NOVEMBER 16
Lord's Prayer (5)
Forgive us our debt as we forgive our debtors

Our devotional today continues with the Lord's Prayer. So far, we've read: "Our Father which art in heaven, Hallowed be thy name. Thy kingdom come. Thy will be done on earth, as it is in heaven. Give us this day our daily bread. And forgive us our debts, as we forgive our debtors." Or, "Forgive us our sins, as we forgive those who sin against us."

Following this, Jesus speaks frequently about forgiveness, emphasizing its importance. He offers several parables as examples. One tells of a servant who owed the king a significant amount, equivalent to millions of dollars in today's terms. When the king demanded repayment, the servant pleaded for mercy, asking for more time to settle his debt. Moved by compassion, the king forgave the entire amount. Yet, this servant, upon leaving the king, encountered a fellow servant who owed him a mere hundred dollars. Despite his fellow servant's pleas for mercy, the unforgiving servant had him thrown into prison.

When the king learned of this, he summoned the unforgiving servant and rebuked him, saying he should've shown the same mercy he was granted. The king then ordered that the servant, along with his family, be imprisoned until the repayment of his original debt.

God has forgiven our innumerable sins through the sacrifice of Jesus Christ. He teaches us that if we don't forgive others, He won't forgive us. Forgiveness is not just a principle; it's a fruit of the Holy Spirit working within us.

So, if someone has wronged us, whether justly or unjustly, our first step should be to seek God's strength to forgive them. And, if possible, we should express this forgiveness directly to them, stating, "Even though what you did to me wasn't right, I forgive you wholeheartedly." As recipients of God's grace, we're called to extend grace to others. Peter once asked Jesus how often he should forgive a brother who wronged him. "Seven times?" he ventured. Jesus replied, "Seventy times seven," signifying boundless forgiveness.

Today, let's take a moment to reflect on any unresolved resentments. Let us seek God's guidance to forgive, to reconcile, and to walk in the footsteps of the Lord. Amen.

NOVEMBER 17
Lord's Prayer (6)
And lead us not into temptation, but deliver us from evil

Our devotional today is the continuation of the Lord's Prayer.

Our Father which art in heaven, Hallowed be thy name. Thy kingdom come. Thy will be done in earth, as it is in heaven. Give us this day our daily bread. And forgive us our debts, as we forgive our debtors. **And lead us not into temptation, but deliver us from evil.**

We've now come to the part that says, "Do not lead us into temptation, but deliver us from evil." The Word of God clarifies that He does not tempt anyone. Instead, it's our heart's desires, worldly allurements, and malevolence that entice us. At times, God might allow temptations to test our faith. Yet, He assures us that with every temptation, there's always a way out. Temptation often begins as a mere thought. I recently read a book titled "Winning the War in Your Mind" by Craig Groeschel, which emphasizes how everything starts with a fleeting idea in our minds. Recognizing and addressing it promptly can prevent us from falling prey to more significant temptations and ensuing repercussions.

So, when faced with temptation, what's our escape route? It's turning to the Word of God, holding onto His promises, and focusing on thoughts contrary to the temptation. Hence, we pray, "Lord, when temptations arise, remind us of Your truth. Show us the escape route. Protect us from being lured into them."

Although temptations are inevitable, with God's guidance, we can prevent them from leading to sin – the ultimate trap set by Satan. Therefore, we beseech, "Lord, don't allow us to enter into temptation. Open our eyes and ears to detect them early. Help us swiftly discern temptations rooted in pride, selfishness, or fleeting desires, and guide us toward salvation, ensuring we don't fall into the devil's grasp."

It's vital to understand that facing temptations isn't sinful. However, our response can either lead us into sin or steer us clear of it. So, when temptation whispers, "You need this," let our firm response be, "No, all I need comes from the hands of my dear Lord." Amen.

NOVEMBER 18
Lord's Prayer (7)
Because the kingdom, the power, and the glory is Yours forever

Hello, friends. Our devotional today continues our reflection on the Lord's Prayer. Our Father, which art in heaven, Hallowed be thy name. Thy kingdom come. Thy will be done on earth, as it is in heaven. Give us this day our daily bread. And forgive us our debts, as we forgive our debtors. And lead us not into temptation, but deliver us from evil: For thine is the kingdom, and the power, and the glory, forever.

We have reached the conclusion: "For thine is the kingdom, and the power, and the glory, forever." We've laid out our praises, our desires, and our needs before You, Acknowledging Your sovereignty and majesty because You are the King, and all dominions of this world are Yours. God, You alone reign supreme. All power is Yours, and all glory belongs to You. We confess, Lord, that no one in this world is mightier or more glorious than You. It is because You are the King, the omnipotent, the magnificent, that we come to You. Yet, in all Your splendor and might, You are our Father—A Father who desires the best for His children. But who can call Him "Father"? Only those who are His children. And when are we His children? When we recognize our sinfulness and grasp that our only path to salvation is through the blood of Jesus Christ shed on the cross and His triumphant resurrection. By accepting Jesus Christ as our Lord, Leader, Savior, and Master, we are no longer just servants but children of God. It's then we can address Him as "Father"—a relationship of deep affection and trust. This powerful, glorious King of Kings is not just a distant deity but a loving Father who seeks intimacy with us. Not just for the present but for eternity. This eternal, glorious, and powerful Father with a kingdom greater than all, cherishes us. He heeds our calls, answers our prayers, and His steadfast love never wanes. Let us, henceforth, pray invoking the Father's name, in the name of Jesus Christ, and incorporate the essence of the Lord's Prayer into our daily supplications. Amen.

NOVEMBER 19
Love one another

Today, our devotional reflects on God's instruction: to love one another, so that when others see this love among believers, they will praise our Father in heaven.

How do we manifest this love towards each other? What kind of love is so evident that, when observed, it leads people to praise God and come to know Jesus Christ? What form of love, shared among believers, has the power to attract unbelievers? A love that makes them yearn for the same connection with both fellow humans and with God?

Paul elucidates this in 1 Corinthians 13.

It's evident when we care for one another, genuinely inquire about each other's well-being, and stand ready to assist. It shines when we refrain from backbiting, and when faced with gossip, choose instead to intercede in prayer for the person being discussed. This love blossoms when we are devoid of pettiness and jealousy, earnestly desiring and celebrating the best for one another. It manifests when, in moments of need, we give generously and selflessly.

Gathering at church strengthens this bond of love. While the Lord emphasizes the importance of not forsaking fellowship, we recognize that in recent times, due to challenges like the Covid pandemic, many have turned to online mediums for worship. While it serves its purpose, we must remember we are inherently communal beings. The collective act of praising, praying, and being in the presence of fellow believers intensifies our spiritual experience.

The Lord assures us, "For where two or three gather in my name, there am I with them." While exceptions arise, such as illness or disability that might prevent attending in person, let's remember the significance of the Lord's Day, especially Sundays, to congregate in His name.

As we draw near to God by loving one another and coming together in worship, He too draws near to us, as James declares. Let's genuinely love, pray for, and uplift each other. Let's prioritize gathering together, never neglecting the Lord's Day, and experience God drawing ever closer to us. Amen.

NOVEMBER 20
God is light and there is no darkness in Him

1 John 1:5

> *This is the message which we have heard from Him and declare to you, that God is light and in Him is no darkness at all.*

"If we say that we have fellowship with him, and walk in darkness, we lie, and do not the truth: But if we walk in the light, as he is in the light, we have fellowship one with another, and the blood of Jesus Christ his Son cleanseth us from all sin."

A believer's life is anchored in truth and righteousness. As Jesus Christ instructed, let our affirmation be genuine and our rejection be clear; let our 'yes' truly mean 'yes' and our 'no' truly mean 'no'.

God embodies light; there's not a shred of darkness in Him. He is the epitome of clarity, unwavering truth, and purity. Consequently, in Christianity, there's no room for 'white lies' or half-truths. We are beckoned to uphold the truth, even if it demands the highest price.

Claiming a bond with God while persistently walking in the shadows of our flawed desires makes us hypocrites. However, if we genuinely strive to walk in His luminous path, He acknowledges our human imperfections. When He sees our earnest efforts, His abundant grace, channeled through the sacrificial blood of Jesus Christ, washes away our sins and illuminates our way.

Being a Christian isn't about static faith; it's a dynamic journey of transformation. With every passing second, minute, and day, we should witness change. If a Christian remains stagnant, it's crucial to introspect the authenticity of that faith. Christianity revolves around metamorphosis — molding us progressively into the image of Jesus Christ.

Today, let's introspect. If there's any lingering darkness within us, let's humbly approach God. Request Him to unveil our hidden blemishes, so we can lay them at His feet. Pray earnestly for His cleansing touch to purify our souls, and seek His guidance to walk hand-in-hand with Him in His radiant light. Amen.

NOVEMBER 21
How to pray?

Today, we will briefly revisit the Lord's Prayer that we discussed a few days ago.

The Lord's Prayer emerged as a response from Jesus Christ to His disciples when they requested Him to teach them to pray, just as John the Baptist had taught his own disciples. This prayer is more than mere words; it is a guideline, a framework for our communion with God. When we pray, our first approach is to acknowledge, honor, and magnify Him.

"Our Father which art in heaven, Hallowed be thy name. Thy kingdom come. Thy will be done in earth, as it is in heaven."

We begin by recognizing God for who He is to us: our cherished Father, the heavenly Father, our Savior, the one who redeemed us with His blood and stamped us with the Holy Spirit to affirm our adoption. We express our primary desire – for God's will and kingdom to take precedence. If our requests are contrary to His will or His kingdom, we ask Him to reveal it to us and steer us away. We seek alignment with His divine intent, trusting that His plans are the best for us.

Having acknowledged and revered God, we then present our needs: "Give us this day our daily bread." We lay forth our physical needs and sustenance. We also present our spiritual and emotional petitions, praying for healing, guidance, or any pressing matter on our hearts.

Yet, our spiritual well-being takes precedence. We ask not only for our daily provisions but also for spiritual nourishment and protection. We seek God's assistance in times of temptation, asking Him to illuminate our path, granting us discernment to quash any negative thoughts at their inception. Moreover, we pray for His protection against malevolent schemes, entrusting Him to shield us from harm.

Forgiveness is paramount. As we've been forgiven, we must also extend forgiveness to others. It's an opportunity to bring forth any unresolved grievances and release them, imploring God, "as we forgive, let us also be forgiven."

In conclusion, our prayers circle back to extolling God, acknowledging that all power, majesty, dominion, and glory are His, now and forevermore. Amen.

NOVEMBER 22

Desire, zeal and prayer for Church

Today, our devotional poses the question: Do you pray for your church? Some might wonder about the nature or frequency of such prayers. The scripture reminds us to be vigilant in our communication with God.

Ephesians 6:18 states, "Praying always with all prayer and supplication in the Spirit, being watchful to this end with all perseverance and supplication for all the saints—." Similarly, 1 Thessalonians 5:17-18 urges, "Pray without ceasing; in everything give thanks; for this is the will of God in Christ Jesus for you."

We are beckoned to pray for our church and its congregation, essentially the body of Christ to which we belong. What should our prayers encompass? Do you intercede for your church's protection, unity, physical and spiritual health? Do you fervently seek God's face for the church to be a sanctuary for the downtrodden, the grieving, and the lost? Do you pray for effective ministry, so the Word of God resonates deeply with every attendee? Do your petitions include your church leaders, that they might be divinely led in all decisions?

Moreover, consider your personal commitment. Do you earnestly pray for other members? Do you yearn for communal worship? The pandemic might have steered some into a casual attitude about attending church, thinking, "I'll attend if time permits or when convenient." Yet, the scripture emphasizes the church as our spiritual refuge and a hub for communal support and growth. We shouldn't approach it as a mere option but rather with anticipation, eagerly saying, "I look forward to Sunday to worship with fellow believers." Unless faced with insurmountable circumstances, our devotion should remain unwavering.

When we embrace this fervor for God and His assembly, our perspective shifts. A passionate commitment emerges, proclaiming, "I will attend church come what may, unless an unforeseen situation arises." May the Lord ignite this passion within us.

Dear Father, instill within us an unwavering desire to gather with Your people. Elevate our spirits and fortify our commitment to fellowship and worship. In the precious name of Jesus Christ. Amen.

NOVEMBER 23
Do Christians celebrate Halloween

Romans 12:2

> *And do not be conformed to this world, but be transformed by the renewing of your mind, that you may prove what is that good and acceptable and perfect will of God.*

A few days ago, the topic of Halloween was raised in our church: What is Halloween, and should we, as Christians, partake in its celebration?

To some, Halloween is viewed as a holiday associated with devil-worshipping practices, even going as far as to claim it celebrates the Devil's birthday. Many in the modern era might be unaware of such associations, as over time, the holiday has taken on a more commercial and secular demeanor, characterized by costumes and candy.

However, upon closer inspection, the themes of Halloween often gravitate towards the eerie, with motifs of ghouls, spirits, and other macabre subjects. Such associations should prompt introspection among the faithful. This is why many Christians choose not to celebrate Halloween.

When one examines crime statistics, it's reported that delinquent activities see a sharp spike on Halloween night, especially in North America. Disturbingly, there are claims of ritualistic practices by devil worshipers on this night, some of which involve sacrificing animals and other heinous acts. Given these associations, should Christians join in this celebration?

The scripture admonishes us, saying, "And be not conformed to this world: but be ye transformed by the renewing of your mind." Elsewhere, it queries, "What fellowship has light with darkness?"

Though we might distance ourselves from the overarching themes of Halloween, should we deny a young child candy when they knock at our door? Most would argue that this act of kindness should persist. If you do give out treats, ensure they're ordinary candies without any questionable imagery. Bless the children and pray for their well-being.

In conclusion, while the world might revel in Halloween, we are reminded that our allegiance lies elsewhere. We are not of this world; we are citizens of heaven. Amen.

NOVEMBER 24

What spirit is from the Lord?

1 John 4:1-3

> *Beloved, do not believe every spirit, but test the spirits, whether they are of God; because many false prophets have gone out into the world.* [2] *By this you know the Spirit of God: Every spirit that confesses that Jesus Christ has come in the flesh is of God,* [3] *and every spirit that does not confess that Jesus Christ has come in the flesh is not of God. And this is the spirit of the Antichrist, which you have heard was coming, and is now already in the world.*

One of the foundational principles of Christianity is the call for believers to scrutinize every teaching, voice, or new doctrine they encounter. On what criteria? Primarily, does this new teaching or prophet acknowledge that Jesus Christ came into the world in human form? Moreover, Christians are urged to weigh every word they hear against the Scriptures, the Bible. What does this imply? Simply, if what is taught or spoken contradicts Biblical teachings, then it isn't of God.

If we discern a voice, thinking it's from God, but its message opposes Scriptural teachings, then it is not divine. Instead, it's a voice influenced by evil spirits, the antichrist spirit, which emanates from Satan. John warns us of false prophets, asserting that they are, in reality, mouthpieces for malevolent spirits. Their primary objective is to estrange us from God's love and our faith in Jesus Christ, who sacrificed Himself for our transgressions and was resurrected on the third day.

Satan's primary scheme is to keep individuals from recognizing and accepting Jesus Christ. Why? If people fail to accept Christ, or if they embrace Him and later renounce Him, they risk sharing Satan's fate. Hence, Christians are encouraged to evaluate all teachings and beliefs against the fundamental truth of Jesus Christ's incarnation, crucifixion, resurrection, and His present role interceding for us at God's right hand.

Today, let us align our beliefs with these truths and progress in our journey of faith. May God be with you always. Amen.

NOVEMBER 25
The Lord knows all our ways

Psalm 139:1-6

> [1] *O LORD, you have searched me and known me.*
> [2] *You know my sitting down and my rising up; You understand my thought afar off.*
> [3] *You comprehend my path and my lying down, And are acquainted with all my ways.*
> [4] *For there is not a word on my tongue, But behold, O LORD, You know it altogether.*
> [5] *You have [l]hedged me behind and before, And laid Your hand upon me.*
> [6] *Such knowledge is too wonderful for me; It is high, I cannot attain it.*

Though we understand that God perceives every word we utter, recognizes our every motion, and discerns our deepest thoughts, there are moments we forget this reality. We momentarily overlook the omnipresence and omniscience of God. Yet, the moment we reflect upon it, we are immediately reminded of His awareness of every nuance in our lives.

When we approach God with transparency, concealing nothing, and particularly when we acknowledge Jesus Christ as Lord, the Son of God, our Savior, who sacrificed Himself for us on the cross, a profound transformation occurs. It's then that God extends His hand over us. Why? He has bestowed upon us His Holy Spirit as a guarantee of His promise. With the indwelling of God's Spirit, we are distinguished from the world, elevated to the status of God's children.

We are not like the multitude. We are His children. Not only does He oversee us, but He also envelops and safeguards us at every juncture. He engulfs us with an immeasurable love and tenderness. Pondering this truth, we realize the astounding love of the Creator of the universe for us—a love so profound that, even when we were at odds with Him, He selflessly laid down His life for us. His affection is such that, according to the book of Hebrews, He has commissioned angels to watch over us.

Such knowledge and consciousness are profound. Contemplating it, we recognize the insurmountability of comprehending this love fully on our own.

Yet, through the Holy Spirit within us, God empowers us to grasp this boundless love. Today, let's progress, keeping in mind our identity as God's children, endowed with the Holy Spirit, assured that God surrounds us with His omniscience.

Whenever we appeal to Him in alignment with His will, He generously responds. Amen.

NOVEMBER 26
The Lord transforms darkness to light

Psalm 139:11-12

> [11]*If I say, "Surely the darkness shall fall on me," Even the night shall be light about me;*
> [12]*Indeed, the darkness shall not hide from You, But the night shines as the day; The darkness and the light are both alike to You.*

Even when the shadows of sorrow, grief, depression, or the pervasive gloom of this world threaten to extinguish our hope and sever our connection to God's light, we must remember: God is with us. In His presence, even the blackest nights are illuminated, for God is light.

Who is the architect of darkness and light, of night and day? It is God. To Him, day and night hold no distinction; He is the radiant beacon in both. Jesus Christ proclaimed, "I am the light of the world." If we've embraced Jesus Christ as our Lord and Savior and have made room for Him in our hearts, allowing His Spirit to reign, then His luminescent spirit resides within us. In the presence of darkness, the brilliance of faith, guided by the Holy Spirit within us and the everlasting glow of Jesus Christ, transforms that darkness into day.

For God, darkness and light are indistinguishable. With a mere gesture, He can reshape everything. He is the God of transformation, moving us from obscurity to brilliance. Satan's enduring goal is to strip us of hope and separate us from the love, companionship, and fellowship of Jesus Christ.

When we are confronted by sorrow, darkness, or despair, we must declare that none of these stems from our Lord Jesus Christ. Our God embodies the light of joy and love, and our hope rests firmly in Him. He reassures us, "I will never leave you. I am always with you."

No matter where we tread, His presence is unwavering because His light has made its home in our hearts. He declares, "I am one with the Father. I am in the Father and the Father is in me. You are in me, I am in you. Together, we are united."

God transforms darkness into brilliance, for He is truly the light of the world. Amen.

NOVEMBER 27
We are fearfully and wonderfully made

Psalm 139:13-14

> [13] *For You formed my inward parts; You covered me in my mother's womb.*
> [14] *I will praise You, for I am fearfully and wonderfully made; Marvelous are Your works, And that my soul knows very well.*

"For thou hast possessed my reins: thou hast covered me in my mother's womb. I will praise thee; for I am fearfully and wonderfully made; marvelous are thy works; and that my soul knoweth right well."

When we reflect upon our lives, our birth, and the marvels around us, we are reminded of God's craftsmanship in it all. Do we recognize the intricate details with which He fashioned us, making us both "fearfully and wonderfully"?

Consider the human anatomy: the complex interplay of organs and systems that, if even minutely disrupted, wouldn't function correctly. Delve deeper into a single cell, and one can only exclaim in awe. Within each cell exists an intricate world: mitochondria, RNA, DNA, cytoplasm, all precisely choreographed for the cell's function.

Now, zoom even further into the realm of molecules, and we discover an entirely new universe, layered and interwoven in complexity. Could all of this truly be the result of mere chance? Mathematicians suggest the odds of humans evolving purely by accident are as unlikely as two cars crashing and producing a fully formed Concorde plane from the wreckage.

God designed you and me with intricate precision. He cradled us in our mother's wombs. When we view the world with an analytical eye, we can't help but marvel at the wonders of God's creation. It resonates deep within our souls that these are the works of His hands.

The author reminds us that in observing nature, we see God's touch everywhere. Do you discern God's imprint when you gaze upon the natural world?

Today, let's observe one another, life, nature, and the universe with this perspective. Such a viewpoint fills our hearts with joy, amazement, wonder, and immense gratitude for the God who not only crafted all these wonders but also loved us so profoundly that He sacrificed Himself on the cross for our salvation. Amen.

NOVEMBER 28
How precious are your thoughts to me, oh God!

Psalm 139:17-18

> [17] *How precious also are Your thoughts to me, O God! How great is the sum of them!*
> [18] *If I should count them, they would be more in number than the sand; When I awake, I am still with You.*

God proclaims that His thoughts and plans for us soar far beyond our comprehension. He consistently ponders about us, continually holding us in His considerations. God has bequeathed to us all His promises through the Lord Jesus Christ. We should embrace Jesus Christ not only as our Savior but also as our Lord. Some accept Jesus Christ merely as their Savior, longing for salvation from their sins, but they don't acknowledge Him as their Lord. They fail to yield their entire lives to Jesus Christ.

When we declare that the Lord Jesus Christ is both our Lord and Savior, it signifies that we surrender the direction of our lives to Him, entrusting Him with full command. We are essentially conveying, "Lord Jesus, you are the pilot of this journey, and I will either sit beside you or in the back."

However, some people, even after accepting Jesus Christ as their Savior, fail to surrender control. They effectively tell Him, "I'll drive this vehicle on my own, while you, Jesus, can take the backseat." So, where do you stand? Have you recognized Jesus Christ as your Savior without relegating Him to a passive role?

Or have you expressed to Him, "The magnitude of Your sacrifice for me is so vast that I not only see You as my Savior but also recognize that Your intentions for me are for the best?" Romans 8:28 states, "And we know that all things work together for good to them that love God, to them who are called according to His purpose." Moreover, Romans also declares, "If God is for us, who can be against us?" God assures us, "My designs and aspirations for you are loftier than you can fathom."

The scriptures say, "How precious also are Thy thoughts unto me, O God! How vast is the sum of them! If I were to count them, they would outnumber the grains of sand." Even upon awakening, He remains beside us. The Lord perpetually stands with us, even more so for those of us who have embraced Jesus Christ as our Lord and Savior.

For we are His children, and the Spirit of God resides within us. Through this Spirit, we become united with Jesus, who is one with the Father. Jesus dwells in the Father and vice versa, and the Spirit is intertwined with Jesus. All three are unified, and we are inextricably linked with them.

So, today, place your faith in God's grand intentions for you. Amen.

NOVEMBER 29

Lord, please guard our lips and tongue

Psalm 141:3-4

> [3] *Set a guard, O* L*ORD, over my mouth; Keep watch over the door of my lips.*
> [4] *Do not incline my heart to any evil thing, to practice wicked works with men who work iniquity; And do not let me eat of their delicacies.*

When discussing the Lord's Prayer, Jesus says, "And lead us not into temptation, but deliver us from evil." James speaks about the power and influence of the tongue, emphasizing the profound impact such a small part of our body can have.

David, in his Psalms, implores: "Set a watch, O LORD, before my mouth; keep the door of my lips." This is a heartfelt prayer for caution and mindfulness about what we utter. As followers of Jesus Christ, it is our duty to be vigilant about our words, ensuring that we always speak life and truth.

James likens the tongue to the bit in a horse's mouth, something small that can control something much larger. Just as we control a horse with a bit, we must control our tongue, which has the power to ignite conflicts or uplift souls.

But David delves even deeper, praying, "Incline not my heart to any evil thing." He is asking God to purify his intentions and desires, to keep him from being drawn towards wickedness or joining those who revel in sin.

It all begins in the mind. Each temptation, each sin, starts as a mere thought. It is our responsibility to intercept and counteract these thoughts as soon as they arise. We should recognize and rebuke them, reminding ourselves that they are not of God but snares of the devil. In these moments, we must arm ourselves with God's Word, which provides the strength and wisdom to combat these errant thoughts.

When the world or our past tries to lure us back into old habits or sins, saying, "You've done this before; it's not a big deal," we must stand firm in our renewed identity in Christ. We must declare that the old self is dead, and we are reborn in Christ.

A single thought, when entertained and nurtured, can lead to an inclination, which can then manifest as actions. Eventually, these actions become habits, ensnaring us in their grip.

Therefore, every time a negative or sinful thought tries to take root in our mind, let's combat it with the truth of God's Word. Amen.

NOVEMBER 30

Have we become lukewarm for Jesus?

Revelation 3:14-17

This is where Jesus Christ tells John about the message to the various churches, and that message is to the Laodicean church.

> [14] *And to the angel of the church of the Laodiceans write, 'These things says the Amen, the Faithful and True Witness, the Beginning of the creation of God:*
> [15] *"I know your works, that you are neither cold nor hot. I could wish you were cold or hot.*
> [16] *So then, because you are lukewarm, and neither cold nor hot, I will vomit you out of My mouth.*
> [17] *Because you say, 'I am rich, have become wealthy, and have need of nothing'—and do not know that you are wretched, miserable, poor, blind, and naked.*

The words of God, timeless and eternal, serve as an anchor for believers throughout history. These warnings and counsel are not merely for the churches of the past but resonate deeply with every believer today. Periodically, it is vital for us to engage in self-reflection and introspection, guided by God's wisdom.

Where do we stand in our relationship with Him? Are we lukewarm in our faith, oscillating between passion and indifference? Do we remember the fervor and fiery love we had when we first believed? Often, as our prayers are answered and our needs met, there's a risk of growing complacent. A false sense of security might lead us to declare, "I am rich, and I need nothing," distancing ourselves from our initial dependency on Christ.

However, Jesus warns against such complacency. If we reach a stage where we feel self-sufficient and drift away from Him, losing the ardor of our first love, it displeases Him. Being lukewarm—neither fervently hot nor refreshingly cold—Jesus says, will lead to being spat out unless we rekindle our passion. He calls us to return, to purchase from Him gold refined in fire, symbolizing true spiritual wealth, and white garments to cover our spiritual nakedness.

But despite our imperfections, the Lord's mercy is boundless. He doesn't forcefully enter our lives but gently knocks on the door of our hearts.

If we hear Him and open up, He promises a union, a fellowship, a communion. If we repent and reignite our love for Him, He promises to sit with us, share a meal, and deepen our relationship.

Today, let's introspect: Have we allowed our fervor for Christ to wane? Have we sidelined our commitment to Him and His church? Simply accepting Jesus in our hearts isn't enough. Faith must be alive, evident in our actions, our deeds, our fruits. Let us reflect on these words and ensure our faith in Christ isn't just in our hearts but evident in our lives. Amen.

DECEMBER 1
The lion of the tribe of Judah and the lamb of God

Revelation 5:1-3

> [1]*And I saw in the right hand of Him who sat on the throne a scroll written inside and on the back, sealed with seven seals.*
> [2] *Then I saw a strong angel proclaiming with a loud voice, "Who is worthy to open the scroll and to lose its seals?"*
> [3] *And no one in heaven or on the earth or under the earth was able to open the scroll, or to look at it.*

And I wept profusely because no man was found worthy to open and read the book, nor even to look upon it. One of the elders said unto me, "Weep not: behold, the Lion of the tribe of Judah, the Root of David, has prevailed to open the book and to break its seven seals." I looked and, behold, in the midst of the throne and of the four beasts, and in the midst of the elders, stood a Lamb as though it had been slain, having seven horns and seven eyes, which are the seven Spirits of God sent out into all the earth. He came and took the book from the right hand of Him who sat on the throne.

And when He had taken the book, the four beasts and the twenty-four elders fell down before the Lamb, each having a harp, and golden bowls full of incense, which are the prayers of the saints. They sang a new song, saying, "You are worthy to take the book and to open its seals; for You were slain and have redeemed us to God by Your blood out of every tribe and tongue and people and nation. You have made us kings and priests to our God, and we shall reign on the earth." When John began to cry, an elder told him not to weep. For who is this? The Lion of the tribe of Judah. Yet, when John looked to identify this roaring lion, what did he see? A lamb appearing as though it had been slaughtered. No one in heaven, on earth, or under the earth was able to open the scroll or look inside it, save for He who holds the highest name above all. Jesus Christ: both the roaring Lion of the tribe of Judah and the Lamb of God, slain for our sins. This Lamb of God shed His blood to usher us into the family of God, redeeming people for God from every tribe, tongue, and nation. This is the God we worship. This is Jesus Christ, who was born roughly 2021 years ago, to save each and every one of us. So today, if we face any challenges, we bring them before Jesus Christ, for He is capable of all things. In Him, all promises are "Yes," and His power is unparalleled. Amen.

DECEMBER 2
The word of the Lord is pure

Proverbs 30:5

> *Every word of God is pure; He is a shield to those who put their trust in Him.*

Every word of God is pure; He is a shield to those who put their trust in Him. All of God's words, everything He has said, all of His utterances are in the Bible. Although the Bible has been written by various authors, the original author is the Holy Spirit. It is the Holy Spirit who gave all these words to the previous prophets and apostles.

All the words of God are practical, pure, clear, lucid, and important. As Christians, one of the foundations of our faith is that the Word of God is pure, always valid, and written by the Spirit of God. The Bible is one of the most important documents and one of the most credible books. To determine if an old book is genuine, scientists check how many copies remain and compare those copies to ensure the contents are consistent. This process validates old documents for us. They can also determine the age of a document using radiocarbon dating. The Gospel, or the Bible, is one of the few ancient books with more than 1,500 volumes remaining, and they are all consistent. Thus, the misconception propagated by adversaries that the Bible has been distorted is utterly false.

The Gospel, the Bible, is an authentic book, the only book that contains all of God's Word, and was written through divine inspiration by the Holy Spirit. The author states that anyone who has this faith and relies on God's word will find that God is their shield and stronghold. In another passage, it says, "God is my stronghold, and I will flee and take refuge in Him; the enemy will not harm me." That's why we must read the Bible daily, familiarize ourselves with the Word of God, understand its message, and use it as a defense against adversaries and misleading thoughts. Through it, we come to understand His will and are reminded to live in His presence and guidance every moment. Amen.

DECEMBER 3

Winning the war in our minds (1)

Introduction

We are about to embark on a series of devotionals focused on "winning the war in our minds." This series is inspired by Craig Groeschel's insightful book, "Winning the War in Your Mind."

Every emotion, every action originates from a thought. The genesis is always in our minds. And it's from these small thoughts that our adversary, the devil, begins his subversive activities.

The Bible, in 2 Corinthians 10:4-5, declares: "...who comforts us in all our tribulation, that we may be able to comfort those who are in any trouble, with the comfort with which we ourselves are comforted by God. For as the sufferings of Christ abound in us, so our consolation also abounds through Christ. For the weapons of our warfare are not carnal, but mighty through God to the pulling down of strongholds; casting down imaginations, and every high thing that exalts itself against the knowledge of God, and bringing into captivity every thought to the obedience of Christ."

Our battle, as believers, is not against humans, but against cosmic forces. Some scriptures refer to these as heavenly and demonic forces. But how do we tear down these strongholds the enemy establishes in us and around us? By divine power. Where does it initiate? It all begins as a fleeting thought. Phrases like, "You are superior; this is your right; why settle?" are seeds the enemy plants. When nurtured, they grow, but the root of all such thoughts is pride.

Anything tinged with pride doesn't come from God. He cherishes humility. Any argument or haughty thought that goes against God's knowledge is not of Him. Sentiments like "You're finished; now you're in despair; you've erred too much for God to act" are contrary to God.

To counteract, we must cast down imaginations and every grandiose notion that opposes God's knowledge. Our immediate response should be to bring every thought under Christ's obedience. Every thought contrary to Christ's teachings should be laid at His feet and negated. Amen?

In the upcoming days, we'll delve deeper into the practical application of these truths as guided by the Word of God. For today, I urge you to remain vigilant about your thoughts. Guard against any that oppose God. The moment such a thought surfaces, immerse yourself in praise and stand firm against it. Amen.

DECEMBER 4
Winning the war in our minds (2)
Principles

What should we do when an intrusive, harmful thought emerges in our minds? This is the thought that the devil implants, and if nurtured and given attention, it sets its roots deep within us, leading to temptation and subsequently, sin. How can we effectively combat this?

A Persian proverb astutely observes, "A first war is better than a last peace." This means that the moment such a thought tries to take root, when the enemy seeks to plant a seed contrary to God's teachings in our hearts, we mustn't merely recognize it but take immediate action.

So, how do we proceed? There are four foundational principles to uphold:

1. **Replacement:** The initial step is to substitute that negative thought with the word of God. If the enemy whispers that we are worthless, we can counteract by recalling, "No, the Scriptures assure me of my immense value in the eyes of the Lord Jesus Christ, so much so that He sacrificed Himself on the cross for me."
2. **Re-wiring:** This is about reshaping our thought processes, steering our minds away from harmful tendencies.
3. **Re-framing:** It entails adopting a renewed perspective, reshaping our mental frameworks to align with God's will.
4. **Ecstasy and Joy:** The final principle revolves around immersing ourselves in the overwhelming joy of what the Lord Jesus Christ has accomplished for us.

When a detrimental thought appears, remember to:

1. Replace it with God's word.
2. Re-wire our thinking.
3. Update our perspective.
4. Revel in the joy the Lord provides.

The Scriptures remind us, "For those who love God, all things work together for good, for those who are called according to His purpose." Amen.

DECEMBER 5
Winning the war in our minds (3)
Principle of replacement

The first principle of winning the war in our mind in replacing lies with truth.

As Jesus told us we know that the father of lies is Satan. Satan is our enemy and his goal is to destroy us. How could he destroy us? With lies, the lies that he plants in our minds, in our thoughts and before us so that we accept those lies instead on the truth, in the same way he deceived Eve with his lie: "Do you really think you shall die if you eat of this fruit? No, if you eat this fruit, you will be able to recognize good from evil and you shall become like God." And Eve believed his lie and ate the fruit. So, you see the work of the devil is to plant a lie in our mind and introduce it to us so we believe it as the truth because if we knew it was a lie we would have never believed it NS ct upon it. So, the work of Satan is to plant a lie in our head and repeat it over and over until we believe it as the truth. So, you may say how do we know what the truth is?

The word of the Lord in Gospel of John tells us: "Know the truth and the truth shall set you free." But what is the truth? Pontus Pilot asked Jesus the same question. All the truths are in the word of God, the Bible and that is the reason why reading the word of God is so important for us as believers. When we learn its truth, we know that the Lord loved us so much that He makes all things work for good for us. When the devil tells us: "You are unworthy", if we know the word of God, we will tell him, "No, I worth so much and the Lord loves me so much that when I was a sinner, Jesus Christ died for me on the cross. Or when Satan tells you, "You are hopeless and depressed." If we know the word of God, we will respond: "No, the Lord has not given me the spirit of fear and depression but the spirit of adoption and courage."

So, you see, whenever the devil put a lie before us and tries to plant it in our mind, if we know the truth, we proclaim it and by this replace the lie by the truth and when we know the truth, the truth shall set us free from the lies of enemy. So, reading and knowing the word of God is very essential. The word of the Lord is like arrows that we use in our bows to bring down the devil. When Jesus was in the desert and tempted by the devil, he responded to him with the word of bible because He knew the truth. So, with truth we can break down the lies and be free.

Lord, please help us to read and understand your words everyday so we can replace the lies of the enemy with your truth and win this war. Amen

DECEMBER 6
Winning the war (4)
Principle of rewiring

Today, we delve into the principle of rewriting or rewiring our minds. Our brain contains neural pathways that form when we repeatedly engage in certain thoughts or actions. These pathways become so well-established that certain actions or thoughts become second nature. Take, for example, an Olympic athlete who practices their routine repeatedly; it becomes so ingrained that they perform it automatically, without needing to ponder each step. Similarly, our thinking patterns can solidify through repetition.

When we consistently focus on a specific thought or immerse ourselves in it, we modify the neural pathways in our brain. These pathways then become readily accessible, and this principle is equally applicable to spiritual matters. When the enemy introduces a falsehood, it's essential not only to replace it with the truth but also to adjust these neural pathways. How? By establishing trenches in our minds filled with God's truth.

Thus, in the face of an enemy onslaught, we're equipped with trenches of truth – fortifications anchored in God's Word. By regularly reading and internalizing Scripture, by committing God's promises to memory, we fortify our defenses. Whenever a lie approaches, it is instantly recognized and countered by our entrenched truths.

The light shines in the darkness, dispelling it. Our illumination comes from the truths contained in God's Word. Therefore, it's crucial to immerse ourselves in Scripture, to memorize it, and to continually reaffirm God's promises within us.

Romans 12:2 reminds us, "And be not conformed to this world: but be ye transformed by the renewing of your mind, that ye may prove what is that good, and acceptable, and perfect, will of God." This transformation is achieved by reinforcing our minds with God's truth.

Further, 1 Peter 5:7 asserts, "Casting all your care upon Him, for He cares for you." Psalm 91:2 proclaims, "I will say of the LORD, 'He is my refuge and my fortress; My God, in Him I will trust.'" Romans 8:28 affirms, "And we know that all things work together for good to those who love God, to those who are the called according to His purpose." Romans 8:31 poses the question, "What then shall we say to these things? If God is for us, who can be against us?" By saturating ourselves in these truths, by continually reaffirming them in our hearts, we create new neural pathways. These pathways enable us to swiftly identify falsehoods and stand resiliently against them. Amen.

DECEMBER 07
Winning the war in our minds (5)
Principle of reframing

Our third principle centers on the idea of re-framing, or altering our intellectual framework. What does this entail? While we might not have control over external events, we certainly wield power over our perceptions and reactions to them.

Inherently, we each possess certain biases or patterns of thought that may distort our interpretation of events, preventing us from seeing the genuine truth. However, we also have the capability to shift these deeply embedded thoughts, refashioning them to alter our perceptions and responses to past and future occurrences.

The Word of God in Proverbs 3:5-6 advises us: "Trust in the LORD with all your heart, and lean not on your own understanding; in all your ways acknowledge Him, and He shall direct your paths."

Consider Paul's situation. He aspired to preach in Rome, but how did he ultimately arrive there? In chains. Although he had yearned to share God's message with kings and even Caesar, his journey to Rome was marked by captivity. Yet, instead of lamenting his circumstance or decrying the difficulty, Paul wrote to the Philippians, sharing, "I want you to know, my brothers and sisters, that what has happened to me has actually served to advance the gospel. As a result, it has become clear throughout the whole palace guard and to everyone else that I am in chains for Christ."

He perceived his situation differently. His chains weren't a setback; they were an opportunity. Soldiers, chained to Paul, became an audience for his message, and with a changing guard, the message spread.

We should strive to adopt a similar perspective, reshaping our viewpoints. Instead of asking, "Why did this happen to me?", we ought to reaffirm that God remains in control, desiring the best for us. By focusing our gaze through the lens of God's promises and designs, we can reframe our mindset.

Transforming our outlook, viewing circumstances through the filter of God's word, paves the way for genuine peace and tranquility. Amen.

DECEMBER 08
Winning the war (6)
Principle of Joy

Philippians 4:4-7

> [4]*"Rejoice in the Lord always; again I will say, rejoice.*
> [5]*Let your reasonableness be known to everyone.*
> [6]*The Lord is at hand; do not be anxious about anything, but in everything by prayer and supplication with thanksgiving let your requests be made known to God.*
> [7]*And the peace of God, which surpasses all understanding, will guard your hearts and your minds in Christ Jesus."*

The next principle of winning the war in our mind is joy. Paul in above verses reveals the secret on how to change our anxiety and reasoning in the hard times and storms with prayers and worship. It is easy to be broken down by circumstances and think that enough is enough and give up. But when these thoughts surround us and try to take us down, we need to proclaim that the Lord is enough for us, and not only that but the Lord is near to us. We need to remember these truths and when we proclaim them it will bring us to pray instead of worry. We bring all our fears and anxieties to the Lord and put them in His mighty hands and trust Him, trust His everlasting love, and trust His provision.

Prayer, worship, and praise transform our minds and thoughts. We worship the Lord for whom He is not for what He would give us. And when we worship him in this manner, He shows up and brings us His peace and rest. So instead of worrying, let us rejoice in our Lord. Let us change our way of thinking and understanding which will take us to prayer and worship that bring us peace, rest, and joy of the Lord to our minds and thoughts. Amen

DECEMBER 09
Winning the war (7)
Who are we?

In the previous devotionals we talked about the 4 principles of winning the war in our minds: Replacing, Rewiring, Reframing, and Joy. So, what do we do with these.

Let us decide today to change our thoughts and will not think the way this world thinks, and Let the Lord renew our thoughts and mind and instead of focusing our eyes on the things of this world, focus our minds and thoughts on Christ Jesus. He is our creator that holds us in His hands and carry us. He is the one who makes us strong and gives us power to do the works he has called us to do. Therefore, let us crush every lie that the enemy whispers in our ears under our feet and overcome them.

We know that we are not the ones that need anyone except the Lord because we know that the Lord is our everything. We are not controlled by fear. We are not fallen. We are not the slaves of our habits. We are not prisoner of our addictions. We are not victim. We are not unlovable. We are not a parasite. We are not what we had done. We are not what others had done to us. We are not what other people say we are. We are not who our wrong thoughts say we are. Our work has not finished. We are who the Lord says we are. Because of Jesus Christ we are lovely. We are forgiven. We are healed. We are renewed. We are repurchased. We are free. We are blessed. We are strong. We are chosen. And we are the righteousness weapon in this dark world.

Let all these truths take place in us and transform us. Our Lord is with us. He never leaves us or forsake us. The Lord is for us. He fights for us and no weapon that is against us shall prosper. Through Him we are greater than this world. The Lord is enough for us and even more than enough.

Nothing can separate us from the love of our God, not death, not the evil spirits, not the present time and not the past, nothing can separate us for the love of God that is in our Lord Jesus Christ.

So, Lord, change our minds and therefore, change our lives. Amen

DECEMBER 10

A new habit, bless the Lord oh my soul

Psalm 103:1-5

> *[1]Bless the LORD, O my soul; And all that is within me, bless His holy name!*
> *[2]Bless the LORD, O my soul, And forget not all His benefits:*
> *[3]Who forgives all your iniquities, Who heals all your diseases,*
> *[4]Who redeems your life from destruction, Who crowns you with lovingkindness and tender mercies,*
> *[5]Who satisfies your mouth with good things, So that your youth is renewed like the eagle's.*

As we usher in a new year, it would be beneficial to cultivate the habit David speaks of. In our previous sessions, we discussed Craig Groeschel's book, "Winning the War in Our Minds."

I encourage you to commit these five verses to memory: "Bless the LORD, O my soul." Let's extol the Lord with all that's within us. This should become a daily practice, praising His holy name in every situation, with every fiber of our being. How can we achieve this? By remembering all His blessings.

As I shared at the outset of this year, Insook and I set aside time at the beginning of each year to reflect on God's deeds in our lives from the preceding year. We enumerate His acts of love, the storms we faced, and how He navigated us through them, expressing our gratitude for each one.

So, let's cultivate a habit of recognizing His benevolence in every circumstance. "He forgives all your sins." Indeed, when we accept the Lord Jesus Christ as our Savior, our sins are not only forgiven, but each time we repent thereafter, He grants us swift forgiveness and salvation. "He heals all your diseases." This refers not just to physical ailments but spiritual afflictions too. Our healing is assured through the stripes He bore for us.

"He redeems your life from the pit." The Lord Jesus Christ delivered us from the grasp of death and hell, offering a once-for-all sacrifice on the cross. Accepting Him as our Lord, Savior, and the Son of God ensures our redemption. "He crowns you with steadfast love and mercy." Our God is a God of boundless love. His love was so profound that He gave His Son for us while we were still His adversaries.

Jesus Christ's love was so immense that He endured the cross for us, even when we were opposed to Him. Upon accepting Him, He declares us as kings and priests, bestowing upon us the crown of love. "He satisfies you with good things." Jacob reminds us that all blessings come from the hands of our God above.

Whenever we witness such acts of grace, our response should echo: "All praise and worship belong to You, O God." Amen.

"And thy youth is renewed like the eagle's." When we embody gratitude for all that God does, when we journey alongside Him, when His presence permeates our lives, God rejuvenates us. He doesn't merely restore our youth; He invigorates our spirits. The way we perceive others, situations, and even challenges is transformed, infusing us with a renewed vigor.

As we step into this year, let's approach Him with hearts full of praise, declaring, "Bless the LORD, O my soul: and all that is within me, bless His holy name." Amen.

DECEMBER 11
Humility of Jesus Christ

Matthew 3

Matthew chapter 3 introduces us to John the Baptist, whom the prophet described as the voice crying out in the wilderness: "Prepare ye the way of the Lord, make his paths straight." As John performed baptisms, Jesus approached from Galilee to Jordan, seeking baptism. John, aware of Jesus' divine nature, hesitated, exclaiming, "I need to be baptized by you, and yet you come to me?"

In response, Jesus said, "Let it be so now; it is proper for us to do this to fulfill all righteousness." Then John agreed.

Who was John the Baptist? He was a relative of Jesus. Delving deeper into their story, we find that the angel Gabriel, when announcing to Mary that she would bear a son, also informed her that her older cousin Elizabeth was expectant. Mary went to visit Elizabeth, who was then six months pregnant with John. Upon Mary's arrival, the unborn John leapt for joy in Elizabeth's womb, filled with the Holy Spirit at the very presence of Jesus. Thus, John the Baptist and Jesus, being only six months apart, grew up together.

John, well-acquainted with Jesus, recognized His divine identity. Yet, Jesus displayed profound humility. Throughout His life, our Savior consistently exemplified and taught humility. The King of Kings chose to be born not in a palace, but in a humble stable amidst animals. Even in His final moments, He embraced the most agonizing death, reminding us that, although He commanded the heavenly hosts, He chose a humble path. As He told Peter, "Put your sword back in its place... Do you think I cannot call on my Father, and he will at once put at my disposal more than twelve legions of angels? But how then would the Scriptures be fulfilled that say it must happen in this way?"

Our Lord Jesus Christ's actions resonate deeply with His teachings. His life serves as a living testament, instructing us to emulate His humility.

Let us pray: Father, in the name of Jesus Christ, we express our gratitude for guiding us from darkness into light. Instill in us the humility exemplified by our Lord Jesus Christ. We reject the spirit of pride and seek to embody humility in Your eyes, today and always. In the name of Jesus Christ. Amen.

DECEMBER 12
Beatitudes, inheritors of kingdom of God (1)

Matthew chapters 5 to 7 encompass one of the most renowned sections of the Bible, commonly referred to as Jesus Christ's Sermon on the Mount. The Lord initiated His teachings with the Beatitudes:

"Blessed are the poor in spirit, For theirs is the kingdom of heaven. Blessed are those who mourn, For they shall be comforted. Blessed are the meek, For they shall inherit the earth. Blessed are those who hunger and thirst for righteousness, For they shall be filled. Blessed are the merciful, For they shall obtain mercy. Blessed are the pure in heart, For they shall see God. Blessed are the peacemakers, For they shall be called sons of God. Blessed are those who are persecuted for righteousness' sake, For theirs is the kingdom of heaven."

The kingdom of God contrasts starkly with the kingdoms of this world. Often, God's kingdom appears inverted, offering unexpected blessings. "Blessed are the poor in spirit, for theirs is the kingdom of heaven." But what does it mean to be "poor in spirit"?

It signifies recognizing one's spiritual deficiency, acknowledging one's meagerness in spirit. Such individuals intensely seek spiritual growth because they recognize their scarcity in this regard. They ardently chase spiritual enlightenment, approaching it with humility, fully aware of their limited spiritual wealth.

In worldly kingdoms, riches often determine power and ownership. Yet, in God's kingdom, it's the spiritually impoverished, those who perceive their lack and yearn for more, who truly inherit His kingdom.

Today, let's turn to God, admitting our spiritual poverty and beseeching, "O God, bestow Your Spirit upon us, enrich us with Your presence. Enlighten us with Your spiritual wisdom and fill our hearts with Your Spirit."

In the name of Jesus Christ. Amen.

DECEMBER 13
Beatitudes, inheritors of kingdom of God (2)

We continue our devotional journey today, diving deeper into the beatitudes from Jesus Christ's Sermon on the Mount. Previously, we reflected upon: "Blessed are the poor in spirit, for theirs is the kingdom of heaven." Today, we'll ponder the next beatitude: "Blessed are they that mourn, for they shall be comforted."

Blessed are those who experience the weight of grief and sorrow. The Lord assures that He will provide comfort to the afflicted. For those who mourn and grieve, the Lord offers His solace. Jesus promises, "I leave with you my peace. It's not as the world gives. It's a peace that only I can offer." The peace the Lord bestows is distinct and unparalleled. He reminds us, "I haven't given you a spirit of fear, but one of adoption."

The Lord, in His divine wisdom and love, bore our burdens. By taking on human flesh, Jesus Christ walked amongst us, sharing in our joys and sorrows. Having witnessed our trials firsthand, He knows precisely how to console our hearts. Even amid despair, challenges, and storms, His peace remains an unwavering beacon, providing a solace that's beyond human comprehension.

Jesus reassures us that in moments of grief and pain, seeking Him brings solace. When facing life's inevitable heartbreaks and losses, turning our gaze to Him offers hope. Because He is the anchor of our souls, our refuge in times of trouble, He brings calm and consolation, providing all that we seek.

This is why Jesus says, "Blessed are the mourners; they shall find comfort." But why does mourning lead to blessing? In our moments of grief, we draw closer to God, seeking His divine comfort. It's a blessing to feel the gentle touch of God, to sense His ever-present comfort and care.

So, if today you find yourself burdened with sorrow or gripped by sadness, lift your hands to the Lord Jesus Christ and say, "O Lord, you promised, 'Blessed are those who mourn, for they will be comforted.' My solace, my peace lies in Your hands. Touch me, Lord." Amen.

DECEMBER 14
Beatitudes, blessed are the meek (3)

Today, we continue with our exploration of the beatitudes that Jesus Christ shared during His sermon on the mount.

"Blessed are the meek, for they shall inherit the earth."

We've previously discussed "Blessed are the poor in spirit" and "Blessed are those who mourn." Now, we turn to understanding the meek. Who are they? The meek are the humble, those who prioritize others above themselves. They are individuals who exhibit selflessness, refraining from elevating themselves above others. They recognize their flaws, their vulnerabilities, and in acknowledging these, they remain humble before both God and His people.

Contrarily, the world often suggests the inverse. It teaches that for prosperity, one must be ambitious, assertive, and, at times, even aggressive. It suggests that you need to assert your rights, even if it means sidelining others. But, as we've seen, the kingdom of God operates on principles diametrically opposed to those of the world. It is the meek, the humble, and those poor in spirit, who are, against worldly expectations, designated as the heirs to God's kingdom.

We should reflect on our nature: Are we humble? Or do we consistently place ourselves above others? When we act, is it solely for personal gain without considering its potential repercussions on others? Are our actions and decisions driven solely by personal benefits, or do we prioritize the welfare of others?

To be "meek" in God's eyes means to respect others' opinions, to value their well-being over our desires, and to humbly consider their needs above our own. Those who embody such virtues, the truly humble and meek, are the ones who will inherit both the earth and the kingdom of God.

Let us move forward today, keeping these teachings close to our hearts. Amen.

DECEMBER 15
Beatitudes, inheritors of kingdom of God (4)

Today, we continue our study of the beatitudes that the Lord Jesus Christ presented in His Sermon on the Mount.

We have already explored: "Blessed are the poor in spirit, for theirs is the kingdom of heaven." "Blessed are those who mourn, for they shall be comforted." "Blessed are the meek, for they shall inherit the earth."

Today, we delve into verse 6: "Blessed are those who hunger and thirst for righteousness, for they shall be filled."

We are beckoned to have a deep longing for justice and righteousness. What kind of righteousness are we discussing here? It is the righteousness of God. And who embodies this righteousness for us? Who justified us? The Lord Jesus Christ. In another part of the scripture, Christ mentions that unless our righteousness surpasses that of the Pharisees, we won't enter the kingdom of God.

It's essential to understand that the Pharisees were devout followers of the Mosaic Law, adhering strictly to its statutes. In this context, Christ speaks of upholding and fulfilling the Old Testament, emphasizing that no commandment will be discarded. We are also called to uphold them.

How then can our righteousness exceed that of the Pharisees? It is because, through our acceptance of the Lord Jesus Christ, believing that He died for our sins and rose on the third day, His resurrection is counted as righteousness on our behalf. It stands as the pinnacle of righteousness and justice in this world.

The righteousness of Jesus Christ is unparalleled. Accepting Him and His sacrifice means being filled with righteousness. When we yearn for Him, we are filled, not just with momentary righteousness but with the everlasting righteousness of God. His righteousness, granted to us through His death and resurrection, is supreme. As we hunger and thirst for Christ, we find ourselves being filled. Yet, paradoxically, this filling also increases our longing for Him.

By embracing Jesus Christ and allowing the Holy Spirit to work within us daily, our thirst for righteousness is quenched, even as our yearning for Him grows. Amen.

DECEMBER 16

Beatitudes, blessed are the merciful and pure in heart (5)

Today, we continue our exploration of the beatitudes that the Lord Jesus Christ presented in the Sermon on the Mount. We'll focus on verses 7 and 8:

"Blessed are the merciful, for they shall obtain mercy." "Blessed are the pure in heart, for they shall see God."

Jesus emphasized mercy in His teachings. In the Lord's Prayer, He instructs us to pray, "Forgive us our debts, as we forgive our debtors." Mercy is a pivotal outcome of the Holy Spirit's work within us. After acknowledging our Father in heaven, Christ delves into forgiveness. He challenges us on whom, how, and how often we should forgive, emphasizing that vengeance is reserved for God alone. Our role? To forgive, to exhibit mercy. Jesus promises, "As you forgive others, so shall your Father in heaven forgive you." Conversely, withholding forgiveness denies us God's mercy. Mercy isn't just a blessing; it's the fruit of the Spirit living within believers.

Following this, Jesus speaks of purity: "Blessed are the pure in heart." How do our hearts become pure? It's not by our own deeds. God, in His grace, took on human form, experienced our struggles, and, sinless, offered Himself on the cross for our redemption. Rising again, He provided righteousness for all who believe.

Accepting Jesus purifies our hearts. This purification, too, is the work of the Holy Spirit. If we find ourselves lacking in mercy or purity, we should earnestly seek God, praying, "Lord, grant me a pure heart and infuse me with Your compassion. Let Your Spirit work in me continuously, for I yearn to see and commune with You."

Through accepting Christ as our Savior, our relationship with God is restored. The veil is torn, allowing us unhindered access to our Father. Amen.

DECEMBER 17

Beatitudes, blessed are the peacemakers (6)

Blessed are the peacemakers: for they shall be called the children of God

Today, we delve deeper into the beatitudes that the Lord Jesus Christ shared in the Sermon on the Mount. We turn our attention to verse 9:

"Blessed are the peacemakers, for they shall be called the children of God."

How are peacemakers recognized as children of God? Who bears the title, the Prince of Peace? It's none other than Jesus Christ. Through His sacrifice on the cross, Jesus reconciled us to God, bridging the chasm and ushering in peace. When angels heralded His birth, their declaration was one of peace on earth.

Jesus is the embodiment of peace. Through His death and resurrection, He mended the relationship between humanity and God. In observing the world, it's evident that true Christians, driven by the Holy Spirit, are frequently the torchbearers of peace. As the Holy Spirit takes residence in our hearts, one of its fruits is peace.

Being peacemakers, standing against anger, animosity, and vengeance, aligns us with the nature of our Savior. It's in these moments that we mirror the Prince of Peace, demonstrating our identity as God's children.

It's our calling to be ambassadors of peace. When faced with conflict, whether at home, within our families, or among peers, we should ardently seek peace, striving to infuse every situation with harmony. We are beckoned to reflect the peace of our Lord and Savior, Jesus Christ, showcasing our lineage as the children of God. Amen.

DECEMBER 18
Beatitudes, inheritors of kingdom of God (7)

Today, our devotional explores the culmination of the beatitudes, imparted by Jesus Christ during His Sermon on the Mount. We turn our attention to Matthew chapter 5, verses 10 to 12:

> *"Blessed are those who are persecuted for righteousness' sake, For theirs is the kingdom of heaven. Blessed are you when they revile and persecute you, and say all kinds of evil against you falsely for My sake. Rejoice and be exceedingly glad, for great is your reward in heaven, for so they persecuted the prophets who were before you."*

It's human nature to feel affronted when someone maligns us due to our beliefs or speaks ill of us behind our backs. While we must remain steadfast in our faith, Jesus doesn't instruct us to abandon our stance or express remorse for our convictions. Instead, He guides us to find joy amidst adversity. For, in facing such trials for righteousness, our eternal reward is bountiful.

Who is the embodiment of righteousness? Jesus Christ. He bore human flesh, suffered on the cross for our transgressions, and with His resurrection, bestowed upon us righteousness and salvation. He is the path of righteousness. In professing our faith in Him, we must understand that persecution will inevitably follow.

If our Savior, during His time on earth, endured persecution, false accusations, public humiliation, and ultimately, a harrowing crucifixion, then it stands to reason that in our journey, we will also encounter adversity due to our unwavering faith.

Yet, as we confront these challenges, Jesus calls us not to bitterness, but to joy. For withstanding such tribulations secures for us a rich reward in heaven. So, if we face slander or abuse, our response should be one of kindness, patience, and prayer. For in doing so, we may lead others to the profound blessings found in the Lord Jesus Christ. Amen.

DECEMBER 19

Worshiping our Lord with our possessions

Proverbs 3:9-10

> [9] *Honor the LORD with your possessions, And with the first fruits of all your increase;*
> [10] *So your barns will be filled with plenty, And your vats will overflow with new wine.*

The proverbs penned by Solomon impart a conversation with his son, and he advises, "Honor the Lord with thy substance, and with the first fruits of all thine increase: So shall thy barns be filled with plenty, and thy presses shall burst out with new wine." In another verse, it is emphasized that God cherishes those who generously give in His name, driven by heartfelt conviction.

As Christians, we are beckoned to contribute joyously from our resources towards God's purpose. But whence come our possessions? They are borne of God's benevolence. While one might argue that personal toil and determination are responsible, the guiding hand of God remains undeniable. As Jacob professed, every blessing, every good thing, is a gift descending from heaven.

Hard work, devoid of divine blessing, may yield little. Dishonest means might bring wealth, but such gains lack God's favor. Ill-gotten wealth, easily acquired, is just as swiftly lost. And what joy does wealth bring if it's shadowed by guilt? Countless tales recount wealthy individuals, even famed artists, succumbing to despair, showing that material abundance without spiritual contentment is empty.

The teachings of Jesus Christ stress not the evils of money, but the perils of its idolization. For, in its unchecked adoration, money becomes a false deity, overshadowing our devotion to the one true God. Our loyalty to Him can be expressed by offering Him a portion of our bounty, acknowledging it as His blessing.

Solomon's counsel to bring forth our "first fruits" to God signifies the importance of giving God precedence in our earnings. Fear not that dedicating a tenth might deplete your resources; for, in God's grace, not only will our barns be filled, but they will overflow.

When we approach God, let it be with genuine gratitude, not measured by the magnitude of our gift, but by the sincerity behind it.

Recall the widow who, amidst the throng of donors in the temple, gave merely two coins. Yet, Jesus extolled her for her offering surpassed all, not in amount, but in intent. For while others donated a fraction, she gave all she had. The essence of our gift, not its size, holds true value.

Today, let's present our offerings to God, reflecting our appreciation for His unceasing blessings and love. Amen.

DECEMBER 20
Wise like the snake and simple hearted like the dove

Matthew 10:16

> *"Behold, I send you out as sheep in the midst of wolves. Therefore be wise as serpents and harmless as doves.*

In Matthew 10, as the Lord Jesus Christ prepares to dispatch His 12 disciples to proclaim the good news to the cities of Israel, He imparts a profound piece of wisdom: "Behold, I send you forth as sheep in the midst of wolves: be ye therefore wise as serpents, and harmless as doves."

This counsel has often piqued my curiosity. What does it truly mean to combine the astuteness of a serpent with the innocence of a dove? When we embrace Jesus Christ as our Lord and Savior, the indwelling Holy Spirit becomes our guide.

Walking with the Holy Spirit, engaging with the Word of God, and living in communion with Him yields numerous spiritual fruits in our lives. Yet, concurrently, God admonishes us to remain vigilant. Elsewhere in the scriptures, we're exhorted to "pray and watch." Not just to offer our supplications but to keenly await God's responses.

A serpent epitomizes alertness. It may remain concealed, yet it is perpetually attuned to its surroundings. We, too, are summoned to such vigilance—not characterized by deceit or malicious intent, but marked by astuteness and a rapid, judicious response.

However, Jesus couples this alertness with the purity and innocence of a dove. While our minds should be sharp and discerning, our hearts should overflow with simplicity and unblemished love. We must observe our surroundings with the shrewdness of a serpent yet react with the genuine and loving heart of a dove.

Today, let's reflect on this profound wisdom from the Lord Jesus Christ. As we navigate our journey, may we embody the vigilance of a serpent, coupled with the purity and love of a dove. Amen.

DECEMBER 21
Whoever confesses me before men

Matthew 10:26-33

> [26]*Therefore, do not fear them. For there is nothing covered that will not be revealed, and hidden that will not be known. Jesus Teaches the Fear of God.*
> [27] *"Whatever I tell you in the dark, speak in the light; and what you hear in the ear, preach on the housetops.*
> [28] *And do not fear those who kill the body but cannot kill the soul. But rather fear Him who is able to destroy both soul and body in hell.*
> [29] *Are not two sparrows sold for a copper coin? And not one of them falls to the ground apart from your Father's will.*
> [30] *But the very hairs of your head are all numbered.*
> [31] *Do not fear therefore; you are of more value than many sparrows.*

Here, Jesus Christ says, "Fear them not, therefore." And who are they? Those who slander and punish Christians. "There is nothing covered, that shall not be revealed; and hidden, that shall not be known. What I tell you in darkness, that speak in light: and what you hear in the ear, preach upon the housetops." We are not called to fear anything or anyone. God instructs us not to be disturbed by what they say against you in secret or by what they do against you. Because nothing will remain hidden; everything that is concealed will be revealed.

He then says, "What I told you in private, through my words, you should proclaim in the light and among everyone. If I whisper something in your ear, you have a duty to announce it to everyone, as if shouting it from the rooftops." He continues, "And fear not those who kill the body but are not able to kill the soul: rather, fear Him who is able to destroy both soul and body in hell." And then, in verses 32 and 33, He says, 32 "Therefore, whoever confesses Me before men, him I will also confess before My Father who is in heaven.

33 But whoever denies Me before men, him I will also deny before My Father who is in heaven." Our duty is to bear witness to the Lord Jesus Christ. It isn't really a duty, but if we genuinely love someone, don't we want to talk about them all the time? Don't we want to share about them with everyone we meet, wherever we are?

Naturally, if we love someone, we want to speak of them wherever we go. How much more so for the Son of God, our Savior, who loves us and died on the cross out of that love? When we love Jesus Christ, we want to proclaim Him everywhere. We want to shout from the rooftops, telling people about His goodness, love, kindness, and grace. If we don't confess Him in front of others, He will not confess us on Judgment Day before God. He will also deny us. There are no white lies in Christianity; there are no lies at all.

The Lord Jesus Christ says, "Do not even swear; let your 'yes' be 'yes' and your 'no' be 'no'." Wherever we are, we are called to be honest, truthful, and righteous. Why should we fear when God is with us? We shouldn't be afraid of people; don't be afraid of someone who can only destroy your body but fear Him who can destroy both body and soul. Our only fear should be of God, and that fear of God is the beginning of wisdom. This fear isn't about being scared that God will harm us. This fear stems from respect and love, a fear of offending God. So today, let's confess our faith in the Lord Jesus Christ to others and tell them about His goodness, love, and grace. Amen

DECEMBER 22

Baptism (1)

Christ invitation and our response

Today, we are initiating a series of devotionals about baptism. We began the baptism class at church yesterday, and through these devotionals, I want to delve into the topic of baptism. The primary message is that Jesus Christ, the eternal Son of God, calls each of us to Him.

John 7:37-38 states: 37 "On the last day, that great day of the feast, Jesus stood and cried out, saying, 'If anyone thirsts, let him come to Me and drink. 38 He who believes in Me, as the Scripture has said, out of his heart will flow rivers of living water.'"

In Matthew 11:28-29: 28 "Come to Me, all you who labor and are heavy laden, and I will give you rest. 29 Take My yoke upon you and learn from Me, for I am gentle and lowly in heart, and you will find rest for your souls."

Have you heeded Jesus' call? Have you discerned His voice and responded to Him? If you've come to Jesus, what should you now do?

In Acts 2:37-38: 37 "Now when they heard this, they were cut to the heart, and said to Peter and the rest of the apostles, 'Men and brethren, what shall we do?' 38 Peter responded, 'Repent, and let every one of you be baptized in the name of Jesus Christ for the remission of sins; and you shall receive the gift of the Holy Spirit.'"

So, what is our role? What represents the stream of water that emerges from our being? It is the Holy Spirit. The Holy Spirit will be the source of peace and tranquility within you once you come to Jesus. When Peter relayed the events to them, they were disheartened and inquired about their next steps. He responded with, "Repent." Approaching Jesus Christ and embracing Him initially might not be comforting; it may evoke feelings of guilt, recognizing that we are sinners and only Jesus can offer salvation. This realization should lead to repentance.

"O God, we acknowledge we are sinners and seek Your forgiveness." After which, everyone must believe in Jesus Christ for the remission of sins. Meaning, first repent, then believe that Jesus Christ died on the cross for our sins and rose on the third day.

Once this belief is established, baptism follows. However, water baptism doesn't grant salvation. Hence, we don't advocate for baptizing infants or sprinkling water on their heads.

First, an individual must recognize their sinful nature. Not because someone else labels them as such. They must confess their sins, seek forgiveness, acknowledge Jesus Christ as the singular path to salvation, and post this acknowledgment, undergo baptism. This is why we don't baptize children; they must come to this realization on their own. Baptism serves as a testimony to God, an affirmation of faith to others.

We symbolically proclaim, "Just as Jesus Christ died and resurrected, I too immerse in water, symbolizing burial, and emerge, symbolizing resurrection." This act is a declaration of Christian faith, expressing wholehearted acceptance and commitment to Jesus Christ. Amen.

DECEMBER 23
Baptism (2)
Who is Jesus Christ?

Today, we progress in our devotional about baptism and baptism classes. Yesterday, we delved into Jesus Christ's invitation. If you've heeded His call, accepted Him, and repented, the next step is baptism. But what prerequisites should one be aware of before baptism? Primarily, one must discern who Jesus Christ truly is.

Who exactly is Jesus Christ? John 1:1-5 and 9-14 elucidate: "In the beginning was the Word, and the Word was with God, and the Word was God. He was with God in the beginning. Through Him, all things were made; without Him, nothing was made that has been made. In Him was life, and that life was the light of all mankind. The light shines in the darkness, and the darkness has not overcome it. The true light that gives light to everyone was coming into the world. He was in the world, and though the world was made through Him, the world did not recognize Him. He came to that which was His own, but His own did not receive Him. Yet to all who did receive Him, to those who believed in His name, He gave the right to become children of God—children born not of natural descent, nor of human decision or a husband's will, but born of God. The Word became flesh and made His dwelling among us. We have seen His glory, the glory of the one and only Son, who came from the Father, full of grace and truth."

Colossians 1:15-20 further describes Him: "The Son is the image of the invisible God, the firstborn over all creation. For in Him all things were created: things in heaven and on earth, visible and invisible, whether thrones or powers or rulers or authorities; all things have been created through Him and for Him. He is before all things, and in Him, all things hold together. And He is the head of the body, the church; He is the beginning and the firstborn from among the dead, so that in everything He might have the supremacy. For God was pleased to have all His fullness dwell in Him, and through Him to reconcile to Himself all things, whether things on earth or things in heaven, by making peace through His blood, shed on the cross."

Hebrews 1:1-3 proclaims: "In the past God spoke to our ancestors through the prophets at many times and in various ways, but in these last days, He has spoken to us by His Son, whom He appointed heir of all things, and through whom also He made the universe.

The Son is the radiance of God's glory and the exact representation of His being, sustaining all things by His powerful word. After He had provided purification for sins, He sat down at the right hand of the Majesty in heaven."

From these sacred verses, we can derive a series of questions. Based on this scripture, who is Jesus Christ? What, according to these passages, is Jesus Christ's mission? What drew you toward Him?

Reflect on this today: Who is Jesus Christ to you? What has He accomplished? And, what about Him beckons you closer? His unparalleled love is often the answer. Amen.

DECEMBER 24
Baptism (3)
Who is Jesus Christ? Athanasius creed

Today marks the third installment about baptism, diving deeper into understanding who Jesus Christ truly is.

Previously, we explored the identity of Jesus Christ, a topic concisely encapsulated in the three creeds of the Christian churches: the Apostles' Creed, the shortest; the Nicene Creed, slightly lengthier; and the Athanasian Creed, one of the most comprehensive. Let's delve into the Athanasian Creed:

Whoever wishes for salvation must adhere to the Christian faith. Without embracing it wholly and unfailingly, eternal damnation is certain. This faith decrees that we venerate one God in trinity, and the trinity in unity, neither conflating the persons nor segregating the essence. For the Father, the Son, and the Holy Spirit are distinct, yet their divinity is singular, their majesty shared, their glory equal.

Each possesses the same qualities. All are uncreated, immeasurable, and eternal, but there is only one being with these attributes. All are almighty and are God, but there's just one Almighty God. While the Father, Son, and Holy Spirit are each termed 'Lord,' there is but one Lord. Christian truth necessitates recognizing each person as both God and Lord, while concurrently affirming there aren't three gods or lords.

The Father isn't derived from another, the Son is begotten solely from the Father, and the Holy Spirit proceeds from both. Thus, there's one Father, one Son, and one Holy Spirit. In the trinity, none precedes or supersedes; all are coeternal, coequal.

Essential to salvation is recognizing this trinity in unity and the unity in trinity. Likewise, faith in the incarnation of our Lord Jesus Christ is paramount. True faith asserts that our Lord Jesus Christ, the Son of God, is both divine and human.

He is God, conceived from the Father's essence, existing before all time, and human, born of His mother in time. Fully God, fully human, with a soul and human flesh, He's divine in comparison to the Father but human in His earthly form.

Despite His dual nature, Christ remains singular, unified not by conversion of divinity to flesh but by God's adoption of humanity.

Comparable to how one person has both a soul and flesh, Christ is both God and human.

For our redemption, He suffered, descended to hell, resurrected, ascended to heaven, and took His rightful place beside the Father. He will return for judgment. At His second coming, everyone will resurrect and be judged by their deeds: the righteous will inherit eternal life, and the wicked, eternal damnation. Firm and faithful belief in this creed is the bedrock of Christian salvation. Amen.

DECEMBER 25
Baptism (4)
Who were we before and who are we after Jesus

Today, we delve deeper into understanding baptism, focusing on the transformational power of Jesus Christ in our lives. Let us turn our attention to Ephesians 2:1-22:

"And you He made alive, who were dead in trespasses and sins, in which you once walked according to the course of this world, according to the prince of the power of the air, the spirit who now works in the sons of disobedience, among whom also we all once conducted ourselves in the lusts of our flesh, fulfilling the desires of the flesh and of the mind, and were by nature children of wrath, just as the others. But God, who is rich in mercy, because of His great love with which He loved us, even when we were dead in trespasses, made us alive together with Christ (by grace you have been saved), and raised us up together, and made us sit together in the heavenly places in Christ Jesus, that in the ages to come He might show the exceeding riches of His grace in His kindness toward us in Christ Jesus. For by grace you have been saved through faith, and that not of yourselves; it is the gift of God, not of works, lest anyone should boast. For we are His workmanship, created in Christ Jesus for good works, which God prepared beforehand that we should walk in them."

"Therefore remember that you, once Gentiles in the flesh—who are called Uncircumcision by what is called the Circumcision made in the flesh by hands—that at that time you were without Christ, being aliens from the commonwealth of Israel and strangers from the covenants of promise, having no hope and without God in the world. But now in Christ Jesus you who once were far off have been brought near by the blood of Christ. For He Himself is our peace, who has made both one, and has broken down the middle wall of separation, having abolished in His flesh the enmity, that is, the law of commandments contained in ordinances, so as to create in Himself one new man from the two, thus making peace, and that He might reconcile them both to God in one body through the cross, thereby putting to death the enmity. And He came and preached peace to you who were afar off and to those who were near.

For through Him we both have access by one Spirit to the Father. Now, therefore, you are no longer strangers and foreigners, but fellow citizens with the saints and members of the household of God, having been built on the foundation of the apostles and prophets, Jesus Christ Himself being the chief cornerstone, in whom the whole building, being fitted together, grows into a holy temple in the Lord, in whom you also are being built together for a dwelling place of God in the Spirit."

Reflect on who we were prior to our encounter with Christ and the transformation that ensued thereafter, as depicted in Ephesians 2. Recognize the profound unity we now share with other believers in Christ. As you ponder, consider the ways in which Christ beckons you to unite with Him. What elements in this passage draw you closer to Him? Amen.

DECEMBER 26
Baptism (5)
The power of our testimonies

Today, as we continue our devotional series on baptism, we delve into the fifth segment, focusing on the significance and power of our testimony.

Romans 10:9-13 states: "That if you confess with your mouth the Lord Jesus and believe in your heart that God has raised Him from the dead, you will be saved. For with the heart one believes unto righteousness, and with the mouth confession is made unto salvation. For the Scripture says, 'Whoever believes on Him will not be put to shame.' For there is no distinction between Jew and Greek; for the same Lord over all is rich to all who call upon Him. For 'whoever calls on the name of the LORD shall be saved.'"

While baptism on its own does not confer salvation, a genuine belief in our hearts that God resurrected Jesus on the third day, paired with an open confession of this faith, is imperative. Jesus declared, "If you deny me before men, I will also deny you before my Father." Isn't it true that when someone is deeply in love, they yearn to share stories about their beloved? They won't shy away or remain silent when the topic of their love arises. They'll proclaim, "I love Jesus Christ, and He is my Savior." Thus, the vocal proclamation and sharing of our transformative journey with Christ becomes paramount.

Revelation 12:10-11 affirms: "Then I heard a loud voice saying in heaven, 'Now salvation, and strength, and the kingdom of our God, and the power of His Christ have come, for the accuser of our brethren, who accused them before our God day and night, has been cast down. And they overcame him by the blood of the Lamb and by the word of their testimony, and they did not love their lives to the death.'"

Our testimony stands as a formidable weapon against the adversary. A testimony about what? About our relationship and transformative journey with the Lord Jesus Christ. Such testimony can be profoundly impactful. By sharing with others our experiences and revelations of God's work in our lives, we bear witness to His glory. Simply undergoing baptism — immersing oneself in water and emerging — does not result in salvation. But when we come forward in faith, testify our commitment, and then receive baptism, that's when the sacrament unveils its true essence. Reflect on today's message. Ponder the question: Why does our testimony about Jesus Christ wield such profound power? May God's grace and guidance be with you always. Amen.

DECEMBER 27
Baptism (6)
What is baptism

Today, in our devotional series on baptism, we dive into the sixth segment. We aim to shed light on the essence of baptism and understand its significance in our faith journey.

Romans 10:9 elucidates: *"That if you confess with your mouth the Lord Jesus and believe in your heart that God has raised Him from the dead, you will be saved."*

Thus, during baptism, we attest that Jesus Christ, the Son of God, in unison with God the Father and the Holy Spirit, has bestowed salvation upon us.

The second dimension of baptism is a symbol of divine forgiveness. Through this sacrament, we acknowledge our purification and redemption by Jesus Christ.

Romans 6:23 proclaims: "For the wages of sin is death, but the gift of God is eternal life in Christ Jesus our Lord."

Furthermore, Romans 8:1 reinforces: "There is therefore now no condemnation to those who are in Christ Jesus, who do not walk according to the flesh, but according to the Spirit."

Baptism signifies that our transgressions have been washed away by the sacrificial act of Jesus' crucifixion. The third element of baptism underscores our eternal bond and commitment to Jesus and His divine congregation. Through baptism, we establish our connection with Jesus' sacrifice for our sins and rejoice in His resurrection, which grants us eternal life. Our immersion in baptismal waters symbolizes our unity with Jesus' death and His subsequent resurrection, purifying us and granting us new life.

So in essence, the act of baptism mirrors our narrative: it portrays our past selves, plagued by sins, and our rebirth through Jesus Christ.

Hence, this act serves a dual purpose: it's a testimony and a symbol. This testimony is paramount as it enables us to declare our redemption by Jesus Christ. It answers essential questions: Who were we before Christ? How has Jesus transformed our lives? What's our path forward in this newfound faith? This testimony stands as our most potent weapon against spiritual adversaries.

Conclusively, baptism is also an affirmation of our forgiveness in Christ. We declare our sins have been absolved by Him. Additionally, it's a testament to our bond with Jesus Christ and fellow believers. We aren't solitary entities in our faith journey; we are members of a vast community, the Church. We are destined to unite, support, and uplift one another and spread the divine message of salvation to the world. Amen.

DECEMBER 28
Baptism (7)
After baptism

Today, our devotional concludes the topic of baptism by delving into what ensues post-baptism.

Acts 2:41-47 enlightens us: *"Then those who gladly received his word were baptized; and that day about three thousand souls were added to them. And they continued steadfastly in the apostles' doctrine and fellowship, in the breaking of bread, and in prayers. Fear came upon every soul, and many wonders and signs were done through the apostles. All who believed were together, had all things in common, sold their possessions and goods, and divided them among all, as anyone had need. Continuing daily with one accord in the temple, breaking bread from house to house, they ate their food with gladness and simplicity of heart, praising God and having favor with all the people. And the Lord added to the church daily those who were being saved."*

Colossians 1:21-23 tells us: *"And you, who once were alienated and enemies in your mind by wicked works, yet now He has reconciled in the body of His flesh through death, to present you holy, blameless, and above reproach in His sight— if indeed you continue in the faith, grounded and steadfast, and are not moved away from the hope of the gospel which you heard, preached to every creature under heaven, of which I, Paul, became a minister."*

So, what transpires after baptism? Is the mere act of baptism the culmination of our spiritual journey? No, it's merely the inception. Baptism marks the onset of our journey with Christ and fellow believers. The subsequent phase encompasses growth and maturation in Jesus.

Nurturing and maturing in Jesus is a continual process. The initiation of faith and the sacrament of baptism are foundational, but they don't signify the end. When one loves deeply, the desire to know more, to deepen the bond, and to share that love with others becomes paramount. Thus, baptism represents the dawn of a profound relationship, marking the commencement of an intimate journey with Jesus and fellow Christians.

Reflect on these pivotal questions: Based on the scriptures, how did God guide the early Christians in their continued growth and maturation in Christ? Furthermore, what steps are you prompted to undertake to nurture your faith?

To address these inquiries, we refer to Acts 2 and subsequently to Colossians 1. How did God steer the early Christians on their path to holistic spiritual development? Moreover, which steps beckon you to foster your faith?

In essence, remember that faith, followed by baptism, sets the stage for a lifelong commitment, partnership, and spiritual growth in Jesus Christ. Amen.

DECEMBER 29
Faith, not positive thinking

Matthew 17:16-22

As Jesus Christ and his three disciples descended from the mountain of transfiguration, they were approached by a desperate father. The man's plea was for his epileptic child, who was often thrown into water and fire due to his condition. The disciples, to their dismay, had failed to heal him. Jesus responded, not just by healing the child, but with a rebuke, exclaiming, "O faithless generation, how long shall I be with you?"

The disciples later sought clarity, questioning their inability to heal. Jesus's reply was direct: their faith was lacking. However, He added, even faith as minuscule as a mustard seed could move mountains. Yet certain spiritual battles, He mentioned, could only be won through prayer and fasting.

The episode offers a deeper understanding of faith. It isn't mere positive thinking or mere optimism. Faith is an intrinsic trust in God, a certainty in the unseen. A year prior, the disciples had been empowered by Jesus, performing miracles and casting out demons. But over time, complacency had seemingly weakened their faith.

The essence of faith is not self-confidence but God-confidence. It's about relinquishing control, seeking God's will, and believing in His omnipotence. Faith is bolstered by prayer, a sacred communication with God, and sometimes fasting. But fasting, in the Christian context, isn't solely about abstaining from food or drink. It can be a break from certain habits, actions, or thoughts. The goal of fasting is to draw nearer to God, filling the void with prayer and reflection.

Jesus emphasizes that sustaining faith requires continuous effort. It's a relationship with God that must be nurtured through constant prayer, sometimes combined with fasting, to grow and flourish.

Today, let's remember that genuine faith in God can achieve the impossible. Our challenge is to cultivate it, nurturing our relationship with God daily. Amen.

DECEMBER 30
Faith like a child

Matthew 18:1-4

> [1] *At that time the disciples came to Jesus, saying, "Who then is greatest in the kingdom of heaven?"*
> [2] *Then Jesus called a little child to Him, set him in the midst of them,*
> [3] *and said, "Assuredly, I say to you, unless you are converted and become as little children, you will by no means enter the kingdom of heaven.*
> [4] *Therefore whoever humbles himself as this little child is the greatest in the kingdom of heaven.*

One day, Jesus' disciples approached Him with a question that reflected their human aspirations: "Who is the greatest in the kingdom of heaven?" Instead of answering directly, Jesus presented a child as a living illustration. He proclaimed, "Truly I tell you, unless you change and become like little children, you will never enter the kingdom of heaven. Therefore, whoever humbles himself like this child is the greatest in the kingdom of heaven."

What makes a child's attitude so distinct and admirable in God's eyes?

Children come with an inherent sense of humility. They don't parade achievements, harbor ambitions, or tout titles. They are, in essence, blank slates, dependent on their caregivers for everything. To a child, their parents are their heroes - omnipotent and ever-present. There's an implicit trust; a belief that when held by a parent, no harm can come to them. This unshakable trust, this unwavering belief in their parents' love and strength, is what Jesus highlighted.

For us to truly embrace the kingdom of God, our faith needs to mirror this childlike trust. We must acknowledge our vulnerabilities, our dependences, and place our complete trust in our Heavenly Father, believing He can do all things. In His hands, we find our strength, our provision, and our protection.

Today, let us aspire to be like children in our faith, simple in trust, humble in spirit, and unwavering in our confidence in God. Amen.

Faith and Works: Intertwined Pillars

Throughout our devotional journey, we've repeatedly delved into the nature of faith. We've recognized the profound simplicity of childlike faith and realized the pivotal role of belief in our salvation. Today, we turn to James 2:14-26, which deeply explores the relationship between faith and works.

Historically, the debate has oscillated between salvation by faith and salvation by works. While some religions lean heavily into the merit of human deeds to attain salvation, James's message stands in stark contrast to such beliefs. This apparent conflict led Martin Luther to question its divine origin, yet James's point is clear and invaluable.

Simply professing belief, while leading a life contradictory to faith's teachings, is a hollow testament. Is such a faith genuine? When we genuinely welcome Jesus into our hearts and let the Holy Spirit guide us, a transformation is inevitable. This transformation doesn't just stop at belief; it seeps into our actions, our choices, and our very being. Our works then become the tangible manifestation of this inner transformation.

James encapsulates this idea powerfully in verse 26: "Faith without works is dead." A body without a soul is lifeless; similarly, faith devoid of works lacks life and vitality. It's not that works lead to salvation but that a true, living faith naturally results in good works.

As believers, may our lives be a testament to our faith, not because we strive to earn salvation through our actions, but because our genuine faith in God's grace compels us to live righteously. Amen.

REFERENCES

1. *Bevere, John (2010). Moments of peace in the presence of God: Morning and Evening Edition. Bloomington, Minnesota: Bethany House Publishers.*
2. *Bevere, John (2014). Bait of Satan. Lake Mary: Charisma house pub.*
3. *Chambers, Oswald (1992). My Utmost for His Highest. the updated edition. Pub: Discovery House Publishers.*
4. *Groeschel, Craig (2021). Winning the War in Your Mind. Nashville: Zondervan*
5. *MacArthur, John (2003). The MacArthur Daily Bible. Bub: Thomas Nelson Inc.*
6. *Spurgeon, Charles H. (2001). Morning by Morning: Daily Devotional Readings. Wisconsin, Abbotsford: Aneko Press.*
7. *Bible, New King James*
8. *Bible, New International Version*

www.ingramcontent.com/pod-product-compliance
Lightning Source LLC
Chambersburg PA
CBHW051256120626
46547CB00015B/1963